Establishing a resource-circulating society in Asia

Sustainability Science Series

This book forms part of a series on sustainability science. The other titles in this series are:

Sustainability science: A multidisciplinary approach, edited by Hiroshi Komiyama, Kazuhiko Takeuchi, Hideaki Shiroyama and Takashi Mino, ISBN 978-82-808-1180-3

Climate change and global sustainability: A holistic approach, edited by Akimasa Sumi, Nobuo Mimura and Toshihiko Masui, ISBN 978-92-808-1181-0

Designing our future: Local perspectives on bioproduction, ecosystems and humanity, edited by Mitsuru Osaki, Ademola K. Braimoh and Ken'ichi Nakagami, ISBN 978-92-808-1183-4

Achieving global sustainability: Policy recommendations, edited by Takamitsu Sawa, Susumu Iai and Seiji Ikkatai, ISBN 978-92-808-1184-1

Establishing a resource-circulating society in Asia: Challenges and opportunities

Edited by Tohru Morioka, Keisuke Hanaki and Yuichi Moriguchi

United Nations University Press

TOKYO · NEW YORK · PARIS

United Nations University Press
United Nations University, 53-70, Jingumae 5-chome,
Shibuya-ku, Tokyo 150-8925, Japan
Tel: +81-3-5467-1212   Fax: +81-3-3406-7345
E-mail: sales@unu.edu   general enquiries: press@unu.edu
http://www.unu.edu

United Nations University Office at the United Nations, New York
2 United Nations Plaza, Room DC2-2062, New York, NY 10017, USA
Tel: +1-212-963-6387   Fax: +1-212-371-9454
E-mail: unuony@unu.edu

United Nations University Press is the publishing division of the United Nations University.

Cover design by Mori Design Inc., Tokyo

Printed in Hong Kong

ISBN 978-92-808-1182-7

Library of Congress Cataloging-in-Publication Data

Establishing a resource-circulating society in Asia : challenges and opportunities /
edited by Tohru Morioka, Keisuke Hanaki, and Yuichi Moriguchi.
    p.   cm.
  Includes bibliographical references and index.
  ISBN 978-9280811827 (pbk.)
  1. Sustainable development—Asia. 2. Natural resources—Asia—Management.
I. Morioka, Tohru. II. Hanaki, Keisuke. III. Moriguchi, Yuichi.
HC415.E5E88 2011
333.7095—dc22   2011000803

Contents

Figures

Tables

Plates

Contributors

Xudong Chen is a research assistant fellow at the National Institute for Environmental Studies, Japan, and a doctoral candidate at Nagoya University. His primary research interests lie in eco-industrial parks and low-carbon city planning. He holds a master's in planning from the University of Waterloo, Canada.

Tsuyoshi Fujita is a research director in the National Institute for Environmental Studies, Japan. He is also a professor at Toyo University and a visiting professor at Nagoya University. His research focuses on industrial symbiosis, eco-industrial planning and environmental technology evaluation. He holds a PhD in engineering from Tokyo University and a master's in city planning from the University of Pennsylvania.

Yong Geng is currently the research director of the Research Group on Circular Economy and Industrial Ecology, Institute of Applied Ecology, Chinese Academy of Sciences, supported by the Hundred Talents Program. He was a research fellow at the National Institute for Environmental Studies in 2008. His main research interests are circular economy and industrial ecology.

Hironori Hamasaki is a PhD candidate at the Graduate School of Policy Science, Ritsumeikan University. He graduated with an MSc from Waseda Okuma School of Public Management. His research area is transboundary water resources management, water governance and social networks among stakeholders in relation to water issues.

Keisuke Hanaki is a professor at the Department of Urban Engineering and an adjunct professor at Integrated Research System for Sustainability Science, The University of Tokyo. After obtaining a PhD in 1980 from The University of Tokyo, he worked for Tohoku University and the Asian Institute of Technology. His research interests include management of greenhouse gas emissions from urban areas and urban material flow analysis.

Keishiro Hara is an associate professor at the Research Institute for Sustainability Science at Osaka University. His research interests include urban environmental management and sustainable resources management. Recently his research has been focused upon sustainability science, paying special attention to sustainability assessment methodologies and future scenario approaches. He received his PhD in environmental studies in 2004 and BSc in environmental engineering in 1999, both from The University of Tokyo.

Yuji Hara is a tenure lecturer at the Department of Environmental Systems, Wakayama University. He graduated from the Department of Geography, and did his master's degree in landscape planning at The University of Tokyo, where he received his PhD in 2007. He specializes in landscape planning and anthropogenic geomorphology, and conducts extensive field research in Bangkok, Metro Manila, Tianjin and other Asian cities.

Ai Hiramatsu is a project assistant professor at the Transdisciplinary Initiative for Global Sustainability, The University of Tokyo. She holds a PhD in environmental engineering from the Department of Urban Engineering, The University of Tokyo. Her research interests are climate change, waste management and sustainability science. She has

been engaged in projects on solid waste management in Bangkok and its vicinity.

Toshiaki Iida is an assistant professor in the Graduate School of Agricultural and Life Sciences, The University of Tokyo. After gaining a PhD from The University of Tokyo, he worked at Yamagata University (Japan) and the Asian Institute of Technology (Thailand). His primary research area is environmental hydrology, and his interest extends to greenhouse gas emission from paddy fields, dissolved ion behaviour in snowpack and river water quality management.

Tasuku Kato is an associate professor of irrigation and drainage in the College of Agriculture, Ibaraki University, Japan. He gained a PhD in agriculture from The University of Tokyo in 1998. His research topics are watershed management for agricultural areas, long-term monitoring of agricultural drainage water and water quality forecast model development.

Yusuke Kishita is a researcher at the Department of Mechanical Engineering, Osaka University, Japan, and a research fellow of the Japan Society for the Promotion of Science. He received his PhD in Engineering in 2010 from Osaka University and has a background in design engineering, more specifically life-cycle engineering. His research interests include design methodology for sustainable society scenarios and sustainable resource-circulation systems, and eco-design of artefacts.

Akio Kobayashi is an emeritus professor at Osaka University,

Japan, and previously worked in the Biotechnology Department of the university. He has promoted a series of research activities on *Eucommia ulmoides* (wood tree), which is a promising resource for rubber production.

Kunishige Koizumi is a visiting researcher at the Ritsumeikan Research Center for Sustainability Science, Kyoto, and visiting lecturer at Ritsumeikan and other universities. His areas of interest include waste management, especially global recycling systems. He holds a master's degree from the Kyoto Institute of Technology and a PhD in policy science from Ritsumeikan University.

Terukazu Kumazawa is an assistant professor at the Research Institute for Sustainability Science, Osaka University, Japan. His research interests include environmental planning, community design and knowledge structuring on sustainability science. He received BEng, MEng and PhD degrees from Tokyo Institute of Technology in 1999, 2001 and 2006, respectively.

Shuji Kurimoto is a professor at the Research Institute for Sustainability Science, Osaka University, and a director of Osaka Prefecture Forest Owners Association in Japan. A forestry specialist, he holds a PhD in sociology from Doshisha University. His research interests are farm and forestry villages and forestry technology.

Takashi Machimura is an associate professor in the Department of Sustainable Energy and Environmental Engineering, Osaka University, Japan. He works on the ecosystem processes of carbon exchange and water redistribution, and their responses to climate change. His research interest includes social and technology relations towards sustainable ecosystems.

Takanori Matsui is an assistant professor of sustainable energy and environmental engineering, Graduate School of Engineering, Osaka University. His primary research topics are sustainability design and risk management for symbiotic system integration with natural ecosystems.

Riichiro Mizoguchi is currently professor of the Institute of Scientific and Industrial Research, Osaka University, Japan. His research interests include non-parametric data analyses, knowledge-based systems, ontological engineering and intelligent learning support systems. He received BSc, MSc and PhD degrees from Osaka University in 1972, 1974 and 1977, respectively.

Yuichi Moriguchi is currently the director of the Research Center for Material Cycles and Waste Management, National Institute for Environmental Studies, Tsukuba, as well as a visiting professor at the Graduate School of Frontier Sciences, The University of Tokyo. His recent research area is industrial ecology. He has been contributing to OECD activities on material flows and resource productivity, and is one of the inaugural members of the UNEP international panel for sustainable resource management. He received his doctoral degree in environmental engineering from Kyoto University.

Tohru Morioka is professor of environmental management and systems at the Faculty of Environmental and Urban Engineering, Kansai University, and also emeritus professor of Osaka University. He received his master's and PhD degrees in sanitary and environmental engineering at the University of Kyoto. He was the director of the Research Institute for Sustainability Science, Osaka University, and also led a risk management training programme funded by the Ministry of Education of Japan at the same university. His research interests include sustainable energy and environmental engineering, environmental management systems and environmental risk management.

Ken'ichi Nakagami is a professor of environmental policy at the College of Policy Science, Ritsumeikan University. He holds a PhD in environmental engineering, and has over 30 years' expertise in water resources and environmental management, sustainable region development using biomass towns and strategic research on mitigation and adaptation for climate change. In 2009 he received academic awards from the Japan Association for Planning Administration and Japan Society of Research and Information on Public and Co-operative Economy.

Toyohiko Nakakubo is a doctoral student at the Graduate School of Engineering, Osaka University. He specializes in material flow analysis, and his primary research interest is

biomass utilization in developing countries.

Yoshihisa Nakazawa is an invited professor at the Hitz Biomass Developing Collaborative Research Laboratory, Osaka University, Japan. He and his laboratory colleagues have established an environmentally sound large-scale production system for Eucommia elastomer and are now developing new technologies for its stable supply and industrial applications.

Youji Nitta is a professor in crop science at the Department of Biological Production Science, College of Agriculture, Ibaraki University, Japan. He earned a PhD in agriculture from the Graduate School of Agricultural Science, Tohoku University, in 1999. His primary research interests are biofuel crop production, morphological analysis of crop production and quality, rice grain ripening and quality and ecological evaluation of starch production crops.

Myat Nwe Khin is a senior project engineer for Memiontec, Singapore. She obtained a PhD degree in Asia-Pacific studies from Ritsumeikan Asia Pacific University. Her research interest is water quality management, security of water resources and water resources management in urban areas in the Asia-Pacific region.

Hiroyuki Ohta is a professor of environmental toxicology and chemistry at Ibaraki University College of Agriculture, Ibaraki, Japan. He gained a PhD in agricultural chemistry from Tohoku

University, Sendai, in 1982. His areas of research interest include soil microbial ecology, environmental toxicology and sustainable soil management.

Mitsuru Osaki is a professor in the Faculty of Agriculture, Hokkaido University, Japan, and a vice-director of the Center for Sustainability Science at the university. He was trained as a plant physiologist and soil scientist, and has also carried out many collaborative research and teaching projects on tropical land management and rehabilitation of tropical forest. He is interested in sustainability from food, food production, bioenergy and *satoyama* perspectives.

Kiyotaka Saga is a postdoctoral researcher in the Biomass Technology Research Center, National Institute of Advanced Industrial Science and Technology, Japan. He gained a PhD in agricultural engineering from The University of Tokyo in 2008. His current research focuses on the economic evaluation of biofuel production systems using process simulation technology.

Toshiki Sato is a postdoctoral fellow at the Center for Sustainability Science, Hokkaido University, Japan. His areas of interest include recycling of organic materials in agriculture, self-sufficiency of food production and regional energy use. He holds a PhD in applied biosciences from Hiroshima Prefectural University, Japan.

Motoyuki Suzuki is a professor of environmental engineering at the Open University of Japan. He has worked at the Institute of Industrial

Science, The University of Tokyo (1969–2001) and also served as a vice-rector at the United Nations University in Tokyo (1998–2003) in charge of the environment and sustainable development programme. His primary research area covers environmental technology development, environmental modelling, zero-emission material cycles and biomass utilization. He is currently serving as the chair of the Central Environmental Council, Japan.

Hiroyuki Tada is a co-founder of the environmental NGO Japan for Sustainability. He previously worked at an electronics company as environmental officer. His interests include environmental management, corporate social responsibility and sustainability vision and indicators.

Masao Takebayashi is a project researcher at Integrated Research System for Sustainability Science (IR3S), The University of Tokyo. He has two main research interests: the development of energy- and resource-saving technology, including the concept of zero emissions; and the formation of a sustainable society using biomass.

Noriyuki Tanaka is professor at the Center for Sustainability Science (CENSUS), Hokkaido University, Japan. He holds a PhD in geochemistry. He is interested in sustainability education and managing all subjects organized by CENSUS.

Kazutoshi Tsuda is a specially appointed researcher in the On-site Research Center for Sustainability Design, Graduate School of Engineering, Osaka University,

Japan. He has a PhD in engineering from Chiba University and was a member of the UNU Capacity Development Course Alumni Association. His research interests include material cycles and design for sustainability.

Nobuyuki Tsuji is employed as an associate professor at the Sustainability Governance Project, Center for Sustainability Science, Hokkaido University, Japan. He has a PhD degree in mathematical ecology, and is studying regional sustainability by mathematical analysis.

Yasushi Umeda is professor of life-cycle engineering at the Department of Mechanical Engineering, Graduate School of Engineering, Osaka University, Japan, and a professor at the Research Institute for Sustainability Science, Osaka University, in charge of research coordination. He obtained a PhD in engineering from The University of Tokyo, Japan, and taught at this university and Tokyo Metropolitan University. His research interests include eco-design, especially product life-cycle design, design of sustainable manufacturing industry, design methodology for sustainable society scenarios, and design theory and methodology.

René Van Berkel is currently chief of the Cleaner and Sustainable Production Unit, UN Industrial Development Organization, Austria, and a visiting senior fellow of the United Nations University Institute of Advanced Studies, Japan. From 1999 to 2006 he was a professor of cleaner production at Curtin University of Technology in Perth. Dr Van Berkel is a Dutch national and holds a PhD in environmental sciences from the University of Amsterdam (the Netherlands).

Helmut Yabar is an assistant professor at the Research Institute for Sustainability Science, Osaka University. His research interests include integrated resource management and its evaluation tools, environmental policy in Asia and the implications of technology innovation for environmental regulations. His most recent research has focused on the design of scenarios and indicator systems for a sustainable Asia. He received his PhD in environmental engineering from Osaka University.

Yugo Yamamoto is a tenure lecturer at the Department of Environmental Systems, Faculty of Systems Engineering, Wakayama University, Japan. His major research areas are environmental systems research and environmental management. He has a PhD in engineering from Osaka University.

Shinya Yokoyama is a professor in the Department of Biological and Environmental Engineering, Graduate School of Agricultural and Life Sciences, The University of Tokyo. After obtaining a PhD from Hokkaido University, he worked at the National Institute of Advanced Industrial Science and Technology in Japan. His main interests are biomass energy conversion technology and bioenergy system analysis.

Noboru Yoshida is an associate professor at the Department of

Environmental Systems, Faculty of Systems Engineering, Wakayama University. He received his PhD degree in environmental engineering at Osaka University. He served as a specially appointed professor of the Research Institute for Sustainability Science, Osaka University. His research interests include industrial ecology and energy and material flow analysis.

Haiyan Zhang is a research fellow at the Research Institute for Sustainability Science. Her research currently focuses on assessment of sustainable urban development, eco-industrial park assessment, circular economy in China and land-use change and sustainable urban development in China. Dr Zhang is a member of the Architectural Institute of Japan, Senri Citizen Forum (Japan) and the Suita City Planning Review Committee.

Weisheng Zhou is a professor of policy science at Ritsumeikan University, Kyoto. He graduated from Zhejiang University, and holds a master's degree from Dalian University of Technology in China and a PhD in engineering from Kyoto University. Generally, by analysing and assessing the economic, social and technical measures for synchronous realization of economic development, stable energy supply and environmental protection, and pursuing the optimum environmental strategies considering fairness, efficiency and regional characteristics, he is researching for an international proposal towards a sustainable and widespread low-carbon society.

Preface

This book forms part of a series on sustainability science. Sustainability science is a newly emerging academic field that seeks to understand the dynamic linkages between global, social and human systems, and to provide a holistic perspective on the concerns and issues between and within these systems. It is a problem-oriented discipline encompassing visions and methods for examining and repairing these systems and linkages.

The Integrated Research System for Sustainability Science (IR3S) was launched in 2005 at The University of Tokyo with the aim of serving as a global research and educational platform for sustainability scientists. In 2006 IR3S expanded, becoming a university network including Kyoto University, Osaka University, Hokkaido University and Ibaraki University. In addition, Tohoku University, the National Institute for Environmental Studies, Toyo University, Chiba University, Waseda University, Ritsumeikan University and the United Nations University joined as associate members. Since the establishment of the IR3S network, member universities have launched sustainability science programmes at their institutions and collaborated on related research projects. The results of these projects have been published in prestigious research journals and presented at various academic, governmental and social meetings.

The *Sustainability Science* book series is based on the results of IR3S members' joint research activities over the past five years. The series provides directions on sustainability for society. These books are expected to be of interest to graduate students, educators teaching sustainability-related courses and those keen to start up similar programmes, active members of NGOs, government officials and people working in industry. We hope this series of books will provide readers with useful information on sustainability issues and present them with novel ways of thinking and solutions to the complex problems faced by people throughout the world.

Integrated Research System for Sustainability Science

Abbreviations

ADB	Asian Development Bank
AF&R	alternative fuels and raw materials
AIT	Asian Institute of Technology
ANS	adjusted net saving
APN	Asia-Pacific Network for Global Change Research
ARRPET	Asian Regional Research Program on Environmental Technology
BAU	business as usual
BDF	biodiesel fuel
BMR	Bangkok metropolitan region
BOD	biochemical oxygen demand
BRT	Bus Rapid Transit
C40	Large Cities Climate Leadership Group
CAD	computer-aided design
CBA	cost-benefit analysis
CDM	clean development mechanism
C&DW	construction and demolition waste
CE	circular economy
CF	carbon footprint
CHP	combined heat and power
COD	chemical oxygen demand
CP	cleaner production
CRT	cathode-ray tube
CS	circular society
CSR	corporate social responsibility
DBO	design, build and operate
DME	dimethyl ether
DMI	direct material input

DO	dissolved oxygen
EF	ecological footprint
EID	eco-industrial development
EIP	eco-industrial park
ELV	end-of-life vehicle
EPR	extended producer responsibility
ErP	energy related product
ESI	Environmental Sustainability Index
ESSP	Earth System Science Partnership
EU	European Union
FAO	UN Food and Agriculture Organization
FCV	fuel cell vehicle
FYP	five-year plan
GDP	gross domestic product
GHG	greenhouse gas
GIS	geographic information system
GRP	gross regional product
GS	genuine savings
GTZ	German Agency for Technical Cooperation
HDI	Human Development Index
HEV	hybrid electric vehicle
ICETT	International Center for Environmental Technology Transfer
ICLEI	International Council on Local Environmental Initiatives
ID	industrial development
IESD	Institute of Environment for Sustainable Development
IGBP	International Geosphere-Biosphere Programme
IGCC	integrated coal gasification combined cycle
IGES	Institute for Global Environmental Strategies
IHDP	International Human Dimensions Programme on Global Environmental Change
IPCC	Intergovernmental Panel on Climate Change
IR3S	Integrated Research System for Sustainability Science
JA	Japan Agriculture
JCPRA	Japan Containers and Packaging Recycling Association
JFS	Japan for Sustainability
JICA	Japan International Cooperation Association
L	litre
LCA	life-cycle assessment
LCAs	life cooperative association
LCCO$_2$	life-cycle CO$_2$
LCD	liquid-crystal display
LCS	low-carbon society
LRT	light-rail transit
MAFF	Ministry of Agriculture, Forestry and Fisheries (Japan)
MAIRS	Monsoon Asia Integrated Regional Study
METI	Ministry of Economy, Trade and Industry (Japan)
MFA	material flow analysis

MFA	material flow accounting and analysis
ML	megalitre
MOE	Ministry of Environment (Japan)
MRV	measurement, reporting and verification
MSW	municipal solid waste
MSWM	municipal solid waste management
NACS-J	Nature Conservation Society of Japan
NBP	net biome production
NCEA	National Commission for Environmental Affairs (Myanmar)
NEP	net ecosystem production
NGO	non-governmental organization
NPO	non-profit organization
NPP	net primary production
NRI	national research institute
OBM	Oboto Bang Maenang (Thailand)
OECD	Organisation for Economic Co-operation and Development
PC	personal computer
PCB	printed circuit board
PET	polyethylene terephthalate
PV	photovoltaic
QOL	quality of life
3R	reduce, reuse and recycle
RCS	resource-circulating society
REDD	reducing emissions from deforestation and degradation in developing countries
RISS	Research Institute for Sustainability Science
RP	resource productivity
RUSLE	revised universal soil loss equation
SBR	styrene-butadiene rubber
SCMS	sound material-cycle society
SCP	sustainable consumption and production
SIDA	Swedish International Development Cooperation Agency
SMEs	small and medium-sized enterprises
SMM	sustainable materials management
SS	sustainability science
START	Global Change System for Analysis, Research and Training
TOD	Transit-Oriented Development
toe	tonnes of oil equivalent
TMR	total material requirement
TV	television
UN	United Nations
UNCSD	UN Commission on Sustainable Development
UNDP	UN Development Programme
UNEP	UN Environment Programme
UNIDO	UN Industrial Development Organization
UNU	United Nations University
UR	urban-rural partnership

USER	Unit for Social and Environmental Research (Thailand)
WBCSD	World Business Council for Sustainable Development
WCRP	World Climate Research Programme
WEE	waste electric and electronic goods
WEO	World Energy Outlook
ZE	zero emissions
ZEF	UNU Zero Emissions Forum

1

Introduction: Asian perspectives of resource-circulating society – Sound material metabolism, resource efficiency and lifestyle for sustainable consumption

Tohru Morioka

1-1 Overview of policy initiatives towards a resource-circulating society

Key concepts appear in developed economies relating to "resource-circulating society"

Overconsumption and inefficient production systems in the last decades have caused pollution, environmental degradation and the depletion of scarce resources in both developed and developing countries. In response, international organizations such as the UN Development Programme (UNDP), the UN Environment Programme (UNEP) and the Organisation for Economic Co-operation and Development (OECD) have promoted the exchange of policy initiatives, action programmes and practices among member countries, industrial associations and academic institutions. For example, UNEP introduced cleaner production (CP), which promotes a shift from end-of-pipe treatment to pollution prevention, while the UNDP has appealed for environmentally sound technology in technology transfer programmes and assistance to developing countries. In the follow-up meeting after the Rio Declaration and Agenda 21, the International Human Dimensions Programme (IHDP) was established as a collaborative platform for social scientists and policy-oriented academics. The IHDP is supported by the United Nations and numerous international associations. Activities of industrial transformation, which is a prioritized domain in the IHDP working team, have implemented a

Establishing a resource-circulating society in Asia: Challenges and opportunities, Morioka, Hanaki and Moriguchi (eds), United Nations University Press, 2011, ISBN 978-92-808-1182-7

number of industrial ecology (or resource metabolism) practices and performances in various regions and nations around the world (IHDP-IT, 2001).

Business leaders and members of the World Business Council for Sustainable Development (WBCSD), which originated from a non-profit organization of business leaders and the International Chamber of Commerce, introduced "resources efficiency" as a means of superseding the monetary efficiency of input-output (Schmidheiny and WBCSD, 1992), while Schmidt-Bleek (1999) of the Wuppertal Institute introduced the factor X approach. While developing ways to steer industrial societies in developed/developing countries towards sustainability, the IHDP-IT group published a simplified booklet (IHDP-IT, 2001) which provided a conceptual basis, analytical tool, evaluation procedure and policy implication methods to reduce our "ecological rucksack" (hidden flows) and improve factor X and resource efficiency in corporations, regions (e.g. eco-towns) and national initiatives. Some studies have also suggested a double decoupling for sustaining resource use: economic growth from resource use (resource efficiency) and resource use from environmental impact (Bringezu, 2006).

Furthermore, in 1998 the World Resources Institute, in collaboration with the WBCSD, launched the GHG Protocol Initiative to provide a credible and transparent method for quantifying greenhouse gas (GHG) emission reduction at any system (WRI and WBCSD, 2004). A carbon footprint (CF), which is defined as the total direct and indirect GHG emissions caused by a person, event, organization or product, is an important tool to monitor the environmental impacts of our activities. The development of an international standard for the concept of a "carbon footprint" may facilitate input-output analysis of material flows and resources accounting at the corporation and/or national level. In 2008 the OECD hosted its second workshop on sustainable materials management and analysed the major initiatives on this topic within the public and private sector and in international organizations (OECD, 2008).

Physical resources consist of a wide range of useful materials and energy that are transformed in urban and national systems in ways that are analogous to ecosystems. The concept of urban metabolism was formulated by Abel Wolmann (1965) in "The Metabolism of Cities", which was followed by Graedel and Allenby (1995) and others. Examining quantitatively the material input-output influencing the efficiency of economic activities over environmental pressure, the characteristics of metabolism are evaluated in terms of economic features, not societal features. In this case, we should distinguish a resource-circulating economy from a resource-circulating society (RCS).

Japan was the first Asian country to address the resource intensity of consumption patterns with its Basic Environmental Law of 1993 and Basic Environmental Plan the following year. Asian policies addressing material efficiency and sound disposal were recognized in the chair's summary at the Asian 3R Conference in 2006, during which the 3R Initiative emphasizing the principles of "reduce, reuse and recycle" clarified the broad concepts of waste avoidance, minimization, treatment and disposal (MOE Japan, 2006). CP, which was promoted in Asian countries through the activities of UNEP, has become a key element of environment-conscious production in changing the current one-way economy towards a closed-loop economy. UNEP also launched the 3R Platform as an implementing mechanism for 3R activities in developing countries of the Asia-Pacific region (UNEP, 2005). Design-for-disassembly was formulated to promote the easy recovery of parts and materials during the product disassembly process, while design-for-environment called for minimizing pollution and promoting resource conservation during product or system design.

Western European countries and other developed countries have paid increasing attention to the environmental impacts derived from consumption-side behaviour such as in purchasing, lifestyle choices and commodity preferences. In product life-cycle considerations, extended producer responsibility (EPR) may be realized in collaboration with intelligent consumer behaviour. The European Union (EU) and WBCSD have shifted the leading concept of a resource-circulating society from sustainable production and consumption in the 1990s to sustainable consumption and production in a "consumer society".

The concept of an RCS, which first appeared in research conducted at Integrated Research System for Sustainability Science (IR3S), embraces a somewhat wider concept than the past Japanese governmental idea of a "recycling society", the "circular economy" concept in China and even the 3R principle-related planning goals of other Asian countries. Recycling alone is a single measure and cannot fulfil the overall goal of achieving sufficient services in a society while minimizing levels of environmental impact from material/resources consumption. Moreover, as a first priority, alternatives emphasizing reduction are preferable to either recycling or resource circulation.

China's decision to promote a circular economy emphasizes efficient use of land and water in addition to material resources. The Japanese Junkan Shakai plan, launched at national and local community levels, stresses community-based recovery, repair by craftsmen, use of eco-bags and *mottainai* (meaning "waste not" in Japanese), embodying a simple life decoupled from material affluence and emphasizing spirituality. Beyond a resource-efficient economy and decoupling, developing an RCS refers to dematerialization of the economy and individual lifestyle change towards collective well-being in the course of the rediscovery of lives sustained by ecosystem services, forests, mountains, stone statues of *jizo*, travellers' guardian deities, and the sense of an animistic universe (see Chapter 6-2).

Why should Asia's approach be focused on RCS?

In a general sense, the rapid growth of industry and the increasing population of Asia are particularly apparent when viewed within the context of future global society. The combined population of China and India is 2.5 billion and represents 37.5 per cent of the world population (UNSD, 2007). Asia has also become the world's biggest supplier of manufactured goods. For instance, production of liquid-crystal and plasma display televisions in East Asian countries (Japan, Korea and Taiwan) accounts for over 90 per cent of the global total, and the total CO_2 emissions of China, India, Japan, Korea and Indonesia formed 30.5 per cent of the 27 billion tonnes emitted worldwide in 2005. The foreign currency reserves of China and Japan, ranked first and second in the world, account for around US$2 trillion and US$1 trillion respectively, followed by export-oriented Asian economies like Taiwan, Korea and India (IMF, 2009). These trends are an indication that Asia will own a large share of the global economy in the future. The huge scale of resource-intensive economies in Asia is the first reason for emphasizing Asia's approach to RCS.

A modern economy is not isolated from direct waste discharge and environmental pollution, which can be measured by CF, total material requirement or ecological footprint (EF) (see Chapters 3-4 and 6-3). Material flow and resource consumption have increased along the product chain of resource exploitation, material processing, manufacturing, assembly, sale and consumption. Labour-intensive industries such as textiles, household goods manufacturers and others are likely to be relocated in the industrial zones of developing countries, such as the Pearl River and Yangtze River deltas. Sometimes collected post-consumer waste is exported from developed to developing countries, as in the case of packaging waste and e-waste (UNEP, 1998; see Chapter 3-3). Emerging economic partnership agreements or active pledges on 3R partnership action in Asia may enable countries to monitor transboundary waste flows and control shadow or invisible environmental loads emerging from sales or consumption phases. Environmentally sound patterns of production and consumption around the world will require a resource-efficient economy in Asia. Attempts to build a model of mutual collaboration between the developed and the developing worlds that is related to resources-circulating economic practices are described below.

Typical partnership actions for resource circulation in Asia are embodied in the 3R Initiative, the zero-emission initiative, the eco-town partnership and the technology cooperation programme. Each of these ideas continues to be practised and promoted. Chapters 3-1, 3-2 and 3-4 discuss both resource-efficiency performance and policy implications. The message from Japan contained in the 3R Initiative proposed during the G8 summit prioritizes reduction over material recycling, and stresses the importance of an environmentally conscious lifestyle that considers avoiding and minimizing garbage disposal. Furthermore, the concept of *mottainai* invokes a feeling of "saving resources while improving our quality of life", even in an affluent society.

A report on the state of the art and policy orientation of a resource-efficient economy in Asia was published jointly by the Asian Development Bank (ADB) and the Institute for Global Environmental Strategies (IGES). Answers to the question "Why should Asian countries care about resource efficiency?" posed in the publication are itemized in nine reasons (ADB and IGES, 2008: 29–31).

- *Tackling local environmental problems* is an intrinsic objective in developing Asia, and of course a universal one with co-benefits for meeting localized concerns. Ways to satisfy basic needs of energy supply and sanitation in rural areas, and sustainable building construction and urban development in Asian megacities, are crucial targets.

- *Addressing climate change* and *ensuring energy security* are stressed in the sense of cross-cutting integration beyond major individual environmental issues. Not only methane discharge reduction in waste disposal sites but also joint attainment of energy and resource efficiency in firms, communities, regions and countries should be taken into consideration. The vision and scenario for a low-carbon society may be shared through the medium-term action of achieving a resource-circulating society.

- *Minimizing disposal costs* and *improving economic competitiveness* are grouped into the promotion of a vitalized economy, even in manufacturing industries, with advantages in competitiveness achieved by means of utilizing recovered and renewable resources, supported by full-cost accounting in waste management.

- *Developing new business opportunities* and *pursuing social benefits* imply the social profitability and beneficial effects derived from resources circulating in new business models and employment in small and medium-sized enterprises (SMEs). The village- or community-based entrepreneur is expected to become increasingly important in Asia.

- *Avoiding resource conflict* and *preserving natural capital* are components of the wider concept of resource conservation. Promoting use of renewable resources and improving resource efficiency in regions should be accomplished on the basis of transgenerational equity, spatial equity and social justice.

The Asian approach is characterized by the integration of Asian socio-cultural characteristics into policy orientation, decision-making and practices for upgrading resource-based services with local variety and/or uniqueness. Despite the variation in climate, geology, ecology and anthropological peculiarities of the arid lands, islands and mountains of the Asian region, rice cultivation supported by irrigation systems exist harmoniously with village forest to embrace sacred shrines. Indeed, this cultural background, consisting of landscapes, ecosystem services and the mental cosmology of rural villages, and sometimes even of urbanized regions, is considered typical of Asia.

The norm, value judgement or behaviour related to the attainment and distribution of renewable/non-renewable resources in Asian communities influences the way in which Asians create rules, spread benefits and award contributions in using common sense with local resources. Further discussions on these topics are introduced in subsequent sections of this volume and in the book *Designing Our Future: Local Perspectives on Bioproduction, Ecosystems and Humanity* (Osaki, Braimoh and Nakagami, eds, United Nations University Press, 2011) which forms part of this series. These sections will also address key concepts like "harmony with nature", "sense of belonging to the community", "beyond direct self-profit", "artisans with folklore" and "pluralism" in Asia.

In spite of the recent rapid urbanization of Asian countries, local towns, villages and rural regions have been able to provide for their residents and support their business sectors. Even in the megacities of Asia, small traditional houses still stand in downtown areas, while commuters emerge from residences in a patchwork quilt including agricultural plantations and open green spaces. Therefore, urban and rural symbioses need to be encouraged more intensively. Whether the primary industries yield it or not, biomass should be regarded as a key element of affordable resources in the region. The exchange of resources between urban and rural sectors for waste minimization and resource utilization has become a major option. In any case, urban-rural symbiosis is a typical example exemplifying Asian features. The papers in Chapter 4 demonstrate urban-rural combinations, as shown in Figure 1.1. In this scheme Morioka and Yabar (2007) identify three systems: biological production ecosystem, urban and industrial systems. The authors outline three possible combinations among the three systems. The lower level outlines the modern industrialized system with economic efficiency. This system is characterized by organic materials recovery in large-scale plantations; frequent renewal for urban centres and suburban development; and mass production/consumption materials recycling in the industrialized world. The middle level outlines an acceptable way of industrial transformation. This system is characterized by

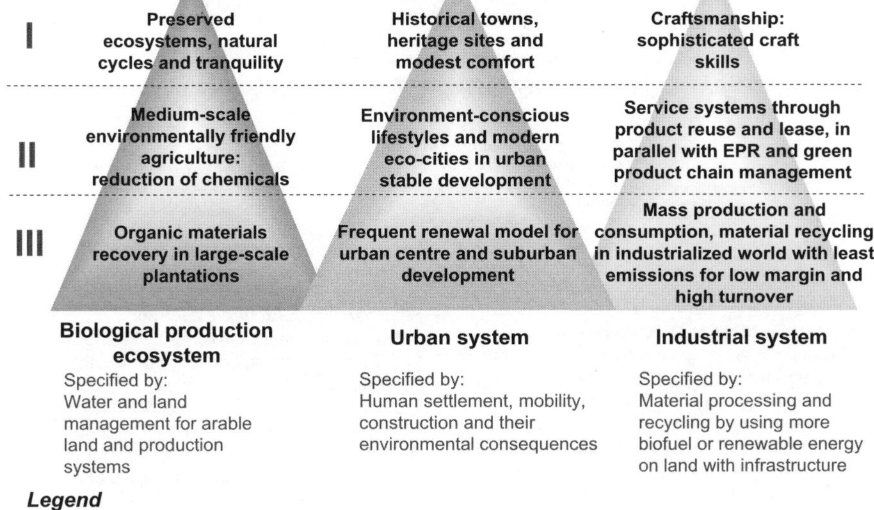

Figure 1.1 Urban-rural-industrial triangle model for Asian concept of resource-circulating society

appropriate-scale and organic agriculture; environment-conscious lifestyles and modern eco-cities in stable urban development; and service systems through product reuse and lease, in parallel with EPR and green product-chain management. The upper level outlines deep ecology, characterized by preserved ecosystems; historical towns, heritage and classic comfort; and craftsmanship and sophisticated craft skills.

1-2 Vision, scenario and programme of a resource-circulating society

Framework of a flagship RCS research project

One approach to developing an RCS is being undertaken by the IR3S flagship research project entitled "Asian challenge to resource-circulating society", a schematic diagram of which is shown in Figure 1.2. The system has three components: designing the *vision for the RCS*, developing a *benchmarking system for sustainability in the RCS* and building a *research network for the RCS*. The concepts and practice of resource circulation in Asia are handled through joint collaboration initiatives, benchmarking with indicators and academic networking.

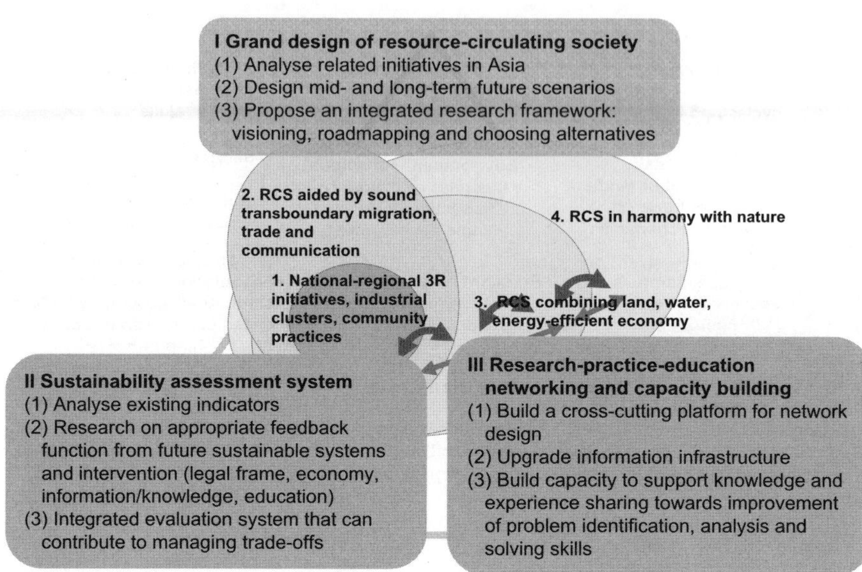

Figure 1.2 Scope of IR3S flagship research project on Asian perspectives for resource-circulating society

The ultimate goal of these activities is the establishment of a sustainable society. The concepts of sustainability and sustainable development originated from the Brundtland Report (WCED, 1987). Since then, many of the concepts of a sustainable society have been identified within the context of evidence-based multidisciplinary academic views, policy-based measures and others. In the IR3S project, resource circulation with minimized emissions and a high level of quality of life can be represented by three lateral pyramids of "low-carbon society", "resource-circulating society" and "nature-harmonious society". While envisioning a future society beyond physical materials recycling, the IR3S working team identified the major domain of RCS in Asia. The hierarchy of goals to create a sustainable society incorporates a resource-efficient economy and considers fundamental targets for appropriate sanitation-based waste management (Figure 1.3). The sanitary treatment and disposal of waste are a concern in developing countries. Community-based recovery programmes for waste minimization, including those incorporating economic gain for firms, have been encouraged in every integrated waste management plan in Asia. For example, waste management strategies in Thailand integrate solid waste and wastewater processing. The implementation of the 3R programme incorporates a hierarchy of management practices, including promotion of source reduction and separation and waste-stream recov-

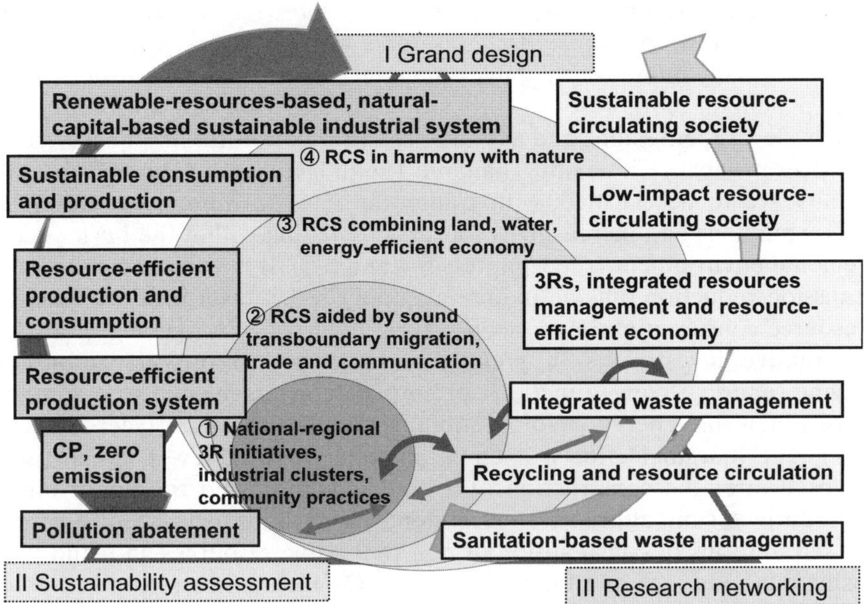

Figure 1.3 Industrial and societal domain of IR3S RCS research project

ery. In this process a set of solid waste management objectives focusing on the 3R approach before final disposal is prepared for the municipal authority. The most fundamental issues of sanitation and basic needs are thus evaluated through national 3R initiatives, the business actions of industrial clusters and community-level practices. Research on recycling of organic waste as biomass in urban fringes in Thailand discusses the dual benefits of energy and material recovery in advanced programmes (Ministry of Natural Resources and Environment, 2006).

Market mechanisms stimulate migration across countries. Voluntary actions for quality inspection and assurance have been required for potentially toxic materials in e-wastes (see Chapter 3-3). The practice of a circular economy in China mainly covers the two areas of production and consumption, including the implementation of CP, construction of eco-industrial parks, environmental labelling of products, certification of environmental management systems for enterprises, comprehensive usage of solid wastes, construction of energy-saving buildings, initiatives on green service and consumption, and the gradual improvement of industrial concepts such as eco-industry, eco-agriculture, recycling and waste decontamination. Furthermore, energy and land conservation are emphasized as part of the circular economy, where the principal guide, as in RCS, is coupling land and water saving with an energy-efficient economy.

The RCS harmonious with nature focuses on mechanisms to create closed-loop resource cycles that resemble natural cycles. This approach will eventually minimize the environmental impact of economic activities. The papers on biotic resource utilization in Chapter 4 deal with reducing life-cycle CO_2 emissions and avoiding capacity deterioration in ecosystem services in Japan, China and Thailand. The judgement criteria for sustainability are to be clarified, with trade-offs between minimized life-cycle CO_2 emissions and increasing resources circulating within the business or regional environment (see Chapters 5-4 and 5-5). It is crucial to prioritize emission reduction outside industrial supply zones, even if direct energy/ resource consumption increases inside an industrial city, when appraising alternative investments in green infrastructures to provide resource-saving (energy-saving) functions, or corporate assets needed to manufacture renewable-energy-yielding equipment and appliances (see Chapter 6-1). The marginal effects of emission reductions achieved in the time elapsed after the construction of a green building, and the opportunity cost derived from alternative investments in other projects, need to be assessed in terms of consumption of non-renewable resources and land use, using methods such as EF and life-cycle CO_2, including emissions related to transport/logistics (see Chapter 6-3).

The following points related to resource-circulating society are addressed in this volume.

- Environmental impact assessment should include indirect impacts as well, such as the damage around dumpsites away from consumption locations, embodied CO_2 (life-cycle CO_2), outbound emission leakage from relocated industries under pressure from strict regulations and the collective influence of degraded ecosystem services.
- Depletion of scarce resources applied in frontier technologies can be easily identified in the resource economy, but invisible ecological impacts along supply chains, especially those associated with resource exploitation, can only be realized in the manner of EF.
- Beyond reactive policies on end-of-life wastes, a proactive paradigm shift needs to be made towards downsizing consumption volumes and innovating product/process design in accordance with sustainable waste management.

Scenario design, benchmarking and research orientation

Who are the key players in the RCS research project? When, what, where and how will they accomplish it? In addition to academia, the stakeholders in an RCS include the citizens, corporations and governments of Asia. In other words, RCS is expected to strengthen collaboration between the supply side and the demand side, the domestic and trade sectors, upstream product chains and downstream retail sectors, manufacturing and agricultural sectors, and urban and rural sectors. The tangible boundaries of Asia are thus most likely dependent upon geophysical or political boundaries. However, this research focuses on conditions and outlooks inside East Asia, especially within the Asian monsoon climate region comprising China, Korea, Japan and other countries. The temporal range considered is two decades, which is similar to the mid-term targets of global warming policies.

The question of what issues are examined has it roots in assessing the differences between the economy and society, or economic efficiency and social welfare. This flagship research project aims not only at engineering solutions, but also developing societal system changes through legal, economic and financial instruments, as well as information-based or voluntary instruments. For example, the 3R Initiative stresses education for reducing adverse behaviour at the source, while the take-back system for discarded home appliances emphasizes extended producer responsibility and other institutional means to meet the aims of the study. The Korean experience since 1992 with waste electric and electronic equipment, using a waste deposit-refund system for the recovery of discarded TVs, washing machines and other appliances, is noteworthy in this regard. The programme was modified in 2006 to include an amendment to the extended producer responsibility system (2003 onwards) for printers and copy machines (MOE Korea, 2006).

Scenario design and creating a roadmap to a target society are the purpose of integrated planning (Chapter 2-1). In general, scenario design has been applied to a wide variety of issues with often-unclear dimensions, levels and interactions of key variables in future outlooks. In global warming, the most-cited pioneering work is the Target Approach of Holland in the 1990s (Loorbach and Rotmans, 2006) and the IPCC report on emission scenarios of 2000 (Kok et al., 2002). In 2005 a Japanese research group (originally called the Sustainable Japan Society) presented a long-term social target to develop a low-carbon society by 2050. The backcasting approach, i.e. envisioning a sustainable society based on defined parameters and designing short- to mid-term strategies towards that end, is perhaps the approach that most ably serves the sustainability goal (Morioka, Saito and Yabar, 2006).

Within the context of RCS there seem to be few reports on backcasting. A primary example is the four-year research project entitled "Designing a resources-circulating society in the Tokyo metropolitan area" (Tanji and Morioka, 2004). In general, patterns of societal goals are distinguished on a two-dimensional horizon. The first dimension is economic growth in terms of gross regional product or population size in urbanization. In the case of a mature economy in a society experiencing a decreasing population, the dichotomy of centralized and decentralized city regions (or national levels) can be applied to scenario design work when assuming robust population estimates. The second dimension involves selecting between technocentric views of development in city regions and intimate community commitment/participation in regional governance.

Four representative patterns in developing countries have been identified by the flagship RCS research project: the business-as-usual scenario, which emphasizes rapid economic growth by extrapolating from previous records; a second pattern emphasizing green manufacturing production and innovation as applied to CP, zero-emission approaches, resources saving and a voluntary top-runner accountability system; a third pattern characterized by increased regulatory oversight, including renewable energy feed-in tariffs or regulations on target setting for resource-efficient production systems; and a fourth option emphasizing urban-rural collaboration schemes (see Chapters 2-1 and 4-1).

The identification of indicators for resource metabolism or circulation is necessary to benchmark performance in a roadmap to an RCS. Long-term RCS planners should pay attention to the distinct differences in the integral or unified indicators used for benchmarking in scenario design for societal goals in global warming policy, and separate them from those used in the RCS scenario design. Carbon emission intensity, CF and complementary balanced volume (as in carbon offsets) are representative indices that are compatible with others in design of a low-carbon economy. As shown in Figure 1.4, a wide variety of indicators exist for benchmarking in the scenario design stage of an RCS, including indicators for resource efficiency, urban-rural symbiosis and ecosystem services with biodiversity. Land-cover change and the associated deterioration of ecosystem services are also evaluated in the domains of mining, plantations, industrial operation, logistics, landfill operations and product and supply chains.

However, only a few of the indicators from the many basic indices are useful for checking and reviewing actions or monitoring and revising the plans for an RCS. Performance in environmental state variables or environmental pressures is measured by waste volume, resources input (direct material input – DMI) and life-cycle CO_2, regardless of how different they may be from the suitable indicators for an optimal decoupling scenario. The most compatible indicator for dealing with the decoupling of environmental impacts from economic development is eco-efficiency, or resources efficiency, which addresses up and down trends of environmental productivity similar to the time-elapsed profile of the Kuznets curve. The production amount, in terms of GDP per unit of solid waste (US$/tonne), has improved in the recent records of Japan and Korea;

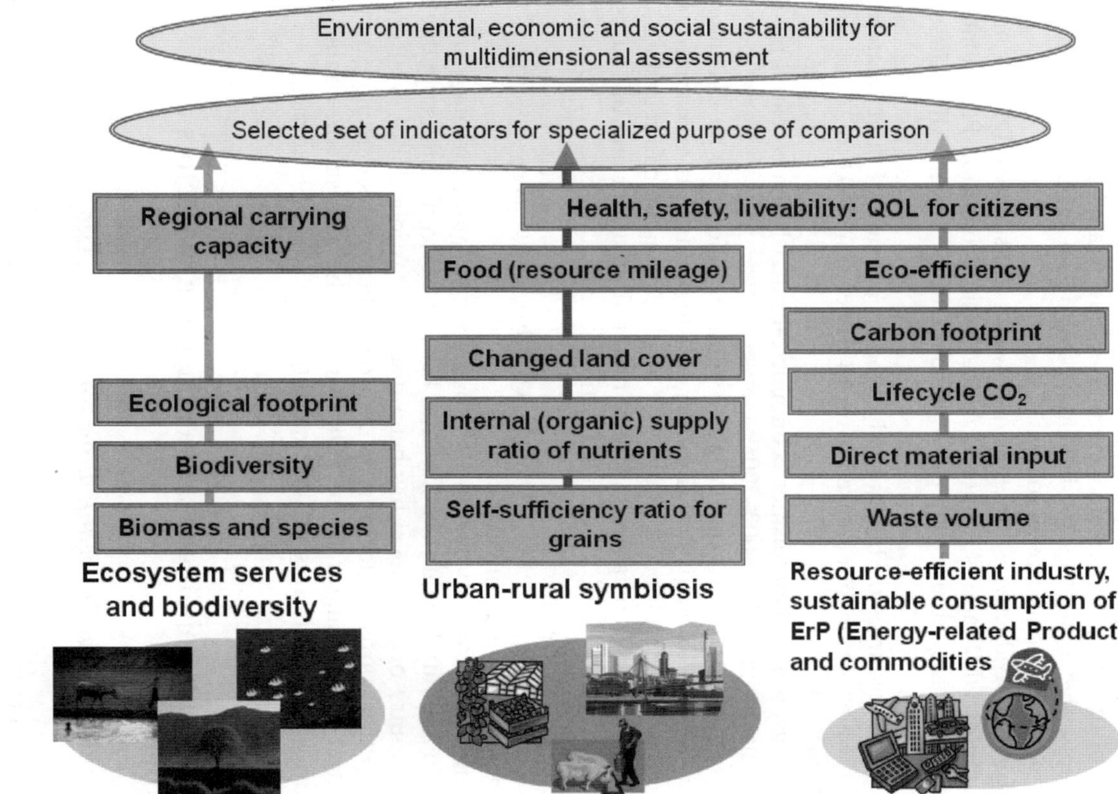

Figure 1.4 Benchmarking and sustainability indicator system in IR3S RCS research

however, since 2005 the situation has become increasingly worse in China, which has experienced a period of rapid economic growth. The experience gained in establishing an international standard for the concept and application of product-based CF, or business-site-based GHG accounting, may contribute to monitoring and evaluation of progress and the comparison of the extent of resource circulation and related sustainability.

The tentative indicators for benchmarking in an RCS or related domains of the 3R policy are as follows.

- Resources productivity or efficiency, which considers GDP per unit volume of DMI, and is proposed in the Basic Promotion Plan related to RCS by the Ministry of the Environment of Japan (MOE Japan, 2009).
- Recycled resources in the national economy per unit of direct material input, which in Japan increased from 14 per cent in 1992 to 21 per cent in 2008.
- Waste disposal in landfills per economic output, which decreased by 40 per cent in the period 2000–2005.
- Recycled resources per unit of waste volume, which may be calculated from 3R-related statistics. However, waste volume is minimized at source in less developed countries by local scavenging and recycling.
- Resource input as measured by total material input per unit of end-use services, which is the conceptual ultimate indicator but the least directly measurable.
- Ratio of actual/potential recycled materials, which considers the performance of a recycling action plan.

Not just sustainability within the domain of resource circulation, but also sustainability beyond the material base of environmental soundness at the country or state level has been discussed. Applicability or affordability with regards to decision-making on indicator systems appears to be central to choosing a set of indicators for the assessment, appraisal, comparison or monitoring of sustainability in nations or regions.

1-3 Capacity building in academia, business sectors and citizenry

Networking research organization for RCS in Asia

There are increasing numbers of institutes engaged in research on RCS in Asia. Cycle economy research or sustainability research units have been established in universities or area-wide joint centres in China. The

Chinese Academy of Sciences and other national research institutions have also been engaged in 3R-related indicator development, biomass utilization system design, cycle economy planning, e-waste regulation programming, etc. Korea's Advanced Research Institute of Science and Technology has developed a variety of environmental technologies for integrated waste management. In the field of solar and renewable energy, the TERI institute of energy and resources in India is a unique research organization, while the Malaysian institute RESTARI is tackling sustainability issues related to industrial waste management. UNEP has worked to enable developing countries to promote and disseminate CP technologies. For example, the Hanoi branch has exchanged experiences and practices on CP inside and outside Viet Nam. The Japanese MOE has provided a training course for researchers and officials in central/local governments to help them master ways of accounting for and evaluating value changes to 3R-related indicators.

Turning to international exchange or collaboration between Japan and Asian countries, Japan's Ministry of Education, Culture, Sports, Science and Technology has long supported bilateral communication in science and technology, and international cooperation has also been promoted on the basis of industrial development by the Ministry of Economy, Trade and Industry. Several types of low-impact environmental technologies, renewable energy production technologies and zero-emission technologies have been examined in Asia within the context of economic cost benefit, institutional intervention and social feasibility. The framework of urban environmental infrastructure, such as sewage and waste treatment, in Asia has been investigated with the support of the Japan International Cooperation Association (JICA), the US Agency for International Development, the German Agency for Technical Cooperation (GTZ), the Swedish International Development Cooperation Association and other international aid organizations.

Recently, multiple-purpose, trans-sector, integrated urban environmental planning schemes, operating on a participatory basis, have been applied to practices prior to the construction of specific infrastructure projects in Asian countries. The integrated urban environmental management plan prepared in 2007 by a team of JICA experts assessed physical environmental conditions, quality-of-life service-level indicators, basic human needs and citizen satisfaction in the areas of sanitation, sustainable waste management and amenity services in subdistricts in Hanoi. Using investigatory methods, they proposed recommendations for revising the medium-term master plan of Hanoi, which is known as the Oriental Pearl City. Sustainability should be taken into consideration at an early stage in any planning process at the city, region and national levels.

Zero Emission Forum and other institutions in Japan undertaking joint initiatives to disseminate a key RCS issue in Asia

The Zero Emission Forum established by the United Nations University has promoted the concept and practice of "zero emissions", which involves decoupling emission discharge from socio-economic development. Through symposiums and workshops, the forum has disseminated information on implementation of such initiatives in Asian countries (Chapter 3-1). The concept of zero emissions, whether gaseous, liquid or solid, has been linked with zero defects in product quality control and zero industrial accidents in workplace safety management. In the course of disseminating the Asian zero-emissions concept, the first international meeting on the subject was held in Jakarta and released the Declaration on Zero Emissions to the world (United Nations University, 1996).

IR3S and RISS planned joint workshops in Viet Nam and China with the collaboration of the Zero Emission Forum. Two workshops held in Hanoi and Ho Chi Minh City, followed by a workshop in Beijing, provided the opportunity to promote a mutual understanding of the situations in developing and developed countries. The practices in China, presented by a steel company, a synthetic fertilizer company and a cement company in Beijing, proved that cost-effective measures for energy saving, recycled resource utilization and waste minimization were both applicable and feasible for developing economies, which require short-term returns from investments. Advanced technology transfer has become a "hot" topic in discussions related to the development of the CDM (clean development mechanism) or other "win-win" systems directed at combating global environmental threats.

As shown in the Beijing workshop in 2006 (Chapter 3-1), there are increasing expectations among engineers regarding the implementation of advanced and highly efficient technologies, such as those used in the furnace-top thermal recovery of steel industries, combined power generation with coal gasification and cement kiln modification for organic waste inputs with high calorific contents. Bottom-up recycling practices were introduced during a seminar convened in Zhejiang in 2008. Bottle-to-bottle PET recycling in the Beijing area was also discussed, with emphasis on how it symbolized a new step for resource circulation in China. Another example is a food waste recycling system developed by a multidisciplinary team of government agencies, corporations and academia; this is similar to an ongoing Japanese project related to methane fermentation and high-speed composting technology with waste recovery logistics and multi-stakeholder collaboration.

These joint initiatives to disseminate key RCS issues have provided opportunities that should mutually benefit frontier and applicable scientific knowledge for all participants. For example, continuous exchanges of knowledge and practices on an RCS between Japan and Viet Nam yield significant academic and practical fruits in the IR3S research project. A Vietnamese research team has examined typical ecosystem services in the wetland conservancy of the Mekong River delta (Triet and Caines, 2007). The harvesting of aquatic plants such as reeds in wetlands was linked to community-based handicraft manufacturing initiatives, which was judged to be an appropriate example of a biomass-based resource-circulating economy. Another example is the attempt to establish a non-governmental organization for public participation in municipal waste recovery. Waste recovery programmes in megacities like Bangkok (Chapter 4-5) need collaboration among industries, government, collection service providers, engineering firms and residents. The waste fund of Ho Chi Minh City, established by academia's commitment in recent years, launched coordination activities for collaboration for waste recovery.

Furthermore, in Viet Nam the communication platforms proposed and supported by institutes in Japan for international cooperation on global or common environmental issues have played a crucial role in empowering researchers and practitioners in the field of resource circulation, sustainable waste management and 3R practices. For example, the UNEP International Environmental Technology Centre, associated with the Global Environment Center in Osaka, has organized international collaboration programmes in the focus area of sustainable production and consumption, especially eco-town promotion in Asia. A publication on eco-towns in Japan (GEC, 2005) shows a step-by-step flowchart for stimulating the roles of legislation, strategic policy-making, finance, capacity building and technology development and transfer among stakeholders, including universities.

The International Center for Environmental Technology Transfer (ICETT) has been engaged in key environmental technology appraisal, technology transfer and capacity building. The centre maintains a database on environmental management and technology, which is focused on CP, eco-efficiency, zero emissions and environmental management. Recently, ICETT has become involved in reducing the energy consumption of Yunnan and Gansu provinces in China, and in the glass and beer industries in Viet Nam, by improving energy efficiency and offering training opportunities. ICETT has conducted studies, proposed improvement options and provided technical guidance for several governments and their local officials. Capacity-building programmes stimulate improvements in environmental conservation, resource conservation, energy efficiency, CP and waste disposal. The Kitakyushu International Techno-Cooperative Association has consulted with Asian city stakeholders on issues related to waste management, recycling and environmental conservation. Recently, high-level discussions were held at Orissa in east India, Haiphong in Viet Nam, Chelyabinsk in Russia, Chonburi in Thailand, Surabaya in Indonesia and Liaoyang and Tianjin in China.

IGES has launched waste and resources projects, some of which have dealt with material flow accounting in selected non-OECD countries, and waste and recycling policy in the regional economic integration of East Asia. The institute's seminal joint publication on 3R (ADB and IGES, 2008) emphasizes eight roles of government in initiatives directed towards the establishment of resource-efficient economies in Asia and the Pacific: adopting integrated approaches to change perspectives and decision-making processes; developing national policy frameworks; building institutional capacity; supporting local action; investing in resource-efficient infrastructure; promoting new technologies and solutions; supporting industry awareness and change; and participating in regional and international initiatives.

This book deals with the academic basis of the RCS concept and provides insights into its achievement. Within a comprehensive perspective of sustainability science, authors from different scientific fields, including environmental engineering, environmental economics, policy science, agricultural science, sociology, etc., explore strategies on integrated management, technology innovation and policy for achieving a resource-circulating and ultimately "sustainable" society in Asia.

The book's intended audience includes experts in the field of resource-circulation systems and university professionals in resource-circulating research. The book is also intended for the business sector working on resource circulation in the Asian region, including those in international cooperation and assistance projects (consultants, NGOs, government organizations, etc.). It provides plentiful case studies of resource circulation for those working in this field, and introduces different scenario schemes (the whole process from conception to planning and implementation) regarding the design of a resource-circulating society. While this book considers scenarios in the broader sense, where necessary and to avoid any misunderstanding we will refer to these as options.

REFERENCES

ADB and IGES (2008) *Toward Resource-Efficient Economies in Asia and the Pacific – Reduce, Reuse and Recycle*. Manila: Asian Development Bank/Institute for Global Environmental Strategies.

Bringezu, S. (2006) "Materializing Policies for Sustainable Use and Economy-wide Management of Resources: Biophysical Perspectives, Socio-Economic Options and a Dual Approach for the European Union", Wuppertal Papers No. 160, June, Wuppertal Institute for Climate, Environment and Energy.

GEC (2005) *Eco-Towns in Japan – Implications and Lessons for Developing Countries and Cities*. Osaka: Global Environmental Center.

Graedel, T. E. and B. R. Allenby (1995) *Industrial Ecology*. Englewood Cliffs, NJ: Prentice-Hall.

IHDP-IT (2001) "Industrial Transformation Science Plan", Report No. 12, International Human Dimensions Programme on Global Environmental Change, Amsterdam.

IMF (2009) *International Reserves and Foreign Currency Liquidity*. Washington, DC: International Monetary Fund.

Kok, M., W. Vermeulen, A. Faaij and D. de Jager (2002) *Global Warming and Social Innovation: The Challenge of a Climate Neutral Society*. London and Sterling, VA: Earthscan.

Loorbach, D. and J. Rotmans (2006) "Managing Transitions for Sustainable Development", in X. Olsthoorn and A. J. Wieczorek (eds) *Understanding Industrial Transformation: Views from Different Disciplines*. Dordrecht: Springer.

Ministry of Natural Resources and Environment (2006) "3R Initiatives in Thailand", paper presented at Senior Officials' Meeting of the 3R Initiative, Tokyo.

MOE Japan (2006) "Chair's Summary", Asia 3R Conference, Tokyo, 30 October–1 November; available at www.env.go.jp/recycle/3r/en/asia/01.pdf.

———— (2009) *Japanese Environmental Statistics*. Tokyo: Ministry of Environment (in Japanese).

MOE Korea (2006) "Policy Direction on E-Waste Recycling in Korea", paper presented at Senior Officials' Meeting of the 3R Initiative, Tokyo.

Morioka, T. and H. Yabar (2007) "Resources Circulating and Sustainable Society in Asia: Concept and Research Scheme", *International Journal of Environmental Technology and Management* 7(5/6), pp. 596–617.

Morioka, T., O. Saito and H. Yabar (2006) "The Pathway to a Sustainable Industrial Society – Initiative of the Research Institute for Sustainability Science (RISS) at Osaka University", *Journal of Sustainability Science* 1, pp. 65–82.

OECD (2008) "Front-runners' Experience on Sustainable Materials Management (SMM)", report of the Second SMM Workshop, OECD Working Group on Waste Prevention and Recycling, Tel-Aviv.

Schmidheiny, S. and WBCSD (1992) *Changing Course: A Global Business Perspective on Development and the Environment*. Cambridge, MA: MIT Press.

Schmidt-Bleek, F. (1999) "The Factor 10/MIPS-Concept: Bridging Ecological, Economic, and Social Dimensions with Sustainability Indicators", UNU/ZEF Discussion Paper Series 2, Doc. ZEF-EN-1999-2, UNU Zero Emissions Forum, Tokyo; available at www.unu.edu/zef/publications_e/ZEF_EN_1999_03_D.pdf.

Tanji, K. and T. Morioka (2004) "Design of Scenario Guidance Type Policy-making Support System for Nature-convivial Basin Management", *Journal of Environmental Information Sciences* 18, pp. 521–526 (in Japanese).

Triet, T. and R. Caines (2007) "Towards Sustainable Rural Development: Combining Biodiversity Conservation with Poverty Alleviation – A Case Study in Phu My Village, Kien Giang Province, Vietnam", in T. Morioka, K. Haruki and H. Yabar (eds) *Transition to a Resource-circulating Society: Strategies and Initiatives in Asia*. Osaka: Osaka University Press, pp. 181–190.

UNEP (1998) "Basel Convention: Guide to the Control System", Secretariat of Basel Convention, pp. 1–51.

———— (2005) "Strategic Elements in Implementing the 3R Platform", UNEP contribution to 3R Ministerial Meeting, Tokyo, April; available at www.unep. or.jp/ietc/SPC/3R_Strategic_Elements.pdf.

United Nations University (1996) *Proceedings of the Second Annual UNU World Congress on Zero Emissions*, Chattanooga, 29–31 May; available at www.unu. edu/zef/publications_e/96_congress_proc.pdf.

UNSD (2007) "Demographic Yearbook Database". UN Statistical Division; available at http://unstats.un.org/unsd/demographic/products/dyb/dyb2.htm.

WCED (1987) *Our Common Future,* Report of the World Commission on Environment and Development. Oxford: Oxford University Press.

Wolman, A. (1965) "The Metabolism of Cities", *Scientific American* 213, pp. 179–190.

WRI and WBCSD (2004) *The Greenhouse Gas Protocol.* World Resource Institute and World Business Council for Sustainable Development; available at www.wri.org/publication/greenhouse-gas-protocol-corporate-accounting-and-reporting-standard-revised-edition.

The Asian approach to a resource-circulating society – Research framework, prospects and networking

2-1

Framework of future vision, scenario and roadmap

Yasushi Umeda, Yusuke Kishita and Tohru Morioka

2-1-1 Introduction

One of the main challenges in sustainability science is to develop visions of a sustainable society. For example, the Japanese government defines the concept of a sustainable society as a combination of a low-carbon society, a resource-circulating society and a naturally symbiotic society. However, a holistic vision integrating these three societal visions has not yet been presented or fully clarified. Developing visions is thus essential to setting targets for a sustainable society as well as for assembling the various technological, political and grassroots measures required to achieve those targets. For this purpose, numerous scenarios have been proposed (IPCC, 2007; Japan LCS Scenario Team, 2008; International Energy Agency, 2004). However, scenarios focusing on a resource-circulating society (RCS) have rarely been put forward. Describing sustainability scenarios is an effective approach in discussions of a sustainable society and for creating a consensus regarding this society. Moreover, by analysing existing sustainability scenarios, we can identify their essential problem structures and develop potential solutions for achieving sustainability.

However, since sustainability scenarios contain future prospects, which inherently contain ambiguity and uncertainty, combined with the fact that they are documents, more holistic and scientific methodologies are required to support the design and analysis of scenarios. This chapter aims at clarifying discussion points on developing scenarios for an Asian RCS from the viewpoint of a computer-aided methodology.

Establishing a resource-circulating society in Asia: Challenges and opportunities, Morioka, Hanaki and Moriguchi (eds), United Nations University Press, 2011, ISBN 978-92-808-1182-7

2-1-2 Review of scenario studies

To clarify requirements for Asian RCS scenarios, the team at the Research Institute for Sustainable Science, Osaka University, investigated existing sustainability scenarios that focus on low-carbon and resource-circulating societies (Hara et al., 2007; Yabar and Hara, 2008). Going back to the history of scenario-based analysis, DeWeerd (1967), who was one of the pioneers of such analysis, discussed political-military scenarios in the context of defence problems and war gaming, and claimed that relevance to research objectives is sometimes predominant over credibility of the scenario. Schwartz (1991) clarified that describing scenarios is a promising approach for drawing visions of various possible futures, and the point of scenarios is to make strategic decisions that will be sound for all plausible futures.

There are many scenario studies, mainly in the areas of climate change and energy demand and supply. However, a few studies have been carried out regarding the RCS. The most famous may be the Intergovernmental Panel on Climate Change (IPCC) assessment reports (e.g. IPCC, 2007), which describe climate change scenarios in the medium (2030) and long (2100) term. The World Energy Outlook (WEO) of the International Energy Agency (e.g. International Energy Agency, 2004) forecasts trends of energy demand and supply. The Japan LCS Scenario Team (2008) depicts low-carbon society in Japan in 2050. This scenario employs the back-casting approach that sets a desirable future in which CO_2 emissions in 2050 have been reduced by 70 per cent, followed by drawing paths between the present and the future. Gallopin et al. (1997) described six scenarios, which are mutually different in terms of population growth, environmental quality, technological change, etc., for discussing the sustainability of the global system. The World Business Council for Sustainable Development designed three global scenarios to explore what human social systems should be established for sustainable development (WBCSD, 1997). Shell's scenarios are also quite famous. Shell developed its first set of global scenarios in 1972, raising the possibility of high oil prices, which happened in 1973 (Shell International, 2003). Scenarios are stories about the future, and their purpose is to help make better decisions in the present. Shell International (2008) also developed "Shell Energy Scenarios to 2050", which consists of two alternative futures called "Scramble" and "Blueprints" for the development of the energy system over the next 50 years. These scenarios predict energy consumption for individual sources, such as oil, gas, coal and biomass. The results differ in respect to, notably, the supply of biofuels. One of the most famous approaches for scenario development is the Shell/GBN matrix, which contains two dimensions of uncertainty; each of the four quadrants in the matrix expresses the kernel of a possible future (Wack, 1985). In terms of scenarios on ecosystems, Cosgrove and Rijsberman (2000) employed the WaterGAP model in describing "world water vision scenarios". The Millennium Ecosystem Assessment research group explores plausible future changes in ecosystem services and human well-being (Carpenter et al., 2005).

Raskin et al. (2005) analysed the structure of six major sustainability scenarios based upon time horizon, covered regions and study focus. Morioka, Saito and Yabar (2006) summarized various international scenario studies in terms of five global challenges: climate change, depletion of energy resources, degradation of ecosystem services, overconsumption of non-renewable resources and decoupling of industrialization from environmental pressure. In this analysis, each challenge was described in terms of four criteria: carrying capacity concept; indicators and targets; major driving forces and policies; and commitment.

One core aspect of resource circulation is how to manage resources in a sustainable manner. Some studies have proposed policy frameworks for sustainable resource management. Bringezu (2006), for instance, proposed a generic policy approach that focuses on increased resource efficiency and reduced use of all primary resources. At a regional level, the European Union (EU) has made many efforts to construct an RCS. The Sustainable Europe Research Institute developed a project called MOSUS (modelling opportunities and limits for restructuring Europe towards sustainability), which designed and applied a global environmental-economic model to quantify the interrelations between socio-economic driving forces and the state of the environment. The model is used to simulate different scenarios for sustainable development in Europe until the year 2020, and evaluated the impacts of policy measures on both economic and environmental indicators (SERI, 2007). This project developed three scenarios: the baseline, in which projections of further trends observed in the last 25 years are made and no particular policy strategies are encouraged; the weak sustainability scenario that reflects policy goals and measures from key EU documents; and the strong sustainability scenario that includes more ambitious policy goals, based on the scientific literature (SERI, 2004).

Scenarios generally employ databases and simulations, in addition to narrative storylines for predicting the future (Alcamo, 2001). For example, simulations play a central role in the IPCC assessment reports. In these scenarios, storylines describe common conditions for simulations, and the branching of the subscenarios corresponds to differences in future visions based on different simulation conditions. The main body of the IPCC reports binds these various simulation results. In contrast, the International Energy Agency WEO scenario does not explicitly mention

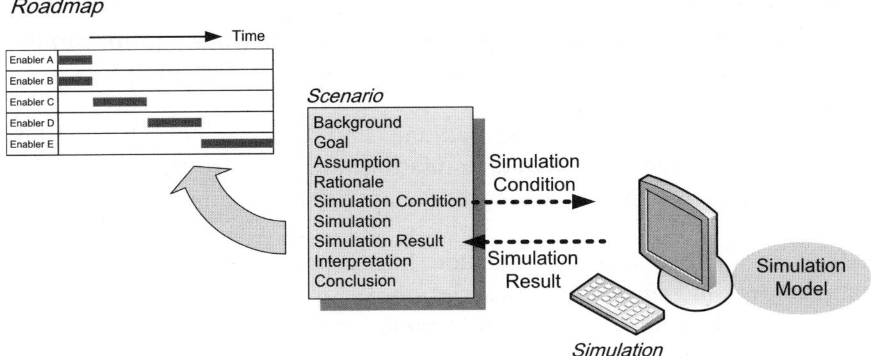

Figure 2.1.1 Scenario, roadmap and simulation

a simulator or simulation results. Instead, the WEO descriptively estimates future trends based on the analysis of large amounts of available data.

Forecasting and backcasting are often applied when composing a scenario. A backcasting scenario explores paths backward from a predetermined future end-point to the present in order to discuss what measures are required to reach that future state (Robinson, 1990). For example, the 2050 Japan LCS scenario uses backcasting. Backcasting is suitable for addressing long-term problems that need drastic changes (Dreborg, 1996), and is thus a distinguishing feature of scenario description.

While scenarios, roadmaps and simulation have some commonality in describing the future, their roles are different (Figure 2.1.1). Firstly, while scenarios may include simulation, simulation cannot include scenarios. Roadmaps may be understood to be a component of a scenario focusing on the route for achieving a vision in the scenario, and describe measures and actions required to realize the vision and their expected results over time. Such measures and actions include political actions, social activities, social system design, institutional design, structure of manufacturing industries, design of resource-circulation systems and environmentally conscious products and their life cycles, and development of enabling technologies. Simulation derives some results based on a certain model from input conditions. In this sense, scenarios and simulation are complementary to each other: scenarios describe plausible measures and actions, and simulation verifies their effects and drawbacks. Note that simulation itself does not explicitly include the model on which the simulation is based, nor does it include assumptions and limitations of the model, assumptions of the simulation conditions or interpretation of the simulation results. This makes reuse and verification of a simulation difficult. Furthermore, from the viewpoint of composing a scenario, simulation is a computerization of forecasting, and it is difficult to execute backcasting with simulation.

This comparison of scenarios, roadmaps and simulation clarifies the importance of the scenario. While simulation and data are the most indispensable elements for describing a scenario, the most important feature of a scenario is that it can descriptively represent what a simulation and data cannot. Such elements include backgrounds and assumptions of data, models and simulations, descriptions of situations and their changes, measures and actions to be taken, simulation conditions, methods of future prospects, and interpretation and analysis of data and simulation results. Thus scenario is inevitably descriptive because these elements can only be presented as text.

2-1-3 The role of descriptive scenarios in seeking an Asian RCS

A scenario is a story that connects a description of the future to present realities within a context of causality (Glenn and Futures Group International, 2003). A sustainability scenario here refers to desirable or undesirable visions of a sustainable society and identifies routes towards the desired visions. Most of the existing scenarios, described in the preceding section, basically follow a common pattern: analysis of the current state of the target system under study based on past trends; identification of the key drivers, which may determine the path of the future of the target system, and assumptions regarding the main sectors of the target system; and description of several future visions of the system, including required key measures and actions based on the results of the first two steps. The significance of scenario description for discussing the Asian RCS can be summarized as follows.

- Scenario description provides a strategic methodology to draw several future visions, assuming uncertainty and ambiguity of the future, and encourages us to discuss measures and actions required for each vision, including technologies, institutions and economic mechanisms. This more or less requires a backcasting approach.
- It facilitates communication among various stakeholders and, as a result, the creation of social consensus regarding directions of the RCS in Asia as well as the measures and actions required for achieving it.
- The process of composing a scenario clarifies the fundamental issues and bottlenecks of the Asian RCS and their critical drivers.
- Since real-world transitions will not always be consistent with the scenario, we can manage transitions toward the Asian RCS by executing

"plan, do, check and action" cycles, in which differences are monitored and analysed, and scenarios and action plans are modified.

- Scenario description provides a method for systematizing knowledge towards visions of a sustainable society. In this sense, it is a useful approach for knowledge systematization in sustainability science.

The scenario description approach is thus suitable for discussing future visions of the Asian RCS, and there might be no other methods. For example, an important question for the RCS is whether a low-carbon society and a resource-circulating society can coexist, particularly in Asia in this context. They must coexist, and such a situation is an indispensable element. However, under the current circumstances we do not have sufficient knowledge to discuss conditions and measures for realizing this coexistence in a general form. We should therefore gradually clarify the conditions and measures needed by collecting examples of success and failure. This is an exact description of the process of creating future visions of the Asian RCS.

However, the issue of the Asian RCS contains a wide variety of topics, including climate change, depletion of energy resources, waste problems and overconsumption of non-renewable resources. Moreover, it covers a variety of regions with drastically different characteristics, and reliable fundamental data are decidedly insufficient. So instead of employing the well-established traditional scenario-based analysis mainly developed in the Western world, we take a bottom-up and flexible approach to describing scenarios. In other words, our description approach may be rephrased as scenario planning or option design for alternative future visions and their valuation. As the first step for an Asian RCS scenario, we should construct firm foundations by collecting concrete elements; in other words, elements for analysis of the current state, identification of the key drivers and assumptions, and descriptions of future visions and required key measures and actions. For this purpose, each chapter in this book provides these elements of the Asian RCS scenarios.

2-1-4 Required research for the Asian RCS scenarios

As discussed, the Asian RCS inherently has a very complicated structure and contains a wide variety of mutually related environmental issues. This implies, on one hand, that there may be plenty of plausible scenarios. On the other hand, it requires a clear representation of each scenario easily understood by scenario readers despite the complicated structure. An approach to solving these two problems is to encourage stakeholders to compose various scenarios in easily understandable representation. We propose a methodology for supporting scenario composition and archiving, the "sustainable society scenario simulator" (Figure 2.1.2). This

Figure 2.1.2 Encouraging stakeholders to compose various Asian RCS scenarios

system, the 3S simulator, archives various scenarios and simulators, and a wide variety of stakeholders can compose sustainability scenarios easily by combining archived scenarios and simulators in a cooperative manner.

- *Scenario writer:* can efficiently compose Asian RCS scenarios by referring to archived scenarios and register his/her scenarios into the archive.
- *Scenario reader:* can search for scenarios that cover his/her interest, understand the scenarios and analyse them.
- *Policy-maker:* can determine policies by investigating, analysing and evaluating archived scenarios and can estimate the effects of policies.
- *Enterprise strategist:* can plan strategies by investigating, analysing and evaluating archived scenarios and estimate the effects of new environmentally conscious products when they are shipped to the market.

It is important to note here that the issue of sustainability inherently requires a multifaceted perspective. Even if we resolve one aspect, another broader aspect may exist, and we may uncover external effects and new problems from this broader aspect. This recursive structure is central to the issue of sustainability. If this is true, no single scenario from a certain viewpoint will provide us with a sustainable solution. Instead, we

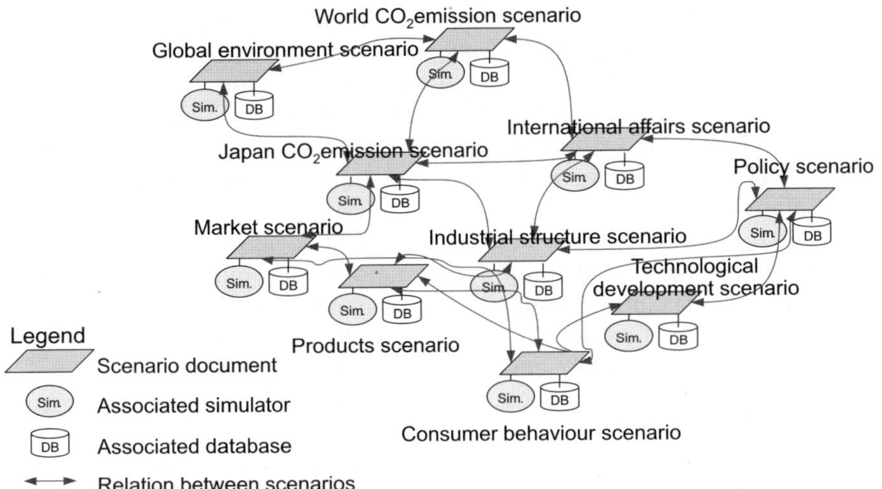

Figure 2.1.3 Multifaceted structure of scenarios used to model the issue of sustainability

should organize various scenarios from different viewpoints by relating them to each other (Figure 2.1.3). This book as a whole provides this multifaceted perspective of the Asian RCS problem, and each facet is an indispensable element of Asian RCS scenarios. According to this discussion, the approach here is to develop methodologies for representing, composing, analysing and structuring scenarios, rather than to describe a holistic and comprehensive Asian RCS scenario. The difference between these two approaches can be explained using a product design analogy: while the latter (describing a comprehensive scenario) corresponds to designing a perfect eco-product, the former (developing methodologies) corresponds to developing design theories and methodologies.

This chapter takes the former approach, because few research efforts have examined this support method, and this approach may lead to a scientific analysis of scenarios and knowledge systematization through the description of scenarios. Thus the aim is to construct an intelligent computer-aided design (CAD) system in the domain of scenario design.

2-1-5 Sustainable society scenario simulator

In order to develop methodologies for representing, composing, analysing and structuring scenarios as described above, we can identify the following problems of current scenario representation methods that employ documents.

- The logical structure of scenarios is not clearly described. For example, assumptions and facts are not clearly distinguished in scenario documents, causing difficulties in rational understanding: it is unclear to what extent a reader can believe in a scenario and where logical jumps exist. This may be serious in describing the Asian RCS scenarios, since they will cover a wide variety of issues related to sustainable resource circulation.
- Scenarios are not connected with their associated simulators, even though scenarios often employ simulators. This makes it difficult to verify and re-examine simulations in original scenarios.
- Scenario CAD methods for supporting the processes of scenario design in a holistic manner have not yet been well formalized.
- No computer-aided methods have been established for analysing scenarios, such as logical structure analysis and "what-if" analysis, in which users can examine changes in a scenario by changing its assumptions.

To develop an intelligent CAD system to be used for scenario design by solving these issues (not automating but supporting a user in representing, composing, analysing and structuralizing scenarios), we propose the 3S simulator (Umeda et al., 2009). We intend to describe our visions of the Asian RCS by structuring various facets described in this book using this system. To develop the system, we have settled on five research topics.

- *Representation methodology of scenarios:* this formalizes scenario representations to clarify their causal structure and relations to associated simulations. This provides us with a computerized way of representing sustainability scenarios.
- *Computer-aided scenario design methodology:* this models the design processes of new scenarios, including forecasting and backcasting, and develops a methodology for supporting the design of new scenarios by reusing archived scenarios and their associated simulators.
- *Dynamic scenarios:* this refers to a structured, computerized scenario representation that maintains dynamic links to its associated simulators. These links enable re-execution of simulations with different conditions and permit the modification of the scenario according to the simulation results.
- *Scenario analysis:* this supports the analysis of described scenarios, including logical structure, "what-if" and sensitivity analyses.
- *Scenario archives:* this focuses on archiving scenarios and their simulators by using structured, computerized representation to facilitate understanding and analysis of existing scenarios, as well the design of new scenarios using existing scenarios.

The architecture of the 3S simulator consists of five components (Figure 2.1.4).

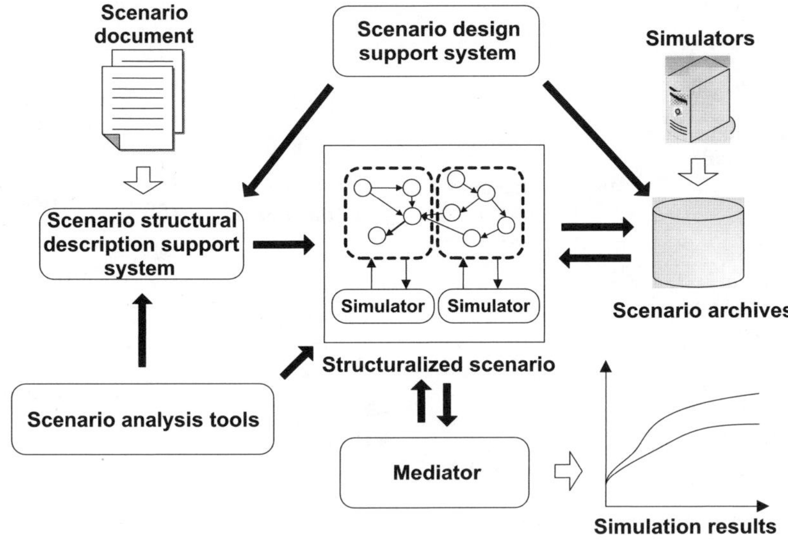

Figure 2.1.4 Architecture of 3S simulator

- *Structural scenario description support system:* structurally supports describing new or existing scenarios.
- *Scenario archives:* archives structuralized scenarios and associated simulators.
- *Scenario design support system:* supports designing new scenarios.
- *Scenario analysis tools:* analyse the logical structure of a described scenario and conduct "what-if" and sensitivity analyses using its simulators.
- *Mediator:* exchanges data among simulators used in a scenario in order to run simulations.

2-1-6 Structural description of scenarios

In general, an Asian RCS scenario inevitably contains ungrounded hypotheses and logical jumps because it involves future predictions. The existence of such hypotheses and jumps in a scenario does not mean it is inferior; rather, they characterize the scenario and often suggest its innovativeness. At the least, it is valuable for understanding a scenario correctly to clarify such hypotheses and logical jumps and rationales (e.g. the references, data and simulations) of the scenario.

For these purposes, we are developing a structural description methodology for sustainability scenarios (ibid.). This methodology presents a

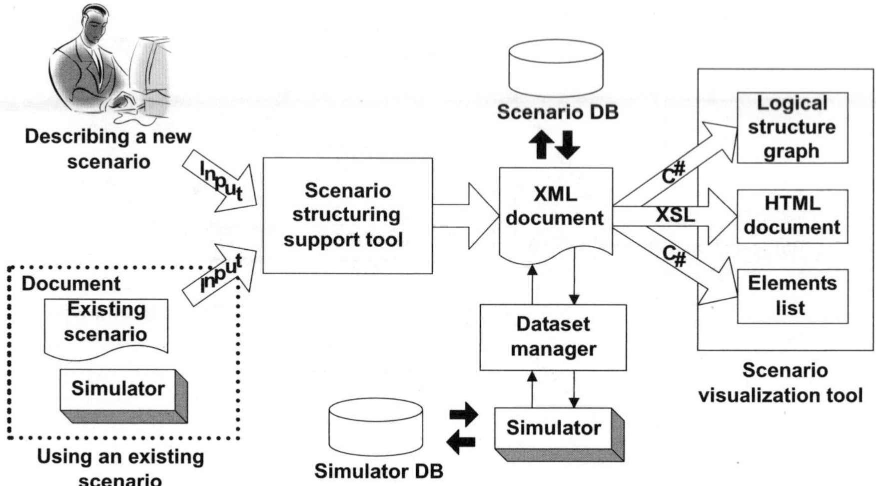

Figure 2.1.5 Architecture of scenario structural description support system
Source: Umeda et al. (2009).

scenario as a directed graph composed of nodes and links in four levels, where a node expresses an element of a scenario, such as a subscenario and a clause, and a link express a relation between nodes, such as causality:

* *scenario level:* expresses the structure of subscenarios
* *expression level:* expresses the structure of clauses in a subscenario
* *word level:* expresses causality among phrases in a clause
* *data level:* expresses the relationship between simulator input and output data.

We developed the scenario structural description support system (Figure 2.1.5) as a part of the 3S simulator (ibid.). This system consists of five components. The scenario structuring support tool supports the structuring of scenarios by inserting XML (Eckstein, 1999) tags into original scenario text in order to indicate node and link types. The scenario visualization tool visualizes a structured scenario as a logical structure graph, an HTML document and an element list. For example, the logical structure graph represents a scenario as a graph based on tags added to the scenario. The remaining three components, the scenario database, simulator database and dataset manager, work in archiving scenarios and describing dynamic scenarios.

For example, Figure 2.1.6 illustrates a structural description of a hybrid electric vehicle (HEV) diffusion scenario, which predicts the number of HEVs in Japan up to 2050 by using the product diffusion simulator (Matsumoto et al., 2008). The figure shows the logical structure graph of the

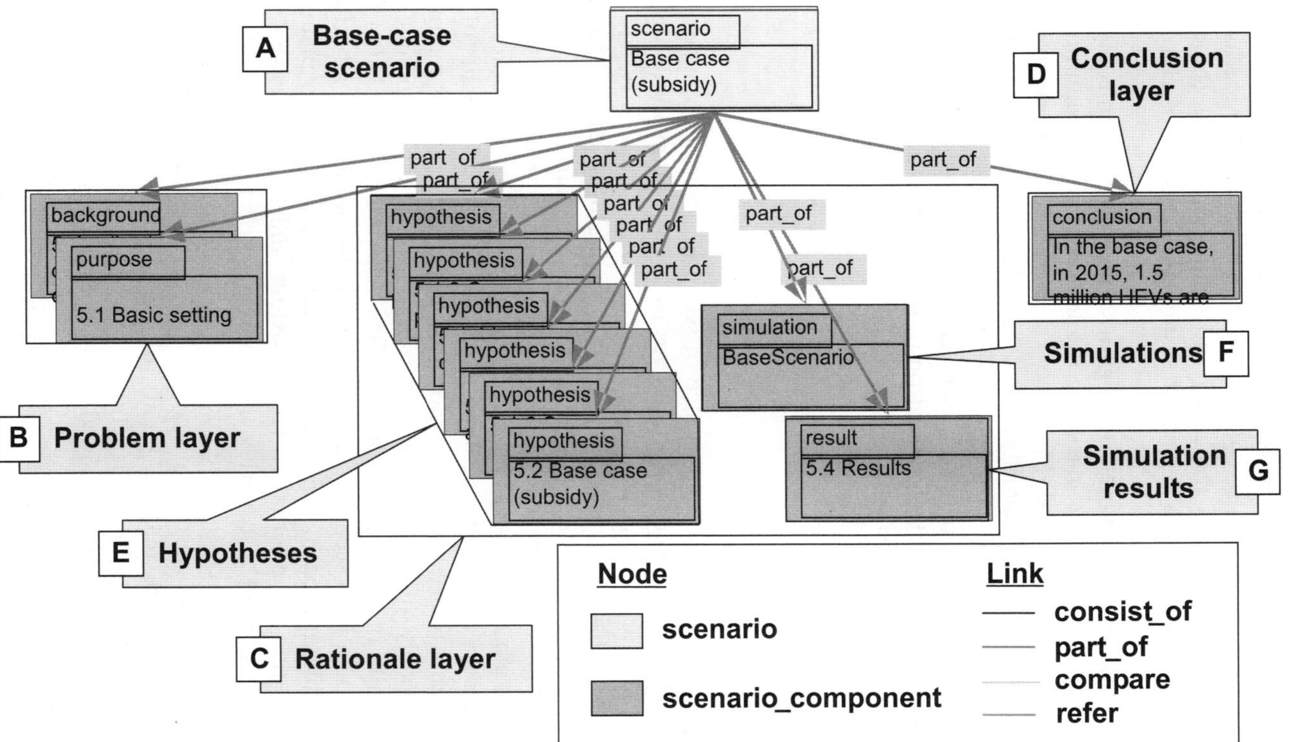

Figure 2.1.6 Structural description of a hybrid electric vehicle diffusion scenario

scenario at the scenario level. The whole subscenario (block A) consists of problem (block B), rationale (block C) and conclusion (block D) layers. The rationale layer also consists of three blocks. These are hypotheses (block E), simulations (block F) and simulation results (block G). Empirically, this structure is typical of sustainability scenarios employing simulators.

By using this description methodology, a scenario writer can compose a sustainability scenario while clarifying the logicality and assumptions on which the scenario is based. Moreover, a scenario can be analysed in terms of logicality, which clarifies the assumptions of the scenario and, therefore, helps a reader to understand it. Since the methodology provides a mechanism for managing data consistency between a scenario and its simulators, it enables verification of the scenario and execution of "what-if" analysis by reusing the scenario and its simulators in a dynamic manner.

2-1-7 Conclusions

This chapter discussed the importance of scenario description in seeking the Asian RCS. Scenario description gives us a strategic methodology to draw several future visions, assuming uncertainty and ambiguity, and encourages us to discuss measures and actions required for each vision, including technologies, institutions and economic mechanisms. Reviewing existing sustainable scenarios revealed that, while there are future scenario studies in such areas as climate change and energy, few studies have been carried out regarding a resource-circulating society. The issue of the Asian RCS inherently contains a wide variety of topics, covers many regions with widely differing characteristics and lacks reliable fundamental data, especially in developing countries. This chapter proposed that, for describing Asian RCS scenarios under these conditions, we take a bottom-up and flexible approach, which may be rephrased as scenario planning or option design for alternative future visions and their valuation. For constructing Asian RCS scenarios, this book lays firm foundations by collecting concrete elements of the current state, key drivers, future visions and required key measures and actions. The features of the Asian RCS also imply that there may be plenty of plausible scenarios, and each would be complicated in its structure. For solving these problems, this chapter proposed a computer-aided methodology for representing, composing, analysing and structuring scenarios; especially, a structural representation method for describing a sustainability scenario. This method provides a clear representation of scenarios easily understandable to scenario readers, with structural analysis of scenarios. The proposed methodology encourages and accelerates various stakeholders in describing Asian RCS scenarios, which will lead us to holistic and comprehensive scenarios.

Acknowledgements

This research is supported by Grant-in-Aid for Scientific Research (No. 20246130 and 21·316) by the Japan Society for the Promotion of Science.

REFERENCES

Alcamo, J. (2001) "Scenarios as Tools for International Environmental Assessments", in T. Ribeiro (ed.) *Environmental Issue Report No. 24*. Copenhagen: European Environmental Agency.

Bringezu, S. (2006) "Materializing Policies for Sustainable Use and Economy-wide Management of Resources: Biophysical Perspectives, Socio-economic Options and a Dual Approach for the EU", Wuppertal Papers No. 160, Wuppertal Institute.

Carpenter, S., P. Pingali, E. Bennett and M. Zurek (2005) *Ecosystems and Human Well-Being: Scenarios – Findings of the Scenarios Working Group*, Millennium Ecosystem Assessment Series Vol. 2. Washington, DC: Island Press.

Cosgrove, W. J. and F. Rijsberman (2000) *World Water Vision: Making Water Everybody's Business*. London: Earthscan/Thanet Press.

DeWeerd, H. (1967) *Political Military Scenarios*. Santa Monica, CA: RAND Corporation.

Dreborg, K. (1996) "Essence of Backcasting", *Futures* 28, pp. 813–828.

Eckstein, R. (1999) *XML Pocket Reference*. Sevastopol: O'Reilly & Associates.

Gallopin, G., A. Hammond, P. Raskin and R. Swart (1997) "Branch Points: Global Scenarios and Human Choice", Polestar Series Report No. 7, Stockholm Environment Institute, Boston, MA.

Glenn, J. and Futures Group International (2003) "Scenarios", in J. C. Glenn and T. J. Gordon (eds) *The Millennium Project Futures Research Methodology V2.0*. Washington, DC: American Council for the United Nations University.

Hara, K., O. Saito, H. Yabar, Y. Yamaguchi and T. Morioka (2007) "Building Future Scenarios toward Resource-Circulating Society – Case Study in Yangtze River Delta", in *Proceedings of 35th Annual Meeting of Environmental Systems Research*. Tokyo: Japan Society of Civil Engineers, pp. 123–128.

International Energy Agency (2004) *World Energy Outlook 2004*. Paris: IEA Publications.

IPCC (2007) "Climate Change 2007, Synthesis Report", contribution of Working Groups I, II, III to the Fourth Assessment Report of the Intergovernmental Panel on Climate Change, Geneva.

Japan LCS Scenario Team (2008) *Japan Scenarios and Actions towards Low-Carbon Societies (LCSs)*. Tsukuba: National Institute for Environmental

Studies; available at http://2050.nies.go.jp/material/2050_LCS_Scenarios_Actions_English_080715.pdf.

Matsumoto, M., S. Kondoh, J. Fujimoto and K. Masui (2008) "A Modeling Framework for the Diffusion of Green Technologies", in M. H. Sherif and T. M. Khalil (eds) *Management of Technology Innovation and Value Creation*. Singapore: World Scientific Publishing, pp. 121–136.

Morioka, T., O. Saito and H. Yabar (2006) "The Pathway to a Sustainable Industrial Society – Initiative of the Research Institute for Sustainability Science (RISS) at Osaka University", *Journal of Sustainability Science* 1, pp. 65–82.

Raskin, P., F. Monks, T. Ribeiro, D. van Vuuren and M. Zurek (2005) "Global Scenarios in Historical Perspective", in *Ecosystems and Human Well-being: Scenarios Assessment*. Washington, DC: Island Press.

Robinson, J. (1990) "Futures under Glass: A Recipe for People Who Hate to Predict", *Futures* 22, pp. 820–842.

Schwartz, P. (1991) *The Art of the Long View*. New York: Doubleday.

Shell International (2003) "Scenarios: An Explorer's Guide"; available at www.shell.com/home/content/aboutshell/our_strategy/shell_global_scenarios/scenarios_explorers_guide/scenario_explorers_guide_30102006.html.

———— (2008) "Shell Energy Scenarios to 2050"; available at www.static.shell.com/static/public/downloads/brochures/corporate_pkg/scenarios/shell_energy_scenarios_2050.pdf.

SERI (2004) "Resource Use Scenarios for Europe in 2020", Working Paper No. 1, Sustainable Europe Research Institute, Vienna.

———— (2007) "Modelling Scenarios towards a Sustainable Use of Natural Resources in Europe", Working Paper No. 4, Sustainable Europe Research Institute, Vienna.

Umeda, Y., T. Nishiyama, Y. Yamasaki, Y. Kishita and S. Fukushige (2009) "Proposal of Sustainable Society Scenario Simulator", *CIRP Journal of Manufacturing Science and Technology* 1, pp. 272–278.

Wack, P. (1985) "Scenarios: Uncharted Waters Ahead", *Harvard Business Review* 63, pp. 73–89.

WBCSD (1997) *Exploring Sustainable Development: WBCSD Global Scenarios 2000–2050 Summary*. London: World Business Council for Sustainable Development.

Yabar, H. and K. Hara (2008) "Backcasting Approach Towards a Resource-circulating Society", in *Designing a Closed-loop Economy with Eco-industrial Technology*, RISS Annual Report, March. Osaka: Osaka University, pp. 136–147.

2-2

Structuring knowledge on a resource-circulating society

Terukazu Kumazawa, Takanori Matsui and Riichiro Mizoguchi

2-2-1 Introduction

Chapter 1 laid out a framework for the formation of a resource-circulating society in Asia. As mentioned in the previous chapter, scenario description provides a strategic methodology to draw several future visions, assuming uncertainty and ambiguity, and encourages us to discuss the measures and actions required for each vision, including technologies, institutions and economic mechanisms. To an extent this requires a back-casting approach. In the scenario approach, process organization precedes vision implementation, so we must deal with the uncertainty and complexity associated with the future. And the very complex task of designing a resource-circulating society has not been clarified yet.

Because of this, decision-makers inevitably go through the decision-making process while exploring problem structuring at the same time. Knowledge should help them gain a deeper understanding of choices and thus yield better results for decision-makers and their constituencies than would be achieved when choices are made without that knowledge (National Research Council of the National Academies, 2009).

While stressing the importance of exploring problem structuring in the decision-making process, this chapter will structure the knowledge related to the design of a resource-circulating society. As a tool capable of dynamic structuring, ontology engineering lays the foundations for mapping tools. By exploring the system, technology and concept dimensions, this chapter aims to clarify the nature of the resulting structure of the

Establishing a resource-circulating society in Asia: Challenges and opportunities, Morioka, Hanaki and Moriguchi (eds), United Nations University Press, 2011, ISBN 978-92-808-1182-7

resource-circulating society as well as recognizing the importance of designing the decision-making process.

2-2-2 Framework for discussion and analysis tools

Classification of levels and dimensions for discussion

To advance the discussion in this book, the authors will clarify the framework of this chapter. When we categorize the purpose and means of measures to implement a resource-circulating society, the most significant ends are the goals: we can use terms such as resource management, environmental conservation, institutional design, technology development, human security and capacity building. This chapter addresses the dimension analysis at the means level, with special focus on the system and technology aspects.

The goal of designing a resource-circulating society at the ends level is an important issue. Let us therefore discuss the terms "circulating" and "society" with a focus on "industrial ecology", as proposed by Graedel and Allenby (2002), as a framework for systematically observing the concept of a resource-circulating society. Industrial ecology is an approach based on mutual interaction between industry and the environment which is beneficial in evaluating and minimizing various future adverse effects. Industrial ecology provides formal definitions at least for resource and material recycling.

However, materials and resources are not necessarily the only aspects of the "circulating" concept, which may be expanded to include all things that circulate, from currency to human resources and even information. Furthermore, assuming that an Asian model of the resource-circulating society exists, some would argue that the Buddhist doctrine of metempsychosis (transmigration of the soul) should also be perceived as a circulating concept, and therefore not only be deemed relevant to the definition of "circulating" but even regarded as comprising its basic framework. But what about the term "society"? If we perceive society as a system composed of actors and actions, then who are the actors involved in the circulating or recycling phenomenon? Does it involve, for instance, a certain industry or multiple industries, or does it extend beyond industry to encompass citizens, non-profit organizations and government? Similarly, are actions restricted to the development of new technologies or do they also include production, consumption and lifestyle? The definition of society differs according to the scope of the actors and actions it comprises.

It is also important to include in the discussion fields related to the Asian concept, such as cultural anthropology, social psychology and literature.

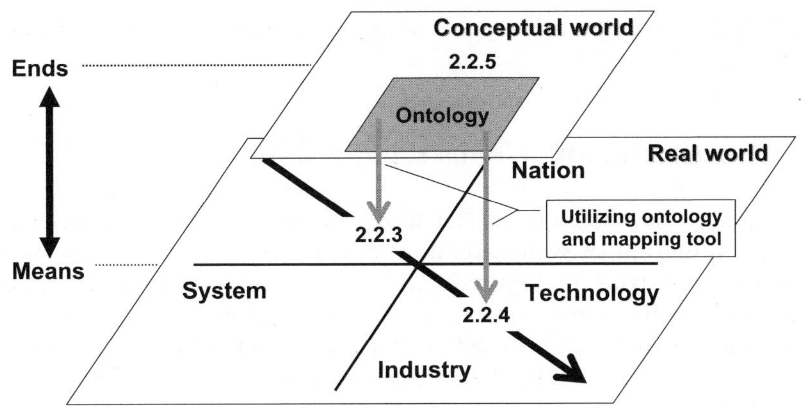

Figure 2.2.1 Framework for discussion

As shown in Figure 2.2.1, following the exploration and analysis of the system and technology dimensions, this chapter conducts an analysis of the conceptual dimensions related to the objective of the means.

Ontology-based tools as analysis tools

Ontology and ontology engineering are covered in the book *Sustainability Science: A Multidisciplinary Approach* (Komiyama, Takeuchi, Shiroyama and Mino, eds, United Nations University Press, 2011) which forms part of this series, so this chapter will provide only brief explanations. "Ontology" is originally a philosophical term which means a "systematic theory of existence". In the position of artificial intelligence, Gruber (1993) defined an ontology as an "explicit specification of a conceptualization", and basic theories and constructive methodologies have been developed as a way of modelling the general/special and total/partial relationships between the conceptual elements that comprise the subject world. The distinguishing feature of ontology is that it can be processed by computers (Mizoguchi, 2005). The Knowledge Structuring Research Group at Osaka University Research Institute for Sustainability Science (RISS) is currently working on the development of ontology in relation to sustainability science – hereinafter "SS ontology" (Kumazawa et al., 2009).

In addition, this group's leader, Riichiro Mizoguchi, and his laboratory members are developing a tool to generate context-compliant maps from ontology. The tool extracts concepts from an ontology and visualizes them as a user-friendly conceptual map that is drawn based on the viewpoints specified by users (Hirota, Kozaki and Mizoguchi, 2008; Hirota et al., 2009). This chapter utilizes this mapping tool for analysis, as shown in Figure 2.2.1.

2-2-3 Structuring of systems relationships

When we set the objective of designing a resource-circulating society, we must pay attention to system relationships not only within countries but also across countries. System regulation is an important issue when dealing with illegal movement of resources across nations.

Three issues have been raised concerning the international transfer of recyclable resources (MOE, 2008). The first issue to be highlighted is that the outflow of resources accompanying recyclable resource exports based on market mechanisms inevitably leads to the stagnation and hollowing out of the domestic recycling industry, and may hinder the stable continuation and enhancement of Japan's waste management and recycling systems which have been built up over many years. Second is the emerging concern that cross-border recyclable resource transfer may cause environmental pollution in importing nations which lack proper waste management systems. The third issue is that this cross-border recyclable resource transfer may be regarded as waste transfer, given the fact that second-hand and recycled goods are cheaply available in importing countries and thus, although effective use of resources may result, these goods may just as easily become waste again in a short period of time.

Based on these and other issues, the authors use the mapping tool to identify the connections between countries' institutions concerned with resource circulation. Using this tool, this section will clarify what types of conceptual linkages exist. As an example, the concept "issue of waste resources" is used as a focal point of the mapping tool. The results are shown in Figure 2.2.2.

The generated chain is mainly classified into two types. One type has the following flow: "waste problem", "waste", "(waste)[RH]@eccentrically located",[1] "developing country", "[name of country]", "[institution or project implemented in a targeting country]". For instance, relating to Indonesia, the following countermeasures are shown: "national action plan",[2] "local government's waste management law", "reusing hazardous wastes", "recycling hazardous wastes", "cleaner production (reuse and recycling of waste and residues)" and "compost subsidy programme". "(waste)[RH]@eccentrically located" was found to indicate the connection between the concepts explaining "waste trade problem", which are "waste" and "developing country". In other words, these concepts were connected through "waste trade problem". To a large extent, SS ontology has been constructed using a white paper and a report published by Japa-

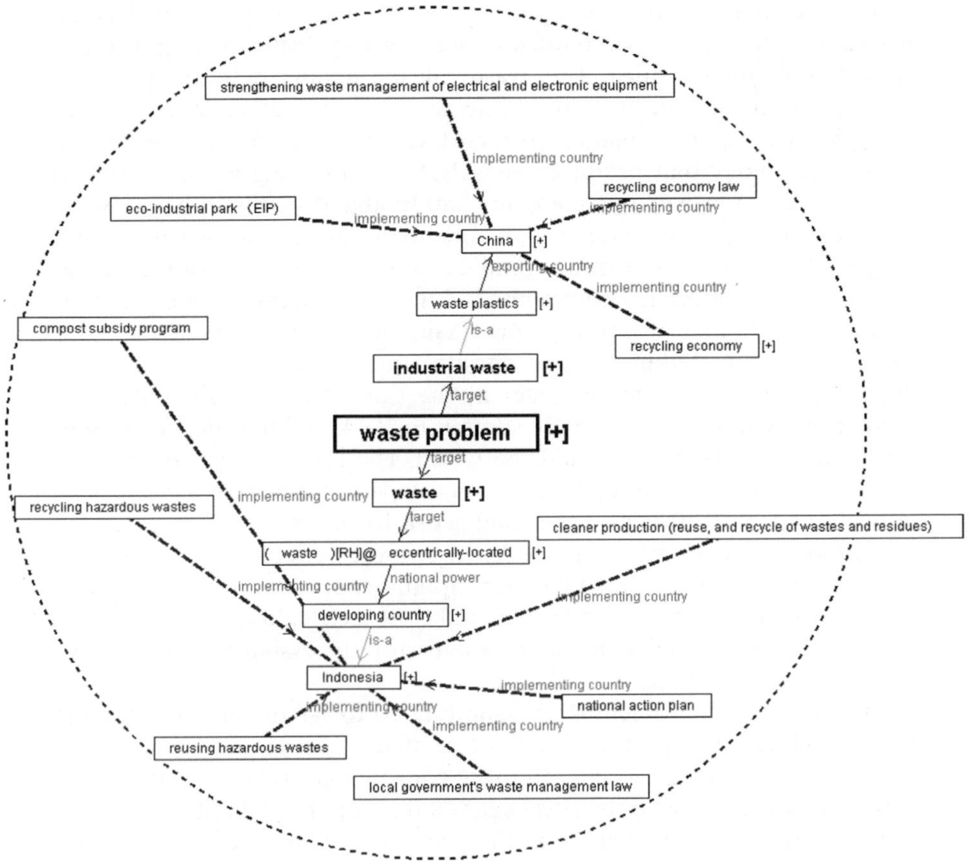

Figure 2.2.2 Extracted chains on systems relationships

nese ministries (MOE, 2008; METI, 2009) as a source of information. SS ontology is currently being developed, but the map reflects this kind of information. This indicates that there are many points that need to be modified towards generalization, but it also indicates the view of the Japanese white paper regarding the Japanese waste problem. For developing countries in general, the map explicitly shows that the Japanese waste problem is connected to institutions in a developing country through the waste trade problem.

The other chain has the following flow: "waste problem", "industrial waste", "waste plastics", "China" and "[institution or project implemented in a targeting country]". The case of China is different from developing countries in general, and the focus is on the import and export of "waste plastics". China imports waste plastic from all over the world, and Japan is one of the exporting countries (see www.cycle.nies.go.jp/jp/project/project4/seika/plastic.htm). This waste plastic export potentially constitutes a limiting factor for promoting domestic recycling in Japan. For example, two Japanese manufacturers developed the so-called bottle-to-bottle technology that produces new PET bottles using waste bottles as raw material. However, one company had to abandon this technology because of the rapid increase in demand for waste plastic in China. This suggests that the current trade trend can not only increase domestic demand for raw materials and resources, but also generate disincentive effects for technological development. Asian-level management of goods and resources, including an appropriate framework for waste trade, is thus necessary. The prime minister at the time, Junichiro Koizumi, proposed the 3R Initiative at the G8 summit in 2004, and this gained consensus among leaders from around the world. The initiative is a framework to be shared as a common principle when Japan or other countries design institutions for 3R. It is also the framework for international partnership and cooperation for building an Asian resource-circulating society. Between China and Japan, such partnership and cooperation are being realized as a concrete project which includes an eco-industrial park (EIP). However, there are all kinds of problems for the Asian region to solve using common methods (see Chapter 3-4).

The waste trade problem is an issue related to Japan and a developing country, while waste plastic is an issue related to Japan and China. When taken together, these two intermediary concepts are related to the issues between two countries only. This suggests that a partnership between two countries is useful for addressing the problems of those countries alone, and not for solving the challenges of the region. Solving the issues in two countries without considering other parts of Asia does not necessarily contribute to solving the challenges the region faces. From the generated map, we can understand the need for proposing strategies that encompass the Asian region, which is consistent with the claim made by Moriguchi in Chapter 3-4.

2-2-4 Structure of technology relationships

The design of a resource-circulating society states that wastes should be considered valuable resources. Individual industries must promote product reuse and recycling, but at the same time we need to promote technology development for industrial symbiosis – in other words, the sharing of wastes and by-products among industries. With the construction of a new stream in the circular flow of goods and services, technology will induce the emergence of new business conditions that will reshape the industrial structure. However, as of yet, the 3R framework has not set up an industry policy.

By clarifying the kind of concepts linking individual technologies to each other in the field of final disposal problems, this section aims to examine how the industries associated with the concepts can cooperate. Focusing on the scale of the Asian region, it becomes essential to determine the type of flows we need to construct, the type of technology development and the measures to promote technology transfer to certain countries in order to solve the final disposal problem. With a view to reducing the amount of product disposal, the authors produced an example map that starts from the final disposal problem viewpoint. The result is shown in Figure 2.2.3.

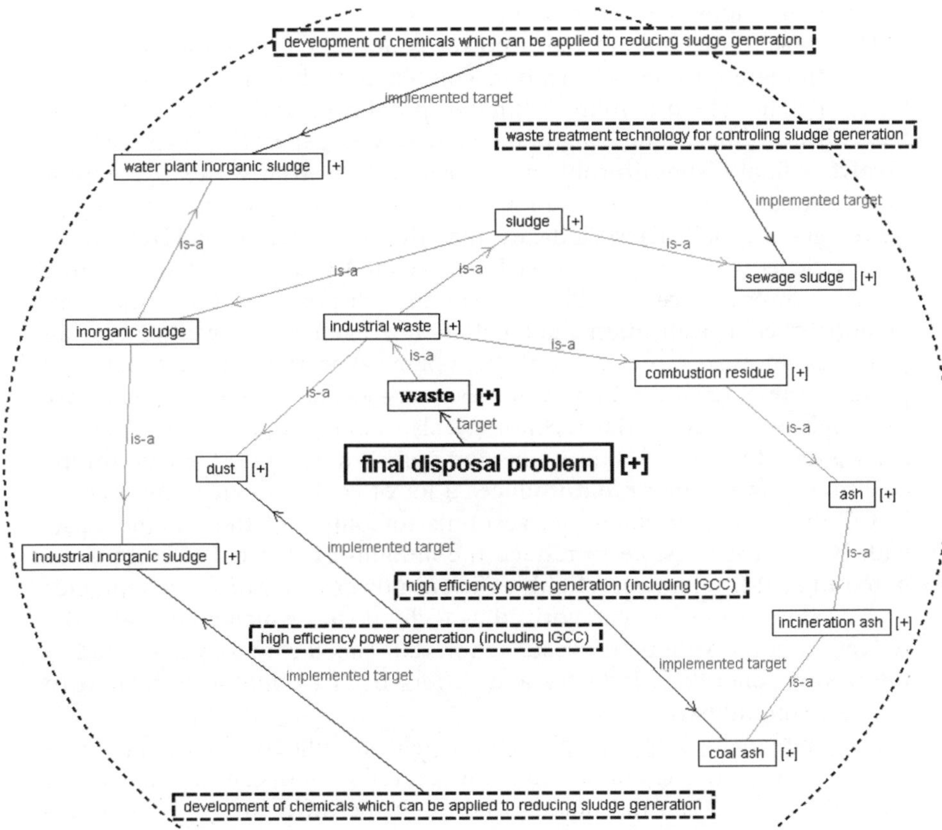

Figure 2.2.3 Extracted chains on technology relationships

From this comes a result chain that produces concepts such as "waste treatment technology for controlling sludge generation" and "high-efficiency power generation technology (including IGCC)". The final concept of "development of chemicals which can be applied to reducing sludge generation" produces two types of chains. The first chain is the final disposal problem, involving "waste", "industrial waste", "sludge", "inorganic sludge", "water plant inorganic sludge" and "development of chemicals which can be applied to reducing sludge generation". The other chain is identical up to "inorganic sludge", and from there leads to "industrial inorganic sludge" and "development of chemicals which can be applied to reducing sludge generation". These expressions indicate that the sludge generated from final disposal is linked with the sludge from water treatment and that associated with the industrial process, wastes and recycling. This explains the technological aspects centred on the sludge concept and the generation control technologies associated with downstream industries and recycling fields.

The concept of high-efficiency power generation technology including IGCC (integrated coal gasification combined cycle) also produces two types of chain. The first follows "final disposal problem", "waste", "industrial waste", "dust" and "high-efficiency power generation"; the second involves "final disposal problem", "waste", "industrial waste", "combustion residue", "ash", "incineration ash", "coal ash" and "high-efficiency power generation". These indicate that the introduction of IGCC technology deals with two important issues related to a resource-circulating society: power generation efficiency and final disposal. In IGCC, the combination of coal gasification and combined-cycle electric power generation produces an even more efficient technology than the existing coal-fired power system (clean coal power – see www.ccpower.co.jp/index.html). The high efficiency of the technology also implies that it is possible to reduce the SO_2, NO_x and dust emission per kWh generated. Furthermore, coal-fired power generation produces a lot of coal ash, but in the case of IGCC the glass slag generated accounts for only half the volume. Also, with IGCC it is possible to reduce the amount of thermal effluent compared to coal-fired power. Highly efficient power generation technologies such as IGCC could be categorized as technologies which contribute to a reduction in the volume of waste generated. This technology is related to the power generation industry and differs from technologies related to downstream industries.

Dust and coal-ash treatment technologies are related to recycling technologies. From the chain we can link recycling and generation control technologies, and see the linkages between the different types of industries. This aspect is discussed in Chapter 5-4, but the structuring position is explained here. Hanaki discusses urban technological linkage in Chapter 5-3.

Since policies for science and technology are often created based on combinations of multiple technology options and diverse alternatives, those who are not familiar with these technologies might have difficulties involving themselves in such policies. In addition, experts who are very familiar with the specific field tend to have views based upon the particular technologies they know well, which often creates barriers in promoting a comprehensive policy for science and technology. However, since the generated map shows the framework for the linkages between 3R and industrial cooperation, as well as the linkages and proposal of options within the technology group, we can start designing a path towards a resource-circulating society.

2-2-5 Structuring of concept relationships

Thus far the authors have proposed the policy framework for building an Asian resource-circulating society from the dimensions of system and technology. However, regardless of their profession, including systems and technology, is it possible for experts to discuss and share the meaning of concepts about a resource-circulating society? When experts from different academic fields cooperate, this question becomes even more pertinent.

Regarding the target to achieve a resource-circulating society, this section clarifies the difference between the concepts and their relationships based on the selection of two experts. The authors show where these concepts were positioned in the hierarchy based on ontological theory, and compare the two maps across the SS ontology's structure. The authors targeted the two maps on which each expert took a top-down approach.

The first is a field indicated by Moriguchi (2003) in his role as director of the National Institute for Environmental Studies Research Center for Material Cycles and Waste Management (Figure 2.2.4). Moriguchi selected the goals of "sustainable production and consumption" using industrial-ecology-related research fields and techniques as the players, then attempted to organize the position of these players. The second is a map created as part of the IR3S flagship research project, "Development of an Asian resource-circulating society", undertaken by Osaka and Hokkaido Universities (Figure 2.2.5). The main creator of this map is Dr Hara at Osaka University RISS.

Dr Moriguchi majors in industrial ecology, material flow analysis and accounting, environmental indicators, life-cycle assessment and long-term

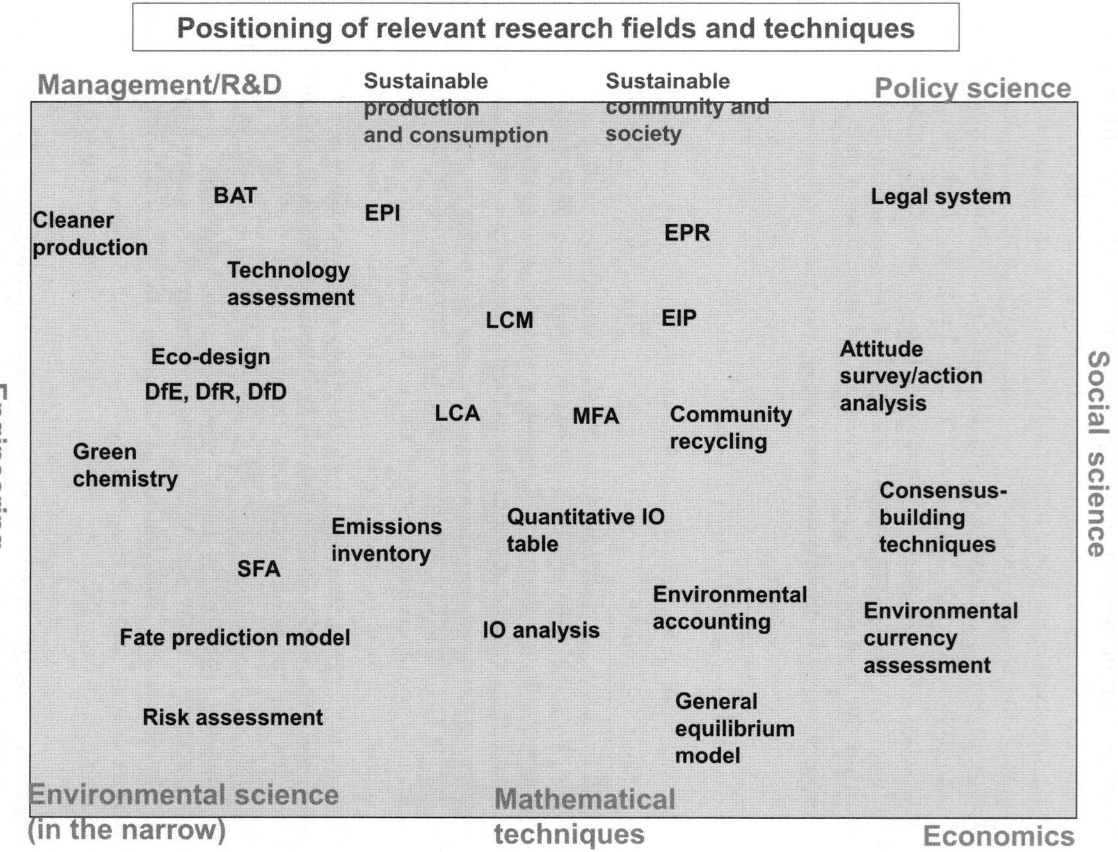

Figure 2.2.4 Position of associated techniques and research fields in industrial ecology

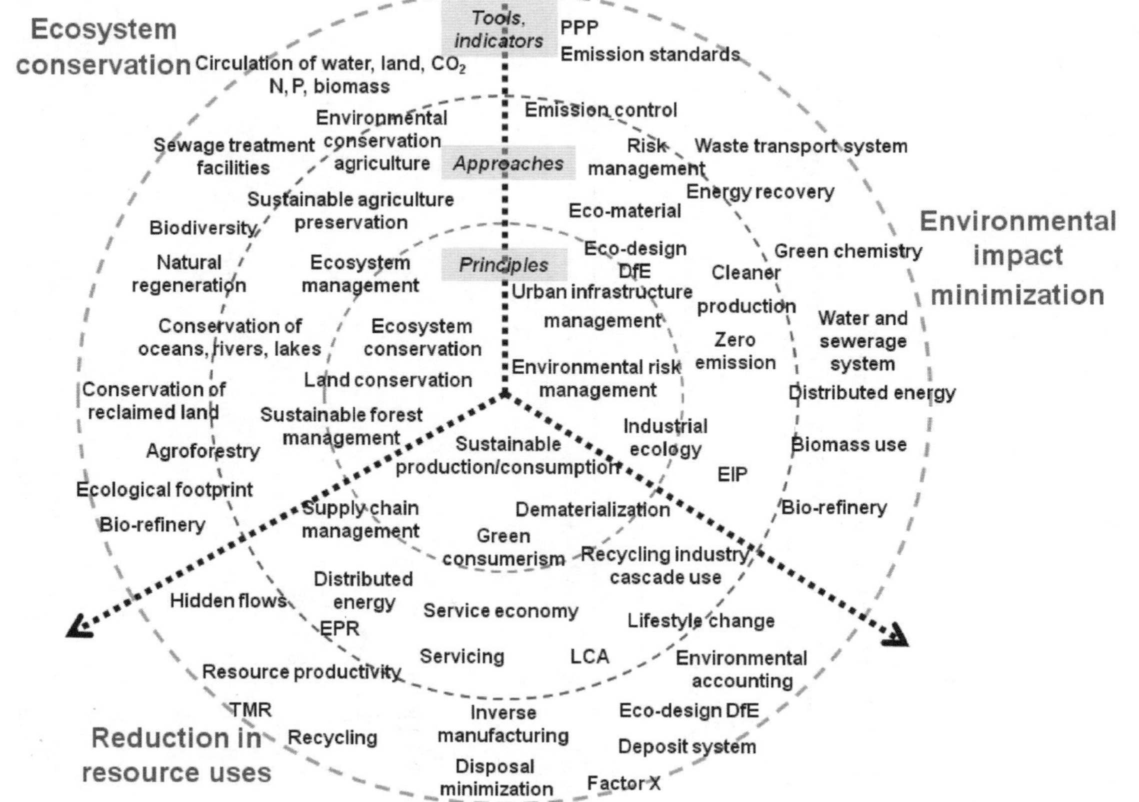

Figure 2.2.5 Mapping the concept of a "resource-circulating society" designed by RISS

Table 2.2.1 Position in SS ontology of the concepts in the map of Moriguchi (2003)

Hierarchy	Depth							
Top-level concept	Under 3	4	5	6	7	8	Over 9	Total
Goal			2	1				3
Problem								
Countermeasure		1	3	6	1			11
Assessment		9	2	1				12
Domain concept			1	2				3
Total		10	8	7	3	1		29

Average depth: 5.2
Most selected field: flow-based evaluation method

Note: The numbers in the matrix show the number of concepts selected by Dr Moriguchi. A blank indicates 0; highlighting indicates the most popular concepts.

Table 2.2.2 Position in SS ontology of the concepts in the map of Hara et al. (2009)

Hierarchy	Depth							
Top-level concept	Under 3	4	5	6	7	8	Over 9	Total
Goal				1	3			4
Problem								
Countermeasure			9	21	9	2		41
Assessment		3	3	1				7
Domain concept				4	2			6
Total		3	12	27	14	2		58

Average depth: 6.0
Most selected fields: management for sustainability; direct approach towards
   lands and living things

Note: The numbers in the matrix show the number of concepts selected by Dr Hara. A blank indicates 0; highlighting indicates the most popular concepts.

vision of an environmentally sustainable society, while Dr Hara majors in urban environmental management and sustainability assessment. Judging from these keywords, their fields are similar and partly overlapping.

The results are shown in Tables 2.2.1 and 2.2.2. Rows indicate the top-level concepts of SS ontology, while columns show the depth of the hierarchy where each of the targeted concepts is positioned. Moriguchi's main concern is the concepts of "countermeasure" and "assessment", while the concepts selected by Hara et al. mainly concern "countermeasure". Regarding depth of hierarchy, the largest number of concepts selected by Moriguchi is at a depth of 4, while the most concepts selected by Hara et al. are at a depth of 6. This indicates that Moriguchi's concepts are more general from the point of view of sustainability, while the concepts selected by Hara and colleagues are more concrete and specific. However, the hierarchy of "assessment" tends to be shallower than that of "countermeasure", so we need to discount the result to a certain extent.

Focusing on the domain type of concepts, in Moriguchi's map concepts on the flow-based evaluation method are intensively selected (number: 7; 24 per cent). In Hara's map the concepts on management for sustainability (number: 7; 12 per cent) and direct approach towards lands and living things (number: 10; 17 per cent) are favoured. Also, because of the rich countermeasures, Hara's map is assumed to cover broader fields when judged from the viewpoint of sustainability.

It should be noted that these maps were created according to set purposes and preconditions, and so this analysis should be treated very carefully. To be precise, map creation and comparison under the right conditions are required, but this analysis suggests that the type, extent and depth of hierarchy of the target field are different, despite the experts having similar backgrounds. These differences are considered to be the major barrier to promoting collaborative work and sharing concepts among experts. The reason for this is not only the different backgrounds of the experts, but also because the experts are conducting different research projects.

There are assumed to be various background causes. But, at the very least, making plenty of time for sharing concepts among experts as the first step in the decision-making process is considered to be really meaningful in order to avoid difficulties caused by differing views at later stages. However, it is extremely difficult to make enough time for concept sharing in the arena of decision-making. Furthermore, decision-makers cannot understand to what extent they attain concept sharing unless they use some supporting tools. Thus it is of particular importance to develop a knowledge-structuring tool and design the decision-making process, both of which facilitate efficient concept sharing and thus lead to better decision-making.

2-2-6 Conclusion

This chapter structured the knowledge related to the design of a resource-circulating society. As a tool capable of dynamic structuring, it focused on mapping based on ontology engineering, and explored the maps in terms of the system, technology and concept dimensions. Through these tasks the chapter showed that knowledge structuring is important for building a resource-circulating society, as using tools based on ontology engineering framed the strategies at the conceptual level. Specifically, the results can be summarized in three points.

First, the map generated based on ontology engineering suggested that a bilateral partnership between countries addresses only the problems in those two countries. Solving issues in these countries without considering other parts of Asia does not necessarily contribute to solving regional challenges. To achieve a balance between the environment and economic development within as well as between countries in the region, proposing strategies that target the whole Asian region is necessary.

Second, the generated map showed the associations between recycling technologies and generation control technologies as well as the linkages between the different types of industries. This indicates that integrating the promotion of industrial cooperation and 3R initiatives is crucial. Proposing such comprehensive strategies would induce the technological developments for meeting 3R targets, leading to the achievement of a balance between environmental and industrial targets.

Third, the comparative analysis of maps suggested that the type, extent and depth of hierarchy of the target field were different even among experts with similar backgrounds. Provided that these differences constitute the major barrier to promoting collaborative work, sharing concepts among experts in the early stages is particularly meaningful.

Of course, there are still many challenges ahead, including structuring institution-industry relationships and institutional design promoting industrial cooperation, and structuring technology-nation relationships including technology development, technology alliance and joint projects under international networks. Nevertheless, utilizing tools of this kind facilitates further understanding among experts and policy-makers. Taking this step could greatly contribute to implementing integrated policies, and even reaching solutions in the work on an Asian resource-circulating society.

Notes

1. "[RH] @" indicates "role holder", a concept proposed in ontology engineering. Role holder means an entity of a basic concept which is holding a role (e.g. teacher). Role concept means a concept representing a role dependent on a concept (e.g. teacher role). Basic concept means a concept which does not need other concepts for definition (e.g. human) (Mizoguchi, 2004). SS ontology is currently being developed, and so fluctuation in the basic concepts is inevitable.

2. A national action plan is being implemented from 2008 to 2015 in Indonesia. This is not a concept, but an instance in the real world. SS ontology includes examples: "local government's waste management law", "compost subsidy programme", "eco-industrial park" and "Recycling Economy Law (under consideration)" in Figure 2.2.2 are also cases.

REFERENCES

Graedel, T. E. and B. R. Allenby (2002) *Industrial Ecology*, 2nd edn. Englewood Cliffs, NJ: Prentice-Hall.

Gruber, T. R. (1993) "A Translation Approach to Portable Ontology Specifications", *Knowledge Acquisition* 5(2), pp. 199–220.

Hara, K., H. Yabar, M. Uwasu and H. Zhang (2009) "Scenarios Design and Assessment towards Energy and Resources-efficient Societies – A Regional Study in China", paper presented at International Conference on Sustainability, Human Geography and Environmental Studies, Imperia, November.

Hirota, K., K. Kozaki and R. Mizoguchi (2008) "Development of a Conceptual Map Creation Tool for Overlooking Ontologies", paper presented at Twenty-second Annual Conference of Japanese Society for Artificial Intelligence, Asahikawa, June.

Hirota, K., K. Kozaki, O. Saito and R. Mizoguchi (2009) "Development of Ontology Exploration Tool for Overlooking Domain-knowledge", paper presented at Twenty-third Annual Conference of Japanese Society for Artificial Intelligence, Takamatsu, June.

Kumazawa, T., K. Kozaki, T. Matsui, O. Saito, M. Ohta, K. Hara, M. Uwasu, Y. Yamaguchi, Y. Yamamoto and R. Mizoguchi (2009) "Development of Ontology on Sustainability Science Focusing on Building a Resource-circulating Society in Asia", paper presented at Sixth International Symposium on Environmentally Conscious Design and Inverse Manufacturing, Sapporo, December.

METI (2009) "Technology Road Map 2009", Ministry of Economy, Trade and Industry, Tokyo.

Mizoguchi, R. (2004) "Tutorial on Ontological Engineering – Part 2: Ontology Development, Tools and Languages", *New Generation Computing* 22(1), pp. 61–96.

——— (2005) *Ontology Kougaku*. Tokyo: Ohmsha.

MOE (2008) *Annual Report on the Environment and the Sound Material-Cycle Society in Japan 2008*. Tokyo: Ministry of Environment.

Moriguchi, Y. (2003) "Industrial Ecology", paper presented at Third Seminar on Environmental Technology R&D, "Towards an Environmental Technology Nation", JET Forum, Tokyo, November.

National Research Council of the National Academies (2009) *Informing Decisions in a Changing Climate*. Washington, DC: National Academies Press.

2-3

Indicator systems as an instrument for establishing sustainable resource-circulating societies

Keishiro Hara

2-3-1 Introduction

Indicators could play an essential role in measuring or assessing the status of society, and eventually guide society towards sustainability. Indicators can also provide important guidelines that assist in the development of strategies and actions, because they indicate the status, progress and failures of measures undertaken for a specific system. They can help to describe accurately, diagnose and clarify the problems of any system or society, and can assist in efforts to design and develop solutions for overcoming such problems. Sustainability indicators are one of the central tools used for sustainability assessments, and are particularly aimed at measuring environmental improvements, social progress and economic development (Hara et al., 2009).

The concept of establishing a resource-circulating society constitutes an important pillar for achieving a sustainable society. Accordingly, I define a "sustainable resource-circulating society" as a broadly sustainable society that incorporates the concept and elements of less environmental impacts, effective resource circulation and resource conservation. Hence, associated indicators for measuring a sustainable resource-circulating society should be sufficiently comprehensive, incorporating socio-economic as well as environmental aspects.

This chapter discusses the utility of indicator systems as essential instruments for envisioning and establishing sustainable resource-circulating

Establishing a resource-circulating society in Asia: Challenges and opportunities, Morioka, Hanaki and Moriguchi (eds), United Nations University Press, 2011, ISBN 978-92-808-1182-7

societies. First, some representative indicator systems designed specifically for the assessment of sustainability status or sustainable development are briefly reviewed. Then a Japanese case is introduced to demonstrate the historical evolution of relevant environmental policies in Japan and how indicator systems have been applied to policy-making, particularly in the context of promoting resource-circulating societies. Additionally, indicator systems applied in environmental policies in China and the European Union (EU) are briefly examined for comparison. Finally, an indicative indicator system with time-series scores that is designed to analyse relative sustainability statuses among regions is introduced, along with an actual case study in China. The results of the case study illustrate how the application of the indicator system could assist in clarifying changes in sustainability statuses in the Chinese provinces. The conclusion argues the importance of such indicator systems in pursuing a sustainable society and their future prospects.

2-3-2 Indicator systems for sustainability assessment

A variety of sustainability assessment tools have been developed and applied to the measurement of the actual sustainability statuses of societies at local, country and regional scales. Yet, importantly, the definitions of sustainability and sustainable development are rather vague. The Brundtland Commission defined sustainable development as "development that meets the needs of the present without compromising the ability of future generations to meet their own needs" (World Commission on Environment and Development, 1987). The International Union for the Conservation of Nature (1991), on the other hand, defines sustainable development as "improving the quality of life while living within the carrying capacity of the supporting system". Hence applicable sustainability indicators can vary, and they should be appropriately devised, developed and applied depending on the purpose and intended scope of the studies.

Several approaches have been devised to categorize such diverse assessment methods or indicator systems. One possible approach would be to classify them into indicative and definitive types. Indicative assessment methods, in principle, aim to analyse the relative status of sustainability or specific components of sustainability, among targeted areas or over a period of time; definitive assessments intend to measure and investigate the absolute status of sustainability. In the following, depending on the classification, I shall discuss the representative indicator systems and the assessment methods.

Indicative type of assessment

A variety of initiatives with indicative indicator systems have been implemented, not only at national and global levels but also at region and city levels. I focus upon initiatives at the national and global levels. The representative indicators for these levels include, but are not limited to, the Environmental Sustainability Index (ESI), the Human Development Index (HDI) and the UN Commission on Sustainable Development (UNCSD) indicators.

The ESI, originally developed by Columbia and Yale Universities, attempts to rank countries in terms of environmental sustainability status, and presented reports of such rankings in 2001 and 2005. The index consists of five components: environmental systems, environmental stresses, human vulnerability, social and institutional capability, and global stewardship. Each component has a group of so-called indicators (21 in total) and each indicator has an associated group of variables, giving a total of 76 variables. The ESI is an equally weighted average of the 21 indicators and five components (Esty, Levy and Srebotnjak, 2005).

The HDI considers three basic dimensions for human development: health (measured in terms of life expectancy at birth), education (measured in terms of adult literacy and primary, secondary and tertiary enrolment) and standard of living (measured in terms of GDP per capita) (UNDP, 2006). As a basic indicator, the HDI ranks countries in terms of human development. Notably, the HDI has been calculated on a yearly basis since 1975.

These indicator systems are designed to show aggregated scores, and this characteristic has strengths and weaknesses. One major merit of this approach is that it can demonstrate environmental and sustainability statuses in the form of aggregated scores, thus making it easier to show statuses at a macro level. However, the performance variations of individual components that constitute sustainability cannot be clearly illustrated and remain hidden behind the aggregated simplified scores. The UNCSD indicators for sustainable development are not integrated or aggregated in any manner (Ness et al., 2007). They are a set of 58 indicators that can be adapted flexibly at the national level. The indicator framework uses the four dimensions of society, environment, economy and institutions. Each dimension is further subdivided into themes, subthemes and indicators. For instance, a theme of the environmental dimension is the atmosphere, which is divided into three subthemes: climate change, ozone layer depletion and air quality. Each subtheme has one or more indicators. In the case of air quality, an example indicator is "ambient concentration of air pollutants in urban areas" (UNCSD, 2001).

In Asia there are some initiatives that aim to assess sustainable development at the country level, applying a set of selected indicators (UNESCAP, 2007). In Thailand, for instance, the government developed a set of indicators that address economic, social and environmental dimensions for assessment purposes and policy planning, and has carried out sustainability assessments. In Korea, the government chose 77 sustainable development indicators under economic, social and environmental dimensions for evaluation. In contrast, Malaysia particularly adopted the term "quality of life" in its development of indicators. To address this, 42 indicators under 11 components were selected for evaluation. "Malaysian Quality of Life 2002", the second in a planned series of reports on the subject, examines the progress and trends in national development for the period 1990–2000, using 1990 as the base year (Economic Planning Unit, 2002). Thus several initiatives for assessment at country level have been promoted in Asia, particularly aiming to apply such assessments in policy planning and analysis.

In sustainability assessments it is essential to be able to assess and monitor interlinks and dynamics of human-environment systems that affect sustainability statuses. The Organisation for Economic Co-operation and Development (OECD) published indicator systems based upon the pressure-state-response framework for environmental performance reviews in 1993 (OECD, 1993). This framework provides the concept of causality, i.e. humans exert pressure on the environment and change its state, forcing the adoption of different types of policy directed at overcoming the situation (OECD, 2003). This framework is applied to the UNCSD indicators as well. It is also important to note that these systems are not the types that set targets and then assess performance to see whether the indicators meet the given targets. Some of the systems applied to policy evaluation, such as the three macro indicators used for promoting the Sound Material-Cycle Society in Japan, which will be discussed later, set targets to investigate performance quantitatively.

Definitive type of assessment

Another classification of sustainability indicators is the capital approach, which is applied to definitive-type assessments. This approach aims to clarify the sustainability level in a definitive manner by emphasizing the clarification of sustainability itself. The capital concept states that capital stocks provide a flow of goods and services necessary for human well-being (Ekins, Dresner and Dahlstrom, 2008). Under this approach, there are in principle four types of capital: natural, human-made, human and social. Natural capital refers to traditional natural resources, both renewable and non-renewable, as well as natural assets to which the assignment of a monetary value is difficult. Human-made or manufactured capital consists of physical or produced assets. Human capital represents the health, well-being and education – or potential productive capacity – of humans as individuals. Social capital addresses the values, norms and trust embodied in institutions and social networks. The traditional approach to capital in economics has tended to focus on the manufactured capital that is necessary to produce goods and services. However, this concept has been expanded to consider the other capital types – human, social and natural (Hara et al., 2009).

In the capital approach, two group types are considered when categorizing indicators: weak and strong sustainability indicators. The weak and strong sustainability concepts differ with respect to the substitutability of natural capital. The weak sustainability approach is based on the neoclassical view, which advocates a constant stock of capital where the substitution of natural capital is possible. In this idea, sustainability is essentially achievable as long as total capital stocks are maintained over time. Indicators categorized under this group include adjusted net saving (ANS), genuine savings (GS), the genuine progress indicator and green GDP. ANS attempts to estimate the wealth of nations based on the four types of capital mentioned previously. Human and social capitals are expressed as "intangible capitals". ANS estimates the total wealth of nations in terms of the present value of future consumption, produced capital in monetary terms and natural capital in terms of its shadow prices. Intangible capital is calculated as the difference between total wealth and natural and produced capital. Yabar et al. (2008) analysed the patterns of GS accumulation and other factors, such as governance conditions, for 84 countries and concluded that governance and population growth are important factors for identifying the accumulation of wealth, and hence the path to sustainable development.

The strong sustainability approach, on the other hand, advocates a constant stock of each form of capital and restricts the substitutability of natural capital. The rationale behind this idea is that non-declining natural capital is essential for socio-economic development and must be maintained for future generations. In fact, this approach argues that nature provides several functions that are essential for human existence, such as climate stabilization and emissions-absorbing capacity. One of the indicators under this group is the ecological footprint, defined as the area required to support human needs in terms of necessary resources and the area required for the disposal of waste. The ecological footprint methodology provides an account of natural capital that can determine how much of nature's endowment can be appropriated for supporting human activities without depleting the natural capital stock (Wackernagel et al., 2006).

As overviewed here, each indicator system has characteristic weaknesses and strengths. It is therefore very important to apply the most appropriate indicators depending upon the purposes and scope of the actual assessment. It is known that some indicators, such as the ESI and ecological footprint, have been primarily used for policy analysis with political orientation. Whatever the purpose of a developed indicator system, however, it is important that the system itself should keep a sound scientific foundation, which will eventually provide the most useful information for such policy judgements.

2-3-3 Indicator systems for environmental policies

Sustainability indicators could provide useful guidelines for policies and decision-making in the pursuit of a sustainable society. This section aims to provide an overview of the evolution of Japanese policies and associated indicator systems in order to demonstrate how indicator systems have been employed and functioned in Japanese policies, particularly in relation to developing a resource-circulating society. Then, for comparative purposes, indicators applied to policies in China and EU countries are briefly reviewed. A common characteristic of the systems proposed here is that a quantitative target is set for each indicator and actual performance progress is monitored and evaluated against the set target.

Environmental policy in Japan: A historical overview

At the beginning of the period of rapid economic growth and rural urban migration in the 1950s, the increasing amount of urban waste became a problem. To deal with this issue, the government introduced the Public Cleansing Law in 1954. The law aimed at the proper treatment and disposal of wastes by means of incineration and home disposal (MOE, 2002). The rapid economic growth of the 1960s led to a significant lifestyle change, which in turn translated into further increases in waste generation. Waste generation exceeded the government's forecast, and the lack of proper treatment and disposal systems for the newly generated waste resulted in illegal dumping in mountainous areas (Yabar et al., 2009).

The severe industrial pollution generated during this period also became a social concern. In view of this situation the government passed the Waste Management and Public Cleansing Law in 1970. For the first time, the law placed responsibility for industrial waste management on the generators, and tasked local governments with dealing with municipal wastes. The 1980s also witnessed impressive economic growth, which translated into further lifestyle changes. Popular demand for diversity in daily items, such as food products, boosted small-volume production, especially for plastic containers and packaging materials. In the 1980s and 1990s concerns over the environment intensified in many parts of the world. The Basic Environmental Law of 1993 addressed environmental degradation on a global scale. Its main principles include environmental preservation for future generations, sustainable development based on environmental impact minimization and international cooperation to promote global environmental preservation (ibid.).

Based upon the "reduce, reuse and recycle" (3R) principles, the government introduced the Law for Promotion of Utilization of Recyclables in 1991. Following this, the government enacted specific laws that promoted intelligent use of resources, including the Containers and Packaging Recycling Law (1995), the Home Appliance Recycling Law (1998), the Construction Materials Recycling Law (2000), the Food Recycling Law (2000) and the End-of-Life Vehicles Recycling Law (2002).

In the year 2000 the government introduced the Fundamental Law for Establishing a Sound Material-Cycle Society, which is the central pillar of efforts leading towards the development of a sustainable society in Japan. The law aims to integrate resource management through optimization of resource use and minimization of environmental impacts. Indeed, under the law, a "sound material-cycle society" is defined as a society in which the consumption of natural resources will be conserved and the environmental load will be reduced to the greatest extent possible, by preventing or reducing the generation of wastes through the cyclical use of products when these products have become circulative resources, or by ensuring proper disposal of circulative resources not put into cyclical use. To achieve these goals, the government passed the Fundamental Plan for Establishing a Sound Material-Cycle Society (MOE, 2003). The plan introduced quantitative and comprehensive indicators based on material flow accounts (discussed below). These indicators not only focus on improving overall recycling levels and final waste disposal, but also target upstream flow through improving resource productivity.

Target setting in relation to Japanese environmental policies

As stated, the emphasis of Japanese environmental policies historically shifted from tackling issues related to public sanitation to the responsive measures of the 1960s and 1970s that introduced waste classification and standards for waste disposal, and then to policies that focused on the 3R principles proposed in the 1990s. The associated indicators and targets also evolved from the waste recycling targets of the 1990s to the current comprehensive indicator systems.

The Law for Promotion of Effective Utilization of Resources of 2001, which is based on the Law for Promotion of Utilization of Recyclables of 1991, aimed at establishing a sound material-cycle economic system by increasing recycling levels of specific wastes through the implementation of collection and recycling systems, waste minimization through promotion of resource saving and ensuring longer product lives, and measures to promote the reuse of parts and implementation of guidelines for industrial waste reduction. Accordingly, the government enacted recycling targets for specific wastes, including containers and packaging, home appliances, construction materials, food and end-of-life vehicles. The law also set waste reduction targets for specific industries, including iron and steel, paper and pulp, chemicals, non-ferrous metal, electricity, automobiles and electronic devices. The targets set for specific wastes have been important because they have driven the design of the technological innovations required to meet recycling targets. Furthermore, these regulations have induced innovation at the product design phase since manufacturing industries realized that designing easier-to-recycle products would eventually reduce the final disposal costs (Yabar et al., 2009). The recycling rates of the most prevalent container and packaging materials have increased steadily since the law was enacted. The case of PET bottles, in particular, shows the positive impact of the law; the recycling rate has increased from 3 per cent in 1996 to 69 per cent in 2007 (Council for PET Bottle Recycling, 2008).

Comprehensive indicators based on material flows in Japan

As stated earlier, the Japanese government designed a plan for establishing a sound material-cycle society in 2003 as its primary strategy for decoupling economic growth from environmental pressure (MOE, 2003). The plan established quantitative indicators derived from material flow analysis. The indicators not only focused on increasing recycling levels and minimizing final disposal wastes, but also on promoting intelligent use of resources in the upstream stages of urban metabolism. The indicators focus on the upstream, circulation and downstream stages of the Japanese material economy and the targets, which have the year 2000 as their basis, must be achieved by 2010 in the following manner:

- *inputs (upstream):* 40 per cent increase in resource productivity (GDP/ direct material input), from approximately ¥280,000/tonne to ¥390,000/ tonne
- *circulation:* 40 per cent increase in recycling levels (total recycled amount/direct material input), from approximately 10 per cent to 14 per cent

- *outputs (downstream):* 50 per cent decrease in wastes transported to final disposal sites, from 56 million tonnes/year to 28 million tonnes/year.

These indicators are being monitored and individual performance evaluations have been conducted against set targets. The concept of resource productivity described in the first item is also reflected in the development process of the Third Basic Environmental Plan proposed by the Japanese government. The indicators considered in the plan include CO_2/ GDP, representing environmental efficiency (or decoupling environmental loads from economic growth), GDP/resource-inputs (representing resource productivity) and ecological footprint (Hara et al., 2009).

The Fundamental Plan for Establishing a Sound Material-Cycle Society (2003) was the first attempt at tackling Japanese production and consumption patterns in a holistic way. To address the pressing global environmental issues, including the extensive consumption of resources and the threat of climate change, the government introduced the Second Fundamental Plan for Establishing a Sound Material-Cycle Society in March 2008. The plan proposed using the same three indicators mentioned in the first plan for the period 2000–2015. The numerical targets are a 60 per cent increase in resource productivity, a 40–50 per cent increase in recycling levels and a 60 per cent reduction in final disposal wastes. The plan proposes specific indices related to the macro indicators, including a 60 per cent reduction in both domestic and industrial wastes. These targets in relation to indicators are considered to play an important role in directing society towards the intended policies.

In 2007 the Japanese government implemented its long-term strategy directed at achieving a sustainable society (Government of Japan, 2007). The strategy proposed comprehensive measures directed at integrating the three main components of a sustainable society: a low-carbon society, a society in harmony with nature and a sound material-cycle society. These components were incorporated into the revised version of the Fundamental Law for Establishing a Sound Material-Cycle Society, along with indicators associated with a low-carbon society. Even so, comprehensive indicator evaluations that consider socio-economic progress are still in the development stage in Japanese policies, and holistic views and multiple indicator systems, coupled with future visions and plausible scenarios towards a sustainable society, are urgently required.

China's circular economy: Evolution of policies and indicators

In recent decades China's economic growth, urbanization and industrialization have been remarkable. However, this rapid development has resulted in resource overconsumption, as well as environmental and socio-economic problems. Given this situation, sustainable development is considered to be the most pressing challenge currently facing the country.

China began introducing five-year plans (FYPs) in 1953 with the aim of promoting economic and social development. Historically, environmental aspects have been taken into account in public policies. Until the end of the 1980s most of the environmental protection laws were restricted to specific issues (Yabar et al., 2009). In 1989 the Chinese government introduced the Environmental Protection Law, which primarily focused on protection and improvement of the living and ecological environments, prevention and treatment of pollution and safeguarding the health of the population (Li and Li, 2004).

Subsequently, the government adopted its Eighth FYP (1991–1995) for environmental protection along with its regular FYP in 1991. It is divided into sector-specific plans: water management in key rivers and lakes, air pollution reduction in specially designated regions, hazardous waste management and nature conservation (OECD, 2006). The Ninth FYP set nationwide goals for controlling ambient pollution by targeting 12 major pollutants in three categories: air pollutants, water pollutants and solid waste (Dudek et al., 2001). The Tenth FYP integrated environmental protection with economic development, and clearly stipulates that local governments must assume primary responsibility for environmental conservation (SEPA, 2001). The Eleventh FYP takes a more proactive approach and stresses the importance of improving living standards, setting long-term strategic policies regarding environmental protection and sustainable use of natural resources. Of particular interest, the Eleventh FYP identifies three main challenges (Yabar et al., 2009).

- The emerging bottleneck of natural resources and energy supply: energy and resource security is needed to sustain economic development.
- Environmental and ecological degradation: water, air and land protection is needed to preserve the environment and human health.
- Social conflicts caused by the unbalanced development pattern.

To tackle these issues, the concept of the "circular economy" (CE) was introduced in China. The CE model aims to decouple economic growth from environmental pressures and is based on Japanese and German environmental policies. Based on the German experience, the CE concept was first introduced by the Shanghai municipal government in 1998. The Chinese national government then promulgated a comprehensive CE strategy in 2005 (Zhang et al., 2009). This model is built on the 3R principle, and focuses on improving resource productivity and eco-efficiency while enhancing the quality of life of citizens (Yabar et al., 2009).

Notably, the Eleventh FYP included both absolute and decoupling targets with specific indicators. These targets are a clear attempt to decouple economic growth from environmental loads, in addition to providing specific targets for pollution control and resource conservation. As an example, target indicators include, but are not limited to, energy intensity (20 per cent reduction between 2005 and 2010) as a decoupling indicator, discharge of major pollutants like SO_2 (10 per cent reduction by 2010) as a pollution prevention indicator and forest coverage areas (increase from 18.2 per cent to 20 per cent by 2010) as a resource conservation indicator. In addition to considering these environmental aspects, the Eleventh FYP includes indicators associated with socio-economic aspects, such as education levels and revenues for farmers, making the indicator lists comprehensive to address sustainable development. The government also set a major mid-term decoupling goal of quadrupling GDP/capita while only doubling energy consumption by the year 2020, compared with the base year 2000. These future targets for energy intensity were proposed based on the 1980–2000 performances (Zhuang, 2008).

The targets serve as the basic driver to direct the society towards sustainable development. However, given the nation's recent rapid economic growth, it remains to be seen whether the targets will be met, particularly with the considerable production currently taking place in energy-intensive industries such as steel and cement. Appropriate policy measures, coupled with diffusion of highly energy-efficient technologies, should therefore urgently be introduced in China.

EU approach and indicator systems in policy-making

An essential aspect of the resource-circulation concept is how to manage or conserve resources in a sustainable manner. The European Union has been making concerted efforts towards promoting sustainable resource management. Under the sixth Environment Action Programme, the European Union developed a thematic strategy on sustainable use of resources. The strategy proposes a double decoupling: economic growth from resource use (resource efficiency increase) and resource use from environmental impacts (Commission of the European Communities, 2005). The resource management perspective is reflected in the EU sustainable development strategies adopted by the European Council in June 2001 in Gothenburg, Sweden, and renewed in June 2006. The renewed strategy reaffirms the overall aim of achieving continuous improvements to quality of life and well-being on Earth, for present and future generations, through the creation of sustainable communities that are able to manage and use resources efficiently, and tap the ecological and social innovation potential of the economy, thus ensuring prosperity, environmental protection and social cohesion (European Commission, 2007). The first monitoring report compiled by Eurostat covers the period up to December 2005 (ibid.); it is expected to be updated and republished every two years. In the first report, 10 headline indicators were introduced: socio-economic development, climate change and energy, sustainable transport, sustainable consumption and production, natural resources, public health, social inclusion, demographic changes, global partnership and good governance. Out of these, the sustainable production and consumption indicator is the one most relevant to the promotion of a resource-circulating society.

The report concludes that out of the 10 headline indicators, four have progressed favourably since 2000: socio-economic development, sustainable consumption and production, demographic change and global partnership. For example, the report states that resource productivity increased by an average of 2.3 per cent a year between 2000 and 2004 in the EU-15, showing decoupling between resource use and economic growth (ibid.). However, the report notes that chronological changes are clearly less impressive for the two indicators related to climate change and energy, as the EU-15 reduction in greenhouse gases and increased use of renewable energy are still far from the targets set in the strategy. In principle, these indicators are to be monitored over time in order to determine the chronological progress of performance.

A summary in the report states that the there are limitations to the analysis of some existing indicators, and some objectives are not adequately monitored due to the lack of appropriate statistics. While some qualitative objectives are difficult to measure based on quantitative information, the sustainable development indicators set is well suited to evaluating the quantitative targets.

Efforts to set targets and monitor the indicators' progress, particularly in terms of sustainable resources management, are currently being undertaken at the country level as well. For instance, the Environment Ministry of Germany drafted an environmental policy programme in which targets were set, and progress towards these targets has regularly been monitored by the Ministry of Economics and the Federal Statistical Office (Bringezu, 2002). The indicators with targets include, but are not limited to:

- an increase of energy productivity by a factor of 2 (1990–2020)
- an increase in non-renewable raw materials productivity by a factor of 2.5 (1993–2020)
- an increase in the share of organic farmland to 20 per cent (by 2010).

Bringezu (ibid.) argues that progress has been made for the majority of these indicator targets, although further action is needed.

As overviewed, indicator systems have been employed in policy analysis and decision-making in various countries as benchmarks. Indicators, together with appropriate targets, could play an essential role in environmental policies and thereby assist in efforts to establish a sustainable society. A comprehensive approach is fundamentally important in developing such indicators to address effectively a sustainable society which consists of various components.

2-3-4 An indicative sustainability assessment

This section discusses how an indicator system can be used for sustainability assessment and policy analysis. In particular, an indicative indicator system based upon the Environmental Sustainability Index is introduced, with a case study in China.

Assessment framework and case study

As explained previously, the ESI is an indicator system consisting of five components: environmental systems, environmental stresses, human vulnerability, social and institutional capability, and global stewardship. A notable strength of the ESI is its ability to demonstrate the relative sustainability statuses of targeted countries and clarify relative sustainability performance. Since the assessment method demonstrates sustainability statuses in the form of aggregate scores, it has the potential advantage of providing a clear message regarding overall relative sustainability statuses across countries, and is therefore considered to be useful for policy evaluations.

Hara et al. (2009) proposed a more robust assessment method with reference to the ESI approach. The basic ESI framework was modified, making the assessment system more flexible and permitting a comparison of relative sustainability statuses of targeted regions for various time periods. The novel aspect of the new method is the calculation of the relative sustainability performance of China's provinces over two different time periods. More specifically, in the calculation framework, performance in terms of relative sustainability status is compared across provinces for the years 2000 and 2005. The method examines the sustainability status of provinces and facilitates investigation of chronological trends in the integrated sustainability status, components and individual variables under each component in each province.

The case study employs the assessment method to analyse the relative sustainability status of the 31 Chinese provinces, autonomous regions and major municipalities. To evaluate China's sustainability at the provincial level, Hara et al. (ibid.) first identified three sustainability components. The selection of the criteria was based on the current situation in China, i.e. the most important challenges that China currently faces and is likely to face in the future. In addition to serious environmental problems, rapid economic growth in China has caused marked disparities in socio-economic performance across regions. Furthermore, efficient resource utilization has been, and will continue to be, one of the most critical issues associated with China's rapid industrialization. Based on these assumptions, three components were selected to address the issue of sustainability status: environment, resources and socio-economic aspects. It should be noted that the second component, "resources", actually refers to the conditions of efficient resource usage and is intended to represent the perspectives of the resource-circulation concept.

With relevance and data availability in mind, 22 variables were selected to represent the three components, and data for the variables were collected from the China Statistical Yearbook for the years 2000–2006 in order to calculate the index scores of the three components for each province for the two time periods. Table 2.3.1 lists all the variables comprising the three components. The socio-economic component, representing quality of life and basic human needs, consisted of seven types of variables, such as access to water. The environmental component, representing the environmental loads associated with economic activities, has nine variables, such as green space, air pollution, water pollution and waste generation. The resource component includes variables related to the efficient use and availability of natural resources, such as energy, materials and water per unit and their availability. After compiling the datasets, the variables and component scores, sustainability index scores were calculated in the following manner.

Step 1: normality test. The sustainability and component scores were calculated by aggregation. However, the aggregation procedure requires that all variables follow a normal distribution. Thus the Skewness-Kurtosis test is conducted first to determine if each variable followed a normal distribution. When the normality test failed (at the 0.05 significance level), the variable was logarithmically or exponentially transformed. A natural logarithm or square root was then applied to all the variables.

Step 2: z-score calculation. A set of transformed variables was produced in step 1. However, these variables have different averages and variances and cannot be aggregated. A z-score for each variable is then computed to control for differences in the absolute values and variances across variables using the following equation:

$$z_{i_t}^{j_m} = \frac{\mu^{j_m} - X_{i_t}^{j_m}}{\sigma^{j_m}} \tag{1}$$

where i_t denotes a province in year t, j_m denotes a variable name within a component $m \in M =$ (environment, socio-economic, resources), X is a

Table 2.3.1 Components and variables

Component	Type	Variable name	Variable definition
Socio-economic	Quality of life	GRP/capita	Gross regional product (GRP)/capita
	Quality of life	Income gap	Ratio between per capita consumption of urban and rural households
	Quality of life	Floor space/capita	Total floor space of residential building/capita
	Basic human needs	Water access	% of population with access to water
	Basic human needs	Gas access	% of population with access to gas
	Basic human needs	Life expectancy	Life expectancy at birth
	Basic human needs	Illiteracy	% of illiterate or semi-literate among population over 15 years old
Environment	Green space	Forest coverage	Forest coverage areas
	Water	COD discharge	Discharge volume of chemical oxygen demand (COD) in urban domestic sewage
	Water	Sewage treatment level	Treatment ratio of urban domestic sewage
	Water	Wastewater discharge/GRP	Total discharge amount of wastewater/GRP
	Air	Gas emission/GRP	Total volume of industrial waste gas emission/GRP
	Air	SO_x emission/GRP	Total volume of SO_x emission/GRP
	Waste	Solid waste discharge/GRP	Discharge amount of industrial solid waste/GRP
	Waste	Solid waste treatment level	Treatment ratio of industrial solid waste
	Soil	Fertilizer usage	Consumption of chemical fertilizer
Resources	Energy	Coal use/GRP	Consumption of coal/GRP
	Energy	Oil use/GRP	Consumption of fuel oil/GRP
	Material/waste use	Solid waste utilization	Utilization ratio of industrial solid waste
	Water	Water supply/GRP	Volume of water supply for productive use/GRP
	Water	Water availability/capita	Total amount of available water resources/capita
	Water	Industrial water use/GRP	Industrial water consumption/GRP

Note: All data were obtained from the China Statistical Yearbook (2000–2006).
Source: Hara et al. (2009); reproduced by permission of Springer Japan.

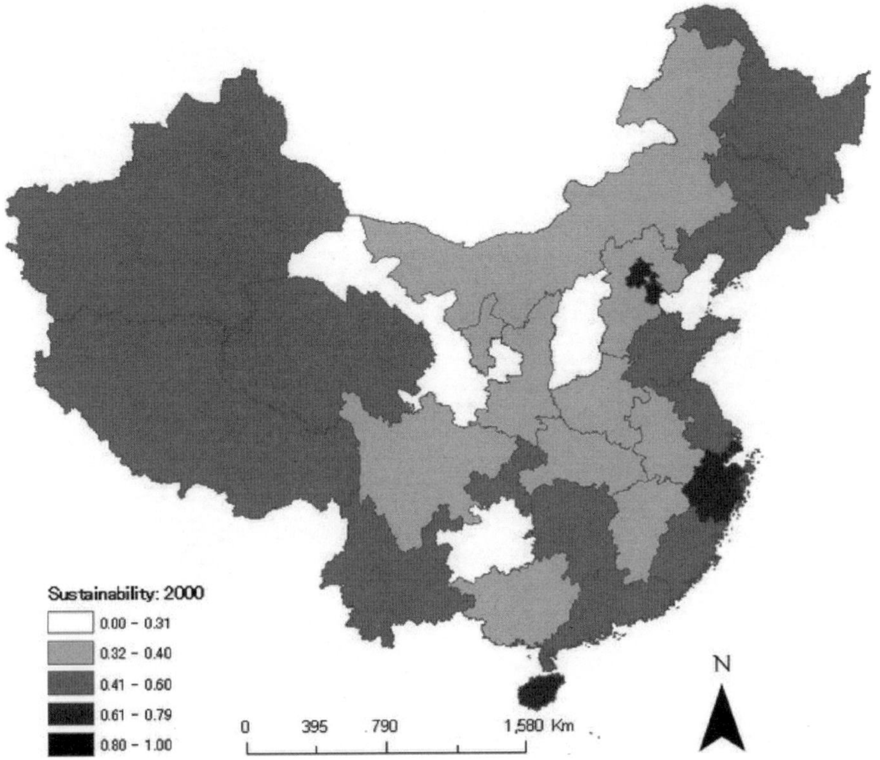

Figure 2.3.1 Sustainability index scores, 2000
Source: Hara et al. (2009); reproduced by permission of Springer Japan.

normalized variable, as described in step 1, and μ and σ are the mean and variance of the transformed variable, respectively. Note that the final sustainability index score is calculated so that the higher the score, the better the evaluation of the province.

Step 3: z-score aggregation. After obtaining z-scores for all the provinces and variables for the two selected time periods, the z-scores are aggregated over the variables within one component using the following equation:

$$I_{i_t}^m = \sum_{j_m} w^m z_{i_t}^{j_m} \tag{2}$$

where w^m denotes a weight for each variable in component m. Equal weight for each variable in the three components is applied. For example, since the environmental component consisted of nine variables, the weight used for the aggregation was 1/9.

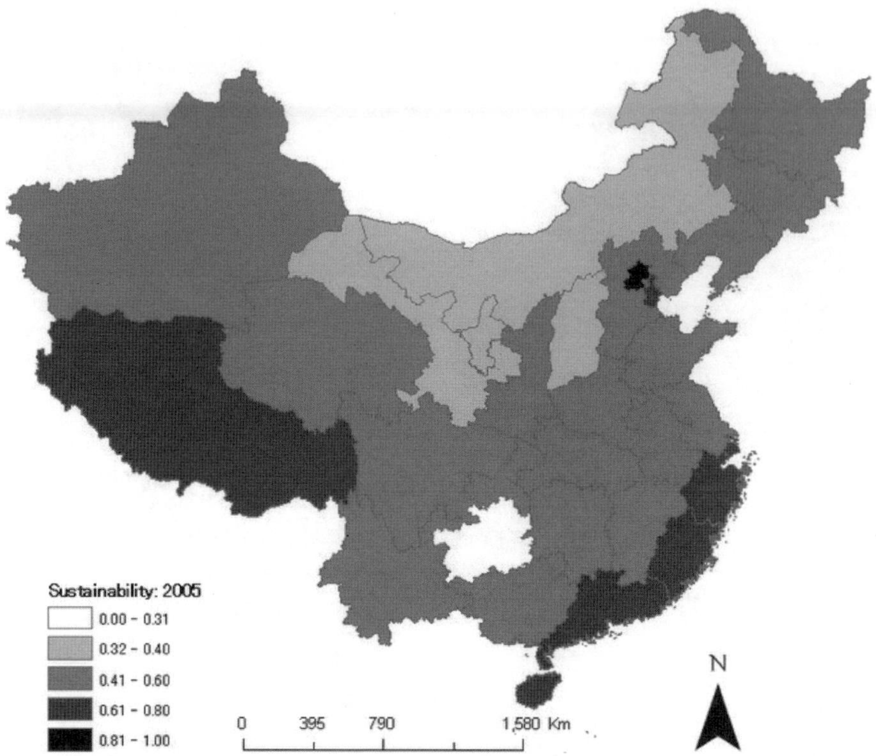

Figure 2.3.2 Sustainability index scores, 2005
Source: Hara et al. (2009); reproduced by permission of Springer Japan.

Step 4: calculation of sustainability index scores. The final sustainability index score for province i is the mean of the three components. A more detailed explanation of the calculation methods and assessment framework is given in Hara et al. (ibid.).

Assessment results and implications

Figures 2.3.1 and 2.3.2 show the calculated sustainability index scores for all examined provinces in 2000 and 2005 using a geographic information system. Figures 2.3.3 and 2.3.4 illustrate the scores for the environment components of all provinces in 2000 and 2005. The results demonstrate a general tendency in which municipalities such as Beijing, Shanghai and Tianjin (most of which are considered economically developed regions and thus relatively affluent) were ranked highly. This is mainly attributed to the fact that the scores for the socio-economic component appeared to

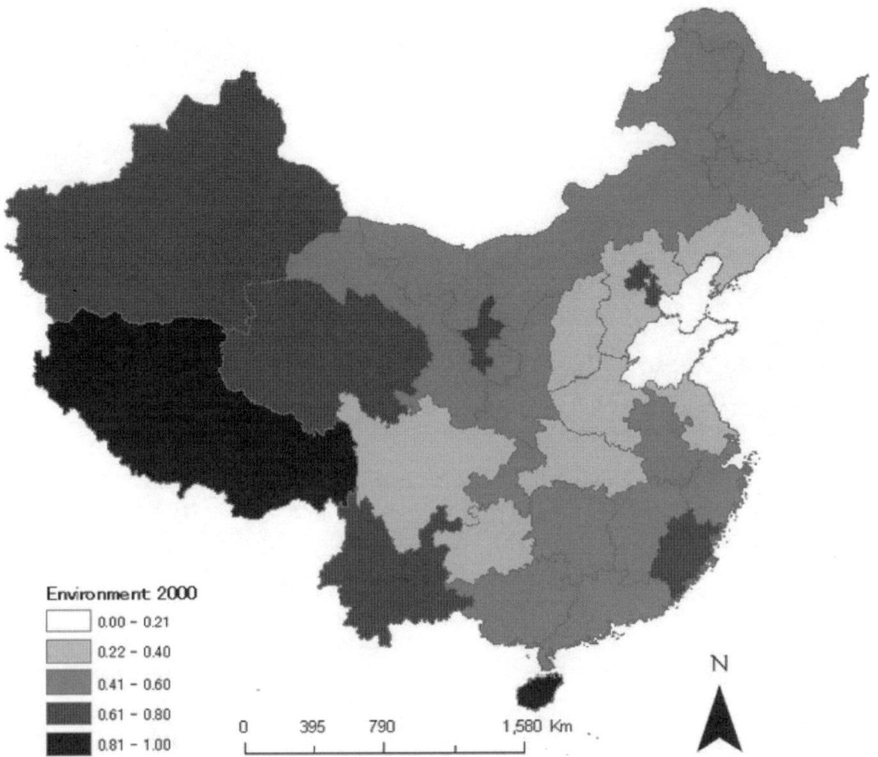

Figure 2.3.3 Environment component scores, 2000
Source: Hara et al. (2009); reproduced by permission of Springer Japan.

be markedly higher in these municipalities when compared to the other provinces. It is important to note that all three components were weighted equally in the present study, and the high scores associated with the socio-economic components affected the final sustainability index scores. Different weights can be applied depending on the purpose and scope of studies.

In addition, the scores for the environment component decreased in several of the provinces over the study period. Figures 2.3.3 and 2.3.4 show that the environmental conditions worsened between 2000 and 2005, particularly in the western and northeastern areas of China. Several provinces around large municipalities, such as Beijing, showed a decrease in values for the environment component.

The method was useful for several reasons. First, it was capable of determining the relative sustainability status, in the form of aggregate scores, of targeted regions for different time periods on a common basis.

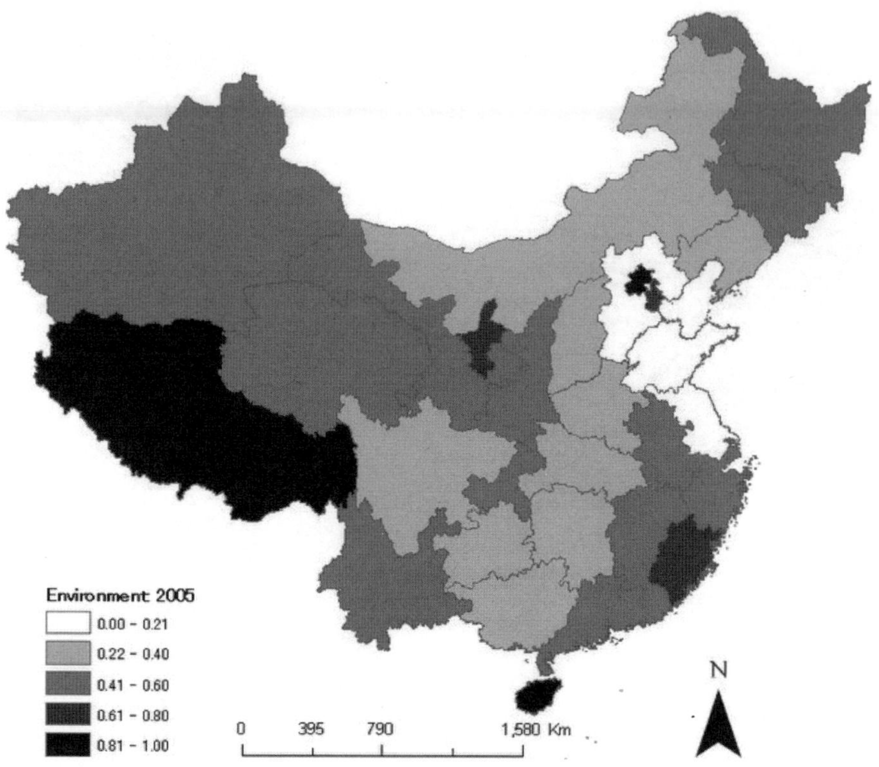

Figure 2.3.4 Environment component scores, 2005
Source: Hara et al. (2009); reproduced by permission of Springer Japan.

Consequently, the results could be used to infer which regions performed well or poorly from the viewpoint of sustainability, as well as the changes in performance over time. These findings could therefore serve as basic information for macro-analyses of indicative sustainability performance. Second, information can be derived from decomposed sustainability elements – that is, the environment, resources and socio-economic components. Thus not only aggregated assessment of sustainability but also investigations using various components are simultaneously possible. Such information derived by the method is useful for obtaining an overview of relative or indicative sustainability status and understanding the level of performance or potential problems in individual provinces from a sustainability perspective. Thus the approach could be useful in policy analysis and for guiding a society towards a sustainable future, although the results are affected by the credibility and availability of the primary data.

2-3-5 Conclusion

This chapter discussed indicator systems and their application to the implementation of environmental policies by reviewing existing sustainability indicator systems and examples where indicator systems have been implemented in environmental policies in Japan, China and the European Union. Subsequently, a novel indicative assessment method, which is useful for macro-analysis of sustainability status, was introduced, along with a Chinese case study. This demonstrated that indicator systems could be very useful in measuring sustainability status that incorporates the resource-circulation concept. By providing objective information on the current status and performance progress of sustainability conditions, indicators – along with certain targets and benchmarks – can be effectively applied to efforts to design and develop sustainable resource-circulating societies. Indicator systems should keep a scientific foundation to provide neutral and useful information. To keep such a scientific basis, two conditions should be prioritized: assessment processes and interpretation of assessment results must be traceable; and regardless of political judgements, the same types of indicators should be selected and assessed over examined periods. For indicator systems to be effective, databases for various indicators should be further enriched in Asian countries – the development of databases is an area in which Asian countries should collaborate.

In terms of resource-circulating societies, the Japanese government adopted three comprehensive indicators: resource productivity, recycling ratios and reductions in final disposals. The government is now implementing efforts directed at making these indicators more comprehensive by combining them with other indicators that are relevant, for example to the promotion of a low-carbon society. Such a holistic approach and multiple or comprehensive assessments are essential in establishing sustainable societies.

REFERENCES

Bringezu, S. (2002) "Towards Sustainable Resource Management in the European Union", Wuppertal Papers No. 121, Wuppertal Institute.

Commission of the European Communities (2005) "Thematic Strategy on Sustainable Use of Natural Resources", COM 670 final, Brussels.

Council for PET Bottle Recycling (2008) "Pet Bottle Recycling Annual Report", CPBR, Tokyo.

Dudek, D., M. Zhong, J. Zhang, G. Song and A. Liu (2001) "Total Emission Control of Major Pollutants in China", China Environmental Series, Woodrow Wilson International Center for Scholars, Washington, DC.

Economic Planning Unit (2002) "Malaysian Quality of Life 2002", Prime Minister's Department, Government of Malaysia; available at www.epu.gov.my/malaysiaqualityoflife2002.

Ekins, P., S. Dresner and K. Dahlstrom (2008) "The Four Capital Method of Sustainable Development Evaluation", *European Environment* 18, pp. 63–80.

Esty, D., M. Levy and T. Srebotnjak (2005) "2005 Environmental Sustainability Index: Benchmarking National Environmental Stewardship", Yale Center for Environmental Law and Policy, New Haven, CT.

European Commission (2007) *Measuring Progress towards a More Sustainable Europe 2007. Monitoring Report of the EU Sustainable Development Strategy.* Luxembourg: Eurostat Statistical Books.

Government of Japan (2007) *Becoming a Leading Environmental Nation Strategy in the 21st Century – Japan's Strategy for a Sustainable Society.* Tokyo: Government of Japan.

Hara, K., M. Uwasu, H. Yabar and H. Zhang (2009) "Sustainability Assessment with Time-Series Scores – A Case Study of Chinese Provinces", *Sustainability Science* 4(1), pp. 81–97.

International Union for the Conservation of Nature (1991) *Caring for the Earth – Strategy for Sustainable Living.* London: Earthscan Publications.

Li, K. and W. Li (2004) "Introduction to China's Environmental Protection Laws", *Chinese Education and Society* 37, pp. 21–25.

MOE (2002) *Quality of the Environment in Japan.* Tokyo: Ministry of Environment.

——— (2003) *Fundamental Plan for Establishing a Sound Material-Cycle Society.* Tokyo: Ministry of Environment.

Ness, B., E. Urbel-Piirsalu, S. Anderberg and L. Olsson (2007) "Categorizing Tools for Sustainability Assessment", *Ecological Economics* 60(3), pp. 498–508.

OECD (1993) *Core Set of Indicators for Environmental Performance Reviews.* Paris: OECD.

——— (2003) "OECD Environmental Indicators: Development, Measurement and Use", reference paper, OECD, Paris.

——— (2006) "Environmental Compliance and Enforcement in China: An Assessment of Current Practices and Ways Forward", Programme of Environmental Cooperation with Asia and the OECD, Hanoi.

SEPA (2001) "The National Tenth Five-year Plan for Environmental Protection", State Environmental Protection Administration, No. 76, Beijing (in Chinese).

UNCSD (2001) "Indicators of Sustainable Development: Guidelines and Methodology", UN Division for Sustainable Development, New York.

UNDP (2006) *Human Development Report 2006: Beyond Scarcity: Power, Poverty and the Global Water Crisis.* New York: UNDP.

UNESCAP (2007) "Expert Group Meeting on Developing Eco-Efficiency Indicators (EEI)", UN Economic and Social Commission for Asia and the Pacific, January; available at www.unescap.org/esd/sustainable/eei/meeting/Jan2007/.

Wackernagel, M., D. Moran, S. White and M. Murray (2006) "Ecological Footprint Accounts for Advancing Sustainability: Measuring Human Demands on Nature", in P. Lawn (ed.) *Sustainable Development Indicators in Ecological Economics.* Cheltenham: Edward Elgar.

World Commission on Environment and Development (1987) *Our Common Future*. Oxford: Oxford University Press.

Yabar, H., M. Uwasu, K. Hara, H. Zhang and T. Kumazawa (2008) "Visioning the Future: Sustainability Pathways and Indicators Based on the Capital Approach", in *Proceedings of Eighth International Conference on EcoBalance*, Tokyo, December. Tokyo: Institute of Life Cycle Assessment, Japan, pp. 158–161.

Yabar, H., K. Hara, M. Uwasu, Y. Yamaguchi, H. Zhang and T. Morioka (2009) "Integrated Resource Management towards a Sustainable Asia: Policy and Strategy Evolution in Japan and China", *International Journal of Environmental Technology and Management* 11(4), pp. 239–256.

Zhang, H., K. Hara, H. Yabar, Y. Yamaguchi, M. Uwasu and T. Morioka (2009) "Comparative Analysis of the Sustainability Indices Systems for Eco-industrial Parks in Baotou, Suzhou and Shanghai", *Sustainability Science* 4(2), pp. 263–279.

Zhuang, G. (2008) "How Will China Move towards Becoming a Low-carbon Economy?", *China and World Economy* 16(3), pp. 93–105.

2-4

International comparison of sustainability indicators and outlook for Asia

Hiroyuki Tada

2-4-1 Why are indicators necessary for an organization like Japan for Sustainability?

The author belongs to the Research Institute for Sustainability Science and also serves as co-representative of the non-governmental organization Japan for Sustainability (JFS). JFS was established in August 2002 and its mission is to build a sustainable world using communication as a driving force.

In the years since JFS was established, it has disseminated information in English on various sustainability initiatives in Japan to 191 countries. We have received numerous comments from these countries and invite you to visit our website (www.japanfs.org). JFS has developed numerous projects around the central theme of sustainability, but the one I would like to introduce here is called the Index Project.

Why are indicators needed today? My thinking on the issue is broadly summarized in three points.

- Conservation activities and initiatives for a sustainable society and centred on the environment are currently being conducted in variety of sectors in Japan. However, most of these are individual, local efforts and do not promote an overall image of the society we should be developing. This may be because there is no clear vision for the direction of the country, and therefore no indicators for measuring progress towards that vision have been clearly formulated.

Establishing a resource-circulating society in Asia: Challenges and opportunities, Morioka, Hanaki and Moriguchi (eds), United Nations University Press, 2011, ISBN 978-92-808-1182-7

- Furthermore, we often follow trends emanating from Western countries, not only regarding the environment but in other areas as well, including corporate social responsibility (CSR). This has meant that we have not yet developed an endogenous method for designing a sustainable society, nor have we conducted the deep philosophical search that would precede such a design. This makes it difficult to claim that we are showing adequate leadership today, even regarding the urgent issue of forming Asian recycling-oriented societies.
- For example, no one can answer the question of whether Japan has moved closer to or further from being a sustainable society in the past 10 years. No analysis has been conducted, and thus no one can verify whether government policies have actually been helpful in moving the nation towards the society we want to have.

It was due to this sense of crisis and government inaction that we decided, through the power of private citizens and civil society, to formulate an index for Japan along with a vision for a sustainable society. The project was inaugurated in 2004 and is currently ongoing.

Around 60 Japanese companies are supporting members of JFS. Almost all of them have an environmental sustainability index already, but have not yet developed others in the CSR area. Although the JFS index targets the country level, it is applicable to business units. Some companies were stimulated by the JFS index to study areas of social and economic well-being. They set an individual CSR index in accordance with the national sustainability index in Japan.

2-4-2 Development of the JFS sustainability index and its contents

Figure 2.4.1 shows an overall image of our index. Due to space limitations, it is not possible to explain the figure in detail; readers are requested to visit the abovementioned website for additional details.

As stated, a key aim was to develop our vision and index together as a set. We started by collating and studying various definitions of basic sustainability, and from these developed our own original definition; the website of Maureen Hart was very helpful in this regard (www. sustainablemeasures.com/). We then established five keys, corresponding to capacity/resources, temporal fairness, spatial fairness, diversity and connection with intent. These keys were linked to the four categories of environment, economy, society and individuals to formulate our initial vision for a sustainable Japan. Simultaneously, the five keys were cross-referenced with the four categories to produce a group of 20 indicators.

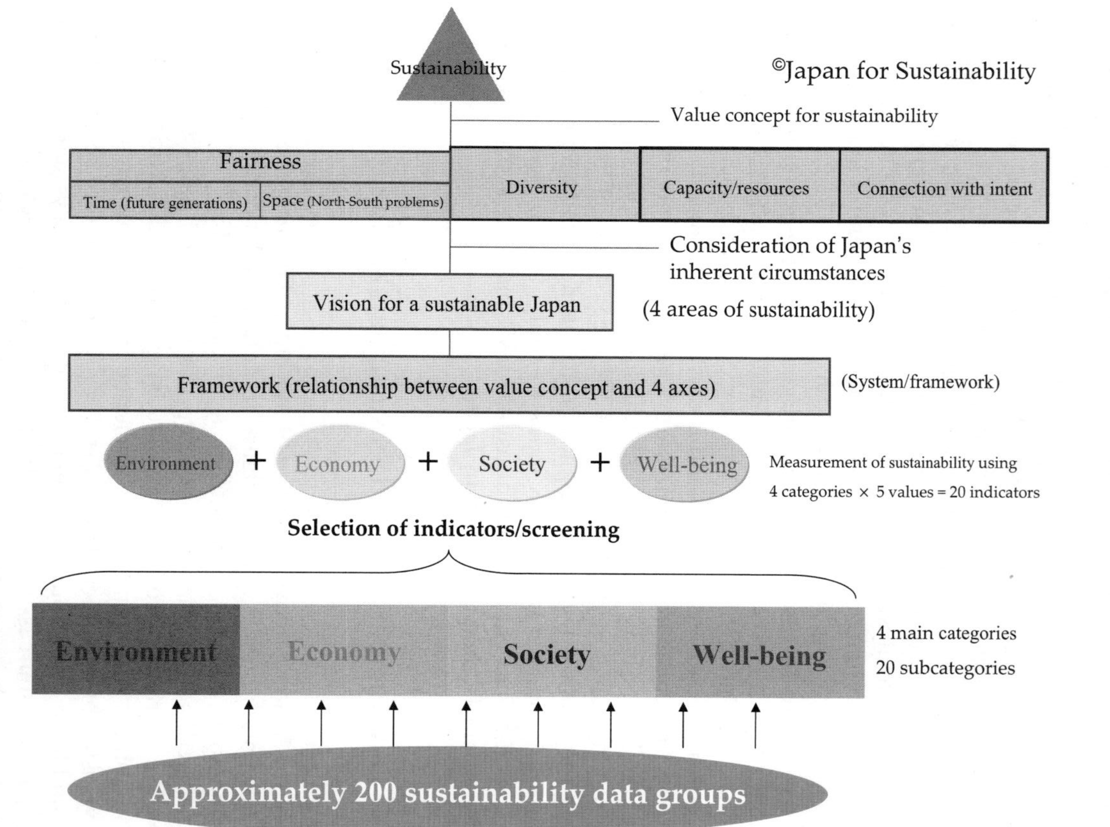

Figure 2.4.1 Overall framework of JFS index

One issue that arose when developing the indicators was that data related to sustainability were unorganized and scattered throughout the various ministries and agencies of Japan. This presented a challenge that differed from the countries described below, and gathering the information for the approximately 200 potential indicator candidates involved a considerable number of work hours. And this was not simply a problem of time; it also highlighted the question of whether one of the important roles of government in creating a sustainable society should be to share information from these individual datasets across agencies (ideally storing them in one place) and provide this information as a public service.

Table 2.4.1 shows the framework for the 20 specific indicators and their overall relationships. The target year was set for 2050, and the trends for the years 1990–2005 were calculated within this framework.

Figure 2.4.2 shows the measurement results for the years 1990–2005. If the weighting is ignored and equivalents are averaged, the total score is 33.5 points, a decrease of 19 per cent compared to 1990, when it was 41.3 points. The results of these calculations mean that we have moved that much further away from being a sustainable society.

2-4-3 Example of an international comparison

What about other countries? Table 2.4.2 shows the results of an investigation that found that 11 countries have sustainability indicators at the national level. All these indicators were created under government direction. (Since then, New Zealand has also formulated an index.) In most of these countries, the number of main indicators is around 20, with a minimum of six and a maximum of 48.

It should be apparent that most of these are European countries and there is not a single Asian country on the list. As an example, therefore, I shall compare the JFS index with those of the United Kingdom and Germany. I would like to make this comparison from the perspectives of the purpose of developing the index, the range and framework of the index and the characteristics of each indicator.

United Kingdom

After first declaring that sustainability = quality of life (QOL), the overall structure of the UK index consisted of 15 headline indicators: economic performance; investment; employment; poverty and discrimination; education; health; living environment; crime; climate change; atmosphere; traffic; water quality of rivers; wildlife; land use; and waste.

Table 2.4.1 JFS sustainability framework and 20 indicators

Four axes	Model for sustainability	Subcategory	Headline indicator	Correlation with sustainability value concept	Type of indicator
Environment	• Coexistence of humans and nature • Concept of "climate" • Preservation of diverse ecosystems and indigenous species • Nature restoration • Emphasis on natural cycles • *Satoyama* (woodland near developed areas) and *Chinju no mori* (tree groves of village shrines)	1) Biodiversity forest 2) Warming 3) Resource recycling/ waste 4) Water/soil/air 5) Environmental education and systems	1) Proportion of falconiformes species that are facing extinction 2) Per capita greenhouse gas output (annual) 3) Amount of waste produced per capita per day 4) Amount of chemical synthetic fertilizers used (exposed vegetables, per 10a) 5) Proportion of green consumers	Diversity Intergenerational fairness Interregional fairness Resources/capacity Resources/capacity Connection with intent	Status Burden Burden Burden Change
Economy	• Self-supporting economic systems • Discrete self-sufficient economies • Environmental efficiency • Resource productivity • Regional development • International contributions	1) Energy 2) Resource productivity 3) Food 4) Finance 5) International cooperation	1) Proportion of reusable and recycled energy 2) Input of GDP/annual energy 3) Food self-sufficiency on a calorie basis (as proportion of GDP) 4) Proportion of aid in gross national income	Diversity Intergenerational/ Interregional fairness Resources/capacity Resources/capacity Connection with intent	Change Change Status Burden Change

Society	• Slow life • Making use of nature • Mutual assistance • Equal opportunities • Local culture • Intercommunication	1) Safety 2) Mobility 3) Gender, minorities 4) Traditions and culture 5) Socially responsible investments	1) General crime rate (number of incidents per 100,000 people) 2) Proportion of people aged 15 years or older whose only means of transportation is a bicycle 3) Proportion of women occupying seats in national parliament 4) Production value of traditional crafts 5) Proportion of SRI (socially responsible investment) mutual funds in net asset value of all mutual funds	Resources/capacity Interregional fairness Diversity Diversity Connection with intent	Burden Status Status Status Change
Well-being	• Smiles • Freedom and citizen participation • Development of abilities and growth • Cultivation of ethics • Health and safety • Natural vocation	1) Life satisfaction 2) Learning/education 3) Citizen participation 4) Mental and physical health 5) Disparities in living standards	1) Proportion of people who are satisfied with their current lives 2) OECD Programme for International Student Assessment 3) Proportion of hours participating in volunteer or social participation activities among number of free hours per day 4) Suicide rate (number of suicides per 100,000 people) 5) Social welfare rate	Intent Intent Intent/diversity Resources/diversity Intent Intergenerational and interregional fairness	Status Status Change Status Status

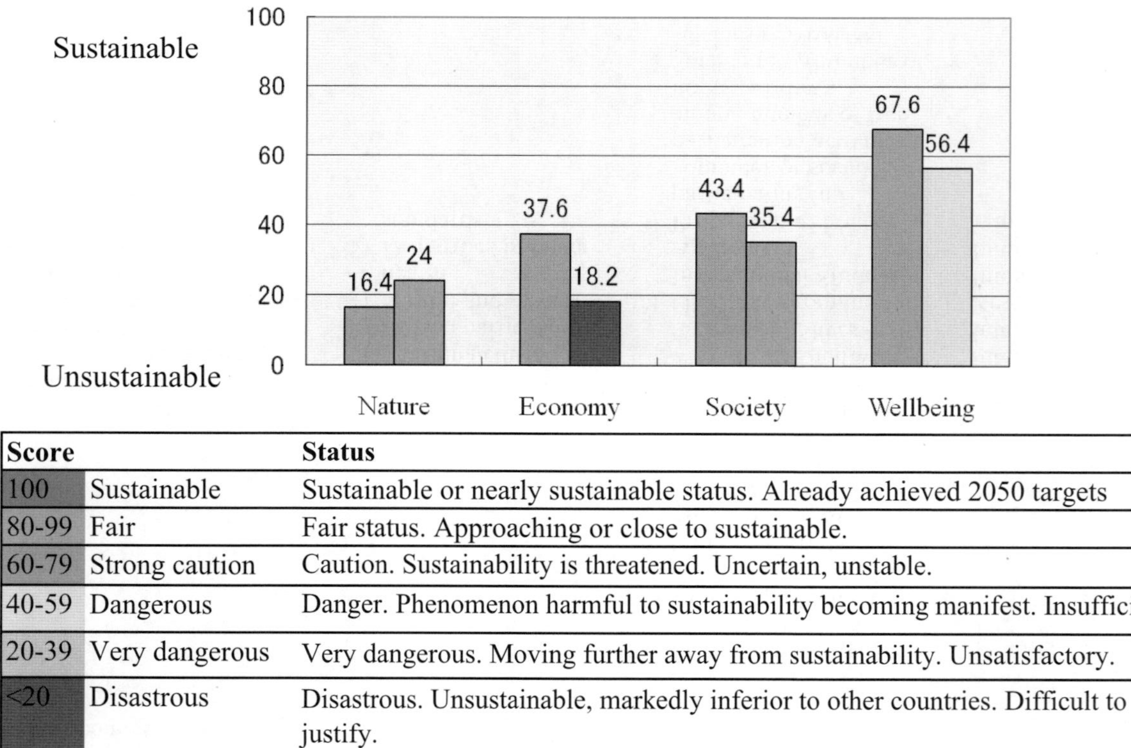

Score		Status
100	Sustainable	Sustainable or nearly sustainable status. Already achieved 2050 targets
80-99	Fair	Fair status. Approaching or close to sustainable.
60-79	Strong caution	Caution. Sustainability is threatened. Uncertain, unstable.
40-59	Dangerous	Danger. Phenomenon harmful to sustainability becoming manifest. Insufficient.
20-39	Very dangerous	Very dangerous. Moving further away from sustainability. Unsatisfactory.
<20	Disastrous	Disastrous. Unsustainable, markedly inferior to other countries. Difficult to justify.

Figure 2.4.2 Results of evaluation of Japan using JFS index
Note: Please see page 427 for a colour version of this figure.

Table 2.4.2 Examples of indices in other countries

No.	Example	Country	Outline
1	Sustainable development index	UK	Graphs using latest data for 15 headline indicators for easy understanding
2	National sustainability strategy	Germany	21 numerical targets established in 3 fields: intergenerational fairness, quality of life, social cohesion
3	Sustainable development index	Sweden	30 indicators established for 4 themes: efficiency; contribution and equality; adaptability and values; resources for the next generation
4	Sustainable development monitoring index	Switzerland	Social, economic and environmental database for sustainable development
5	Sustainable development index	Finland	64 indicators established in 8 categories, including intergenerational fairness and global responsibilities
6	National sustainability strategy	Denmark	14 main indicators based on 8 fundamental principles; additional indicators set for various fields including climate change and ecosystem preservation
7	Environmental and sustainable development index	Canada	6 indicators established centred on natural capital (air environment, water environment, greenhouse gases, forest destruction, wetlands, academic achievement)
8	Sustainability index	Australia	24 indicators established as national strategy for sustainable development
9	National sustainability strategy	Austria	48 indicators based on 20 basic policies
10	Sustainable development index	United States	39 indicators established in the 3 areas of society, economy and environment, with 3 respective categories of long-term resources and debts, progress and current results

With a focus on ease of understanding, one of the main purposes has been to make sustainability itself more widely known in society. Meanwhile, advances since 1990 have been assessed as a "quality of life barometer". There is also a mechanism for strategic feedback. Although there is no categorization, the range of the index not only covers the environment but also includes the economy and society. Characteristics of the index include a primary emphasis on establishment of subindicators under the headline indicators and attempts to ensure the accuracy of measurements. It attempts to develop a broad understanding among the nation's citizens that the environment and QOL are synonymous rather than in conflict (www.sustainable-development.gov.uk/performance/indicators-home.html).

Germany

Twenty-one indicators were established in four categories: intergenerational fairness, QOL, social cohesiveness and international responsibility. Intergenerational fairness includes resources, climate stability, reusable energy, land use, biodiversity, issuance of national bonds, policies and measures for economic stability, technical innovation and education. QOL includes economic growth, transport, food, atmosphere, health and crime. Social cohesiveness includes employment, family, equal opportunities for men and women, and opportunities for foreign nationals. Responsibilities to international society include development assistance and open markets.

Unlike the United Kingdom, the German sustainability index places more emphasis on ensuring closeness with the German sustainability strategy than on ease of understanding. In addition, this index addresses many facets related to sustainability while placing continued importance on QOL. Examples are the family, gender equality, equality among diverse people (including foreign nationals) and emphasis on cohesion. In addition, two indicators are allocated to the questions "Is it acceptable for Germany alone to become sustainable while other countries are sacrificed?" and "Who is sustainability for?" Another commendable aspect is that, while efforts are government-led, private citizens participate in the formulation process (http://nachhaltigkeisrat.de/english.html).

International comparison

Comparisons between the JFS index and that of the United Kingdom revealed a similar purpose for establishing the index. These indicators also share the ideal of making the concept of sustainability, which is not much talked about among the population as yet, well known to everyone.

Of the three indexes, the range covered by the indicators is nearly universal, with all three employing a triple bottom line. However, among the 11 countries previously mentioned, several formulated indexes based on the single premise that "sustainability = environment". Each index has its own characteristics, but all countries are influenced by what can be referred to as their sustainability circumstances, and any attempt to make international comparisons between the indicator groups of different countries' national indexes is tenuous. I also feel that nothing positive can be gained from such attempts.

2-4-4 Overall direction and significance of the developmental process for indicators in the European Union

I have examined and considered several index system groups, including those in Japan. In addition to the resulting comparison of the selected indicators, I consider it to be equally (or more) important to focus on the process used to develop indicators, as was mentioned above for Germany.

I participated in the "Beyond GDP" conference in Brussels, Belgium, in November 1997; over a period of three days, participants discussed whether to develop a new type of index, centred on the European Union, that would go beyond the traditional measure of GDP. While the European Union considers this conference to be a milestone in its medium- to long-term sustainability strategy, it was also open to all other regions. For details of the discussion, I refer you to the website (www.eea.europa. eu/highlights/beyond-gdp). However, here I would like to share some insights I gained through renewing my awareness of this project.

- From the environment to QOL: the tendency in developed countries has been to consider the environment to be the "trigger" for moving towards sustainability, but in the ultimate definition there is a trend towards seeing this as stemming from QOL. Even the current concept of the triple bottom line – environment, economy, society – is becoming obsolete.
- Approaches to policy-makers: the sponsors of this conference included the EU Commission, European Parliament, Organisation for Economic Co-operation and Development, Rome Club and the World Wide Fund for Nature. However, after taking the trouble to develop this index, the obvious major issue of creating understanding and awareness of the index among policy-makers, so that it could be implemented, was left unresolved. The opinion was also expressed that the mass media should have been involved to a greater extent.
- From the perspective of understandability, the concept of an ecological footprint needs to permeate each country and region, not just the European Union overall. Using this concept separately from macro-environmental accounting, priority is placed first on the infrastructure for sustainability and understanding the EU ecosystem.

- Creating both subjective and objective indicators will be important in the future.
- Who should contribute to the process of formulating indicators? Something that surprised me was the very large number of participants (dozens), mainly from European countries, who belonged to the statistics bureaux of their respective countries. Statistics were not investigated after the index had been created; rather, people whose job is dealing with numbers were involved in the discussions as the index was being formulated. I recognized again the importance of their contribution into the process.

2-4-5 Possibility of developing an index in Asia

How will indicators contribute to a sustainable Asia? In the Asian region, development of the comprehensive indicators described above will remain difficult at the national or regional level for some time. The uniqueness of the economies and societies makes Asia completely different from the European Union. Many countries are still developing and the region's economies (or economic growth) and ecologies are still considered to be antagonistic entities.

However, I do not think that we should give up on developing a regional index. The region's economic growth continues each year and it supports one-third of the world's population, as well as more than half of the world's industrial output. Asia bears a large responsibility for the sustainability of the entire Earth, for which it must make a paradigm shift and aim at building true recycling-oriented societies.

No benchmark has been established for Asian countries. However, with reference to JFS and other countries, it is possible that if an index were to be developed in one country, the development of indicators would spread from one country to another. We must chart a course for this.

There is a high possibility of achieving this goal if we start from a focus on environmental sustainability. For this purpose, it will be very important to develop a definition that can be shared among the countries in the region. This definition can then be used as the starting point of one path; after the establishment of reliable environmental databases in as many countries as possible, this path can then be undertaken.

In line with building a resource-circulating society, I believe resource-related data are one of the most important elements to be considered. As can be seen in section 2-4-3, space/resources in the JFS index, waste in the UK index and resources in the German index were all considered key parameters.

Not limited to resources, most Japanese companies which launched their production in Asia acquired ISO 14001, and already grasp whole-environment sustainability data. It is key that they conduct supply-chain management globally, including Asia. Local components and parts vendors follow this line in gathering their own environmental data. I suggest collaboration between public sector and business units beyond boundaries, so that Asian countries can collect these data properly.

2-4-6 Conclusion

The areas where Japan could show leadership include sharing what we have learned from previous examples with other Asian countries, as well as with Europe, and taking the initiative in establishing an environmental database that would cover the entire Asian region. We can start by assisting with the establishment of baseline data. This should be followed by the internal development of indicators in each country that reflect its individual circumstances. I do not think it will be too long before a country with a vision, and which has created a sustainability index, emerges in Asia.

2-5

Research and networking initiatives on resource circulation in Asia

Helmut Yabar, Haiyan Zhang and Keishiro Hara

2-5-1 Introduction

One of the primary challenges currently facing modern societies is how to decouple economic development from the environmental pressure conferred by the limits of the Earth's carrying capacity. This global challenge prompts the question of whether our dealings with nature are sustainable and we will be able to decrease our reliance on nature despite increasing trends in population and economic activity. In this sense, sustainable development is achieved if intergenerational well-being is at least maintained over time (Arrow, Dasgupta and Maler, 2003). According to Dasgupta and Maler (2000), to sustain intergenerational well-being each generation should bequeath to its descendants a productive base at least as large as that which it inherited from its predecessor. An economy's productive base is composed of its institutions (social infrastructure) and capital assets (natural, human and manufactured capital) (Dasgupta, 2007). If we can properly manage natural resources in a way that yields economic profits and increase the other types of capital, we will be on a sustainable path. This chapter analyses the different international research initiatives directed at the development of an Asian resource-circulating society, with particular emphasis on China, focusing on mutual objectives, research themes and networking initiatives. It stresses the vital role of the international research institutions of the developed world in supporting these initiatives through funding, research networking and capacity building.

Establishing a resource-circulating society in Asia: Challenges and opportunities, Morioka, Hanaki and Moriguchi (eds), United Nations University Press, 2011, ISBN 978-92-808-1182-7

2-5-2 Regional strategies towards a resource-circulating society: Research network initiatives in Asia

The ever-increasing and highly inefficient demand for natural resources is already damaging the planet (Hawken, Lovins and Lovins, 1999). One of the primary drivers underlying the demand for resources is the needs of urban inhabitants for food, water, shelter, energy and mobility. Sustainable resource management and resource-circulating societies focus on finding ways to minimize our footprint on nature at city-region, national and international levels. A number of international research initiatives have attempted to integrate these different spatial scales. The Earth System Science Partnership (ESSP), formed after the Amsterdam Declaration on Global Change in 2001,[1] is perhaps one of the first integral research initiatives on global environmental change. The ESSP is a coalition of four research programmes: Diversitas, which focuses on biodiversity, the International Geosphere-Biosphere Programme (IGBP), which focuses on the interactions between physical, chemical and biological processes that define Earth system dynamics, the International Human Dimensions Programme on Global Environmental Change (IHDP), which focuses on the understanding of global environmental change, and the World Climate Research Programme (WCRP), which focuses on the effect of human activities on climate.

The ESSP encourages researchers from diverse fields to engage in integrated study of the Earth system in terms of its structure and functions, the changes occurring in the system and the implication of those changes for regional and global sustainability. The ESSP has conducted various activities including joint projects, integrated regional studies and capacity-building initiatives. The IHDP industrial transformation project identified industrial transformation as the key to sustainability and established five research projects towards that end: energy/material flows, food, cities (transportation and water), information and communication technology, and governance and transformation processes (IHDP-IT, 2001).

At the international policy level, Japan proposed the "reduce, reuse and recycle" 3R Initiative at the G8 summit in 2004 as a way of steering production and consumption patterns towards sustainability. The Japanese government has begun implementation of the 3R Initiative, which aims at sharing experiences among developed and developing countries regarding their environmental and 3R-related policies and actions (Yabar et al., 2009). At the same time, universities and research institutes have come to understand the importance of research collaboration towards a resource-circulating society. For example, the Integrated Research System for Sustainability Science (IR3S), a coalition of five universities and several research institutions, has as a primary goal the promotion of a multidisciplinary research platform in the emerging field of sustainability science. As we will see, Asia has witnessed an increasing number of research initiatives similar to the IR3S. This chapter focuses on some of the most important and comprehensive international research initiatives to address issues related to human-environment linkages in Southeast Asia. The selection of the initiatives was based on three major factors.

- *Interdisciplinary research:* initiatives that cover a wide range of research fields with special focus on the challenges of human-environment relationships in Asia, such as production and consumption systems, land-use change and urbanization.
- *Transboundary research scope:* research themes that cover issues affecting more than one Asian country or having regional impact.
- *International networking:* research initiatives that have networking systems and/or funding cooperation with not only Asian countries but other parts of the world as well.

Monsoon Asia Integrated Regional Study

The Monsoon Asia Integrated Regional Study (MAIRS), which is the first integrated regional ESSP study, focuses on the resilience of the monsoon system to human transformation and the vulnerability of society to its changes. MAIRS, established in 2003, was implemented by the Global Change System for Analysis, Research and Training (START[2]) and the START Temperate East Asia Regional Center. Figure 2.5.1 shows the framework of the MAIRS programme. The international programme office, which supports and promotes MAIRS's full implementation, is part of the Institute of Atmospheric Physics of the Chinese Academy of Sciences.

Research objectives

With 479 people per square kilometre, the Southeast Asian monsoon region has a very high population density (United Nations, 2005), and the area has experienced rapid economic development over the last few decades. Since it is expected that these trends will continue, human activities in the area will have global as well as regional impacts. To address these challenges, MAIRS has set the following objectives:

- understanding how human activities in the region affect the natural variability of the atmospheric, terrestrial and marine components of the monsoon system
- developing a predictive capacity for estimating changes in global-regional linkages in the Earth system and projecting the future consequences of such changes
- developing scenarios for the monsoon area region in 2050 through analysis of the consequences of projected changes.

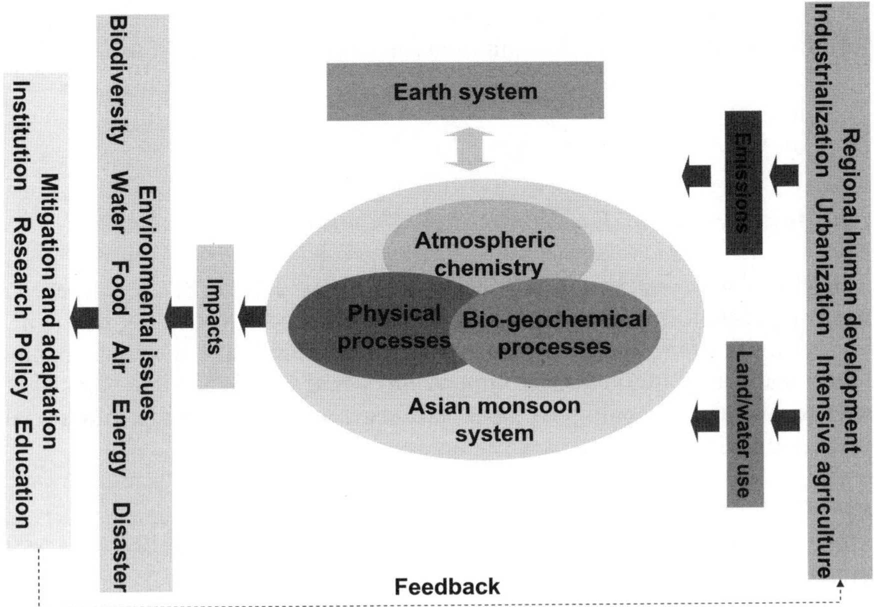

Figure 2.5.1 MAIRS research framework

Research programmes

MAIRS identified six important issues related to environmental change: water, energy, food security, air quality and health, natural disasters and biodiversity. It also established that the importance of these issues is relative to the different geographical zones. To answer questions about these key issues in an integrated manner, MAIRS established four research themes (Fu, Zhang and Yan, 2006):

- coastal zones: rapid transformation of land and marine resources
- high mountain zones: multiple stresses on ecosystems and the biophysical resources within ecosystems
- semi-arid zones: vulnerability of ecosystems resulting from changing climate and land use
- urban zones: changes in resource use and emissions due to rapid urbanization.

Networking

Being the first integrated regional ESSP study gives MAIRS access to an extensive network of institutions. Each of the four global environmental programmes (IGBP, IHDP, WCRP and Diversitas) organizes research activities and capacity-building initiatives and assists MAIRS in establishing scientific networks. MAIRS also has a range of sponsor institutions through which it maintains networking links. These include START, the Chinese Academy of Sciences, the Chinese Ministry of Science and Technology and the Asia-Pacific Network for Global Change Research (APN).[3]

Unit for Social and Environmental Research

The Unit for Social and Environmental Research (USER) is a research network affiliated with the Faculty of Social Sciences at Chiang Mai University in Thailand. USER's mission is multidisciplinary research on the identification of human-environment links and the necessary steps that will contribute to ecological sustainability, human well-being and social justice in the Southeast Asian region.

Research objectives

USER conducts field-based research on the linkages of our lifestyles and social institutions with the environment. The main objectives of USER can be summarized as follows:
- facilitate and conduct interdisciplinary research on complex social-environmental interactions
- improve the quality and use of research-based knowledge in decision-making at local, national and global levels
- conduct assessment and scenario exercises along with field-based research activities.

Research programmes

USER's current interests include investigating the resilience of social-ecological systems, the importance of cross-scale interactions, understanding production-consumption chains and methods for integrated regional assessment. These research activities are organized through five programmes implemented by combining separately funded projects and building and supporting collaboration through networks and partnerships (SARCS, 2008).
- *M-POWER – Mekong Program on Water, Environment and Resilience:* aims to improve livelihood security as well as human and ecosystem health in the Mekong region through democratic water governance.
- *U-TURN – Urban Transformation and Urbanization Research Network:* explores innovative ways to decouple environmental changes from social change through regional development strategies, policies and participatory processes that influence urban transformation and the urbanization process.

- *SPACES – Sustainable Production and Consumption Systems:* focuses on the challenges and opportunities that arise from treating commodity chains as integrated systems, i.e. from inputs through distribution, consumption and disposal.
- *WALKS – Well-being, Alternative Livelihoods and Knowledge Systems*: focuses on improving the well-being of disadvantaged and vulnerable groups through participatory action research, partnerships and capacity building at grassroots and local government levels.
- *ERA – Exploring Regional Alternatives*: focuses on integrated analysis and participatory assessment and deliberation of alternative objectives, strategies and investments in regional development. The programme also explores alternative regional futures through the design of goals, visions and strategies for sustainability.

As shown in Figure 2.5.2, these programmes are carried out based on three major themes: knowledge (effective use of diverse systems of knowledge for sustainability), governance (governance transformation to

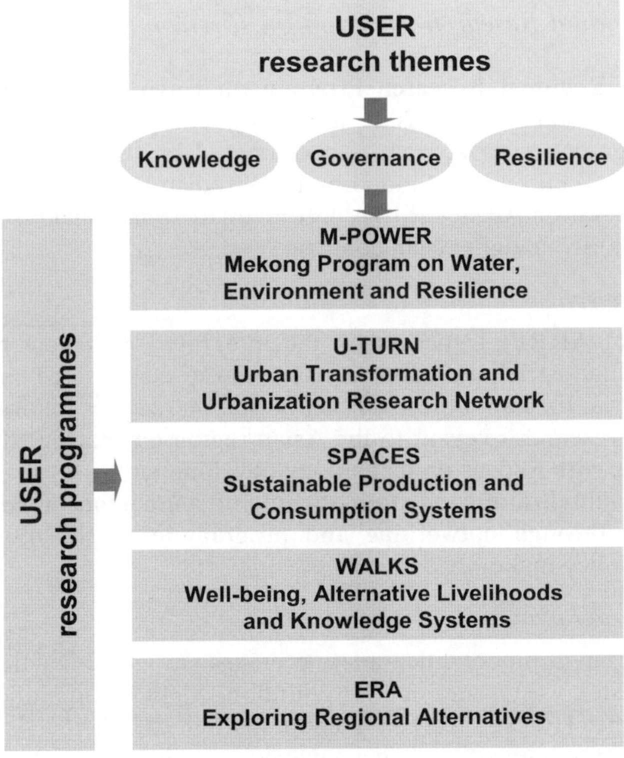

Figure 2.5.2 USER research framework

improve well-being and social justice) and resilience (enhancing capacity to manage the resilience of human-environment systems).

Networking

USER has an extensive research and development network in Southeast Asia. Through M-POWER, SPACES and the Southeast Asian Committee for START, it builds and supports several collaborative networks. For example, M-POWER network strategies include equitable and transparent distribution of research grants, engaging decision-makers, information sharing and communication (monthly research updates, web communication tools, visual aids, etc.) and promoting grassroots research and capacity building in the region. USER contributes to the new IHDP Earth System Governance project, which focuses on global, national and local institutions and governance systems in relation to the natural environment. It is also engaged in a collaborative research project called Rewind, funded by the APN, focusing on the benefits and limitations of multi-stakeholder participation in river basin management.

Asian Regional Research Program on Environmental Technology

The Asian Regional Research Program on Environmental Technology (ARRPET), established in 2001, assesses growing concerns on environmental degradation in Asia. It is coordinated by the Asian Institute of Technology (AIT[4]) and is funded by the Swedish International Development Cooperation Agency (SIDA[5]). It involves 18 national research institutes (NRIs) from eight Asian countries.

Research objectives

Research at ARRPET focuses on the integrated management of solid wastes and industrial and agro-based wastewater, as well as air pollution issues in Asia. Its main objectives can be summarized as follows:
* advance research relevant to the Asian region on specific environmental issues, with a focus on technology development
* capacity mobilization and strengthening of competence in NRIs
* research through networking and programme results dissemination among policy-makers.

Research programmes

To address environmental degradation in Asia, especially in areas related to solid wastes, wastewater and air pollution, ARPPET identified four research themes (Rakshit, 2009; Visvanathan et al., 2007).
* *Wastewater treatment and management.* Covers treatment and management of domestic and agro-based industrial wastewater. Specific

research topics include technology development for nitrogen removal from wastewater and sustainable practices in agro-based industries.

- *Sustainable solid waste landfill management in Asia.* This theme investigates suitable methods for solid waste landfill management in the region, including landfill gas, leachate, liners and covers, as well as pre-treatment, fermentation and compositing of wastes.
- *Improving air quality in developing Asian countries.* The first phase included topics such as assessment of air pollution status, air pollution control technologies and modelling tools for integrated air quality management. The focus of the second phase is long-term monitoring of toxic air pollutants and their potential health effects, and appropriate control technologies.
- *Industrial and hazardous waste treatment and management.* This focuses on efficient methods and strategies for hazardous waste management. The research places particular emphasis on the removal of heavy metals and chlorinated organics from industrial processes.

Networking

The ARRPET research network consists of 18 NRIs from eight countries (China, India, Indonesia, Malaysia, the Philippines, Sri Lanka, Thailand and Viet Nam) that are engaged in the four research themes; Figure 2.5.3 shows the research institutes involved in this network. In addition to this extensive network of Asian institutes, ARRPET benefits from the AIT and SIDA research networks.

2-5-3 China's research initiatives based on the circular-economy approach

Similar to what happened to Japan in the 1960s, the rapid economic growth of China in the last few decades has resulted in resource overconsumption and environmental degradation, including air and water pollution and desertification (Feng and Yan, 2007). To address these challenges, the government introduced the circular-economy (CE) approach in its Eleventh Five-Year Plan (FYP). The CE is a mode of economic development based on the circulation of resources: CE aims at sustainable growth by means of rational use of energy and resources and ecological preservation, while ensuring continuous economic development (Yabar et al., 2009). The CE framework consists of three levels, small, medium and large circulations, which relate to individual enterprises, eco-industrial parks (EIPs) and cities, provinces and regions, respectively (Zhang et al., 2008). The small circulation approach is based on promoting cleaner production at the individual enterprise level. More than 8,000 enterprises in

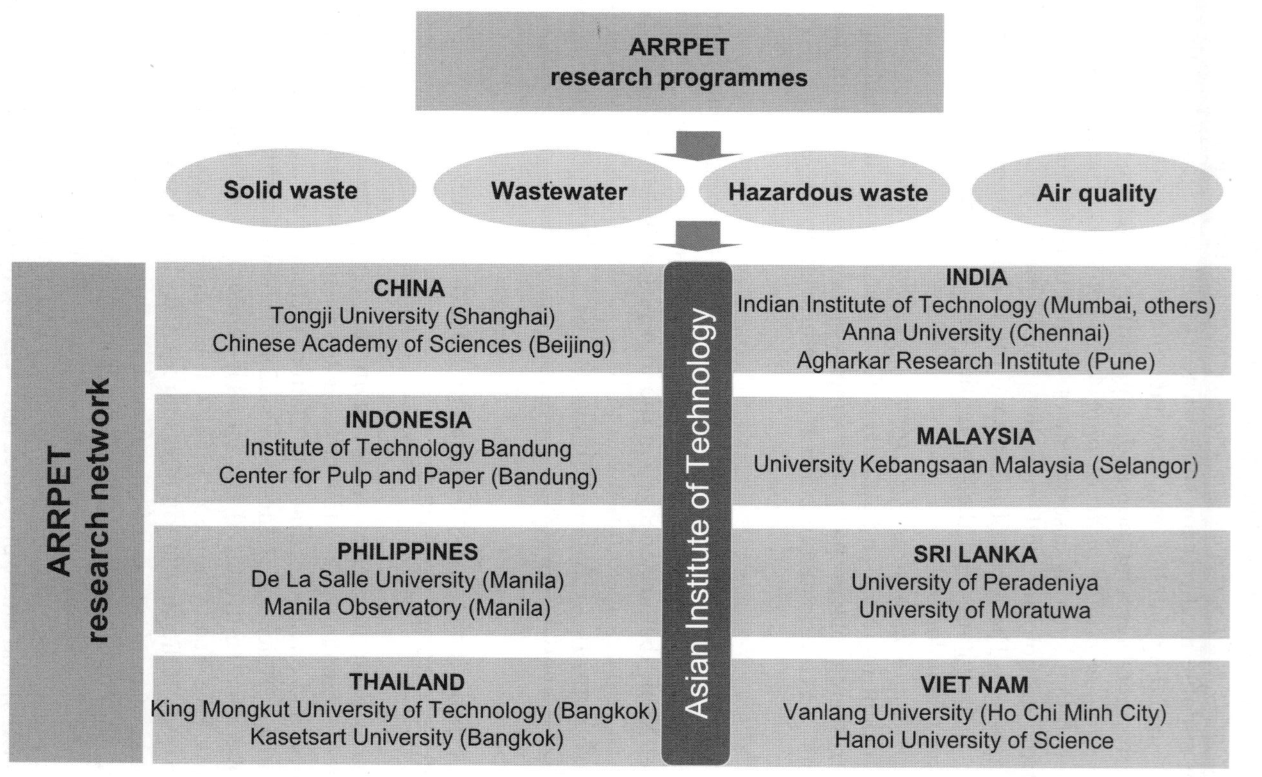

Figure 2.5.3 ARRPET research and network framework

China are registered under ISO 14000 standards (Yabar et al., 2007). The medium circulation approach is based on promoting CE implementation through EIPs. Between 2001 and 2007 the State Environmental Protection Administration approved 26 EIPs in China (SEPA, 2007). The large circulation approach promotes CE implementation at the city and provincial levels (Zhang et al., 2009).

Universities in China have been conducting research on sustainable resource management since the late 1970s. The outcomes of these efforts have provided strong theoretical support for CE in achieving the aims of sustainable development in China. For example, the Department of Environmental Science & Engineering at Tsinghua University has addressed the issue of environmental degradation by undertaking hundreds of research projects on environmental management in the areas of water pollution control, wastewater treatment, air pollution control and solid waste management and reclamation (Tsinghua University, 2009). The department has also established research networks with leading international universities, including Harvard and Yale in the United States, Aachen University of Technology and Delft University of Technology in Europe and The University of Tokyo and Kyoto University in Japan. Tsinghua and Yale also established a three-year programme in 2005, the Yale-Tsinghua Environment & Sustainable Development Leadership Program, to teach Chinese municipal officials in charge of urban planning and development how to promote economic development in sustainable ways. The education programme included sessions in China and the United States where participants held meetings with senior American officials from cities and corporations.

Another example of international research collaboration is the UNEP-Tongji Institute of Environment for Sustainable Development (IESD) established in 2002 by UNEP and Tongji University. The institute promotes education, research and outreach in collaboration with the academic, government and corporate sectors. It conducts various research programmes, including water environmental studies, eco-city planning and waste management. As part of its education and outreach activities, and in order to provide education and training skills to the future leaders of Asia, the IESD launched the Asia-Pacific Leadership Programme on Environment for Sustainable Development in 2004, and the International Masters Programme in Environmental Management and Sustainable Development in 2006.

More recently, numerous top Chinese universities have established research centres to implement the CE concept. Table 2.5.1 shows some of the CE and sustainable-development-related centres established in China over the last decade. These research institutions provide strong theoretical support for directing CE towards sustainability in terms of policy-making and technology innovation.

Table 2.5.1 Circular economy and sustainable development centres in Chinese universities

Centre name	Year	Outline	Projects
Cleaner Production and Circular Economy Center, Chinese Research Academy of Environmental Science	2005	Carry out research to support environmental policy in: • circular economy • eco-industry • cleaner production	• Study on production and emission coefficient of industrial pollution • Environmental protection of circular-economy development of major industries • 25 industrial cleaner production standards • Implementation mechanism for circular economy • Guidelines for EIP design planning
Research Center for the Social and Economic Development of the Yangtze River Delta (YRD), Nanjing University	2001	Establish a scientific network in socio-economic and environmental development by establishing innovative research mechanisms and keeping up with leading domestic institutions	• Strategy for socio-economic development in the YRD • Study on influence of development of information technology on economic growth • Analysis of the urbanization patterns in the YRD
UNEP-Tongji Institute of Environment for Sustainable Development	2002	Promote education, research and outreach in fields of environment and sustainable development in collaboration with academia, government and corporate sectors	• Research programmes in water environmental studies, eco-city planning and waste management • Education and outreach activities to provide education and training skills: Asia-Pacific Leadership Programme on Environment for Sustainable Development
Yale-Tsinghua Environment and Sustainable Development Leadership Program	2003	Education programme for Chinese municipal officials in charge of urban planning and development, focused on how to promote economic development in a sustainable way	Develop skills on applications of concepts of sustainable development to specific urban concerns such as water supply and quality, energy, pollution reduction, waste management and other urgent urban environmental issues

| China-US Center for Environmental Remediation and Sustainable Development, Rice and Nankai Universities | 2007 | Develop the innovative and practical technology and policies that China and the United States must have to support both economic growth and environmental protection in the twenty-first century | • Research and technology development: nanotechnology application for environmental protection, air pollution control, environmental policy and regulation, etc.
• Technology transfer: conferences, publications, short courses, etc.
• Education: internships and student exchange programmes |
| Joint Research Center of Urban Environment and Sustainable Development, Ministry of Education | 2005 | Inter-university programme (network of 11 universities) focusing on postgraduate studies in sustainability-related fields | Inter-university postgraduate programmes in sustainable development |

2-5-4 Discussion and conclusion

This chapter addressed the current trends in Southeast Asian research initiatives towards sustainability, with special emphasis on the impact of human activities on the environment. In general the initiatives have both theoretical and practical dimensions. From the theoretical perspective, the initiatives analyse and assess the influence of human activities on the environment, particularly in highly populated areas, and explore the use of both policy and strategic solutions to overcome the specific challenges. The initiatives also have a practical component, consisting of efforts to address the challenges the region is facing, including solid waste and wastewater management, air quality and ecosystem degradation, especially in the monsoon and Mekong Delta areas. Asian research institutions such as the AIT and the Chinese Academy of Sciences play a central role by providing their research and management experience to facilitate these initiatives. Another characteristic of Asian research initiatives is the importance of international institutions in the developed world: these not only provide support through funding, but also access to their research networks and capacity building.

The most effective way to promote a transition to sustainable development is perhaps to manage our limited natural resources in a way that yields economic benefits while improving the other types of capital for future generations. While developed nations such as Japan are promoting the sustainable use of natural resources with strategies such as streamlining resource productivity, products and service systems (Yabar et al., 2009), developing countries are still trying to improve their pollution control and waste management strategies. Initiatives like the ones introduced here play a central role to bridging this gap between developed and developing nations. The next steps towards successful implementation of initiatives like these include the following.

- Designing a central database that not only includes the information related to these institutions in terms of their research activities, but also their research outcomes (scientific articles, books, conferences, etc.). This will make it possible to promote knowledge exchange in terms of specific research experiences and stimulate the creation of other research networks.
- Encouraging the participation of government officials in these initiatives. Engaging officials in these research initiatives and the knowledge-exchange process will promote the development of faster and more robust links between research and policy.
- Research collaboration among different initiatives. In addition to knowledge and information sharing, it is equally important to promote the exchange of researchers and conduct joint studies in order to improve the networking system and move towards sustainability.

Notes

1. The Amsterdam Declaration on Global Change was signed at the Global Change Open Science Conference in Amsterdam by 1,400 participants from more than 100 countries. The declaration recognized the threat of climate change and the increasing human influence on the global environment. To address these challenges the declaration called for strengthening the cooperation among the four global environmental research programmes (Diversitas, IGBP, IHDP and WCRP) and promoting integration across disciplines, including environment and development issues and the natural and social sciences.
2. The Global Change System for Analysis, Research and Training (START), which is sponsored by the ESSP, provides an international framework for capacity building on the causes and impacts of regional and global change in developing countries.
3. The APN is an intergovernmental network that promotes research on global change and the linkages between science and policy-making in Asia.
4. The AIT, based in Bangkok, promotes technological change towards sustainability in the Asia-Pacific region through higher education, research and outreach.
5. SIDA is a government agency that focuses on international development through cooperation and partnerships with organizations and government agencies in developing countries.

REFERENCES

Arrow, K. J., P. Dasgupta and K. G. Maler (2003) "Evaluating Projects and Assessing Sustainable Development in Imperfect Economies", working paper, Beijer International Institute of Ecological Economics, Stockholm.

Dasgupta, P. (2007) "Measuring Sustainable Development: Theory and Application", *Asian Development Review* 24(1), pp. 1–10.

Dasgupta, P. and K. G. Maler (2000) "Net National Product, Wealth, and Social Well-Being", *Environment and Development Economics* 5, pp. 69–93.

Feng, Z. and N. Yan (2007) "Putting a Circular Economy into Practice in China", *Journal of Sustainability Science* 2, pp. 95–101.

Fu, C., R. Zhang and X. Yan (2006) "Introducing a New International Program: Monsoon Asia Integrated Regional Study (MAIRS)", *Particuology* 4(6), pp. 352–355.

Hawken, P., A. Lovins and L. Lovins (1999) *Natural Capitalism: Creating the Next Industrial Revolution.* Boston, MA: Little, Brown.

IHDP-IT (2001) "Industrial Transformation Science Plan", Report No. 12, International Human Dimensions Programme on Global Environmental Change – Industrial Transformation Project, Amsterdam.

Rakshit, S. (2009) *Climate Change Adaptation – Challenges and Opportunities in Higher Education.* Bangkok: Asian Institute of Technology.

SARCS (2008) "SARCS Annual Report 2006–2007", Southeast Regional Committee for START Secretariat, Taipei.

SEPA (2007) "List of National Ecological Industrial Demonstration Parks in China", State Environmental Protection Administration, Beijing, May (in Chinese).

Tsinghua University (2009) "About the Department of Environmental Science and Engineering"; available at http://env.tsinghua.edu.cn/Eng/about%20DESE/Welcomespeech.aspx.

United Nations (2005) "Statistical Indicators for Asia and the Pacific", UN Economic and Social Commission for Asia and the Pacific, New York.

Visvanathan, C., K. Joseph, C. Chiemchaisri, G. Zhou and B. Basnayake (2007) "Integrated Networking for Sustainable Solid Waste Management in Asia", in *Proceedings of the International Conference on Sustainable Solid Waste Management*, Chennai, India. Chennai: Centre for Environmental Studies, Anna University, pp. 27–33.

Yabar, H., K. Hara, M. Uwasu, Y. Yamaguchi, H. Zhang and T. Morioka (2009) "Integrated Resource Management towards a Sustainable Asia: Policy and Strategy Evolution in Japan and China", *International Journal of Environmental Technology and Management* 11(4), pp. 239–256.

Yabar, H., K. Hara, M. Uwasu, Y. Yamaguchi, T. Murayama, H. Zhang and T. Morioka (2007) "Strategies towards a Resource-circulating Asia: Design of a Sustainability Assessment Framework", paper presented at EcoDesign 2007, fifth international symposium on environmentally conscious design and inverse manufacturing, Tokyo, pp. 1–8.

Zhang, H., K. Hara, H. Yabar, Y. Yamaguchi, M. Uwasu and T. Morioka (2009) "Comparative Analysis of Socio-economic and Environmental Performances for Chinese EIPs: Case Studies in Baotou, Suzhou and Shanghai", *Sustainability Science* 4(2), pp. 263–279.

Zhang, H., M. Uwasu, K. Hara, H. Yabar, Y. Yamaguchi and T. Murayama (2008) "Analysis of Land Use Changes and Environmental Loads during Urbanization in China", *Journal of Asian Architecture and Building Engineering* 7(1), pp. 109–115.

3

Initiatives and practices for a resource-circulating society

3-1

Zero-emission initiatives in Asia: Communication and partnership

Motoyuki Suzuki and Masao Takebayashi

3-1-1 Introduction

In Western countries the phrase "zero emissions" (ZE) has two meanings: reduction of harmful chemical substances, and an industrial symbiosis that promotes the mutual use of waste and by-products. The United Nations University (UNU) Zero Emissions Forum (ZEF) constructed a wider-ranging concept to expand the one used in Europe and America. It covers reduction of energy and materials consumption, reuse of used products, recycling of materials, use of renewable energy and zero waste from factories. In addition, ZE is designed to create a recycling society; the concept involves not emitting polluting gases or sewage and waste from the community.

Many corporations and regional governments have embraced this concept in their management activities and play an important role in improving the environment and providing economic benefits. Ricoh, the world's largest maker of photocopiers, and many other international companies are now implementing environmental management systems based on the zero-emission concept. At the government level, the Ministry of Economy, Trade and Industry and the Ministry of the Environment in Japan and the governments of China and Korea have also incorporated this concept in their policies, along with the 3R (reduce, reuse and recyle) principle.

In 1992 Brazil hosted the UN Conference on Environment and Development, commonly known as the Earth Summit, and the action plan

Establishing a resource-circulating society in Asia: Challenges and opportunities, Morioka, Hanaki and Moriguchi (eds), United Nations University Press, 2011, ISBN 978-92-808-1182-7

Agenda 21 was adopted, aiming for the development of a circulating society. To that end, UNU passed a resolution for an environmentally sustainable development programme (UNU Agenda 21) in 1994, and has established the Zero Emissions Research Initiative in accordance with this. The initiative has been consolidated under the leadership of its proponent, Gunter Pauli (then presidential senior adviser), Tarcisio Della Senta (chief of the UNU Institute of Advanced Studies) and Motoyuki Suzuki (UNU vice-rector).

In Japanese universities, two major projects were promoted: "Establishment of element circulating aiming at zero emissions (1997–2000)" and "Establishment of Yakushima Island model of a circulating-society system (2000–2003)". These projects involved the participation of more than 100 university researchers and the establishment of 138 business-academia collaboration committees in the Japan Society for the Promotion of Science; both maintained close cooperation with the activities of ZEF. Inspired by an international conference concerning ZE in 1999, ZEF began to promote ZE further in 2000 by establishing a network between industries, local governments, NPOs (non-profit organizations) and academies to promote ZE activities as a composite forum.

To commemorate the tenth anniversary of the work on ZE, which began in 1994, the Wise Men's Forum was held at UNU in 2004 with the participation of Motoyuki Suzuki and Tadahiro Mitsuhashi (professor, Chiba University of Commerce, representative/director of ZE Municipal Network) as co-chairmen, Hans van Ginkel (rector, UNU), R. K. Pachauri (chairman, IPCC, TV participation), Tomonobu Imamichi (philosopher), Hiroyuki Fujimura (second-generation chairman, ZEF), Joan Martinez-Alier (professor, Universitat Autonoma de Barcelona, economic science), Friedrich Schmidt-Bleek (president, Factor 10 Institute) and Karl Henrik Robert (chairman, Natural Step International). The forum's themes were "Global civilization in the future" and "The economic system and the roles of corporations tomorrow", and the discussion provided many interesting implications for consideration in establishing a future direction.

Since then, Japan has been making progress in forming a sustainable society comprehensively based on a low-carbon, recycling and naturally symbiotic society, and following the same path as the goals of ZE. The Japanese government, industries and UNU have also supported and cooperated with efforts by Asian countries in ZE initiatives.

3-1-2 Zero-emissions concept

The rapid and continuous economic growth of the 1960s and 1970s caused severe damage to our natural ecosystem. This huge consumption of

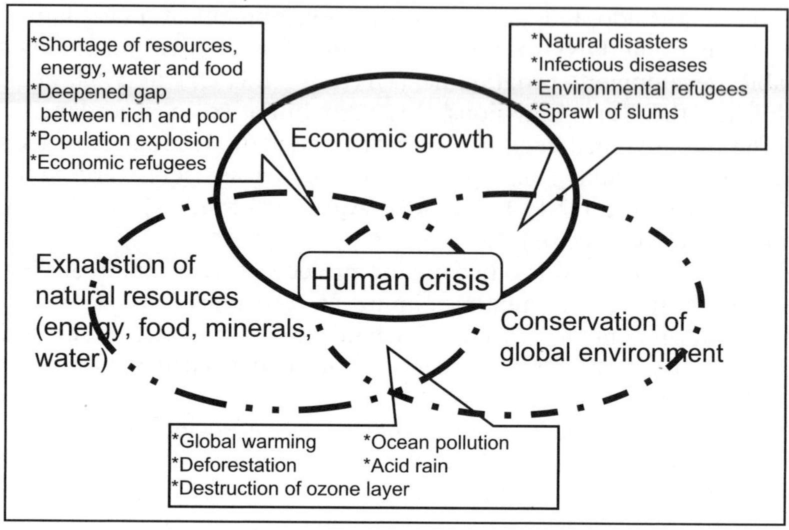

Figure 3.1.1 Global tri-lemma

energy and resources continued in the 1980s and 1990s, causing global problems including ozone layer depletion and more recently climate change. During this period, global environmental change became evident, and was enforced by Hansen's testimony to the US Senate Committee in 1988. The same year, the Intergovernmental Panel on Climate Change (IPCC) was established. With this background, rapid progress in information technology and the enhancement of computer capabilities have led to new developments in testing future predictions of global climate change.

At this time, various problems caused by the global expansion of human activities were discussed, including the conflict in three fields – environmental problems, economic situation and limited resources – recognized as a "tri-lemma" (Figure 3.1.1), and the mechanisms to design structural change of conventional industrial society. The discussions incorporated the environmental standpoint (global warming, increase in natural disasters, deforestation, destruction of the ozone layer, marine pollution, acid rain, etc.), the economic standpoint (especially food shortages and starvation with developing countries in mind, disparity in wealth between rich and poor, increase in population) and the resource standpoint (depleted underground resources such as fossil resources, competition for resources, energy shortages, conflicts over water, securing of food resources, etc.).

The proposition is that risks caused by economic development, environmental deterioration and depleted resources bring crisis to humankind and are not a problem of only one region or country, but a problem for all mankind, and as such must be solved by both developed and developing areas as one body. A root cause of this problem is the two-sided issue of material prosperity brought about by modern industrialization and the expansion of human activity, and the idea that industrialization brings human happiness. However, it has been recognized that the development of modern industry has led to mass disposal and mass energy consumption along with mass resource mining, mass production and mass consumption, resulting in environmental destruction in various regions, resource depletion and change in the global environment. Various proposals have been made as to how to solve these issues.

As examples of movements aimed at the improvement of industrial process, the cleaner production system proposed by organizations like the UN Environment Programme and the UN Industrial Development Organization is an initiative to minimize disposal from the production process, and Inverse Manufacturing proposed the "reverse factory" initiative for the reduction of materials and resources from raw materials to the final product.

"Zero emissions" is often recognized as zero waste products (garbage), but actually has a broader meaning. At UNU, ZE has been used as the concept of complete utilization of resources since 1994. In 1995 UNU hosted the First Annual UNU World Congress on Zero Emissions and publicized the word ZE and its concept as coming from UNU/Japan to the world.

In the industrial production process, materials and auxiliary materials are necessary and the parts that are not included in end products are released as waste. Since the amounts of materials and end products never match, it is impossible not to produce waste, which limits the success of cleaner production. The definition of "waste products" is unnecessary items without economic value. However, even if the material is unnecessary in that particular production process, it can still be utilized as material in another process or to produce other valuable resources. From this point of view, by considering a combination (cluster) of production processes to use waste products actively in other areas or industries, efforts to produce no waste products outside the system as whole can result in achieving zero in the industry. This idea is shown in Figure 3.1.2: by forming a network of material circulation between different industries, resources can be effectively transformed into valuables without creating waste products, thereby reducing production costs and creating a new industry and employment.

ZE is a necessary concept to construct a sound material-circulation system not only in industrial processes but also within consumption systems and the natural ecological system. This can achieve efficient utilization and application of resources in society as a whole, as well as the

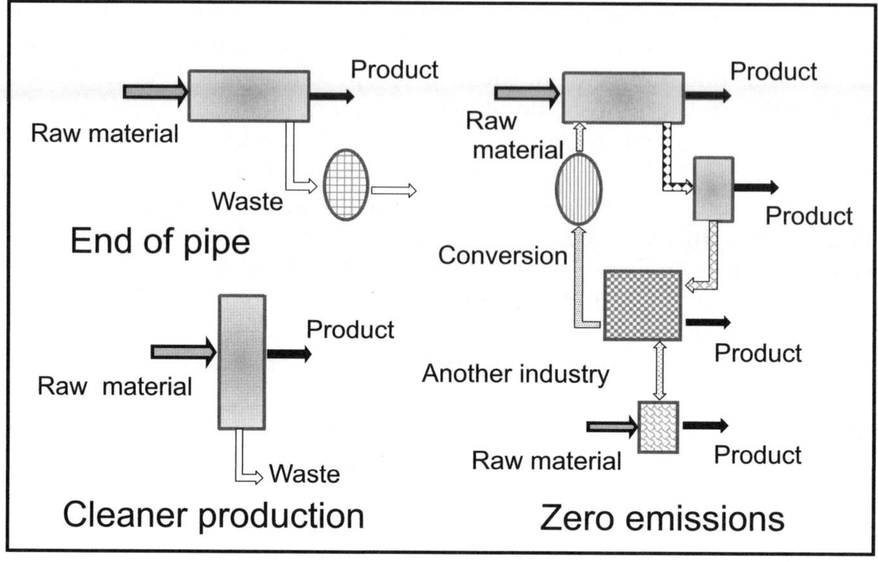

Figure 3.1.2 End of pipe, cleaner production and zero emissions

reduction of environmental load and construction of overall sustainable human activities.

ZEF, formed in 2000 with such a goal, has expanded this concept in various networks through exchange with other nations. At the international conference for the establishment of ZEF hosted by UNU in 1999, Karl Henrik Robert of Natural Step International, an NPO in Sweden, listed four system conditions for a sustainable society.

- The concentration of substances extracted from the Earth's crust does not continue to increase in nature.
- The concentration of substances created by human society does not continue to increase in nature.
- Nature does not deteriorate by physical methods.
- Situations that hinder actions that satisfy the basic needs of man should not be created.

This idea harmonizes with the basic thinking in ZEF activities. Schmidt-Bleek of the Factor 10 Institute in France also proposed an index of factors that tend to raise productivity of resources, which is important in the thinking to promote ZE activities.

Later, ZEF published various guidelines and activity principles to assist the continuation and implementation of ZE activities, accomplish the goals of sustainability and environmental improvement, and achieve ZE. First, Tadahiro Mitsuhashi (2001) proposed six principles of action.

- Do not consume more renewable resources than the amount of resources that can be renewed.
- For non-renewable resources, improve productivity. Develop renewable clean alternative resources and limit consumption to within the range of the production amount.
- Do not emit more waste products than the environment can accept.
- Seek to reduce material usage as much as possible in economic and everyday activities.
- Seek to use the above-ground stock resources effectively.
- Internalize environmental costs and create a market economy with high environmental efficiency.

The first three principles were proposed by Herman Daly, in consideration of economics under a steady state, and are fundamental when considering resource circulating for zero emissions.

Next, Keizo Yamaji (2001) proposed five forms of action.

- To solve both environmental and economic problems simultaneously, consider changing from large-scale mass production and integrated processing to a distributed style, pursuing energy consumption controls and utilizing biological resources and natural energy.
- Set high goals, seeking to reach the maximum limit of technology and methodology.
- For improvement of the environment and economy, recognize each related person as a colleague – it is important to remove all frames of organizations, regions, theories, etc.
- Accumulate best practice.
- There are numerous examples of ZE. Those who are resolving problems can imitate the best practice most appropriate to the issue, exercise greater ingenuity and add the completed solution to ZE, to be used as a benchmark for others.

Following this, he suggested practical step-by-step promotion of "effective methods to utilize resources and energy, factory ZE activities, ZE design, green procurement, whole company ZE activities which include ZE evaluation, creation of sustainability reports, information disclosure, making ZE clusters with a region and/or other industries". In addition, in order to create a ZE society, reform of the tax system based on taxation of the "bad" and tax reduction for the "good", changes in human lifestyles, etc., have been proposed.

Also, since factories and businesses are limited in what they can do by themselves to implement ZE, forming a network that includes different industries in industrial parks and regions, and the application and promotion of ZE activities by local governments in their plans to boost development of the area are thought to make implementation easier and lead to larger effects. To that end, points to consider in progressing from ideas and concepts to execution were published by the Zero Emissions Manual Drafting Committee (2003). Three principles, four steps, the PDCA (plan, do, check, action) cycle, etc. are explained in an easy-to-understand way.

The Japanese government has accepted the ZE concept as proposed by UNU, and has promoted the ZE initiative since 1997. It has also introduced the Eco-Town Project, a new plan to create environmentally friendly towns for the twenty-first century. Twenty-six industrial parks are implementing the initiative at present, and projects such as Kitakyushu and Kawasaki eco-towns have become examples of success. In 2008 Chinese President Hu Jintao toured these areas and gave them a high evaluation.

3-1-3 ZE dissemination activities in Japan and regions in Asia, and the trend in forming a circulating society

Activities in Japan

In 2001–2002 UNU hosted four workshops on the theme of regions in order to disseminate ZE research results. Kyoto and Numazu cities, Shizuoka, Tokushima, Mie and Iwate prefectures, and Itabashi ward in Tokyo, etc., were introduced, and views were exchanged between government, academia, NPOs, civil society, etc. Since then, local government interest in ZE has increased, and in response to requests ZEF hosted symposia on the subject in 25 municipalities across Japan from 2003 to 2009. The purpose of these symposia was to continue efforts to disseminate ZE thinking in consideration of regional characteristics. Towards this end, leading members of ZEF gave keynote addresses and led discussion regarding ZE activities that combine regional life activities, with the goal of a wide exchange with local citizens, representatives of the local governments, etc. These actions have contributed towards the provision of various options in the regions.

In addition, ZE has demonstrated great environmental and economical efficacy at general assemblies and international symposia. Forum records were organized by ZEF.

International activities of ZEF

Early developmental stage of ZEF

Transmissions and exchanges with regions in Asia by ZEF are actively carried out in various ways. Let's take an overall view of the major activities performed since the ZE initiative was born.

The first ZE international conference was held in 1995 at UNU and the second in 1996 by videoconference between UNU and Chattanooga, TN, in the United States. Since then ZE activities, such as in Indonesia and Namibia, have gradually increased in international recognition.

The International Conference on ZE Societies in Industrialized Society, held at UNU in 1999, had great meaning for the establishment of ZEF. The conference covered the latest thinking at the time, positioning it as historically important. The keynote address, "Efforts in ZE toward a circulating society", was given by Motoyuki Suzuki. There were also discourses by 13 others, including Karl Henrik Robert and Friedrich Schmidt-Bleek, and two panel discussions. In response to this conference, UNU's ZE activities were organized as ZEF.

Since then, many joint-hosted ZE conferences have been held with countries from Southeast Asia, including China and South Korea. Since 2006 symposia have been held in collaboration with the Integrated Research System for Sustainability Science (IR3S).

Exchange with China

China has made rapid progress in economic development by adopting a market economy, but this has been accompanied by worsening environmental problems. Around the year 2000, interest in a circulating society began to surface. In 2001 an exchange on the development plan for an industrial park in Tianjin city was held at ZEF. Although there were high concerns regarding the environment, participants were unfamiliar with concepts such as ZE. In the Tianjin Economic Technology Development Zone, a sewage facility and a pharmaceutical plant were inspected. Introduction of the ZE concept was considered to be something for the future, and effort was directed towards expanding the special economic zone.

In 2002 the Japan and China Environment Symposium, a science technology exchange project commemorating the thirtieth anniversary of normalization of diplomatic relations between Japan and China (1972), was held. At the conference, the talk "Aiming to create a circulating economy/society" was given, and three concurrent symposia focused on circulating society and waste products, the water environment and the air environment. Reports by researchers such as Motoyuki Suzuki, Koichi Fujie, Akiyoshi Sakoda, Masao Takebayashi and others caught the attention of China. At this conference, the Chinese presentation used the term "circulating economy", and its definition and thinking received great interest. However, the concept seemed to lack sufficient understanding, and the term was used to express a vague idea of an economy which supports a sustainable society. It gave the impression of an economic system with the purpose of achieving resource circulation as shown by ZE. Later, in

Kiyo in 2004, the Zero Emissions Investigative Commission was held, and construction in the new city centre was examined. General improvement of the city infrastructure was mainly considered, but a ZE framework was not introduced. Relevant information, such as on Japanese eco-town projects, was obtained, and planning of a new city centre with an environmental model city framework began with Japanese support.

In 2007 Beijing hosted a conference on resource circulating and the circulating economy, jointly hosted by UNU ZEF and the National Development Reformation Committee, Agent for the Comprehensive Use of the Environment and Resources of the central government. The themes of the conference were threefold: energy conservation systems, the latest technology trends and environmental-economic balance for pollution and global warming. A seemingly high degree of interest in energy conservation and environmental business by both sides could be seen at a meeting between Japanese Prime Minister Abe and Chinese President Hu Jintao, and at the consultation between Japanese Minister of Economy Akira Amari and the Chinese Secretary-General of the State Council Ma Kai that took place the previous year. There were speeches from a broader point of view, such as "A circulating economy and zero emissions" and "Expanding the concept of zero emissions into Asia". The keynote addresses, "3R policy" by the Japanese government and "Sustainable development by the advancement of a circulating economy" by Qian Yi (professor, Tsinghua University), demonstrated an increase in awareness and standards of the environment and circulating economy. There were talks about the Kitakyushu eco-town project, and reports were given on energy conservation in the steel industry by the Japan Iron and Steel Federation and ZE efforts by other businesses. Converting awareness from an attitude of conventional pollution avoidance to one of sustainability has made great progress, shown in the presentation from local administration and businesses of China, and a special economic circulating zone was introduced.

The next conference was held in Hangzhou in 2008. Although only a year had passed, overall awareness of a sustainable society had become even stronger than awareness of the environment. There was broader participation as well, including members of central and local administrations, universities and environmental organizations. Reports on the application of circulating from industrial groups, such as the Association of Resource Comprehensive Utilization and China National Resources Circulating Association, demonstrated improvements in standards and expansion of environmental efforts in China. The greetings by the central government, "The Eleventh Five-Year Plan: Opinions of the leaders on resource comprehensive utilization", clearly identified a leading ideology, priority areas and important projects, with an investment of approximately 650 million yuan in the government budget. Comprehensive resource utilization in 2,000 sites throughout the country and model projects on energy and water conservation have been set into motion. Also, the Circulating Economy Promotion Law was enacted in August 2008, with implementation in January 2009. As of 2007, circulation and use of renewable resources, including imports, reached 180 million tonnes, the stock of waste steel was 1.38 billion tonnes and waste aluminum 14.7 million tonnes, and disposed home electronics totalled 1.6 million units and disposed cars 4 million units. With the improvement in quality of life, a tremendous amount of waste was generated; some reports now seem to express a resolve for an environmentally conscious society and further energy conservation and resource circulating.

Exchange with China is expected to evolve slowly according to the needs of China, and with its expansion as an economic power, exchange among individual researchers will become even deeper and more profound. We have reached a time when we can look forward to planning the shape of science and technology and environmental exchange between Japan and China in the future.

Cooperation with South Korea

In South Korea awareness of resource circulating developed relatively slowly. Although an international conference on eco-industrial parks held in Seoul in 2003 was organized by the Attached Research Institute of the South Korean Ministry of Commerce and Industry, and introduced the concept of ZE, South Korea seemed to stagnate at the point of learning from various advanced examples. Later, the South Korean Economic Federation showed strong interest in ZE and resource circulating, and hosted ZE seminars in South Korea in 2007 and 2008 consecutively. Like Japan, South Korea has few natural resources and must rely on value-added product exports; thus it pushes to make further use of resource circulation and improved efficiency in resource productivity. At the 2007 UNU ZEF Environmental Symposium for the Realization of a Resource Recycling Society, "Towards the establishment of a resource-circulating society" by Kazuhiko Takeuchi (vice-rector, UNU) and other talks, including "Kawasaki eco-town", "A resource-circulating system in the mining industry" and "Zero emissions of OA devices", all received good reviews. A report on environmental policies was presented by the head of the South Korean Ministry of Environment at both this seminar and the 2008 UNU ZEF symposium, also held in Seoul. How a future cooperative system should be constructed, and how a Japanese-South Korean coalition which especially takes in the industrial cultural aspects of community should be advanced, are dependent on how much passion South Korea has to use and apply the experiences of Japan.

Countries in Southeast Asia

Countries in Southeast Asia are completely different to industrialized countries, and the viewpoint regarding the beneficial application of biomass centring on agriculture and forestation is important. This is a common issue for tropical and semi-tropical regions, which may or may not be affected by monsoons. To achieve a sustainable society/life, it is necessary to narrow the theme down into the effective use of regional biomasses, and there is especially strong interest in bagasse, palm oil, cassava and inedible biomass derived from rice production in some regions, and in some cases ways to produce alternative fuels from agricultural products, sustainable systems, etc. Cooperation from Japan, such as providing proposals for ZE activities, developing human resources to expand understanding of the ZE concept, etc., is needed. While there is great interest from academics and the government regarding the relationship between ZE and biomass, this has not been reflected in ZE concepts for industrial activities.

Since 1997 continued exchange has been carried out with Indonesia, Malaysia and Viet Nam. In 1997 Indonesia hosted the Third Annual UNU World Congress on Zero Emissions, during the infancy of ZE; in addition to an explanation of the basic idea and concept, a concrete framework of ZE-style production was reported by UNU. For example, wastes emitted during beer production at breweries in Fiji were used for mushroom cultivation, and then the wastes from mushroom cultivation were used as cattle feed, biogas or fish food. Vegetables (aquatic fungi) were cultivated in fish-cultivating ponds, and so on. In a 2006 seminar in Jakarta on Sustainable Society Achievement by Biomass Effective Use there were motivated presentations by Indonesian government officials and the University of Lampung on the effective application of biomass for the realization of a sustainable society. A seminar in Malaysia, hosted by businesses, focused on biomass and ZE.

The first seminar held in Viet Nam was in 2005. Prior to that, the deputy leader of a 2004 economic environmental delegation from the Ministry of Economy, Trade and Industry visited Hanoi and inspected local industries, collection of waste products, landfill spaces, etc., as well as asking government personnel about conditions in industry and the environment. At that stage the situation was similar to Japan in the 1960s, and there was no awareness of sustainability, etc. To encourage consideration of ZE, an exchange of ideas regarding an implementation plan for water, sewerage and facilities to process waste products was carried out. In line with this, ZE seminars in 2005 and 2006 reported on sewage and composting waste products, and circulating technology by methane fermentation and gasification. The abundance of biomass in the nation was considered, and refining using biomass as the source material was also reported upon.

Trends in forming a circulating society in Asia

In Asian countries it cannot be denied that severe environmental pollution has occurred along with the development of industry. As such, support from organizations like the World Bank, Asian Development Bank and Japanese official development assistance, which provide financing for the establishment of infrastructure and development projects, has emphasized environmental conservation.

Most Asian industries are primary, and secondary industries are still growing, especially companies with subcontracts from international corporations seeking to enter the Asian market. These corporations have followed the environmental standards of their home country and wish to comply with the minimum standard, but since a local industry standard has yet to be implemented, the creation of a sustainable society appears to be still far from reality. However, the ZE concept, which has a co-benefit approach against global warming and for environmental improvement, has been under consideration. Construction of water treatment plants, power generation by burning residue and composting have been started in large-scale sugar and palm-oil plantations. However, it has been recognized by corporate heads that further ZE development and installation of industrial facilities which consider circulating concepts are needed.

Public interest in the environment is high, and the number of companies responding to such interest has also increased. This includes regional and industrial park development by central and local governments, and the start of efforts advocating ecological developments which preserve the environment. In private facilities, economic interest takes priority and it is difficult to receive government funding for environmental projects, so the overall situation is still weak. Although sewage and household garbage circulation and power generation by burning waste products have slowly taken root, they are still tasks for the future. Asia is waiting for support from developed countries, and providing systems that sufficiently consider environmental aspects such as ZE and 3R is deemed important.

Future challenges include the provision of drinking water, and water for agriculture and industry will significantly dry up. Effective utilization of water and water circulation using filters will continue, but maintenance and water creation must be urgently addressed.

At the very start, using ZE as an approach to solve issues such as pollution was suggested. However, in recent years this has changed: attempts to tackle issues such as global warming have been set as personal tasks, and a circulating economy that focuses on the relationship between the environment and economy, the creation of an ideological sustainable society, etc., has been extensively and profoundly discussed.

Furthermore, some countries have started to develop industries that recycle resources, as well as extensive entrepreneurial environment-related industries, such as the construction of water treatment facilities, methane fertilization, composting, waste incineration, etc. Frontier businesses, such as the steel industry, have promoted the elimination of pollution and resource and energy conservation, starting with process improvement, which results in lower costs, and have begun taking action in recognition of the connection to forming a sustainable society. Methane fermentation facilities have been introduced in the food industry, with a view to processing biomass-related waste products and recovering energy. In recent years, since the sudden increase in the price of energy and the depletion of mineral resources have become global issues, and the finite nature of natural resources is especially discussed, the introduction of environmental accounting has been promoted, along with material flow, reduction of process-related resource use and in-process circulating, resulting in some corporations approaching the standard of developed countries over the past 10 years. Their quick cooperation with developed countries and attempts to design a sustainable society are commendable. Unfortunately, the lack of participation from citizens, NPOs, non-governmental organizations, etc., suggests problems in the administrative process, calling for creativity.

Although governments have belatedly implemented environmental laws, these cannot keep up with the circulation and sustainability concepts. Standards such as ISO are well known and have been obtained by major enterprises, and information on extended producer responsibility and corporate social responsibility is available. Today, legislation has proceeded and industry seems to comply where possible.

ZEF's activities in Asia over the past 10 years basically have not changed – the goal is still instruction and dissemination of ZE ideas, concepts and methods of implementation. However, great changes in society, including issues such as global warming, competition over resources, the rising price of oil and continued population growth, have damaged the environmental and natural ecological systems. In consideration of this, seminars on environment education, capacity development, coexistence with nature, lifestyles, shift to a low-carbon society, economic systems and utilization of natural capital and energy have been widely referred to. The attitude towards the environment of individual countries has progressed from learning to practising, and to a circulating economy, and they have started to consider benchmarks for achievement, incorporating Japan's 3R policy.

3-1-4 Representative example of business activities concretely incorporating the zero-emission concept

Many corporations internationally are tackling zero emission. One example is the world's largest photocopier manufacturer, Ricoh (110,000 employees, sales of ¥2 trillion). Ricoh has been selected as one of the "global 100 most sustainable corporations" by the Davos Conference for five consecutive years. In the United States and Germany the company has been highly evaluated and given a top ranking for its corporate and social responsibility in the electronics, equipment and IT industry divisions (see www.oekomresearch.de/index_jp.php?content=ratings-assessments).

Ricoh established its Environmental Promotion Office in 1976 and the Corporate Center for the Community Environment in 1998 to carry out activities to achieve both environmental and economic goals. As seen in Figure 3.1.3, it promotes product creation that considers life-cycle environmental load to carry out environmental management.

It has expanded its sustainable society formation concept, commonly called the Ricoh Comet Circle (Figure 3.1.4), to related companies around the world. To achieve a sustainable society, it has clarified and expressed a general idea of recycling which:
- prolongs utilization of photocopiers through maintenance
- recovers those which are no longer in use
- recycles and sells them as products
- removes parts from products and merchandises these parts by installing them in new products
- recycles them as materials to create products with these installed as parts
- returns to the original materials and reuses them.

For example, by dismantling and recycling parts of used imagio Neo 751 photocopiers in a recycled model, the imagio Neo 751RC, 88 per cent of their parts are reused, achieving a total 11.9 per cent material reuse and energy recovery rate and only about 0.1 per cent buried in landfill or incinerated. In the early 1990s the landfill rate for the entire Ricoh Group including its overseas members was 35 per cent, but by 2008 this was down to 0.4 per cent. Comparing the quantity of CO_2 emissions required to manufacture the recycled machine with that for a new photocopier revealed a reduction ratio of approximately 80 per cent. In addition, this machine has achieved a significant reduction in standby electric power with reduced recovery time from sleep mode: capacitors are used to set photocopiers in sleep mode and sharply cut electricity consumption during standby. As a result, for each photocopier annual electric power consumption was cut by 270 kWh and CO_2 emissions were reduced by

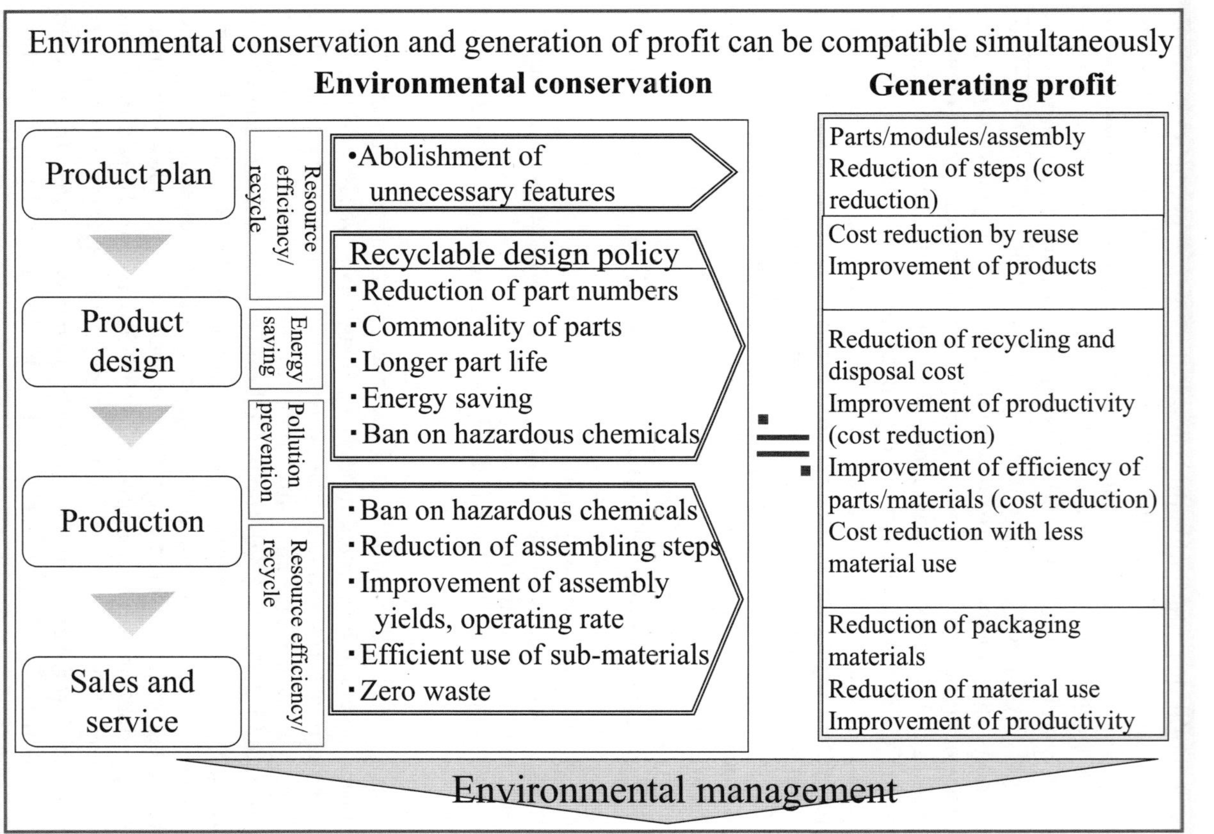

Figure 3.1.3 Considering product life-cycle environmental impact

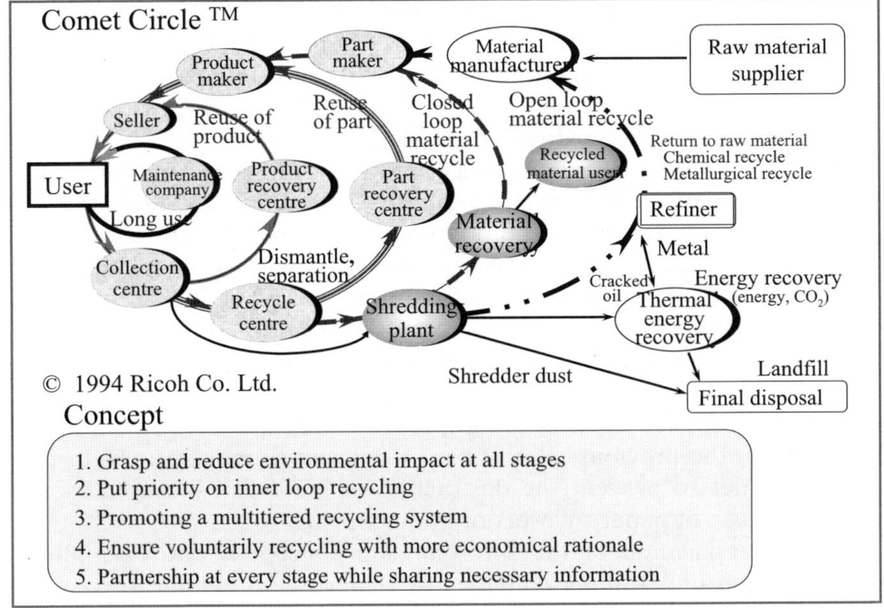

Figure 3.1.4 Concept for establishing a sustainable society

106 kg. The CO_2 emission reduction company-wide target for 2010 is 12 per cent compared to 1990 levels. The company's future sales increase rate is set at 4 per cent for 2010 – a big number which will in itself result in 61,000 tonnes of additional carbon emissions. So the target is an ambitious undertaking, and corresponds to double Japan's emissions reduction target of 6 per cent.

Next, we examine the creation of "zero-waste plants" at Ricoh's global centres. Zero waste has been achieved at 28 production centres and 280 non-production centres around the world, including the Georgia plant in the United States and the Shanghai plant in China. At one plant, an investment of $50,000 resulted in cost reductions of $500,000, or 10 times the investment, through cutting waste, selling valuables, green procurement and so on. Waste production was reduced by 265 tonnes, and final disposal in landfill was lowered to zero. The Shanghai production centre became a zero-waste plant in 2004, gaining economic benefits equal to about $50,000. Highly effective cost benefits are being obtained by achieving zero waste through total environmental education, the use of clear waste categorization tables, installation of clearly marked waste disposal sites and disposal routes by category, a continuous movement to cut the quantity of waste discharged, and tangible resource recycling including composting of organic refuse produced by the centre's dining room, thereby creating a zero landfill disposal and resource recycling consciousness among employees.

According to the Ricoh Group's 2008 environmental account, its environmental expenses (expenditure) were \$172.6 million, while its economic effect (income) on the environment was \$358.2 million.

Ricoh has prepared and announced its 2050 long-term environmental vision. Its achievement goal is to reduce resource use, fossil energy use and atmospheric/water pollution to one-eighth by 2050 in three areas: resource conservation and recycling (compared with 2007), energy conservation and global warming prevention (compared with 2000) and pollution prevention (compared with 2000). To achieve this, it has begun implementing the backcasting approach based on the scenario method. Incidentally, its CO_2 environmental load emitted from all its business centres in 2008 was 294,888 tonnes, representing a reduction of 28,183 tonnes from the previous year. It has also begun to make efforts to perform activities to prevent the destruction of biodiversity caused by the large-scale use of paper by users of photocopiers.

Ricoh's application of the zero-emission concept is one example of a corporation undertaking activities to achieve zero-landfill, zero-waste plants not only in Asia but around the world, thereby contributing to the creation of a sustainable society. Through the UNU ZEF, such approaches are being exchanged in Asia and implemented widely.

3-1-5 Conclusion

Since expansion of human activities in the world as a whole is recognized as having already exceeded the service ability the Earth can provide, we are facing many serious issues, such as what kind of sphere of human activity should be constructed in regions where there is a limited capacity, and what is the future of developing countries in Asia, especially those with growing populations. The thinking of ZE will continue to be extremely important in indicating the ideal direction of human society.

In order for the ZE system to achieve an expanded area where the natural ecosystem and human activities can coexist, efforts to form a nationwide vision to handle problems that affect our future way of life are needed.

UNU, in collaboration with IR3S and other institutions, must work towards further evolution and improvement, and consideration of design for sustainable goods, social systems, etc. Creating a coalition network between UNU and various Asian countries, and a framework for the creation of a sustainable society, is important. It is unfortunate that Asia does not yet have a position on the matter. The time seems to be right for reconstruction of the flow, including how to impart higher ZE ideas and put these into practice, and identification of those who will actively carry out these duties.

REFERENCES

Mitsuhashi, Tadahiro (2001) *Guidelines for Zero Emissions – Aiming for an Economic Society that Generates No Wastes*. Tokyo: Kaizosha (in Japanese).

Yamaji, Keizo (2001) *Practical Methods for Environmentally Conscious Management – From ISO 14001 to Zero Emissions*. Tokyo: Kaizosha (in Japanese).

Zero Emissions Manual Drafting Committee (2003) *Zero Emissions Manual*. Tokyo: Kaizosha (in Japanese).

3-2

Regional management of waste circulation and eco-industrial networks

Tsuyoshi Fujita, René Van Berkel, Yong Geng and Xudong Chen

3-2-1 Waste circulation through industrial symbiosis

Industrial and urban symbiosis are widely considered as among the most effective policies and business concepts in Asian metropolises to realize sustainable resource circulation through collaborative networks among industries and between industries and urban groups, including households, offices and retail shops (Van Berkel, 2006; Fang, Cote and Qin, 2006; Chertow, 2007; Van Berkel et al., 2009b). This reduces local and global environmental emissions while offering attractive profits and motivations for business sectors, municipalities and citizen groups (Chertow and Lombardi, 2005; Van Berkel et al., 2009a). Kalundborg is arguably the most publicized example of the implementation of industrial symbiosis, which materialized over a period of several decades (Jacobsen, 2006; Chertow, 2007). A number of eco-industrial parks (EIPs) and eco-industrial developments (EIDs) are planned or developed in various parts of the world (Deutz and Gibb, 2004; Van Berkel, 2006; Chertow, 2007), and Asian governments in particular have strong interest in practical applications of EIDs (Fujita, 2006; Geng, Zhang and Cote, 2009). Various types of EIP were planned as a key policy solution to keep sustainable industrialization within local and global environmental limitations. A number of demonstration EIPs were planned and developed in many Asian countries and regions from the late 1990s; most of the later projects are based more on single-stream industries or material flows, unlike the earlier Kalundborg case.

Establishing a resource-circulating society in Asia: Challenges and opportunities, Morioka, Hanaki and Moriguchi (eds), United Nations University Press, 2011, ISBN 978-92-808-1182-7

A particular feature of Asian EIPs is urban and industrial symbiosis, where new symbiotic opportunities have been generated from the geographic proximity of urban and industrial areas by linking municipal solid waste management (MSWM) with local industries (Van Berkel et al., 2009b). This provides environmental and economic efficiencies in sustainable resource circulation in Asian cities by transferring physical resources from urban refuse directly to industrial applications, thereby improving the overall eco-efficiency of the city and the region as a whole. Sustainable MSWM has been accepted and practised by city managers for some time in several Asian countries, most prominently in the Japanese eco-town scheme (GEC, 2005; Fujita, 2006). However, with different social and economic realities, consumption patterns and technological development levels, municipalities in different countries have adopted varying approaches. These mainly involve the use of landfill levies and restrictions and incentives for recycling and recovery. Due to increasing environmental pressure and decreasing landfill capacity, prevention of MSW (municipal solid waste) and promoting reuse, recycling and recovery have become priorities for policy-makers and city administrators alike.

This chapter summarizes the results and experiences of Japan's waste circulation through industrial symbiosis in its eco-town programme. This programme has been unique in expanding its focus (Fujita, ibid.) from initially site-specific initiatives (typically cleaner production or eco-efficiency – Van Berkel, 2007a) to industrial symbiosis and urban-industrial interactions. The term *urban symbiosis* was therefore introduced (Van Berkel et al., 2009a) as an extension for industrial symbiosis. It refers specifically to the use of by-products (wastes) from cities (or urban areas) as alternative raw materials or energy sources for industrial operations. The chapter also provides an evaluation of an innovative waste management initiative by a scenario simulation model based on life-cycle assessment (LCA). Results show that obvious environmental and social benefits can be gained through urban symbiosis, helping to realize the goal of establishing a low-carbon city.

3-2-2 Conceptual theories of resource circulation as industrial symbiosis

Industrial ecology uses an ecosystem metaphor and natural analogy to study and improve resource productivity and reduce the environmental burden of industrial and consumer products and their production and consumption systems (Van Berkel, 2007b). One of its principal applications is industrial symbiosis. At its core industrial symbiosis is concerned with ways to close material cycles by using the wastes from one facility as an alternative input for another facility. Industrial symbiosis is defined as encouraging traditionally separate industries to adopt a collective approach with competitive advantage by physical exchange of materials, energy, water and by-products (Chertow, 2000; Liamsanguan and Gheewala, 2008). The keys to industrial symbiosis are collaboration and the synergistic possibilities offered by geographic proximity (Chertow, 2007). In this way, firms in diverse urban areas can benefit from concentrated intermediate inputs that are not specific to any particular industry, such as reuse and recycling of MSW and shared public infrastructure, accounting services and labour market. Municipal governments can receive both economic and environmental benefits from exchange of by-products between firms and between some industries and municipalities. This means that industrial symbiosis need not occur within the strict boundaries of an industrial park or zone, despite the popular usage of the term eco-industrial park to describe a cluster of organizations that are engaged in exchanges of waste materials, water and/or heat. Urban symbiosis is an extension of industrial symbiosis. Similar to industrial symbiosis, urban symbiosis is based on the synergistic opportunity arising from geographic proximity of urban and industrial areas to transfer physical resources (urban refuse) to industrial applications for environmental and economic benefit. This is of particular relevance in Japan, where the proximity principle, namely management of waste close to source, has been a central value in MSWM for over 30 years (Okuda and Thomson, 2007).

In the United States the Presidential Council for Sustainable Development launched a national pilot programme on eco-industrial parks in 1997 (PCSD, 1997). The Netherlands (van Leeuwen, Vermeulen and Glasbergen, 2003) and the United Kingdom (Mirata, 2004) launched similar demonstration programmes on eco-industrial parks and industrial symbiosis respectively. China also established demonstration sites for EIPs under its circular-economy policy (Fang, Cote and Qin, 2006), and has recently launched a standard for eco-industrial parks (Geng, Zhang and Cote, 2009). While good progress has been achieved in improving the environmental amenity of existing industrial areas, the success of government programmes in achieving actual resource exchanges or synergies between industries has been modest at best (Deutz and Gibbs, 2004; Heeres, Vermeulen and de Walle, 2004; Van Berkel, 2006; Chertow, 2007). Generally, the EIPs in Europe have been more successful than their US counterparts. After reviewing the establishment and development of 61 EIPs in the West, Gibbs, Deutz and Proctor (2005) found that only six out of 35 EIPs in the United States and 16 out of 26 in Europe were actually in operation, whereas 16 EIPs in the United States and three in Europe have never emerged as real projects in operation.

A relatively small but compelling set of practical examples of industrial symbiosis have been described in the international literature as reviewed by, for example, Bossilkov, Van Berkel and Corder (2005), Van Berkel (2006) and Chertow (2007). More detailed case studies can be found in the literature on Denmark (Kalundborg – Jacobsen, 2006), the Netherlands (Rotterdam Harbour and Industrial Complex – Baas and Boons, 2007), the United Kingdom (Harris and Pritchard, 2004; Mirata, 2004), Australia (Kwinana and Gladstone – van Beers et al., 2007), the United States (Texas – Mangan, 1998), Puerto Rico (Chertow and Lombardi, 2005) and China (Guigang – Fang, Cote and Qin, 2006). The Japanese government initiated eco-town projects in 1997, and these have had a positive impact in promoting industrial symbiosis at the city level. Most Japanese municipalities have established well-designed source-separation systems for their MSW. With proactive planning, valuable MSW can be efficiently collected and delivered to the appropriate sites for reuse and recycling (Fujita, 2007).

Several quantitative studies have been conducted to assess the environmental benefits of industrial and urban symbioses in selected industrial areas. These studies were reviewed by Van Berkel et al. (2009a), who confirmed that reductions in demand for water, raw materials and energy and reduced emissions of various air pollutants and greenhouse gases are among the major benefits (Table 3.2.1).

3-2-3 Waste circulation policies and eco-town programmes in Japan

In the late 1990s and early 2000s various recycling laws were enacted in Japan, including the Containers and Packaging Law, the Electric and Household Appliances Recycling Law, the Food Recycling Law, the Automobile Recycling Act and the Construction Materials Recycling Law (Okuda and Thomson, 2007). This legal system forms a solid foundation for material recovery. Despite this, incineration remains the dominant MSW management method in Japan. This is because it saves landfill space and generates power or heat which, if produced by conventional energy sources such as fossil fuels, would cause emissions of greenhouse gases (Yoshida, 2005). The main concern is that incineration cannot realize the material recovery potential of MSW as resources (Nakanishi, 2004). Urban communities often consider incineration facilities as sources of pollution and oppose local placement of new plants. As a result, new incineration plants are often located in less populated areas. Because demand for heat in such areas is limited, a large amount of the heat generated these incinerators is not efficiently recovered and used (Sakai, 1996).

Table 3.2.1 Major environmental benefits documented in the literature

Case studied	Environmental benefit	Quantity	Note	Reference
Kawasaki	Landfill avoidance	565 kt/yr	Five by-product exchanges and two recycling industries	Van Berkel et al., 2009a
	Raw material saving	490 kt/yr		
Guayama	Reduction in SO_2	1,978 t/yr	Exchange of steam	Chertow and Lombardi, 2005
	Reduction in NO_x	211 t/yr		
	Reduction in PM_{10}	123 t/yr		
	Reduction in CO	−15 t/yr		
	Reduction in CO_2	51,000 t/yr		
Kalundborg	Conservation of surface water	500,000 m^3/yr	Using cooling water for steam production	Jacobsen, 2006
	Reduction in CO_2	154,788 t/yr	Steam and heat cogeneration	
	Reduction in SO_2	−304 t/yr		
	Reduction in NO_x	389 t/yr		

Incineration impedes the reuse and recycling of many valuable solid wastes that can substitute virgin raw materials. Therefore, the national government decided to adopt another approach: to replace natural resources by MSW for energy generation and material processing. This new approach can reduce both total greenhouse gas emissions and the total amount of waste destined for landfill.

A comprehensive legal framework to that effect is now in place. The foundation was laid by the Fundamental Law for Establishing a Sound Material-Cycle Society, which was came into force in January 2001 (METI, 2004; Morioka et al., 2005). It was developed under the Basic Environmental Law, and provides quantitative targets for recycling and reducing material use in Japanese society. Compared to 2000, it aims by 2010 to improve resource productivity by about 40 per cent (to ¥390,000/ tonne) and recycling by about 40 per cent (to 14 per cent of total materials use) and decrease landfill by about 50 per cent (to 28 million tonnes/ year). Two complementary laws were enacted under the Fundamental

Law for Establishing a Sound Material-Cycle Society (METI, 2004; MOE, 2007). The Waste Management Law (2003 amendments) sets aims and objectives for waste management and defines roles and responsibilities regarding waste prevention and management for waste generators (commercial, industrial and construction wastes) and prefectures (garbage collection, intermediate treatment/incineration and final disposal within the local government boundaries). The Law for Promotion of Effective Utilization of Resources (2001) designates key products and industries for resource saving, and has since been implemented with product-specific laws which set recycling targets for categories of wastes, to be realized through product stewardship schemes, levies and voluntary initiatives of government, producers and consumers.

A comprehensive system of recycling targets is now in place (METI, ibid.; MOE, ibid.), by both product group/waste category (ISC, 2001b) and industry sector (ISC, 2001a). A key project in Japan's effort to become a recycling-oriented society is the Eco-Town Programme (GEC, 2005; Fujita, 2006). Launched some five years before the formal enactment of the Fundamental Law for Establishing a Sound Material-Cycle Society, the programme aimed to develop innovative recycling industries, particularly in towns with ageing industrial infrastructure, through voluntary initiatives and financial support from the national government. The status of the Eco-Town Programme was evaluated in 2006 on behalf of the Ministry of Economy, Trade and Industry (METI), which also provided the main share of the programme funding (Fujita, 2006, 2008). The main findings from this evaluation were analysed by Van Berkel et al. (2009b) to provide insight into the diversity of results and experiences gained in eco-towns since the programme launch in 1997.

3-2-4 Analysis of characteristics of eco-town programmes

Eco-towns in Japan have been developed through a national initiative inaugurated by the Ministry of Health, Labor and Welfare (responsibility for waste management was taken over by the Ministry of Environment in 2001) and Ministry of International Trade and Industry (present METI) in 1997. The aim was twofold: to extend the life of existing landfill sites and revitalize local industries. Japan faced in the late 1990s a serious shortage of landfill sites. In 1997 existing landfill sites for industrial wastes were estimated to be filled within 3.1 years if no measures were taken, and in the Tokyo metropolitan area this would only take 0.7 years. At the same time, local industries experienced economic stagnation triggered by the burst of the Japanese bubble economy after 1991. The Eco-Town Programme aimed to tackle these two challenges simultaneously under the slogan of "zero emissions". This is a concept of an alternative industrial system in which, in principle, all wastes generated by one industry are usefully applied elsewhere. This concept has been promoted by UNU's Zero Emissions Research Initiative with support from the government of Japan (Kuehr, 2007).

The operation of the programme is illustrated in Figure 3.2.1 (Van Berkel et al., 2009b). Under the Eco-Town Programme, local governments (city or prefecture level) formulated eco-town projects in consultation with local stakeholders from the private sector, research institutes, community groups and citizens. Upon submission, the eco-town plans were reviewed by the national government and, if considered appropriate, jointly endorsed by METI and the Ministry of Environment (MOE). The eco-town plan would typically be a combination of town planning, community recycling and outreach activities (jointly termed the "software" project) and proposals for specific innovative recycling plants (commonly known as the "hardware" project).

Upon approval of the eco-town plan, the MOE provided a grant to the local authority to execute the town planning, community recycling and promotion and outreach activities, in collaboration with citizens and non-profit organizations (NPOs). The grant was limited to maximum of 50 per cent of the project costs, typically in the range of ¥3–5 million/year (US$30,000–50,000/yr) for a three- to five-year period (GEC, 2005). Simultaneously, METI provided investment subsidies in the range of ¥100–7,000 million (up to US$70 million) to private enterprises willing to invest in the innovative recycling projects included in the eco-town plans (Fujita, 2006; Van Berkel et al., 2009b). The METI grant was supported by an investment subsidy from the local government, typically in the range of 1–10 per cent of the METI grant (GEC, 2005; Van Berkel et al., 2009b).

During the programme's 10 years of operation, 26 eco-town plans were approved and endorsed for implementation by local government authorities. Figure 3.2.2 maps the geographic locations of these eco-towns, and shows the extensive coverage of all key regions of Japan by the Eco-Town Programme.

Half of the eco-towns were approved and established in the first four years of the programme: four in its first year (1997) and three each in the following years (1998–2000). The other eco-towns were approved and established between 2001 and 2006: four in 2003, three in 2002, two each in 2001 and 2005 and one each in 2004 and 2006. The *administrative responsibility* for 13 eco-towns rests with a municipality and the other 13 with a prefecture. There is considerable differentiation in the *geographic target area* of the projects, as we analysed before (Van Berkel et al., 2009b). Six plans cover a metropolitan area (Chiba, Kawasaki, Kitakyushu, Osaka, Sapporo and Tokyo). These are all focused on setting up recycling infra-

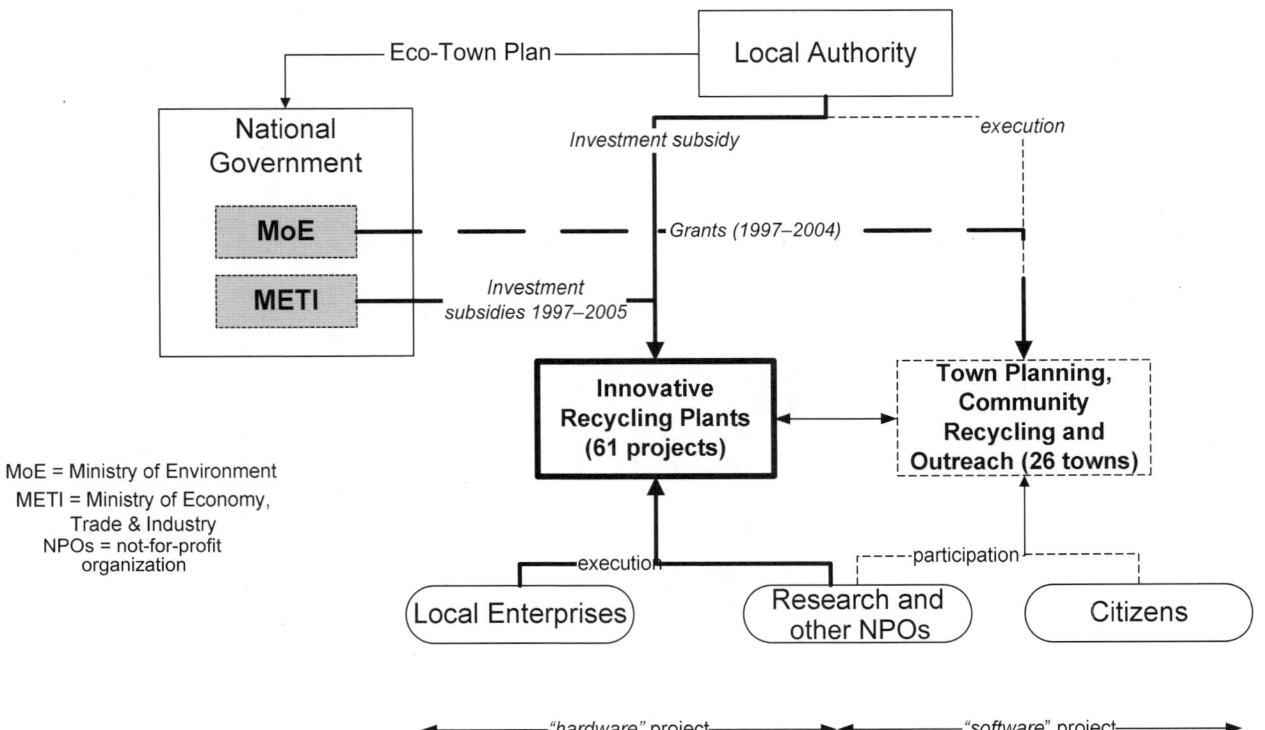

Figure 3.2.1 Operation of the national Eco-Town Programme
Source: Van Berkel et al. (2009b).

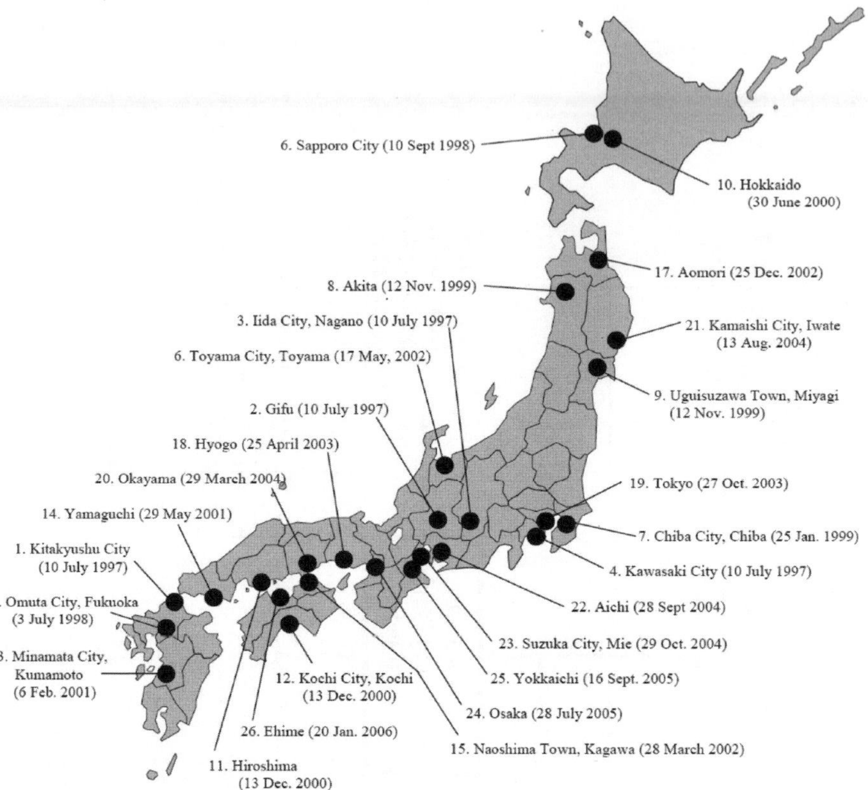

Figure 3.2.2 Map of eco-town locations
Source: www.env.go.jp/en/press/2006/0120a-01.pdf.

structure for different parts of the urban waste stream, including household recyclables, commercial, construction and demolition waste, etc. Six plans cover a region including several towns and/or villages: Aichi, Akita, Ehime, Gifu, Hyogo and Omuta. A common objective for these eco-towns is coordination of waste handling and recycling at the regional level to achieve economies of scale. Two eco-towns cover an island – respectively Hokkaido (large) and Naoshima (small). The largest group of 10 eco-towns has a city, or part thereof, as its target region. These eco-town plans are quite diverse, and typically include a combination of community-based initiatives for improved recycling, environmentally conscious town planning and creating clusters of recycling businesses. The final two eco-towns have an industrial or port area as the target region (Kamaishi and Okayama). These eco-towns have been set up to establish new recycling-oriented businesses in existing industrial complexes for rejuvenation and diversification among established heavy industries.

Table 3.2.2 Categorization of eco-towns

Type and number of eco-towns (based on Sato, Ushiro and Matsunga, 2004)	Eco-towns
1. Promotion of environmental industries (14)	**Aichi**, Akita, *Aomori,* Bingo, **Ehime**, Kawasaki, Kitakyushu, Kurihara, **Okyama**, Omatu, **Osaka**, Toyama, Yamaguchi and **Yokkaichi**
2. Treatment of wastes (7)	Chiba, *Hokkaido,* Kochi, Naoshima, **Suzuka**, Sapporo and **Tokyo**
3. Community development (5)	*Gifu,* **Hyogo**, Iida, **Kamaishi** and Minamata

Note: Eco-towns in **bold** were not included in Sato, Ushiro and Matsunga (2004). Eco-towns in *italics* have been assigned to different categories on the basis of additional information in Fujita (2008).
Source: Van Berkel et al. (2009b).

Sato, Ushiro and Matsunga (2004) proposed categorizing eco-towns in three types: promotion of environmental industries (type 1), treatment of wastes (type 2) and community development (type 3). We expanded and revised this categorization, on the basis of information available in 2006. Table 3.2.2 categorizes all 26 current eco-towns (Van Berkel et al., 2009b). Just over half (14 of 26) of the eco-towns are of type 1. All these have a strong emphasis on environmental innovation in existing industries by applying their core technology and competencies for environmental purposes and/or establishing niche operators that can process wastes available in the region into valuable alternative raw materials for the existing industries. The other eco-towns are almost evenly split between type 2 (waste processing in seven eco-towns) and type 3 (community development and engagement of citizens and businesses in five eco-towns).

Designation as an eco-town provided access to investment subsidies for priority innovative recycling projects. Government subsidies were provided to private sector parties which invest in the establishment of recycling facilities and own and operate them upon completion. The total investment for these plants was reported by Fujita (2008) to be ¥165 billion (Figure 3.2.3). Government public initiatives in a series of recycling laws and national subsidies of ¥59 billion induced as much as 2.8 times more private investment.

The investment per plant ranged between ¥63 million and ¥20.33 billion, with an average of ¥2.71 billion per project (Van Berkel et al., 2009b). The total investment in subsidized recycling plants in each eco-town ranged between ¥75 million and ¥43.37 billion, with an average of ¥6.6 billion per eco-town. The investment was unevenly spread among

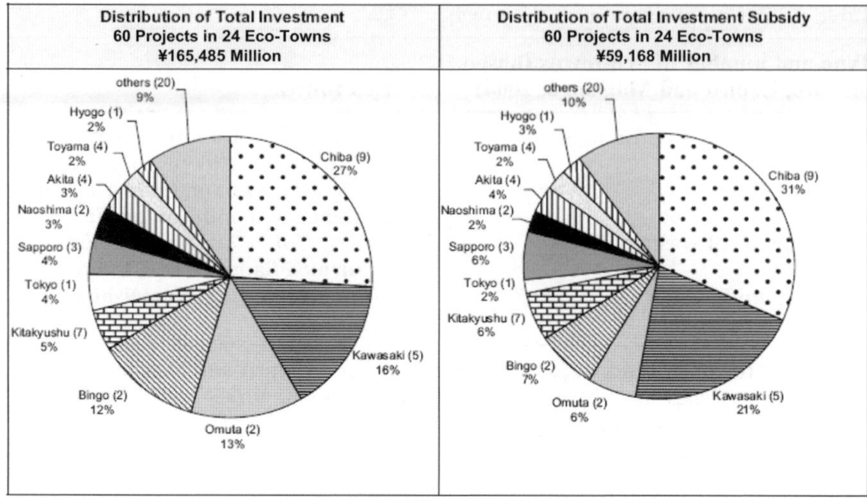

Figure 3.2.3 Levels of subsidies and total investments by eco-towns
Source: Van Berkel et al. (2009b).

the eco-towns (Figure 3.2.3). Over a quarter of the total was invested in one eco-town (Chiba), and collectively four eco-towns (Chiba, Kawasaki, Omuta and Bingo) absorbed two-thirds of the total investment.

The level of subsidy by the national government was in the range of 14–50 per cent of the total investment, with an average of 36 per cent (ibid.). The national government provided a total subsidy of ¥59 billion (approximately US$590 million) (Figure 3.2.3), on average just under ¥1 billion per recycling plant. (This excludes data on subsidy for one relatively small plant in Kamaishi, which had a total investment of only ¥300 million.) The subsidy was provided by METI (87 per cent) and the MOE (13 per cent). National subsidies were matched by local government subsidies, reported to be in the range of 1–10 per cent of the national government subsidies (GEC, 2005). However, no detailed data were available. It is thus likely that the average subsidy percentage for the plants might have been slightly higher, in the range of 36–40 per cent (Van Berkel et al., 2009b). The subsidies followed the investment pattern, and were also not evenly spread over the eco-towns (as illustrated in the right-hand pie chart in Figure 3.2.3). The total subsidy per eco-town varied between ¥25 million and ¥18.82 billion, with an average of ¥2.37 billion (averaged over the 24 eco-towns for which subsidy data are available).

The 2006 summary profiles of the eco-towns presented in Fujita (2008) revealed that the motivation for local governments to develop an eco-town plan had been quite divergent between the various eco-towns. Five categories of motivation emerged from the analysis of the 26 programmes (Van Berkel et al., 2009b).

- *Waste management:* in particular the growing concerns about the availability of landfill space (and/or other treatment and disposal options) to deal with the growing volumes of urban and industrial wastes. This is a shared concern of local government (responsible for garbage collection and disposal) and waste-generating businesses (responsible for collection and disposal of commercial, industrial, construction and other wastes). Waste management is based on the proximity principle, which essentially states that waste generated within one local government area should be disposed off within the boundaries of that jurisdiction; in other words, wastes cannot be transferred from one town to another town for treatment and disposal.
- *Development of recycling industry:* in particular the need to create infrastructure and facilities to reach the mandatory recycling targets set for various product categories under the umbrella of the Fundamental Law for Establishing a Sound Material-Cycle Society.
- *Industry modernization*: many heavy process industrial areas in Japan have experienced downturns over the past two decades, due to deregulation and opening of the economy (leading to greater international competition, for example from China), ageing of industrial facilities, changes in production and consumption patterns (e.g. greater material competition between metals and with plastics) and depletion of local mines (for industries relying on mining activities). Some eco-town projects were established to counter these trends and develop environmental businesses that utilize technological resources available to existing industries for new environmental applications.
- *Environmental remediation:* the presence of an environmental black spot, like a polluted river or abandoned hazardous waste site, has encouraged local governments to develop eco-town plans as a practical way to regain confidence among residents and improve their quality of life.
- *Town planning and community development and engagement:* launching environmental initiatives which involve local residents can strengthen their sense of place in and belonging to the town and gradually improve credibility for the local governments involved.

The 2006 survey (Fujita, 2008) also established that the Eco-Town Programme had triggered investments in at least another 147 recycling plants. This analysis was bound by limitations, however (Van Berkel et al., 2009b). The inventory of additional recycling facilities may not have been complete, as it relied essentially on knowledge and readily available information from local government representatives. For some eco-towns it is known that more recycling projects have been implemented, for example the use of a range of alternative fuels and raw materials for cement production in Kawasaki.

An analysis was also made of the total set of 207 recycling projects reported for the 26 eco-towns, based on the type of waste materials and/or processing involved (ibid.). To this end, they were divided into 12 categories.

- *Alternative fuels and raw materials (AF&R):* use of alternative fuels (organics, plastics, wood, etc.) and alternative raw materials (e.g. shells, ash and slag in cement making).
- *Construction and demolition waste (C&DW):* recycling inert waste from the construction sector, including roads and infrastructure, most commonly for reuse as coarse aggregate.
- *End-of-life vehicles (ELVs):* dismantling and recycling of automobiles, including their components, in particular tyres and batteries.
- *Glass:* reuse and/or recycling of glass, mainly as bottles.
- *Industrial waste:* advanced treatment of wastes from industrial operations (e.g. slag, ash, etc.), including treatment of residues from recycling or incineration operations.
- *Metal recovery:* advanced processes for recovery of precious and/or hazardous metals from complex wastes, such as shredder residue from ELVs and/or WEE (waste electric and electronic goods).
- *Municipal solid waste:* intermediate treatment of garbage collected by municipality, typically involving sorting with metal recovery and incineration with heat recovery for power generation, or production of an intermediate fuel (e.g. refuse-derived fuel).
- *Organics:* recycling of organic matter (e.g. food waste, fishery processing waste from fishery industry) through anaerobic digestion (production of biogas) and/or composting (for soil improvement).
- *Paper:* recycling of paper, cardboard and related products for reuse of fibre and manufacture of recycled paper or paperboard.
- *Plastics:* recycling of various sorted and/or unsorted plastics, in particular from packaging applications, either for direct reuse (down-cycling of mixed plastics) or for recovery of original plastic or for production of intermediate synthesis or fuel gas (for example as alternative reductant in chemical or metallurgical applications).
- *Waste electric and electronic goods (WEE):* dismantling of electric and electronic appliances (including home, office and medical appliances and amusement machines) for recovery of bulk materials. Also includes recycling facilities for fluorescent tubes (glass, aluminum and mercury recovery) and dry-cell batteries.

- *Wood:* recovery of waste wood for chipping and reuse in wood products.

The classification of recycling projects is displayed in Figure 3.2.4 (ibid.). By far the largest group was plastics recycling projects, with 35 implemented projects (of which 20 were subsidized) and 11 planned. This was also the most diverse group in terms of complexity and innovativeness. It included novel chemical separation and recycling processes (e.g. for PET-to-PET recycling, oil liquefaction) as well as relatively simple grinding and pelleting projects for mixed plastics. The next largest groups were organics and MSW, both with 23 implemented projects, followed by WEE (19 implemented projects) and industrial waste (13 implemented projects).

We also provided a conceptual impact diagram to illustrate the diversity of the 26 eco-town projects in Japan (ibid.). The four quadrants in the diagram (Figure 3.2.5) cover different aspects of the environmental and sustainability agendas for government, business and society at large (see e.g. WBCSD, 2001; Dunphy, Griffiths and Benn, 2003; Hargroves and Smith, 2005). These are characterized in the figure by means of the four circles:

- *eco-efficiency:* producing less waste and using less materials in productive activities (see e.g. Van Berkel, 2007a)
- *corporate social responsibility:* improving the well-being of employees, their families and communities (see e.g. WBCSD, 2000)
- *environmental restoration:* reversing environmental damage from past activities to levels that are no longer harmful to humans and ecosystems
- *environmental innovation:* using environmental issues as a driver for developing new technologies, products and services (see e.g. WBCSD, 2002).

Figure 3.2.5 also illustrates that the top right-hand triangle is the working area for *industrial symbiosis* (Chertow, 2000) and the bottom left-hand triangle could then be considered as the working area for *urban symbiosis.*

Using the pseudo-quantitative axes, all 26 eco-towns have been characterized on this conceptual impact map, as in Figure 3.2.6 (Van Berkel et al., 2009b). The largest group is in the eco-efficiency quadrant (12 eco-towns), followed by the environmental restoration quadrant (seven eco-towns) and the environmental innovation and corporate social responsibility quadrants (two eco-towns each). A residual group of three eco-towns does not fit comfortably in any of the quadrants, due to more or less balanced involvement of civil society and the private sector (eco-towns on the horizontal axis) and/or a balanced focus between amenity and productivity (eco-towns on the vertical axis). The figure also shows that in 16 eco-towns the private sector is a more important actor than

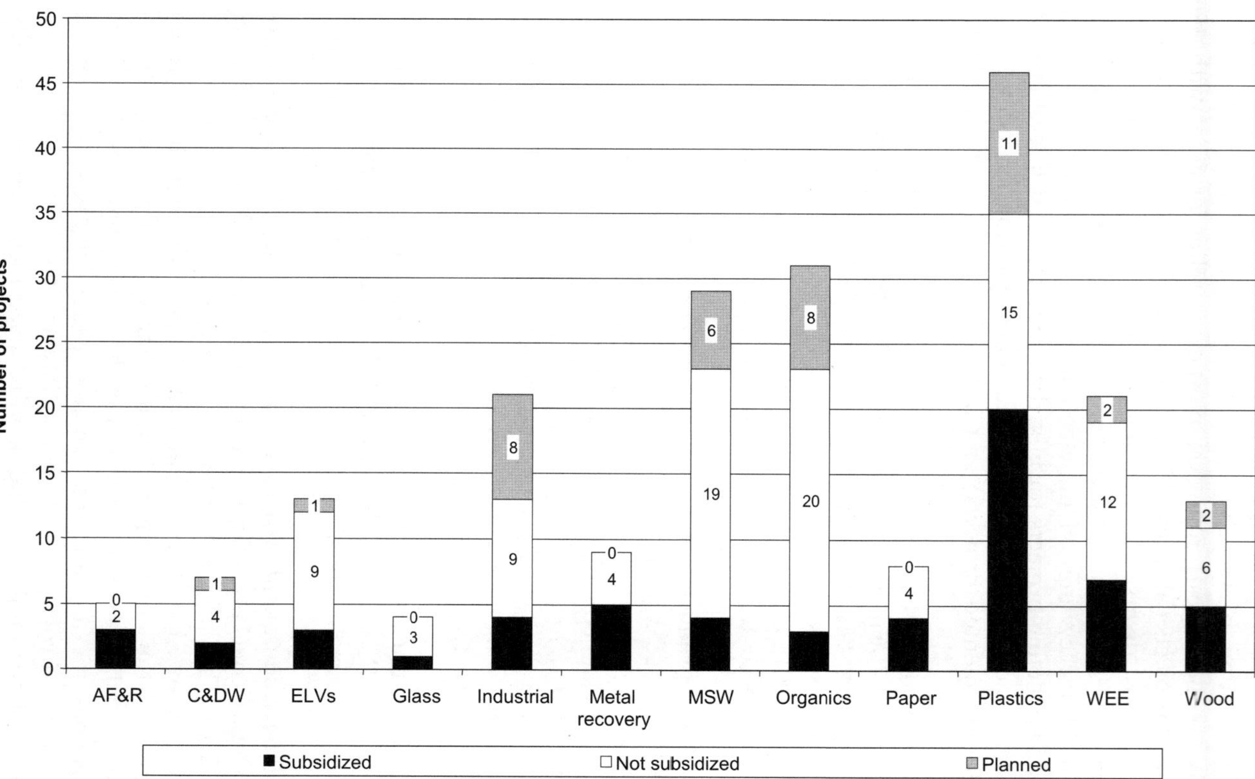

Figure 3.2.4 Recycling projects in eco-towns by category (total of 61 subsidized projects, 107 unsubsidized projects and 39 planned projects)
Source: Van Berkel et al. (2009b).

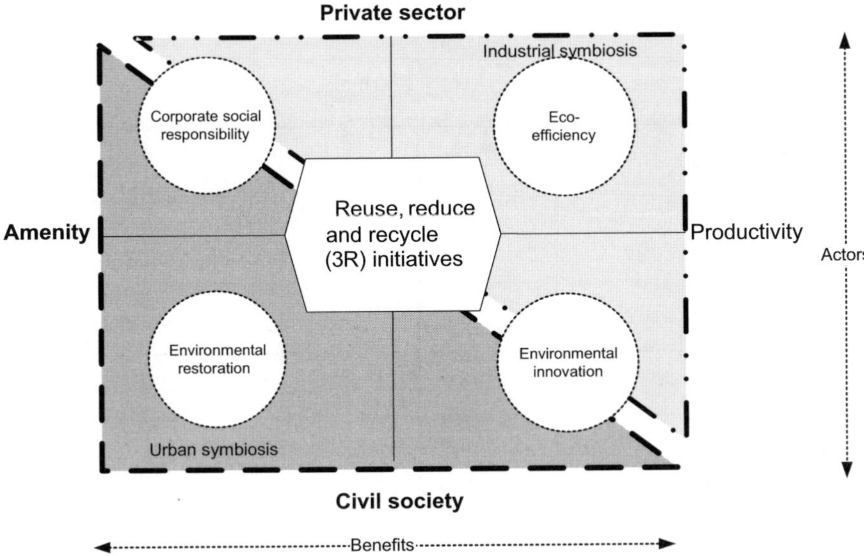

Figure 3.2.5 Contribution of eco-towns to sustainable industrial development
Source: Van Berkel et al. (2009b).

civil society, and that for 14 eco-towns productivity benefits are more important than amenity benefits. The impact map thus confirms that overall the Eco-Town Programme provided a platform for the private sector to innovate using 3R as the guiding paradigm, and thereby contribute to maintaining and where possible improving its competiveness and productivity under tightening environmental regulations.

3-2-5 Linking MSWM with local industry in Kawasaki eco-town

As mentioned, eco-town projects are typically a combination of town planning, community recycling and outreach activities ("software") and proposals for specific innovative recycling plants ("hardware"). The selected city governments formulate their own eco-town plans in consultation with local stakeholders from the private sector, research institutes, community groups and citizens.

Kawasaki was one of the first Japanese cities to initiate an eco-town project (Van Berkel et al., 2009a). The project was approved in 1997, with a total investment of ¥25 billion from government. Five facilities were subsidized: a recycling system using waste plastics as an input to the blast furnace; a paper recycling facility; a PET-to-PET recycling facility; a

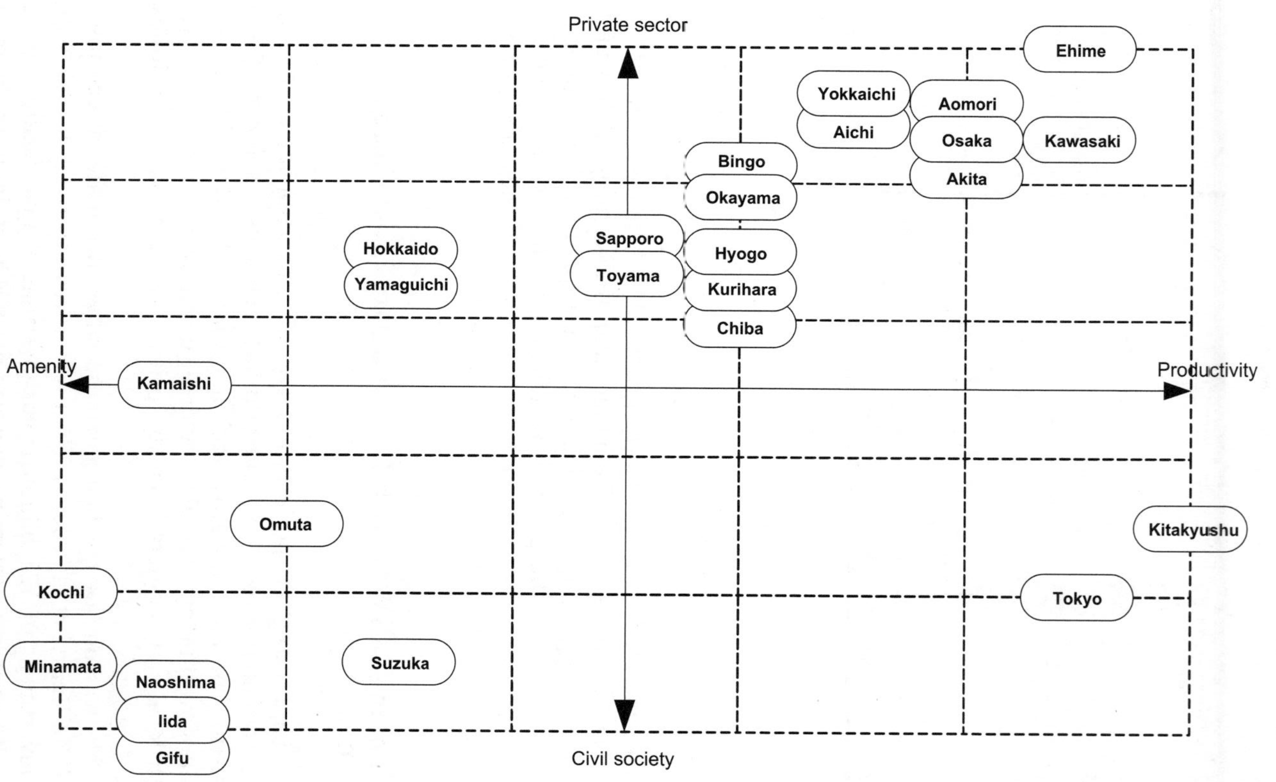

Figure 3.2.6 Qualitative characterization of 26 eco-towns
Source: Van Berkel et al. (2009b).

recycling system for utilizing waste plastic as raw material to make ammonia; and a facility to transfer waste plastics into concrete-setting frames (wall-board) (GEC, 2005). Other key facilities which were not subsidized include a home appliance recycling facility and a cement plant with recycling processes. The main mission of the project was to encourage industrial and urban symbiosis activities and improve the overall eco-efficiency of the coastal industrial area, aiming to develop a zero-emission park.

The eco-town project is not limited to the coastal industrial area. To promote the concept of eco-industrial development further, the city government investigated the possibility of extending its efforts on a larger scale by linking MSWM with local industries. With planning and coordination, several urban-industrial symbiosis activities have taken place between local industries and the city government. Figure 3.2.7 shows current urban-industrial symbiosis in Kawasaki (Van Berkel et al., 2009a). For instance, the cement company is currently recycling sewage sludge from urban areas as a substitute for clay, and waste wood, plastic, tyres and oil as substitutes for coal. The blast furnace slag from a steel manufacturing company located within Kawasaki eco-town is used as a raw material for making cement. The steel company receives iron and non-ferrous metals from the home appliance recycling facility as a substitute for raw iron. In addition, waste plastic collected from home appliance recycling and the urban area is utilized as deoxidization matter for making steel products. The paper recycling plant, Corelex Papers, is the first such facility in the world to succeed in achieving zero emissions. It can treat almost all kinds of wastepaper, including magnetic train tickets, photographic printing paper, paper containers with aluminium and laminate layers and used paper with mixed plastic and staples. Contaminated metals, films, plastic and paper sludge and fluorescent and other ink can be removed from paper sources using innovative technology. Paper sludge and plastic separated in the process are used as fuel for operating its boilers.

3-2-6 Scenario design and analysis

With the establishment and operation of recycling facilities for treating MSW, particularly replacing raw materials with MSW, both economic and environmental benefits can be gained. These include reduction of natural resource consumption, reduction of the total solid waste volume, reducing the burden on local landfill and reduction of resource and solid waste treatment costs, as well as environmental liability and insurance costs relative to solid waste issues. Despite this, public controversy on the appropriateness of such an approach remains. A quantitative evaluation of

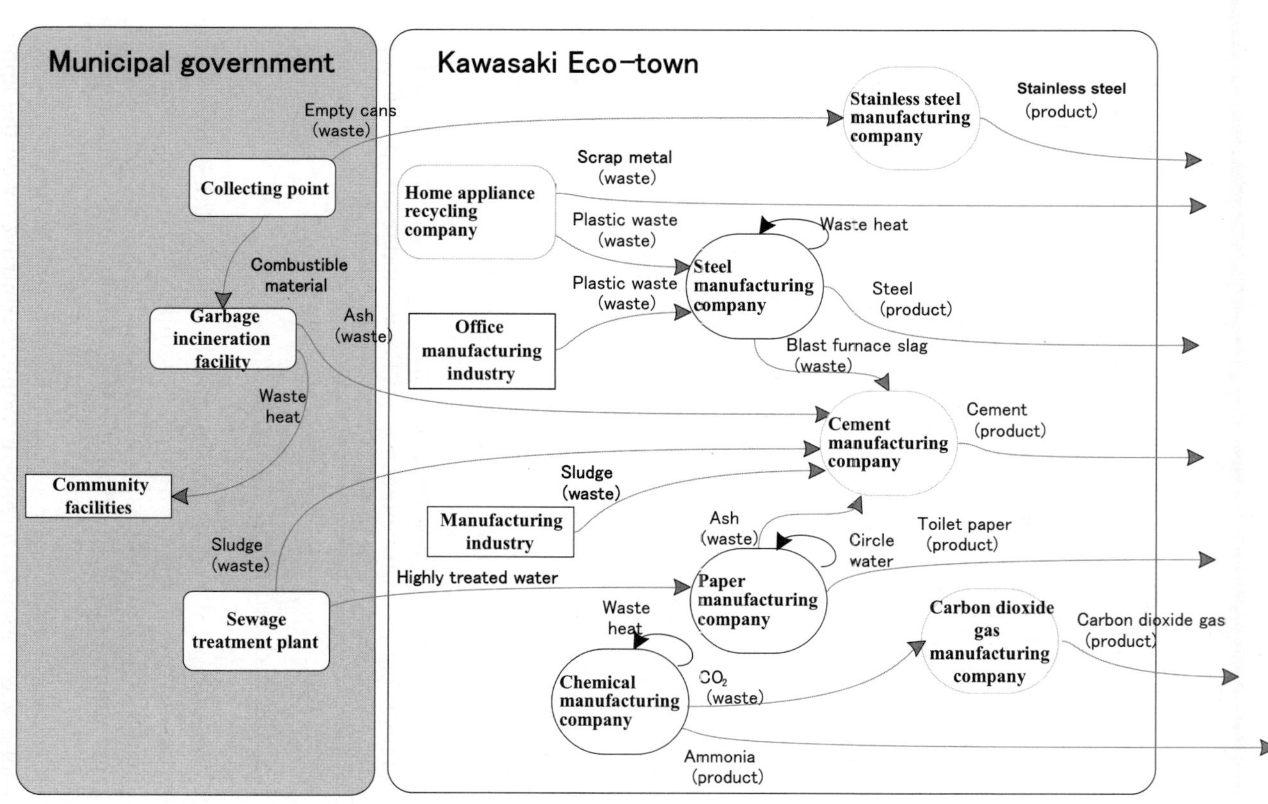

Figure 3.2.7 Current urban-industrial symbiosis in Kawasaki
Source: Geng, Fujita and Chen (2010).

138

different policy scenarios is thus required. Such an evaluation should be able to test the overall eco-efficiency of different policy options, including the potential for reduced MSW amount to landfills, CO_2 emission and total cost.

Several evaluation methods have been developed. Life-cycle assessment is a common methodology for impact assessment of MSWM at the city level. Eriksson et al. (2005) used a sophisticated LCA-based model, ORWARE, to evaluate waste treatment policy scenarios with different combinations of technology applications in Uppsala, Stockholm and Alvdalen in Sweden. Finnveden et al. (2005) used LCA to examine the effectiveness of waste management hierarchy: they proved that recycling is preferable to incineration, and incineration preferable to landfill. Habara et al. (2002) evaluated the environmental impact of energy consumption and the cost of collection and transportation for a regional solid waste management system, in which several municipalities share one centralized treatment facility so as to reduce the total cost. Thus we adopted the LCA approach for our scenario design and evaluation. As defined by the Society of Environmental Toxicology and Chemistry, "the assessment includes the entire life cycle of the product, process or activity, encompassing extracting and processing raw materials; manufacturing, transportation, and distribution; use/re-use/maintenance; recycling; and final disposal" (Graedel and Allenby, 1995: 108). One feature of the model used here is to apply this LCA approach to assessing environmental and economic effects of urban symbiosis. Urban symbiosis pertains to multiple life-cycle stages of various products. It also concerns multiple stakeholders from residential, business and industrial sectors who generate recyclable wastes, and manufacturers who take these wastes as input to production using innovative symbiotic technologies. The assessment boundary of the model includes the processes of both waste management and production.

First, by surveying manufacturers who accept recyclable wastes, we compared the differences between the conventional production process and the process designed to utilize wastes as inputs, and further calculated the difference of CO_2 emissions between the two processes. The comparison and calculation included the embedded CO_2 emissions of relevant raw materials and utilities.

Second, based upon our investigation of waste collection and transportation activities, we developed a spatial database for the MSW generation and collection network in Kawasaki. This database can help determine MSW collection boundaries for different collection centres and recycling facilities, based on transportation distances. We then designed four different scenarios with individual recycling options. The baseline scenario (scenario 0) involves the incineration of mixed waste without any recycling or recovery activities. Scenarios 1 to 4 are set to test various combinations of and trade-offs between incineration and various symbiotic technologies. In scenario 1, mixed wastepaper is recycled by Corelex Papers and directly used in toilet paper production. In scenario 2, waste packaging plastics are recycled and utilized as a reductant in steel production. In scenario 3, organic waste from business sectors is recycled by the local biogas plant, and fermentation residues are further used in cement production. In scenario 4, all three recycling options are combined. In the latter four scenarios, all mixed garbage remains are to be sent to the four incinerators in Kawasaki with electricity generation and heat recovery. In order to realize these scenarios, several new facilities need to be constructed. For instance, for scenario 1 two new pre-treatment centres that can separate, compress and package different wastepapers are required. For scenario 2, two new pre-treatment centres that can separate, compress and package different waste plastics are required. For scenario 3, a biogas plant that can produce power by using methane from the fermentation process of organic waste is required. Thus the construction and operation costs of these new facilities need to be considered for scenario analysis. Figure 3.2.8 illustrates MSW processing flow scenario analysis in Kawasaki.

The next step was to calculate CO_2 emissions, the total input to local landfills and the total cost of MSWM. By applying the LCA method, we could see that CO_2 emissions come from waste collection and transportation processes and construction and operation of recycling facilities. Thus, relevant formulae are required. Through interviewing local industrial engineers and checking Japanese literature, appropriate formulae were developed. We detail all calculation processes below.

The total CO_2 emissions Q_i under scenario i were calculated by the following equation:

$$Q_i = QT_i + QC_i + QO_i - QSub_i$$

where i: scenario index ($I = 0$ to 4); QT: CO_2 emissions from waste collection and transportation; QC: CO_2 emissions from the construction of new waste treatment facilities, including two paper recycling facilities, two plastic recycling facilities and one biogas plant; QO: CO_2 emissions from the operation of waste treatment and disposal facilities, including four incinerators, one transportation and compressing centre, two paper recycling facilities, two plastic recycling facilities, one biogas plant and one landfill site; and $QSub$: reduction of CO_2 emissions due to the substitution of raw materials, including raw pulp (by wastepaper), cokes (by waste plastic) and limestone and clay (by residue from the biogas plant).

By using the original data on waste from the Kawasaki city govern-

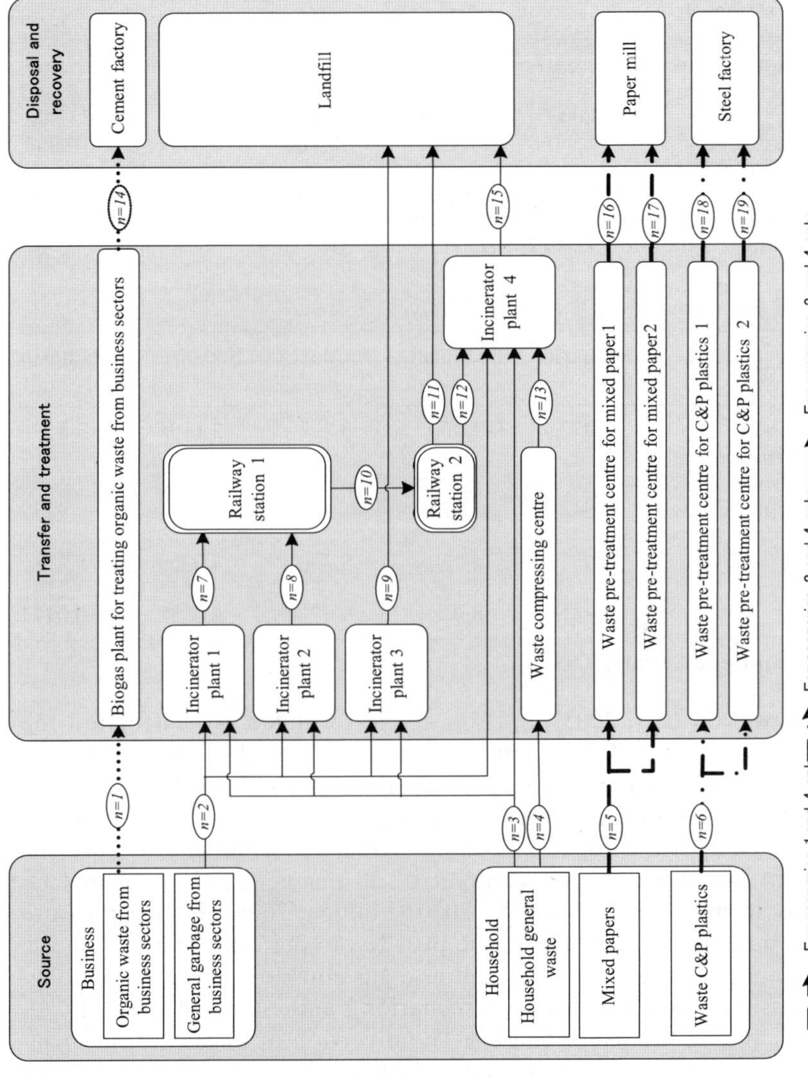

Figure 3.2.8 MSW processing flow scenario analysis in Kawasaki
Source: Geng, Fujita and Chen (2010).

141

Table 3.2.3 Total CO_2 emissions from each scenario (t/yr)

Emission source	Scenario 0	Scenario 1	Scenario 2	Scenario 3	Scenario 4
Collection and transportation of waste	1,650	1,810	19,430	1,790	2,230
Construction of new plants	0	105	463	296	863
Operation	113,000	97,000	51,900	95,500	53,300
Reduction due to substitutive effect	0	126	−10,700	−283	−10,900
Total	114,000	99,100	43,600	97,300	45,500

Source: Geng, Fujita and Chen (2010).

Table 3.2.4 Total cost of each scenario (¥m/yr)

Cost source	Scenario 0	Scenario 1	Scenario 2	Scenario 3	Scenario 4
Collection and transportation of waste	2,972	3,060	3,297	3,119	3,558
Construction of new plants	842	824	911	879	929
Operation	5,037	4,930	5,200	4,936	5,371
Commission	0	105	63	51	219
Total cost	8,851	8,919	9,472	8,985	10,077

Source: Van Berkel et al. (2009a).

ment (Kawasaki City, 2005) and the above formulae, we calculated the total CO_2 emissions of different scenarios (Table 3.2.3), as well as the total cost of each scenario (Table 3.2.4). The results show that the application of urban symbiosis can significantly reduce total CO_2 emissions. This is very important for Japanese municipal governments, because the Cabinet of Japan has set up a target of 20 per cent reduction in CO_2 emissions from the 1990 level by 2020 (Fukuda, 2008). Under pressure from the national government in the post-Kyoto period, all cities face the challenge of reducing overall greenhouse gas emissions to meet the long-term emission target. In this study, scenarios 2 and 4 have the lowest CO_2 emissions among the five scenarios. The diversion of plastics from incineration contributes the most to the reduction of CO_2 emissions because they are not carbon neutral in incineration and, by symbiotic technology, can substitute cokes in steel production. Through such a process, cokes are conserved and removed from combustion. The results of scenarios 1 and 3 show that recycling mixed wastepaper and organic wastes could not significantly reduce CO_2 emissions, unlike recycling plastics. This is mainly because what these two types of wastes substituted in industrial production is not as carbon intensive as cokes. Moreover, conventional paper production considered in this study already uses residues with high heat value, such as black liquor, as carbon-neutral energy sources in production, whereas recycling hard-to-recycle paper requires more energy in pre-treatment processes.

The implementation of urban symbiosis will cost more money in the short term due to the operation of waste separation programmes and the construction of new storage and pre-treatment facilities. The cost of reducing CO_2 emissions through urban symbiosis as discussed here, approximately US$91/t-$CO_2$ in scenario 2 and US$185/t-$CO_2$ in scenario 4 (at an exchange rate of ¥96/US$), is also higher than the price of carbon credits in the international market. However, such an investment is worthwhile because Kawasaki can gain additional environmental benefits through urban symbiotic activities, e.g. saving landfill space and conserving non-renewable natural resources. Compared with the baseline scenario, such symbiotic activities in scenarios 1–4 would reduce waste input to landfill by 3,177 tonnes, 2,714 tonnes, 2,278 tonnes and 8,161 tonnes, respectively. In addition, most incineration facilities require renewal after 20–30 years depending on operation levels. By sending less waste for incineration, renewal costs of these plants can be reduced in the long term. Due to the target of reducing greenhouse gas emission and other unquantified environmental and social benefits, recycling more wastes through urban symbiosis should be an optimal future scenario for Kawasaki.

With such environmental, economic and social benefits, the Kawasaki case study findings can be applied in other Asian cities. In Asian urban development, residential communities, commercial services and primary/secondary industrial activities often coexist. However, a holistic approach wherein the consumption pattern of the residential community interacts with the production pattern in commercial and industrial areas rarely exists. Traditional industrialization has been characterized by urban economic growth and environmental degradation. The major way by which the industrial system is restructured to reduce the discharge of hazardous materials from the production process is to apply end-of-pipe cleaning and/or cleaner production technologies. These technologies can only be employed at the firm level. Urban symbiosis presents a new model for more sustainable urban economic and industrial development at a regional level. Through adequate and appropriate policies, flexible organizational structure and effective tools for integrated resource management, urban symbiosis aims to achieve simultaneous positive outcomes for the economy, society and the environment. Particularly with the rapid growth of industrialization and urbanization, sustainable MSWM is of critical importance for city managers. By avoiding production of waste at source as well as turning waste into resources, innovative MSWM through urban symbiosis can reduce both the amount of waste to be disposed and resource consumption, helping reach the target of sustainable development in urban areas. The process of identifying the most appropriate urban symbiosis methods for different cities requires understanding and information exchange on background conditions, local policies and a myriad of other factors.

REFERENCES

Baas, L. and F. Boons (2007) "The Introduction and Dissemination of the Industrial Symbiosis Projects in the Rotterdam Harbour and Industry Complex", *International Journal of Environmental Technology and Management* 7(5/6), pp. 551–577.

Bossilkov, A., R. Van Berkel and G. Corder (2005) *Regional Synergies for Sustainable Resource Processing: A Status Report*. Perth, WA: Centre for Sustainable Resource Processing.

Chertow, M. (2000) "Industrial Symbiosis: Literature and Taxonomy", *Annual Review of Energy and Environment* 25, pp. 313–337.

——— (2007) "Uncovering Industrial Symbiosis", *Journal of Industrial Ecology* 11(1), pp. 11–30.

Chertow, M. and D. Lombardi (2005) "Quantifying Economic and Environmental Benefits of Co-Located Firms", *Environmental Science and Technology* 39(17), pp. 6535–6541.

Deutz, P. and D. Gibbs (2004) "Eco-Industrial Development: Industrial Ecology or Place Promotion?", *Business Strategy and the Environment* 13, pp. 347–362.

Dunphy, D., A. Griffiths and S. Benn (2003) *Organisational Change for Corporate Sustainability*. London: Routledge.

Eriksson, O., M. Carlsson Reich, B. Frostell, A. Bjöklund, G. Assefa, J. O. Sundqvist, J. Granath, A. Baky and L. Thyselius (2005) "Municipal Solid Waste Management from a Systems Perspective", *Journal of Cleaner Production* 13, pp. 241–252.

Fang, Y., R. Cote and R. Qin (2006) "Industrial Sustainability in China: Practice and Prospects for Eco-industrial Development", *Journal of Environmental Management* 83, pp. 315–328.

Finnveden, G., J. Johansson, P. Lind and A. Moberg (2005) "Life Cycle Assessment of Energy from Solid Waste – Part 1: General Methodology and Results", *Journal of Cleaner Production* 13, pp. 213–229.

Fukuda, Y. (2008) "Towards a Low-carbon Society, Japan"; available at www.kantei.go.jp/jp/hukudaspeech/2008/06/09speech.html (in Japanese).

Fujita, T. (ed.) (2007) *Eco-Town Projects/Environmental Industries in Progress: Environment Conscious Type of Town Building*. Tokyo: Ministry of Economy, Trade and Industry (in Japanese).

GEC (2005) *Eco-Towns in Japan: Implications and Lessons for Developing Countries and Cities*. Osaka: Global Environment Centre.

Geng, Y., T. Fujita and X. Chen (2010) "Evaluation of Innovative Municipal Solid Waste Management through Urban Symbiosis: A Case Study of Kawasaki", *Journal of Cleaner Production* 18(10/11), pp. 993–1000.

Geng, Y., P. Zhang and R. Cote (2009) "Industrial Ecology in China: The National Eco-industrial Park Standard", *Journal of Industrial Ecology* 13, pp. 15–26.

Gibbs, D., P. Deutz and A. Proctor (2005) "Industrial Ecology and Eco-industrial Development: A Potential Paradigm for Local and Regional Development?", *Regional Studies* 39(2), pp. 171–183.

Graedel, T. E. and B. R. Allenby (1995) *Industrial Ecology*. Englewood Cliffs, NJ: Prentice-Hall.

Habara, H., T. Matsuto, N. Tanaka and M. Inoue (2002) "Comparative Study on Regional Solid Waste Management Systems of Cost and Energy Consumption", *Environmental Systems Research* 30, pp. 323–332.

Hargroves, K. and M. Smith (2005) *The Natural Advantage of Nations: Business Opportunities, Innovations and Governance in the 21st Century*. London: Earthscan Publications.

Harris, S. and C. Pritchard (2004) "Industrial Ecology as a Learning Process in Business Strategy", *Progress in Industrial Ecology* 1(1), pp. 89–111.

Heeres, R. R., W. Vermeulen and F. de Walle (2004) "Eco-industrial Park Initiatives in the USA and the Netherlands: First Lessons", *Journal of Cleaner Production* 12(8/10), pp. 985–995.

ISC (2001a) *Guideline for Waste Treatment/Recycling by Business*. Tokyo: Industry Structure Council.

———— (2001b) *Guideline for Waste Treatment/Recycling by Commodity*. Tokyo: Industry Structure Council.

Jacobsen, N. (2006) "The Industrial Symbiosis in Kalundborg: A Quantitative Assessment of Economic and Environmental Aspects", *Journal of Industrial Ecology* 10(1/2), pp. 239–255.

Kawasaki City (2005) "Annual Statistics Report", Kawasaki City Government.

Kuehr, R. (2007) "Towards a Sustainable Society: United Nations University's Zero Emissions Approach", *Journal of Cleaner Production* 15, pp. 1198–1204.

Liamsanguan, C. and S. H. Gheewala (2008) "LCA: A Decision Support Tool for Environmental Assessment of MSW Management Systems", *Journal of Environmental Management* 87, pp. 132–138.

Mangan, A. (1998) *By-product Synergy: A Strategy for Sustainable Development – A Primer*. Austin, TX: Business Council for Sustainable Development – Gulf of Mexico.

METI (2004) *Handbook on Resource Recycling Legislation and 3R Initiatives*. Tokyo: Ministry of Economy, Trade and Industry.

Mirata, M. (2004) "Experiences from Early Stages of a National Industrial Symbiosis Programme in the United Kingdom: Determinants and Coordination Challenges", *Journal of Cleaner Production* 12(8/10), pp. 967–983.

MOE (2007) *Technologies to Support a Sound Material-Cycle Society; Development of 3R and Waste Management Technologies*. Tokyo: Ministry of Environment.

Morioka, T., K. Tsunemi, Y. Yamamoto, H. Yabar and N. Yoshida (2005) "Eco-Efficiency of Advanced Loop Closing Systems for Vehicles and Household Appliances in Hyogo Eco-Town", *Journal of Industrial Ecology* 9(4), pp. 205–221.

Nakanishi, J. (2004) *Environmental Risk Assessment*. Tokyo: Nippon-Hyouron-Sha.

Okuda, I. and V. E. Thomson (2007) "Regionalization of Municipal Solid Waste Management in Japan: Balancing the Proximity Principle with Economic Efficiency", *Environmental Management* 40, pp. 12–19.

PCSD (1997) *Proceedings of the Eco-Industrial Parks Workshop*. Virginia: President's Council on Sustainable Development.

Sakai, S. (1996) "Municipal Solid Waste Management in Japan", *Waste Management* 16, pp. 395–405.

Sato, M., Y. Ushiro and H. Matsunga (2004) "Categorisation of Eco-Town Projects in Japan", paper presented at International Symposium on Green Technology for Resources and Materials Recycling, Seoul, 24–27 November.

van Beers, D., G. Corder, A. Bossilkov and R. Van Berkel (2007) "Industrial Symbiosis in the Australian Minerals Industries: The Cases of Kwinana and Gladstone", *Journal of Industrial Ecology* 11(1), pp. 55–72.

Van Berkel, R. (2006) *Regional Resource Synergies for Sustainable Development in Heavy Industrial Areas: An Overview of Opportunities and Experiences*. Perth, WA: Curtin University of Technology.

—— (2007a) "Cleaner Production and Eco-Efficiency", in D. Marinova, D. Annandale and J. Phillimore (eds) *The International Handbook of Environmental Technology Management*. Cheltenham: Edward Elgar, pp. 67–93.

—— (2007b) "Industrial Ecology", in D. Marinova, D. Annandale and J. Phillimore (eds) *The International Handbook of Environmental Technology Management*. Cheltenham: Edward Elgar, pp. 13–32.

Van Berkel, R., T. Fujita, S. Hashimoto and M. Fujii (2009a) "Quantitative Assessment of Urban and Industrial Symbiosis in Kawasaki, Japan", *Environmental Science & Technology* 43(5), pp. 1271–1281.

Van Berkel, R., T. Fujita, S. Hashimoto and Y. Geng (2009b) "Industrial and Urban Symbiosis in Japan: Analysis of the Eco-Town", *Journal of Environmental Management* 90, pp. 1544–1556.

van Leeuwen, M., W. Vermeulen and P. Glasbergen (2003) "Planning Industrial Parks: An Analysis of Dutch Planning Methods", *Business Strategy and the Environment* 12, pp. 147–162.

WBCSD (2000) *Corporate Social Responsibility: Making Good Business Sense*. Geneva: World Business Council for Sustainable Development.

—— (2001) *Sustainability through the Market: Seven Keys to Success*. Geneva: World Business Council for Sustainable Development.

—— (2002) *Innovation, Technology, Sustainability and Society*. Geneva: World Business Council for Sustainable Development.

Yoshida, F. (2005) "Case Studies of Environmental Politics in Japan", in M. A. S. Hidefumi Imura (ed.) *Environmental Policy in Japan*. Cheltenham: Edward Elgar, pp. 185–214.

3-3

Management of transboundary flows of recyclable end-of-life products and recovered by-products in Asia – A study of the construction of a win-win global recycling system between Japan and China

Kunishige Koizumi and Weisheng Zhou

3-3-1 Introduction

This study specifically considered the material circulation of international recyclable waste material as a global recycling system. The aim of the study was to assess the current global recycling system and develop a legal and safe material trading scheme between Japan and China so each nation can work towards having low carbon output.

The disposal of waste material requires a landfill site or an incineration treatment facility. Waste disposal has considerably high treatment costs, but waste material can also possess value as resource materials for reuse and/or recycling. Many in Japan consider waste material an unpleasant issue, regardless of whether it requires treatment. In contrast, many in China consider waste materials to have market value. In addition, globalization of what has been referred to the material "venous circulation system" (recycling) has come about (Koizumi, Zhou and Obata, 2003). Instead of a closed circulation system designed for Japan alone, Japan should consider establishing an open material circulation system between multiple trading nations.

If the trade in recyclable waste material can lead to a reduction in natural resource consumption, then a global recycling system will have met the goal of Japan's Fundamental Law for Establishing a Sound Material-Cycle Society (2000) as an instrument for achieving waste reduction. In Asia, recent reports have highlighted the issue of pollution by the treatment of electronic waste (e-waste). An example of this is the reclamation

Establishing a resource-circulating society in Asia: Challenges and opportunities, Morioka, Hanaki and Moriguchi (eds), United Nations University Press, 2011, ISBN 978-92-808-1182-7

of gold-bearing components (the process produces toxic fumes and water-polluting acid) from electric circuit boards, assembled home appliances or electrical instruments that are exported as second-hand commodities and/or components.

Japanese government policy on the issue of international trade in recyclable waste material is that it is controllable, and that natural resource consumption must be reduced in the region. One objection to this policy is that Japan should prohibit the trade of international waste material because pollution exports to developing countries can, at times, be secretive and uncontrollable (Citizens Against Chemical Pollution, 2005).

After 2005, Japanese recycling factories could not buy recyclable waste materials because Chinese buyers purchased them at higher prices, and some Japanese recyclers went bankrupt. Recently, however, Japanese waste materials have overflowed because the Chinese stopped buying them in the recession after the global financial crisis. This study considers new policy directions for the governments of both Japan and China regarding the construction of a sustainable material circulation system between the two countries as a countermeasure to increase recyclable waste material trade.

In addition, we discuss the export of large amounts of material waste from Japan to China, including wastepaper, polyethylene terephthalate (PET) bottles, electric appliances and pachinko machines (Japanese pinball and slot game machines). The term e-waste in this study refers to a category of electrical items that includes home and electric appliances, pachinko games machines with intact circuit boards containing rare metals such as platinum, cathode-ray tube (CRT) displays, liquid-crystal display (LCD) panels, steel components and finally non-steel metals, such as the copper wire found in motors, copper cords and aluminium heat-exchangers.

3-3-2 Definition and objective of a global recycling system

Objective of a global recycling system

Like many countries in Asia, China's rapidly growing economy requires various resources to meet industrial demands, both domestically and for producing products for export to world markets. Since 1998 China has imported recyclable waste material, which has included steel, copper, aluminium, plastics and wastepaper, for use as resources, with the amount increasing by 30 per cent per year. Many regions outside China handle material wastes through a mechanized process. In China there is a high recycling rate, largely due to a manual recycling process that is supported through the use of cheap migrant labour. Because Chinese recycling centres are able to employ rural migrant workers, the Chinese government has promoted the recycling industry as a way of securing employment for these workers. However, several challenging issues have periodically arisen in this industry, including the illegal export of waste material, illegal forms of waste treatment and employee health problems.

We hypothesize that the international trade in recyclable waste material, or the "global venous system" (waste → collection → recycling), developed naturally as the industrial commodities trade, or "global arterial system" (manufacturing → distribution → consumption), expanded towards various trading systems like the international division of labour. Specifically, because people of advanced countries had not developed ways to recycle wastes, and because the regulations governing the trade of recyclable wastes had not been studied, illegal exports and pollution problems arose. By formulating international rules for trading recyclable waste, a new recycling system incorporating the "global venous system" can be constructed (Koizumi, Zhou and Obata, 2003).

Definition of a global recycling system

Although regional factors are addressed in detail below, one of the four important factors for realizing a resource-circulating society and economy is the demand for recycled materials (ibid.). Recently, the treatment of waste generated over a wide area and between distant municipalities has generally been implemented from the viewpoint of high-level waste treatment and its increasing processing costs; an example is PCB (polychlorinated biphenyl) waste treatment facilities, of which there are only five in Japan. This affects the recycling system and wide-area recycling, as shown by the gradual introduction of the concept of the ecological industrial park where many environmental industries use locally accumulated technologies to reduce waste generation and increase waste recycling on site. As shown in Figure 3.3.1, we propose a global recycling system coupled to international trade that also considers local and wide-area recycling (ibid.).

The recycling of food waste and industrial wastes from industrial parks at the local and international levels and between municipalities involves spent batteries, old appliances and other waste materials, and represents a wide area of recycling. As a result of increased international trade, offshore production in Asia and imported commodities from the region, it is difficult to sell recycled materials on the Japanese market; these materials are typically incinerated or deposited in landfills. Consequently, global recycling is a realistic concept incorporating consumer countries that export end-of-life products and recyclable materials to producer countries that require materials. The material flow of the global recycling system concept is shown in Figure 3.3.2.

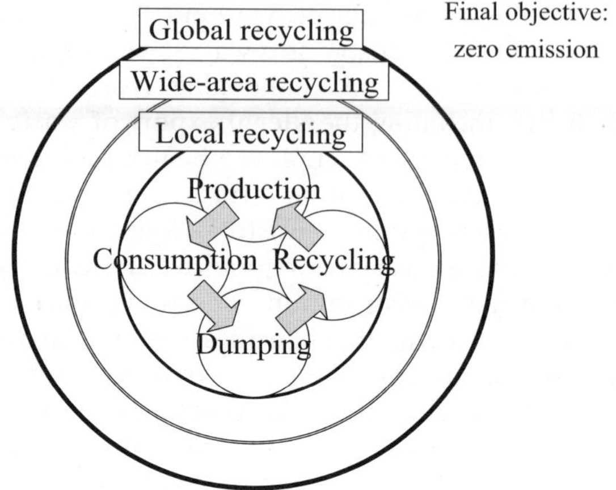

Figure 3.3.1 Concept of global recycling system A (area)

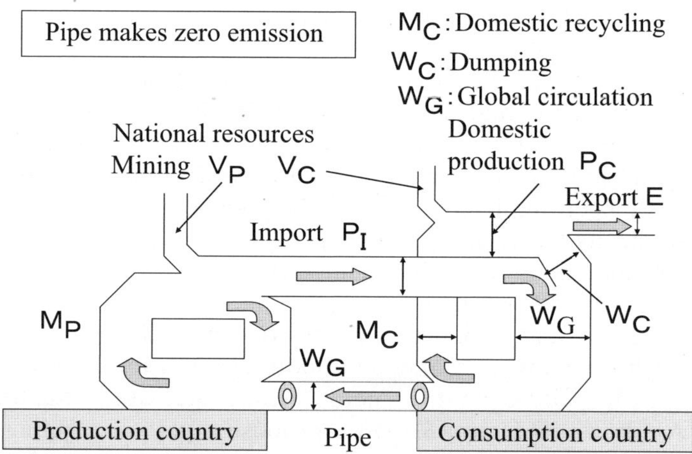

Figure 3.3.2 Concept of global recycling system B (material flow)

3-3-3 Current realities and issues in the Japanese recycling society

Enactment of Japan's Fundamental Law for Establishing a Sound Material-Cycle Society and other recycling laws

The amount of waste produced in Japan remained at high levels after the 1980s (the period of the bubble economy), with household waste produced at a rate of 50 million tonnes per year and industrial waste at 400 million tonnes per year. The recycling rate in 1996 remained at the level set by law (approximately 10 per cent of household waste and approximately 42 per cent of industrial waste). In 1978 the remaining availability of landfill space was estimated at just 8.8 years for household waste and 3.1 years for industrial waste. The Japanese government needed to enact policies to overcome the obstacles to construction of waste treatment facilities posed by the "not-in-my-backyard" mentality in communities, as well as the problem of illegal dumping. So Japan's Fundamental Law for Establishing a Sound Material-Cycle Society was enacted in 2000, designed to ameliorate the problems brought on by mass production and mass consumption and construct a sound material-cycle society with a low environmental impact in which natural resource consumption could be restrained and efficient use of materials and recycling, from production to distribution, could be promoted.

In 2000 Japan amended the Law for the Promotion of Effective Utilization of Resources and the Law for Promotion of Sorted Collection and Recycling of Containers and Packaging, which was known by its abridged name, the Containers and Packaging Recycling Law. Packaging includes PET bottles, aluminium cans, paper and plastic packs. The Home Appliance Recycling Law was enacted in 1998. This research reviews whether resource consumption was reduced after enactment of recycling laws, and examines how these laws and regulation of enterprises can be used to address the problems that have developed.

Current state of container and packaging recycling

Containers and packaging account for 61 per cent of household waste by volume and 24 per cent by weight, with the weight of discharge increasing slightly since the first enactment of the Containers and Packaging Recycling Law in 1995. The objective of such laws is to reduce the consumption of natural resources. As Figure 3.3.3 shows, household waste has not decreased, so the law has been criticized as having merely created a society based on mass production and mass recycling. This law was based on the extended producer responsibility (EPR) policy of the Organisation for Economic Co-operation and Development (OECD), which was drafted to address the waste problems of developed countries. The EPR policy states that a producer is just as responsible for waste treatment as it is for the production process (Research Group for Requesting Revision of the Law for Promotion of Sorted Collection and Recycling of Containers and Packaging, 2003).

Figure 3.3.4 shows the amount of PET bottles produced and collected in Japan for the period 1993–2005. It can be concluded that beverage

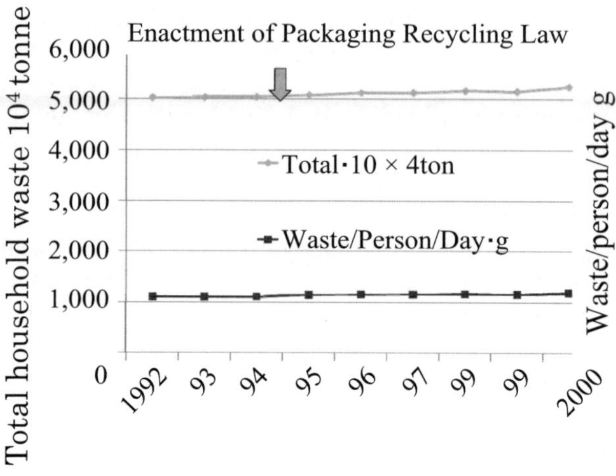

Figure 3.3.3 Total household waste production over time

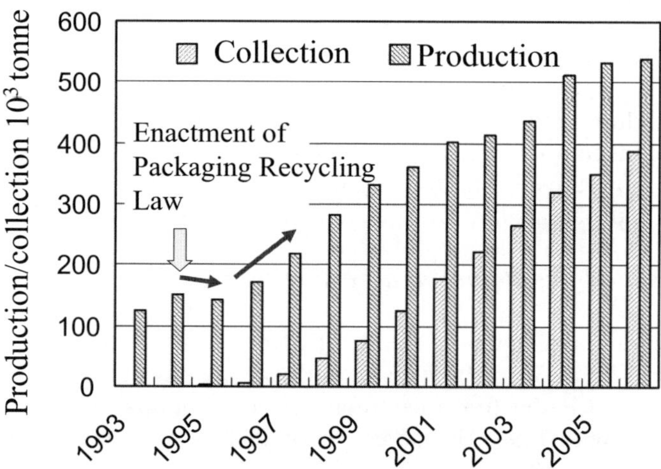

Figure 3.3.4 Annual PET bottle production in Japan

makers exercised some self-control to limit production before enactment of the Containers and Packaging Recycling Law, but after the law took effect the production of PET bottles increased rapidly. As a result, the law has been criticized for promoting an increase rather than a decrease in the consumption of one-way bottles (ibid.).

Local governments are charged with collecting household waste, which is primarily treated by incineration or deposited in landfills. The Containers and Packaging Recycling Law prescribes that producers must be charged with some of the recycling costs. However, collection accounts for 70 per cent of waste treatment costs and local governments are saddled with the greatest share. After one-time use, PET bottles are sorted and washed by the consumer, then collected by local governments using funds derived from taxes, at no cost to the producers. This system discourages the use of returnable glass bottles (reusable bottles), which could help reduce the consumption of natural resources.

Returnable bottles can be recycled after they have been used and re-used approximately 20 times. Producers using returnable bottles for beer, milk, soy sauce and Japanese sake pay the collection costs themselves. In contrast, liquid commodities packaged in single-use bottles are inexpensive and do not entail collection costs for the producer. Furthermore, commodities packaged in returnable bottles that entail collection costs to the producer are more expensive, which discourages consumers from buying them. Consequently, producers continue to resist using returnable bottles. Japan's Fundamental Law for Establishing a Sound Material-Cycle Society states that, of the "reduce, reuse, recycle" (3R) principles, "reduce" has the least adverse environmental impact. The current Containers and Packaging Recycling Law, which overly emphasizes "recycling" and underemphasizes "reduce" and "reuse" (return), is thus in serious need of review.

Current state of home appliance recycling

The Home Appliance Recycling Law (1998) applies to four appliance types: CRTs and televisions (TVs), air conditioners, refrigerators and washing machines. Its objective is to reduce natural resource consumption and, as a policy, to address the lack of landfill space. Despite the sheer volume of such waste and the difficulties associated with disassembly, it also sought to prevent the leakage of hazardous materials (such as lead) into the environment, and to recover the fluorocarbons used for insulation and as refrigerants in refrigerators and air conditioners, which damage the atmospheric ozone layer.

Under the principle of "let the polluter pay", this was the first law in Japan that placed the burden of recycling costs on the consumer of home appliances. Thanks to the principle of extending the producers' responsibility, by tasking them with the responsibility for physical recycling, the recycling rate has increased beyond the targets set in 2008 (50 per cent for refrigerators and 60 per cent for air conditioners) to 74 per cent for refrigerators and 89 per cent for air conditioners – demonstrating that this law has contributed to maximizing the utilization of natural resources (Association for Home Appliances, 2008).

The number of collected appliances has increased from $8,549 \times 10^3$ units in 2001 to $12,112 \times 10^3$ units in 2007. However, illegal dumping has increased somewhat, and the costs to local governments to deal with this problem have also increased, although the costs incurred by local governments for collection, recycling and final treatment have decreased dramatically. The law can be seen as mostly successful because it has had the effect of providing incentives to use environmentally friendly designs that minimize the size and weight of commodities and make for their easy disassembly. However, only 50 per cent of appliances are collected through designated recycling channels, and attention is being focused on the invisible flow of the remaining 50 per cent of appliances into other channels.

Current realities of pachinko machine recycling

Pachinko games machines are one of 35 designated commodities listed in the recycling guidelines of the Industrial Structure Council of the Ministry of Economy, Trade and Industry (METI) as requiring recycling, and producers and pachinko halls are expected to recycle the machines voluntarily. The target recycling rate has been set at 2.95 million pachinko machines and 1.63 million pachinko-slot machines annually. A total of 4.58 million machines (pachinko and pachinko-slot machines are referred to hereafter as pachinko machines) were operating in 2007, and a total of 4.91 million new machines are sold each year (Yano Research Institute, 2007).

Because of constant consumer demand for new games, the life cycle of a pachinko machine is only 0.9 years, and 5 million machines are discarded every year. After an illegal dumping incident in Tochigi prefecture in 2001, the Japan Pachinko Hall Association, organized by the pachinko industry, began to introduce voluntary collection and recycling channels to prevent illegal dumping. The association established Yuko Repro as a company specializing in pachinko machine recycling, and recycling facilities have been constructed in the Kitakyushu eco-industrial park and Saitama prefecture. In Japan there are two voluntary recycling channels for pachinko machines: Yuko Repro, and recycling plants that are registered with the Japan Pachinko Manufacturers Association.

Although the capacity of the Yuko Repro recycling plants is 2 million machines in Kitakyushu and 1.4 million in Saitama, totalling 3.4 million, only 1 million machines (20 per cent of the total discarded machines) are collected and recycled by Yuko Repro annually (ibid.). Furthermore, only 0.9 million machines (18 per cent) are collected and recycled by the plants registered with the Japan Pachinko Manufacturers Association, which estimates that approximately 3 million machines (60 per cent) are disposed of using other invisible channels. Some machines are partially rebuilt as part of producers' efforts towards environmentally conscious design, and the LCD panels and motors are also occasionally reused.

3-3-4 Circulation of recyclable waste between Japan and China

The previous section introduced the current recycling realities of PET bottles, home appliances and pachinko machines, and the fact that recycling rates currently exceed targets. However, some PET bottle recycling companies have gone into liquidation because they were unable to obtain the amount of waste materials expected to support business growth. Large amounts of PET bottle waste were being exported to China, and the current Containers and Packaging Recycling Law only applies to the circulation of recyclable waste within Japan.

The first waste problem to attract attention was wastepaper. Wastepaper was already widely utilized before the recycling laws were enacted, but increased exports of wastepaper from Japan to China have resulted in shortages of wastepaper in Japan. Subsequently, PET bottles and e-wastes such as home appliances and pachinko machines have become an issue. Each waste type presents unique problems because of the recycling situation in Japan, and we focus on these problems in the next subsection.

Wastepaper export to China

Figure 3.3.3 illustrates the problem that has arisen over time caused by the change in the amount of wastepaper exported. Before 1996 there was a glut of wastepaper on the market. However, between 1997 and 2000 most of this paper was exported to China, resulting in a shortage of wastepaper in Japan. Figure 3.3.5 shows the changes in waste collection and utilization rates in Japan after 1977. From the late 1970s to the late 1980s there were wastepaper surpluses due to increasing collection rates fostered by the group collection system promoted by municipal governments. At this time, collection rates increased and collection costs reduced with the cooperation of parent-teacher groups and informal children's groups (Koizumi, Zhou and Obata, 2004).

Because of delays in the development of good-quality paper with high recycled-paper content, and lack of effort on the part of producers to use recycled paper, there were wastepaper surpluses and wastepaper collection companies were near bankruptcy because they could only sell the collected waste at extremely low market prices. Local governments were

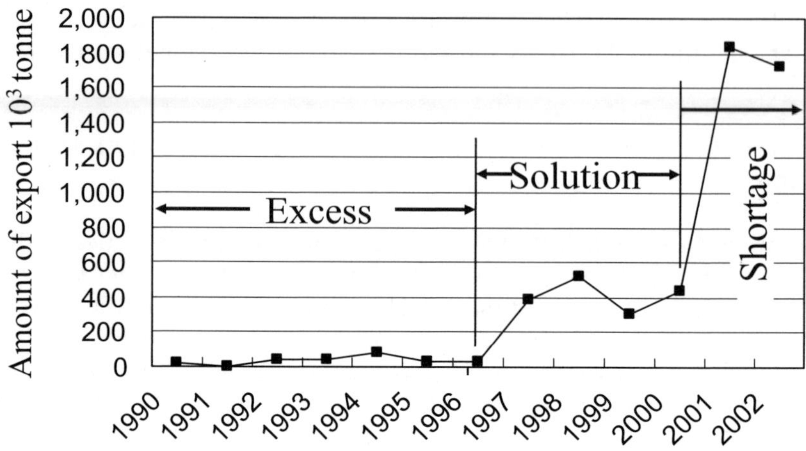

Figure 3.3.5 Transition of wastepaper exports from Japan
Source: Waste Paper Recycle Center.

forced to incinerate collected wastepaper because of the difficulties associated with selling it.

In an effort to facilitate the sale of wastepaper by collection companies to China, local governments supported the construction of warehouses at ports and exported wastepaper at low cost. As a result of these efforts, large amounts of wastepaper were exported to China after 1997, just as the nation's development was accelerating, and the surplus wastepaper problem was resolved. The collection companies recovered and the Japanese paper recycling system has continued to grow because of the demand from countries such as China. However, in 1999 the Green Purchase Law was enacted to promote the recycled commodities market, and as the quality of recycled paper and copy machines improved, many companies began to purchase recycled paper in increased amounts. As a result, the demand for wastepaper has increased in Japan.

However, with the growth of the Chinese economy and its increasing demand for paper to package the increasingly large amounts of clothing, household goods and food that country exports annually, wastepaper shortages have arisen in Japan since 2000. The price for wastepaper has risen considerably and Japanese paper makers find it difficult to buy wastepaper – even when they bid high – because Chinese buyers make higher offers. Consequently, a period of structural wastepaper shortages has begun.

Considering the CO_2 emissions caused by consumption of energy in transportation, one view is that export of wastepaper to China is not a good idea for preventing global warming. According to a life-cycle assessment simulation, which is an assessment tool that analyses the environmental load of a product throughout its entire life cycle, from natural resource extraction to production, usage and then waste processing, CO_2 emissions from paper production are higher than those associated with transportation. However, the use of Japanese wastepaper at Chinese paper plants, which emit more CO_2 as a result of their use of coal-powered generators, contributes less to mitigating global warming than using Japanese wastepaper at more energy-efficient Japanese paper plants (ibid.).

Wastepaper recycled into corrugated cardboard is used in returnable containers travelling between China and Japan. As of 2002, Japan is estimated to import approximately 770,000 tonnes of cardboard annually in the form of packaging for clothing, home appliances, fruit, vegetables and other products. Interestingly, much of that cardboard is destined to return to China in the form of wastepaper for further use as resources (Koizumi, 2004).

Export of waste PET bottles to China

There are two waste PET bottle collection routes in Japan: the bottlers' route (in which bottles are collected from containers next to vending machines) and the local route (in which bottles are sorted by citizens at home and collected by the local government).

According to research by the Japanese Council for PET Bottle Recycling, in 2008 571,000 tonnes of PET bottles were sold and 446,000 tonnes of waste PET bottles were collected (284,000 tonnes through local collection and 162,000 tonnes through the bottlers' collection route), which amounts to a collection rate of 77.9 per cent overall. Of this, 217,000 tonnes (38 per cent) went to domestic use, 268,000 tonnes (46.9 per cent) were exported and 86,000 tonnes (15.1 per cent) are unaccounted for. The share of exports to China was 94 per cent.

In 1995, when the Containers and Packaging Recycling Law took effect, PET bottles were considered nuisance waste and local governments paid for recycling treatment, the cost of which was decided by public bidding. However, with the entry of numerous new recycling companies into the business, the cost of recycling has decreased year on year and recycling treatment went from being a cost to being a source of income for local governments as the demand for recyclable waste resources in China increased. In other words, Japan had previously treated waste PET bottles as valueless nuisance materials to be disposed of at cost, while China has treated them as a desirable commodity and a valuable resource to be paid for. In both countries, the waste PET bottles are used as raw materials for textiles. Where Japanese recycling companies had invested in expensive machinery to produce high-quality textiles for workplace uniforms, Chinese recycling companies had invested in low-cost operations to make low-quality textiles for uses such as filler materials for stuffed toys. The phenomenon of being replaced by Chinese textile companies that employ low-paid workers has affected many textile companies around the world, including Japan, and is rapidly taking place in the venous system (waste treatment and recycling business). Prefectural governments were at first hesitant to sell to Chinese buyers, citing concerns about exporting garbage. However, most eventually relented, not only because of a desire to decrease public expenditure, but also to increase income. Currently, more than half the waste PET bottles collected by bottlers are sold to Chinese buyers, who offer premium prices.

Forced to purchase waste PET bottles at a higher price, several Japanese PET bottle recycling companies filed for liquidation or left the business. This, in turn, caused some worry that, if labour costs in China were to rise and Chinese companies stopped purchasing waste PET bottles from Japan, an overflow of waste PET bottles would result because so many Japanese recyclers had already left the business. With the global financial crisis of 2008–2009, Chinese companies actually did stop purchasing waste PET bottles and China's exports of items such as stuffed animals decreased dramatically. Japanese recycling companies are thus once again able to purchase waste PET bottles, but because of the economic recession the demand for recycled textiles has decreased and sales have declined – resulting in a recycling crisis caused by a currently ongoing surplus of waste PET bottles in Japan.

Current state of PET bottle recycling in China

Collection systems for household waste have not been formally established in China. Although discarded wastepaper, clothing, plastics and home appliances can be sold to recyclers as resources, the main collection system is one in which migrant workers from rural areas collect waste by going house to house on bicycle-drawn carts.

Although the figures are somewhat dated, approximately 220×10^3 tonnes of fibre were produced from waste PET bottles in China in 2002. Because of the rise in crude oil prices and increasing demand for PET bottles, 500 ml waste PET bottles were sold at a price of 2 jiao (around ¥3) per bottle to recyclers. The mean weight of a PET bottle is 28 grams, which translates to 36×10^3 bottles/tonne and $¥108 \times 10^3$/tonne (¥108/kg) (PWMI, 2009).

The maximum price for waste PET bottles purchased by Chinese buyers was $¥45 \times 10^3$ per tonne in 2008. In China the price of waste PET bottles had risen sharply, even with the added export transfer fee. The price of virgin PET reached ¥171/kg in 2007, and that of recycled PET flakes reached ¥100/kg (high-quality recycled PET flakes for fibre reached ¥125/kg). However, due to the global financial crisis, the price of virgin PET fell considerably to ¥65/kg and PET for fibre fell to ¥53/kg in November 2008. Furthermore, following the recent financial crisis, export demand has decreased due to the economic recession in advanced countries (MOE, 2009).

Although recycling laws such as the Japanese Containers and Packaging Recycling Law have not been enacted in China, the Circular Economy Promotion Law took effect in January 2009. Article 15 of the new law stipulates that regional governments must supply funds to promote recycling (NDL, 2009). The state established a list of "recycling-mandated products and packaging" that manufacturers must collect and recycle, or render harmless in cases where the product is technologically unsuitable or economically unfeasible for recycling. Thus it is expected that a recycling policy for packaging, including PET bottles, will be implemented in the near future.

Domestic recycling and export of e-waste to China

E-waste refers to waste electric home appliances and electronics or parts. Discarded home appliances include TVs, air conditioners, refrigerators and washing machines. Waste electronics are personal computers (PCs), electronic games, cellular phones and the electronic components of items such as pachinko machines. However, some items, such as electric cords, are not classified as e-waste as they are not covered by a strict definition. Many small-scale recyclers have formed recycling markets in countries such as China and the Philippines. Recyclers can earn a significant amount of money by removing expensive copper wire from the cords in e-waste and the radiation-condensing coils attached to TV CRTs. Copper and aluminium can be reclaimed from air-conditioner heat-exchangers and compressors, and gold from integrated-circuit chips soldered on to circuit boards can be reclaimed with strong acid, after which it will fetch a substantial price.

Problems caused by low recovery rates of waste home appliances and pachinko machines

Waste home appliances

Japan enacted the Home Appliance Recycling Law, but the collection rate for waste appliances is only 50 per cent using the burdensome collection channel designated by METI (the recycling fee is ¥2,520 for washing machines and approximately ¥4,830 for refrigerators). As a result,

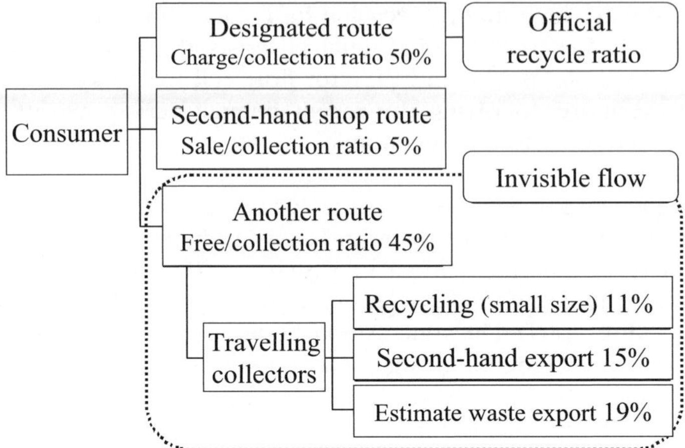

Figure 3.3.6 Flow of waste home appliances

invisible collection channels have become a problem, with waste appliances being collected as second-hand appliances or as recyclable materials by foreign enterprises that often produce pollution. As shown in Figure 3.3.6, the collection rate for waste appliances using unsanctioned channels is 50 per cent of a total 22.87 million discarded or used home appliances, according to an investigation by the Ministry of Environment in 2007 (METI Central Environment Council, 2007). Of these, 2.54 million units (11 per cent) were recycled by other recyclers; 1.02 million units (4.5 per cent) were sold as used appliances; 7.71 million units (33.7 per cent) were exported overseas as used appliances or recyclable materials; and 3.37 million units (14.7 per cent) passed through customs as exported used appliances. Thus 4.34 million units (7.71 million less 3.37 million, or 19 per cent) are estimated to have been exported as recyclable materials.

Yoshida and Terazono (2010) reported that 3 per cent of the TVs collected in Japan and exported to the Philippines were broken, but the remaining 97 per cent were in usable condition and were sold on the second-hand market. This indicates that exporters select only working TVs for export, because they intend to sell them. Their remaining operating life is short, but because exporters supply used TVs that are affordable to poor people, this export for reuse is recommended from the standpoint of the 3R principles.

In a research report issued by the Ministry of Internal Affairs and Communications (1998) prior to enactment of the Home Appliance Recycling Law, usable appliances made up 10–42 per cent of the waste appliances discarded for reasons other than mechanical breakdown, for example after buying a new larger-sized TV set or when moving house (air conditioners 42 per cent; TVs 12 per cent; refrigerators 10 per cent; washing machines 19 per cent).

In the ideal recycling scenario, all broken appliances in Japan would be recycled through the channel designated by METI, and operable appliances would be sold on the second-hand market. The Home Appliance Recycling Law dictates that recyclers must recycle all collected waste appliances, and prohibits them from selling usable units on the second-hand market. Under the current law, if consumers wish to reuse an appliance, they can choose to sell it at a recycling shop, or deliver it to a retail store for reuse free of recycling fees or to one of the private waste appliances collectors that make rounds through Japanese neighbourhoods by truck.

The number of units (4.34 million, 19 per cent) thought to be exported as recyclable resource materials is estimated by subtraction. In actuality, the exact number of waste appliances being exported has not been determined. However, field researchers have found Japanese waste appliances, as well as associated pollution, in countries such as China and the Philippines (Basel Action Network, 2001).

Let us consider the basic reasons why only 50 per cent of waste appliances were recycled at designated facilities. The first is that recycling fees are expensive. The second reason is that the current system is one in which fees are charged for disposal. If the system called for the recycling fee to be charged at the time of purchase, most people would choose the designated channel, and it is probable that only a few would use informal channels. The third reason is the existence of other informal-channel recyclers who charge lower fees – the minimum recycling rate provided by law or no fees at all; because they make rounds of residential neighbourhoods in collection trucks, they are very convenient. Choosing a cheap and convenient route over an expensive route for disposing of appliances is only natural. At the time of the enactment of the Home Appliance Recycling Law, as well as at a review five years later, home appliance manufacturers' associations objected to a system that would charge recycling fees at the time of purchase. Their objection centred on the question of who would pay the cost of recycling appliances that had been sold in the past. But as long as recycling fees continue to be charged at the time of disposal, flow to other channels cannot be avoided.

Waste pachinko machines

Pachinko machine production is an endemic industry in Japan: there is no pachinko machine trade and a venous system operates between Japan and China. According to a detailed report by the Chinese government on imported commodities covered under the Basel Convention (MOE, 2000), pachinko machines accounted for 7,844 tonnes of a total 19,292 tonnes, which amounts to a 41 per cent share. The total amount of export commodities designated by the Japanese government was 7,448 tonnes, but pachinko machines were not included (METI, 2004). The Chinese government has not reported the number of pachinko machines imported from Japan since 2001, when it listed such waste appliances and electric parts as materials prohibited for import. However, a TV programme claimed that pachinko machines had, in fact, been recycled in China, by first exporting the used machines to Hong Kong and then shipping them to the mainland. The existence of this underground channel has subsequently been confirmed (Yuko Repro, 2006).

The reason why many pachinko machines do not enter the voluntary pachinko machine recycling channel, like the home appliance recycling system, is that they can be sold to brokers at a higher price (ranging from ¥100 to approximately ¥8,000) than through the recycling and reuse route (where the price ranges from zero to approximately ¥4,000). The Chinese government does not permit importation of waste electric parts, but in the case of the Hong Kong channel, because pre-inspection before shipping is not required, brokers can import via Hong Kong and then transport inland to small-scale Chinese recyclers who earn money by scavenging and reselling motors, circuit boards, copper wire and plastics.

The problem of the Chinese prohibition on importing waste appliances and electric parts

The Chinese government classified waste appliances and electric parts as prohibited materials registered by the Basel Convention in 2001, and banned the importation of these goods after an environmental NGO successfully prosecuted a small-scale recycler for illegally dumping lead and plastic-residue-laden CRTs once the valuable components had been extracted. The Chinese government said the reason for the ban was that the technical level of small-scale recyclers and final treatment companies was low, and their awareness of environmental conservation was poor.

Before the Chinese government prohibited the import of waste electric appliances, several Japanese recycling factories had exported difficult-to-disassemble compressors (black motors) to Chinese recycling facilities, established partially with Japanese capital. At the time of the ban, copper for compressors and motors was not recycled into pure copper. Instead, it was mixed with iron for use as weights in heavy construction machinery, which caused a new problem: the Japanese recycling system was not decreasing copper consumption.

Securing rare metals and resource circulation between Japan and China

China has the largest number of rare metal (including rare earths) mining companies in the world, which means that it has an advantageous resource negotiating position and can use embargoes or export restrictions for rare metals to manipulate market prices. Rare metals are used in products such as fuel-cell batteries (lithium, neodymium, dysprosium, cobalt), catalysts in catalytic converters (platinum) and LCDs (indium).

Japan, which developed under the business model of importing resources from foreign countries and exporting value-added commodities, has begun to find it increasingly difficult to import rare metals. Yet significant amounts of rare metals remain embedded in the e-waste stockpiled in various cities, and the process of reclaiming these is now referred to as city or urban mining. Compared to production from natural mining, recycling rare metals from e-waste would reduce environmental loads and consumption of natural resources, conforming to the stipulations of the Fundamental Law for Establishing a Sound Material-Cycle Society.

Japan must now consider a resources security policy that can be implemented to secure rare metals and prevent flows outside the country, because the nation has negligible deposits of rare metals. While export for reuse remains acceptable, it is necessary to prevent e-waste exports through invisible channels. It is said that e-waste trade to China was previously motivated only by economical principles; now, however, this has moved to a new stage of assigning priority to resource security.

Home appliance recycling in China

Sales of home appliances in China have already exceeded those in Japan because of the rise in demand brought on by China's economic growth. It is important to understand home appliance recycling trends in China: if we are to construct a "win-win" resource circulation system between China and Japan, we must also construct a system that contributes to Chinese material recycling.

Approximately 182 million home appliances (TVs, washing machines, refrigerators, air conditioners and PCs) are produced and 28 million home appliances are disposed of in China annually (METI, 2005). The Chinese government is making efforts to enact a home appliances law for these five commodities and construct home appliance recycling facilities. Haier, a major home appliance manufacturer, has constructed a recycling facility in Qingdao, and the Tianjin city government has constructed a similar facility in Tianjin Ziya Environmental Protection Industry Park.

Plate 3.3.1 Second-hand appliance market, Tianjin
Note: Please see page 431 for a colour version of this image.

Although there are numerous rural areas where home appliances have not come into wide use, most appliances disposed of in urban areas are sold as second-hand products after undergoing maintenance. Furthermore, there are numerous used appliance markets in urban areas, as shown in Plate 3.3.1. The second-hand appliances used in urban areas are resold as third-hand appliances in rural areas. Thus the numbers of recycled appliances are small and there are few home appliance recycling facilities in operation at present. This situation can be expected to change in the near future, as significant numbers of appliances will soon reach the end of their service lives and will need to be disposed of.

3-3-5 Future of construction of a recyclable waste material circulation system between Japan and China

Wastepaper

Trade in wastepaper promoted by principles of economics and subject to market prices is an attractive prospect because it does not cause pollution in the importing countries. Recyclable waste trade should be treated as the globalization of the venous system, and we should consider wastepaper to be a resource traded at international market prices, much like the iron scrap that Japan imported from America and used to build its economic growth after the Second World War. Because the paper market in Japan is not expected to grow, Oji, a Japanese paper manufacturer, is constructing a new factory in suburban Shanghai. Both Japan and China must secure their supplies of wastepaper.

Here we consider the construction of a "win-win" wastepaper circulation system between Japan and China. The wastepaper collection rate in Japan is 63 per cent, which along with those of Korea and Germany is among the highest in the world. However, the collection rate in China is only 45 per cent. China can therefore gain insights from studies of the Japanese waste collection system. For example, in one incentive scheme, local governments coordinate mass wastepaper collection activities with parent-teacher groups and small youth organizations, and pay them a subsidy to increase their collection rates. Currently, Chinese wastepaper collection depends on small-scale, informal, private recyclers, but if local governments introduced mass collection, a sustainable wastepaper collection system could be constructed.

Waste PET bottles

Since the global financial crisis, because the demand for waste plastics in China has greatly decreased, Japanese PET bottle recyclers have be able to buy stocks readily. However, the recycled PET pellet market has contracted and sales have decreased, leaving governments with growing stockpiles of collected PET bottles that no longer have buyers. Thus it is realistic to say that the Japanese waste PET bottle recycling system has stopped functioning. Nevertheless, a sustainable way of recycling PET bottles is clearly desirable.

There are two PET bottle recycling channels: the designated channel (the Japan Containers and Packaging Recycling Association: JCPRA), and the self-reliance channel. The JCPRA invites bids for recycling cost (or purchase price) from recycling companies and buyers once a year. Beverage manufacturers pay the recycling cost, conforming to the extended manufacturers' responsibility principle (low risk, low return). By taking the self-reliance channel, local governments can negotiate the sales price with buyers individually. When waste PET bottles can be sold, they can make a profit, but if recycling costs are payable, they receive no contribution from beverage manufacturers (high risk, high return).

After the global financial crisis, the Japanese government demanded that the JCPRA should accept surplus waste PET bottles. Many local governments used this emergency system. In addition, emergency action to review the previous bidding price was taken for 2009 to prevent bank-ruptcy among recycling companies.

The designated recycling collection channel is more sustainable be-cause beverage manufacturers pay recycling costs when necessary. As many local governments have already expressed a wish to adopt this des-ignated channel after 2010, this waste PET bottle recycling system will be maintained.

Despite the need to emphasize the basic principles of Japan's Funda-mental Law for Establishing a Sound Material-Cycle Society, it continues to be more profitable under existing laws for Japan to continue mass pro-duction and mass disposal of PET bottles instead of using returnable bot-tles, and large amounts of one-way, single-use, high-quality PET bottles continue to be produced. The Japanese government must recognize the need for a faster way to achieve reductions in natural resource consump-tion. Unfortunately, the truth is that unless the recycling law is changed, incentives for producers to make reusable and returnable PET bottles rather than single-use PET bottles will not work.

It is therefore desirable for Japan to follow free market trade princi-ples in the area of recyclable waste, such as steel scrap. Also, Japan should change the policy that charges producers with collection costs for return-able PET bottles to reduce the production of single-use PET bottles. Some life cooperative associations (LCAs) are experimentally promoting returnable PET bottle usage because such bottles would reduce CO_2 emissions more effectively than one-use bottles. The LCAs believe we must do this in order to achieve greenhouse gas emission targets.

In constructing a "win-win" sustainable PET bottle circulation system between Japan and China, the country that introduces a returnable sys-tem first will take the initiative. Because realization of this system de-pends on drastic changes in society, rather than changes in technology, China, through government leadership, may accomplish this sooner than Japan.

Waste home appliances

We must consider the 50 per cent of appliances that go through the des-ignated home appliance recycling channel separately from those that go through other channels. When considering the construction of a "win-win" sustainable home appliance recycling system between Japan and China, we should note that the recycling rate for manual dismantling of difficult-to-dismantle parts, such as compressors and motors, by Chinese migrant workers from rural areas is higher than that of Japanese recy-cling facilities that depend on machine power. Considering the policy for reducing natural resource consumption in the Japanese Fundamental Law for Establishing a Sound Material-Cycle Society, recycling in China is more rational.

We recommend construction of a high-performance and pollution-free international recyclable waste circulation system through a work-dividing system using Chinese recycling facilities located in pubic recycling industrial parks, with the difficult-to-dismantle parts disassembled by Japanese home appliance recycling facilities. The business of manual dismantling of recyclable waste depends on cheap Chinese migrant labour, but as labour costs rise, the number of low-paid workers will decrease in the near future. However, home appliance recycling businesses will not disappear because they will form the foundation of a large number of recycling systems in the near future and must be encouraged to develop in this direction. The work-dividing system is a sustainable business model that promotes the technical transfer of home appliance recycling from Japan to China.

Japan's problem is that the excessive number of used home appliances diverted to foreign countries through invisible channels accounts for 50 per cent of the nation's discarded appliances, and this trade will not be eliminated simply by implementation of the joint circulation recycling system. To prevent the export of home appliance waste, the objectives of recycling and the recycling fee system must be radically changed from a disposal-pay system to a prepayment system. The total recycling cost for previously sold home appliances, if life cycles are 10 years, is estimated as ¥600 billion (approximately $6 billion) ([total annual appliance sales: 20 million units × mean recycling fee ¥3,000 = ¥60 billion/year] × [life cycle: 10 years]) and it is unrealistic to force producers to bear the cost of recycling alone, or to continue the current disposal-pay system.

Before enforcement of the Home Appliance Recycling Law, local governments bore the costs of collection, recycling and final treatment – a total that approximated the above calculation. After the law came into effect, local governments were exempted from paying these costs. Unless a new policy is introduced in which local governments contribute money to fund the conversion to a prepayment system, no such system will be implemented. Home appliance producers must accept that their responsibility for recycling also extends to appliances sold in the past, and adopt a realistic approach in which they will set aside funds to pay some of the expenses of a desirable new policy.

The Chinese home appliance recycling law is an intelligent policy that includes a prepayment system in which consumers pay recycling fees as costs incorporated into the sale price. Even though special circumstances exist in China, where selling waste home appliances on second-hand markets is currently more profitable to consumers than recycling them, Japan, which has allowed the continued diversion of such appliances into invisible channels, should learn from the Chinese system.

E-waste

We must consider how to deal with e-waste from the viewpoint of reduction of Chinese environmental pollution and Japan's rare metals resource security. Due to low domestic recycling rates, it is clear that e-waste is primarily being exported to other nations where recyclers recover gold and other high-value metals from PCBs. However, because such recycling makes no contribution to reducing resource consumption and often contributes to serious environmental pollution, we must prevent e-waste exports that are based solely on market principles. By doing so, we can also prevent the secondary export of rare metals to other countries.

To build a "win-win" sustainable e-waste resource circulation system between Japan and China, Japanese electronic companies must have facilities in China and should construct a recycling system in China for defective PCBs. Dowa Metals & Mining is currently building a recycling plant for waste PCBs in China and transferring reclamation technologies for rare metals.

Yuko Repro, the pachinko machine recycling company, already exports and recycles dismantled electrical cords from waste machines in China. Thus the first circulation pipeline between Japan and China has already been connected. However, systems for recycling e-waste other than electrical cords have not yet been constructed because of Chinese laws restricting imports of e-waste. The construction of a work-dividing recycling system between Japanese recycling factories and Chinese public recycling facilities is desirable. However, while the Chinese government prohibits the import of e-waste, it does allow imports to recycling facilities in municipal eco-industrial parks if technology transfer is included. This provides an opportunity for a "win-win" sustainable resource circulation system for e-waste to be constructed between Japan and China.

3-3-6 Conclusion

The current export of wastepaper to China from Japan contributes to the effective use of natural resources. In constructing a "win-win" global recycling system between Japan and China, the Japanese collection system for wastepaper is superior to the Chinese system, and the transfer of know-how about Japanese mass collection to China is a good first step.

Regarding the trade of waste PET bottles, both Japan and China must change from single-use bottles to a returnable (reuse) system in order to

Table 3.3.1 Considerations of a "win-win" global recycling system between Japan and China

Recycled item	Factors
Wastepaper	Transfer Japanese mass collection system to China
Waste PET bottles	Change to a returnable system as soon as possible
E-waste	Develop a collaboration system between Japanese home appliance and pachinko machine recycling facilities and Chinese public or designated private recycling facilities Adopt China's prepayment system for home appliance recycling in Japan

comply with the basic premise of a recyclable society. Neither Japan nor China has any experience with such a system, so neither has the know-how to share with the other. The Chinese government currently prohibits the import of e-waste, such as waste home appliances and pachinko machines. To increase the reclamation of material resources, the development of a collaborative system between Japanese home appliance and pachinko machine recycling facilities and the Chinese public or designated private recycling factories is desirable. China will avoid adopting the inherent weaknesses of Japan's Home Appliance Recycling Law by rejecting the disposal-pay recycling system and instead adopt a prepayment system with the fee incorporated in the sale price. Japan must learn from the strengths of the Chinese system.

Table 3.3.1 shows the conclusions discussed above.

REFERENCES

Association for Home Appliances (2008) "Transition of Recovery Ratio of Each Appliance", in *Handbook of Home Appliances*. Tokyo: Association for Home Appliances, p. 116.

Basel Action Network (2001) "Exporting Harm: The High-Tech Trashing of Asia"; available at www.ban.org/E-waste/technotrashfinalcomp.pdf.

Citizens Against Chemical Pollution (2005) "Problem of 3R Initiative and the Ministerial Conference on the 3R Initiative"; available at www.ne.jp/asahi/kagaku/pico/basel/G8_3R/G8_3R.html.

Koizumi, K. (2004) "The Structure of Production System Involving Global Resources Circulation", *Study of Industrial Management* 18, pp. 124–128 (in Japanese).

Koizumi, K., W. Zhou and N. Obata (2003) "Global Recycling System of Waste: Case Study on the Recycling of Home Appliances in Asia", *Policy Science: Ritsumeikan University* 11(1), pp. 43–49 (in Japanese).

——— (2004) "Economical and Environmental Assessment of Wastepaper Export", *Policy Science: Ritsumeikan University* 11(2), pp. 35–44 (in Japanese).

METI (2004) "Realization of Sustainable Material Circulation Economics and Society in Asia. Commodities Exported from Japan Applied Basel Convention", Reference Paper 14; available at www.meti.go.jp/policy/recycle/main/3r_policy/policy/pdf/grobal/ref_14.pdf.

——— (2005) "Research Paper on the Increasing of Modern Activity Technology and Globalization of Recycling System of Enterprises", Mitsubishi Research Institute; available at www.meti.go.jp/policy/recycle/main/data/research/h16fy/161012-3_mri_0.pdf.

METI Central Environment Council (2007) "Estimation of Waste Home Appliance Flow", Reference Paper 3; available at www.meti.go.jp/committee/materials/downloadfiles/g70928c04j.pdf.

Ministry of Internal Affairs and Communications (1998) "Research on Trend in Consumer Consciousness on Consumption", October; available at www.esri.cao.go.jp/jp/stat/shouhi/quarter/19990129shouhi/19990129shouhi2.html#7.

MOE (2000) "On the Current Data of Law of Hazardous Waste Exporting/Importing Limitation"; available at www.env.go.jp/recycle/yugai/h12_jokyo/jyoukyo-s.pdf.

——— (2009) "Transition of Price and Quantities of Recyclable Waste Resources"; available at www.env.go.jp/council/04recycle/y040-49/mat02.pdf.

NDL (2009) "Information of Enactment, the Circular Economy Promotion Law in China", National Diet Library; available at www.ndl.go.jp/jp/data/publication/legis/23701/02370109.pdf.

PWMI (2009) "Current State of Plastics Recycling in China", Plastic Waste Management Institute Public News; available at www.pwmi.or.jp/public/news200903.html.

Research Group for Requesting Revision of the Law for Promotion of Sorted Collection and Recycling of Containers and Packaging (2003) "Problem of Law for Promotion of Sorted Collection and Recycling of Containers and Packaging, Citizens Research Group"; available at www.citizens-i.org/reuse/matigai.html.

Yano Research Institute (2007) *Trend and Market Share of Pachinko Game Machine Producers*. Tokyo: Yano Research Institute (in Japanese).

Yoshida, A. and A. Terazono (2010) "Reuse of Secondhand TVs Exported from Japan to the Philippines", *Waste Management* 30(6), pp. 1063–1072.

Yuko Repro (2006) "Why Recycle? Pollution in China Caused by Waste Pachinko Game Machines"; available at www.yuko-repro.co.jp/contents/index.php?PHPSESSID=746566107a5efa2738e64c0ebca0d960.

3-4

National policies and international initiatives for sustainable management of waste and resources

Yuichi Moriguchi

3-4-1 Introduction

In today's industrialized society, people are increasingly seeking affluence. In December 1994 the Japanese government established the Basic Environment Plan, which follows the provisions of the Basic Environment Law promulgated in 1993. This plan outlines the overall and long-term policies of the government regarding environmental conservation. In its foreword, the plan recognized that socio-economic activities based on "mass production, mass consumption and mass disposal" were common driving forces behind various environmental problems. The transition from such a society to a sound material-cycle society (SMCS) has been one of the top priorities of the Japanese environmental policy agenda.

At the international level, "sustainable consumption and production (SCP)" is recognized as one of the core elements necessary to achieve sustainable development. However, the recent rapid growth of Asian economies has led to an increase in the demand for primary and secondary material resources. In addition to the external cost of environmental degradation related to extensive resource use, the supply of resources itself is regarded as a significant economic issue and is also linked to the social dimension of sustainable development; that is, the equity of resource use across regions and generations. The efficient use of material resources is thus relevant to the full scope of sustainability in its environmental, economic and social dimensions; the SMCS, which integrates environmentally sound management of solid wastes and efficient use of

Establishing a resource-circulating society in Asia: Challenges and opportunities, Morioka, Hanaki and Moriguchi (eds), United Nations University Press, 2011, ISBN 978-92-808-1182-7

material resources, is increasingly expected to provide a long-term vision for society within the broader context of sustainable development.

In this chapter, recent conceptual and practical progress in national policies and international initiatives for sustainable management of resources and wastes will be highlighted. Even though some do not directly focus on Asia, but rather on Japan or its involvement in international activities, lessons learned by Japanese cases and international initiatives have implications for Asia.

3-4-2 Broader scope of a resource-circulating society – A conceptual discussion for sharing a common vision of a "circular society" in Asia

Environmentally sound material cycle, waste, resources and life cycles

The Japanese phrase *junkan-gata-shakai*, which literally means "circular society" (CS), is officially translated by the Japanese government as "sound material-cycle society"; previously it was translated as "recycling-based society". It is not easy to find a perfectly suitable English translation of this key phrase, which is one of the core concepts of recent Japanese environment policy.

During the evolution of Japanese environmental policy, the CS concept was first introduced primarily to support the reduction of solid wastes requiring treatment, because Japan faced a shortage of waste disposal capacity. In this context, recycling was one of the most practical measures to be taken, and this is why the English translation "recycling-based society" was initially adopted. However, recycling is not the ultimate goal of a CS; rather, it is just one of the key measures necessary to accomplish the ultimate goal.

Nevertheless, waste separation by consumers for recycling is a visible and easy-to-understand action, and its promotion has been successful not only in reducing actual amounts of waste but also in highlighting ongoing needs to improve traditional wasteful consumption patterns. The principle of "reduce, reuse, recycle" (3R) has become an alternative key phrase aimed at extending the scope of a "recycling-based society" to incorporate measures that prevent waste generation.

One of the most essential features of the SMCS and 3R is to provide a chance of linking downstream waste issues with upstream resource issues. Waste and resource issues are often discussed separately because they are managed by different authorities, handled by different industries and

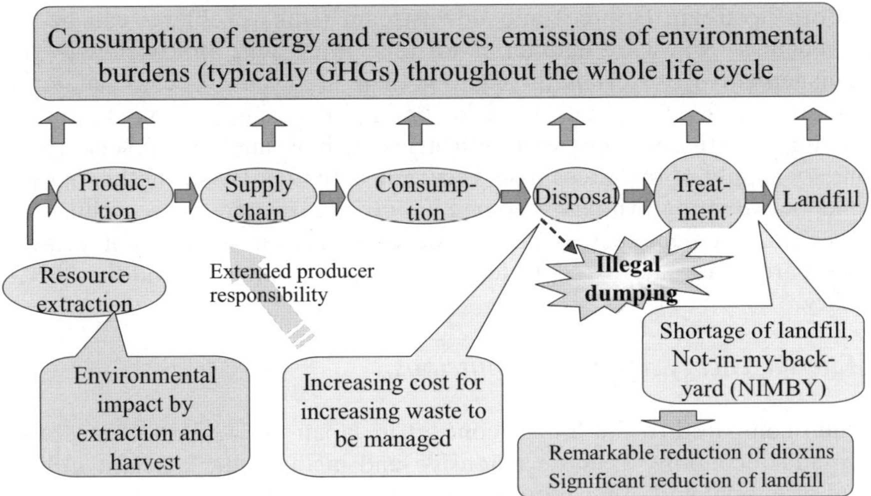

Figure 3.4.1 Environmental implications of mass production and mass consumption

studied by different schools. Japanese environmental policy did not explicitly address the reduction of natural resource use before the enactment of the Fundamental Law for Establishing a Sound Material-Cycle Society in 2000: Japanese resource supply is highly dependent on imports, and the possible negative environmental impacts associated with the extraction and harvesting of natural resources in foreign countries were mostly outside the scope of Japan's environmental policy. The SMCS, at least conceptually, incorporates the indirect impacts of our socio-economic activities in these upstream areas.

Furthermore, the combination of upstream and downstream problems makes it easier to maintain an awareness of the relevant issues throughout full product life cycles. A typical example is the emission of greenhouse gases throughout the life cycle of a product, as shown in Figure 3.4.1.

Currently, it is widely understood that waste minimization is not only useful to prevent environmental burdens associated with waste treatment processes, but also to reduce the amounts of resource consumption and problems associated with the life cycle of the resources used. The amount of solid waste generated by material resource consumption is often interpreted as a symbolic indicator of a society's affluent consumption pattern. Prevention of waste generation contributes to resource conservation, and a reduction in resource consumption contributes to the prevention of waste generation. This fundamental logic is why "reduce" is positioned as the first of the "Rs" in the 3R principle.

Both upstream (source) and downstream (sink) problems can be resolved in a "win-win" manner if we take integrated approaches to the management of materials throughout their life cycles. Because material resources such as metal ores are becoming increasingly scarce, there is a greater incentive for upstream industries, such as smelters, to seek a secondary supply of resources from recycling activities. By strengthening the links between the primary resource supply sectors and the recycling and waste management sectors, both resource supply and waste management issues are better addressed. Indeed, this is the rationale behind the SMCS policy.

Material, energy and GHG emissions

When compared to the SMCS concept in Japan, the Chinese concept of "circular economy" is more extensive and includes the efficient utilization of energy and other natural resources. As mentioned above, the Japanese CS policy originated from problems associated with the mass disposal of solid waste, which has meant that the issue of "solid materials" has been the primary target. However, the mass production and mass consumption of materials are also associated with extensive energy consumption, which almost inevitably accompanies extensive CO_2 emissions. The production of steel and cement for infrastructure projects in developing economies is a typical example. Thus even when narrowly defined, as with the SMCS, the CS is closely associated with the low-carbon society (LCS) concept and low energy consumption. In 2008, five years after the adoption of the first SMCS plan, the fundamental plan for establishing an SMCS in Japan was revised. The revised plan addresses the need for integrating the SMCS and LCS; consequently, a new indicator with a numerical target directed at measuring reductions in CO_2 emissions from the waste management sector was introduced.

Numerous linkages between material and energy use have been identified, and a common framework of material and energy flow analysis has been applied to describe both from a methodological perspective. The majority of raw material industries are both energy and carbon intensive, which implies that any reduction in raw material consumption through the application of the 3R principle contributes to mitigating greenhouse gas (GHG) emissions. There are numerous opportunities to obtain a win-win relationship between resource and energy saving by means of 3R activities. However, some of the technologies used for GHG mitigation may result in a trade-off with resource savings. The increasing demand for rare metals used in highly energy-efficient technologies is a typical example.

Recyclables and renewables

In the context of low-carbon energy, use of biotic resources is attracting increasing attention. Energy recovery from biotic wastes such as construction and demolition wood, animal faeces and organic sludge has been examined and implemented within the scope of effective waste utilization. Energy generation using wood may also be included in an extended scope of sound material cycles. Biofuels made from crops for automobile use have also attracted considerable attention. However, these fuels should be subjected to careful sustainability assessments, as several potential problematic issues have been identified (Searchinger et al., 2008).

In addition to the use of biotic resources, low-carbon energy technologies such as photovoltaic and wind power generation are included in renewable resources. In SMCS planning discussions, these renewable energy technologies are often mentioned because the use of "natural" energy appears to be compatible with the broader conceptual understanding of resource cycles. The original narrower scope of sound material cycles focused primarily on recyclable materials, but a broader CS scope may include renewable energy technologies and renewable material resources. Since both recyclable materials and renewable energy are regenerative, they mesh well with the concept of a circulative and sustainable society. There have been numerous proposals to add other "Rs" to the current 3R principle, with "renewable" considered a good candidate for inclusion.

More integrative view towards an environmentally sustainable society

Japan's Strategy for a Sustainable Society, which was adopted by a cabinet decision in June 2007, proposed the integration of three aspects of a sustainable society. In addition to the concepts of SMCS and LCS, the concept of a "society in harmony with nature" was introduced as the third aspect. Essentially, the primary aim is to enjoy and pass on nature's endowments. In order to realize a society in harmony with nature, sound management of land and ecosystems is required, and harvesting of biotic resources should not conflict with this central requirement.

This integrative view of three aspects is compatible with a CS in a very broad sense, moving towards an environmentally sustainable society. To achieve this vision, sustainable management of natural resources including metals, minerals and natural biomass, as well as natural capital inputs such as land and ecosystems, is critical.

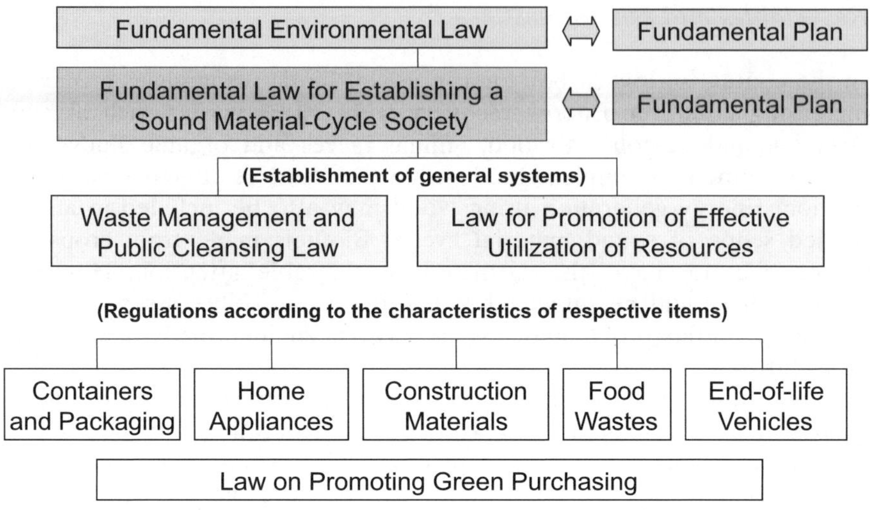

Figure 3.4.2 Structure of laws for a sound material-cycle society

3-4-3 Japanese experience in the implementation of policies for a sound material-cycle society

Legislative framework of SMCS policy

Despite the possible conceptual extension of CS as discussed above, the actual coverage of Japanese SMCS policies is rather limited because of the positioning of the SMCS in the overall hierarchy of Japanese environmental policy. The Fundamental Law for Establishing a Sound Material-Cycle Society enacted in 2000 provides a conceptual basis and framework for SMCS policies, and the Fundamental Plan for Establishing a Sound Material-Cycle Society set the direction of national efforts. The first plan was formulated in 2003 and the second was promulgated in 2008 (Figure 3.4.2).

The fundamental law defined a principle to prioritize methods of handling products, waste and recyclables. First priority was given to "reduce" or prevention, then to "reuse" and "recycle", followed by energy recovery. Only if these "cyclical uses" are impossible can the waste be disposed of. Despite the application of this principle, recycling often attracts greater attention. This is because several individual recycling laws for specific products and sectors were enacted – a number of them even before the fundamental law. A typical case is the Containers and Packaging Recycling Law, which was enacted in 1995 and has been enforced since 1997.

Indicators, target setting and annual review of the plan

In the first Fundamental Plan for Establishing a Sound Material-Cycle Society, a set of three economy-wide material flow indicators was introduced, and numerical targets were set for each. One of the indicators selected was resource productivity (RP), expressed as GDP per unit of direct material input. The adopted target for this indicator was set as a 40 per cent improvement between 2000 and 2010. The other two indicators were the rate of cyclical use of materials and the total amount of solid waste at final disposal (i.e. landfill). These three indicators capture the inflows, cyclical flows and outflows of materials.

Effort indicators and targets were also set in order to review the achievements of entities such as businesses, citizens, non-profit organizations (NPOs) and non-governmental organizations (NGOs), as well as local and national governments.

These indicator sets and their targets were adopted to facilitate the mandated annual quantitative review of the plan. At the time of the annual review of the first plan, it was found that the improvement in the RP indicator had been significantly affected by decreased construction demand. To reduce this influence, another RP indicator excluding construction minerals was introduced, along with targets, in the second plan. RP in terms of fossil-fuel resources was also added to monitor the trends. Figure 3.4.3 shows the trends of these three RP indicators. There are

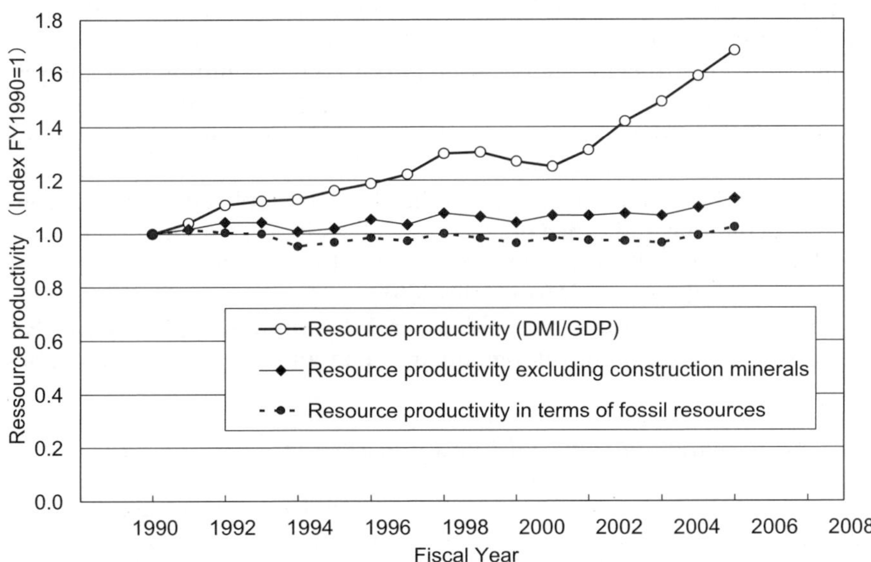

Figure 3.4.3 Trends of resource productivity indicators

significant differences between the trends. In particular, RP in terms of fossil-fuel resources does not show improvement. This unfavourable trend is consistent with the fact that Japanese CO_2 emission reduction over the last two decades has not been successful. Unfortunately, so far the improvement in overall resource productivity has not led to a reduction of CO_2 emissions.

Stakeholder practices have also been reported to the annual review process. It was recognized that the dissemination of reliable information has become a fundamental requirement for collaboration among the multiple stakeholders. Even in Japan, the statistical basis required for backing up such policy-relevant information has been insufficient. Internationally, the availability of quantitative data for solid waste management and recycling processes is considerably more limited, particularly in developing countries. This is a fundamental challenge for Asian countries in strengthening the environmentally sound management of solid waste.

3-4-4 Recent international initiatives and Japanese contributions towards resource productivity/efficiency

Progress and policy-relevant use of material flow analysis

The flows of material resources, products and wastes have been intensively studied over the last decade in order to characterize the physical dimensions of the economy. Some of these studies were directed at establishing targets for the sustainable use of material resources. From an academic viewpoint, recent studies on material flow accounting and analysis (MFA) may be seen as a reinvention, because MFA is based on a well-known, simple and generic methodological adaptation of mass balance or the mass conservation principle. Nevertheless, considerable progress in the area of MFA has been made regarding its application to environmental, economic and other policies, as well as in the compilation of data by official statistical institutions, in attempts to enhance the relevance of this system-analytic tool (Moriguchi, 2007).

This section reviews recent progress in MFA and its application to RP indicators, focusing on developments in Japan and intergovernmental activities.

OECD activities on material flows and resource productivity

The year 2003 was a significant milestone for policy-relevant uses of MFA and RP indicators. In Japan, the first fundamental plan for an SMCS including a set of MFA indicators was adopted. In parallel with this progress at the national level, the Japanese government took a leading role in an international policy forum when environment ministers of the

G8 nations and the European Commission met in April 2003. During this meeting, a communiqué was adopted that included a paragraph related to sustainable production and consumption:

> We recognize that it is essential to improve resource productivity. In that regard, we note with interest Japan's proposal to launch an international joint research project on economy-wide material flow accounts to develop a common measurement system of material flow, building on existing work at international level. (G8 Environment Ministers, 2003)

In June 2003 G8 leaders confirmed the leadership role of the Organisation of Economic Co-operation and Development (OECD) in the research and development of RP and MFA. In response to this request, the OECD's first council recommendation for material flows and resource productivity was adopted in 2004, and the second recommendation on resource productivity was adopted in 2008.

After the adoption of the first recommendation, two working groups under the OECD Environmental Policy Committee played major roles in promoting MFA activities in member countries. They covered both the supply and the demand sides of material flow studies.

Four documents were published in 2008 as the major outputs of the first phase of OECD MFA-related activities: a synthesis report, an OECD guide, a volume on the accounting framework and an inventory of country activities. These documents are useful references to support compilation and policy-relevant use of MFA not only in OECD member countries but also in non-member countries (OECD, 2008).

OECD initiative on sustainable materials management

In parallel with the work on material flows and RP, the OECD initiated work on sustainable materials management (SMM), based on the OECD working definition of SMM: "SMM is an approach to promote sustainable materials use, integrating actions targeted at reducing negative environmental impacts and preserving natural capital throughout the life-cycle of materials, taking into account economic efficiency and social equity." The origin and coverage of issues by SMM are fundamentally consistent with the SMCS in Japan.

Convergence of concepts and practices towards resource efficiency

In April 2008 the Conference on Resource Efficiency was co-organized by the OECD and UN Environment Programme (UNEP) in Paris. The conference brought together relevant ministers, senior government officials, experts, businesses and NGOs from around the world. The participants affirmed the importance of sharing the best practices on national initiatives and continuing efforts to improve resource efficiency. Co-chairs of the conference concluded that several different concepts and approaches were converging:

- reduce, reuse, recycle (3R); sound material-cycle society (SMCS)
- circular economy
- integrated or sustainable waste management
- sustainable consumption and production
- life-cycle management
- sustainable materials and resource management.

All of these aim at similar objectives and require similar actions by the various stakeholders. A major part of the concept and practices represented by the term "resource-circulating society" in this volume is also convergent with these concepts and approaches.

Establishment of the International Panel for Sustainable Resource Management

In MFA studies, attention has primarily been directed at the size of material flows. The RP indicator, in its simplest form, measures all resources by a single unit of physical weight without considering the differences in the environmental impact of specific resources. Although "dematerialization" is a simple, robust and easy-to-understand message, we need to prioritize the kinds of material/resource use that need to be reduced based on reliable scientific knowledge.

Based on a proposal by the European Commission, the International Panel for Sustainable Resource Management was established in November 2007, with UNEP assuming the role of secretariat. The overall objective of the panel is to provide independent, coherent and authoritative scientific assessments of policy relevance on the sustainable use of natural resources, in particular their environmental impacts over the full life cycle, and to contribute to a better understanding of how to decouple economic growth from environmental degradation.

Several experts from Asia participate in the panel. Its outputs are expected to support the transition towards a resource-circulating society.

3-4-5 Strengthening networks to exchange practical experience and knowledge for a resource-circulating society

Efforts for 3R by international organizations and Japan

Japan has experienced serious waste management problems, such as shortages of final disposal sites and large-scale illegal dumping. Due to policy reforms implemented to resolve these problems, Japan is currently a leader in the establishment of the SMCS. Given the nation's success in this regard, the Japanese government proposed the 3R Initiative at the G8 Sea Island Summit in 2004. This initiative was directed at the international promotion and establishment of the SMCS through 3R activities. Building on this proposal, the Ministerial Conference on the 3R Initiative was convened in Tokyo in April 2005 to launch the initiative (MOE, 2009), and several high-level meetings have been organized and held under this initiative to date.

Japan has been supporting activities in the Asian region since the launch of the 3R Initiative. This includes assisting countries in developing their own 3R plan or strategy and providing information on 3R systems, technologies and experience. Such activities have laid the groundwork for the establishment of an SMCS on an Asian scale.

To promote this idea, the Asia 3R Conference was convened in Tokyo in 2006 and in 2008, with the participation of 19 Asian countries, a number of G8 members and international organizations. The conferences provided a platform to share each country's experiences and lessons learned, discuss national and international 3R strategies, exchange views on specific issues (municipal organic waste, medical waste, e-waste, etc.) and facilitate regional cooperation.

Based on these activities, the Kobe 3R Action Plan was adopted at the G8 environment ministers' meetings during the Japanese G8 presidency in 2008. The action plan referred explicitly to the need to support capacity development in developing economies. It also encourages each country to set RP and other targets. An outline of the plan is shown in Table 3.4.1.

Sharing practical experiences for 3R in Asia

To support 3R policies and practices in Asia, a comprehensive report was compiled by the Asian Development Bank (ADB) and the Institute for Global Environmental Strategies (2008). It is intended to provide guidance to policy-makers in the developing countries of Asia and the Pacific regarding the economic and environmental significance of resource efficiency, and describe options for encouraging efficiency improvements. The report also provides practical and useful examples, quantitative data and inputs from subregional workshops in South and Southeast Asia.

A joint regional knowledge hub on 3R was initiated by the ADB, the Asian Institute of Technology, the UNEP Regional Resource Centre for Asia and the Pacific and the UN Economic and Social Commission for Asia and the Pacific.

Most recently, a high-level 3R seminar on Asia was held in Tokyo in March 2009, attended by senior government officials of 11 Asian

Table 3.4.1 Outline of Kobe 3R Action Plan

I. Prioritize 3R policies and improve resource productivity
1. Prioritize implementation of 3R policy
2. Improve resource productivity and set targets
3. Pursue co-benefits between the 3Rs and GHG emission reductions
4. Promote science and technology and create a market for 3R-related products
II. Establishment of an international sound material-cycle society
1. Collaborate to promote sound international resource circulation
2. Promote international trade of 3R-related materials, goods and products
III. Collaborate for 3R capacity development in developing countries
1. Promote collaboration with developing countries
2. Promote technology transfer, information sharing and environmental education
3. Promote partnership between stakeholders
IV. Follow-up on G8 activities based on the action plan

countries, nine international organizations and experts on 3R and sustainable resource management from around the world. During this event, the establishment of a regional 3R forum in Asia for the facilitation of policy dialogues on 3R issues and providing a platform for functions supporting the adoption of 3R in Asia was proposed and agreed. The first forum met in November 2009.

As mentioned previously, reliable quantitative data for capturing the state of the resource use and waste management are essential to supporting policies and practices involving resource circulation. Transboundary flows of primary and secondary resources are likely to increase further as Asian economies increase in size. However, as exemplified by the invisible flows of end-of-life products discussed in Chapter 3-3, there are significant gaps in the availability of reliable data. Consequently, efforts directed at improving environmental and resource accounting at both national and international levels should also be strengthened.

3-4-6 Conclusion

The case of a Japanese SMCS is a unique example of putting the concept of a resource-circulating society into practice by national policies. As in the case of progress in MFA and its application to RP indicators, there is room for experts to play catalytic roles in the domestic policy planning process as well as in dissemination of national experiences to other countries through international initiatives.

Cooperative efforts by experts and policy-makers through recent initiatives, including those focusing on Asia, demonstrated that an integrated approach linking upstream resource issues and downstream waste issues through 3R or the circular economy/society concept attracts increasing attention to the more sustainable management of materials. The exchange of data, knowledge and practical experiences in the field of resource and waste management is a fundamental step for realizing the concept of a resource-circulating society.

REFERENCES

Asian Development Bank and Institute for Global Environmental Strategies (2008) *Toward Resource-Efficient Economies in Asia and Pacific*. Manila and Hayama: ADB/IGES.

G8 Environment Ministers (2003) "Communiqué", Paris, 27 April; available at www.g8.fr/evian/english/navigation/news/previous_news/ministerial_meetings _communiques/g8_environment_ministers_meeting_in_paris_on_25__26 _and_27_april_2003.html.

MOE (2009) *The World in Transition and Japan's Efforts to Establish a Sound Material-Cycle Society, 2008*. Tokyo: MOE.

Moriguchi, Y. (2007) "Material Flow Indicators to Measure Progress toward a Sound Material-Cycle Society", *Journal of Material Cycles and Waste Management* 9(2), pp. 112–120.

OECD (2008) "Measuring Material Flows and Resource Productivity: Synthesis Report; Volume I – The OECD Guide; Volume II – The Accounting Framework; Volume III – Inventory of Country Activities"; available at www.oecd. org/document/47/0,3343,en_21571361_40266644_40464047_1_1_1_1,00.html.

Searchinger, T., R. Heimlich, R. A. Houghton, F. Dong, A. Elobeid, J. Fabiosa, S. Tokgoz, D. Hayes and T. Yu (2008) "Use of U.S. Croplands for Biofuels Increases Greenhouse Gases through Emissions from Land-Use Change", *Science* 319, pp. 1238–1240.

4

Characterization and local practices of urban-rural symbiosis

4-1

Potential accounting of regional urban-rural partnership for constructing resource-circulating systems – A case study of Zhejiang province in China

Kazutoshi Tsuda, Toyohiko Nakakubo, Yasushi Umeda and Tohru Morioka

4-1-1 Introduction

National and local governments have begun constructing low-carbon societies by setting medium- and long-term goals for each sector of concern. Design of regional systems for circulating natural resources across urban and rural boundaries is a promising measure for decreasing greenhouse gas (GHG) emissions as well as extending co-benefits, such as pollution prevention and social development, into rural areas. However, primary sectors with weak economic bases are exempt from requirements to set GHG emission reduction targets. In addition, resource exchange between rural and urban areas is insufficient. For example, in Japan, up to a century ago, considerable amounts of night soil generated in urban areas were collected and transported to rural areas for use as fertilizer. Then agricultural products such as rice and vegetables grown with this fertilizer were consumed by people in urban areas, later becoming night soil again. However, because of urbanization and the prevalence and effectiveness of chemical fertilizer etc., this resource-circulating system fell into disuse. Urban-rural issues are also becoming important outside Japan. For example, in China the income gap between urban and rural areas has been increasing simultaneously with rapid economic growth and urbanization. Therefore, as a measure for building low-carbon societies, we should reconsider the relationship between urban and rural areas and propose plausible forms of partnership between them. For this purpose, it is necessary to model and assess these partnerships, estimate the

Establishing a resource-circulating society in Asia: Challenges and opportunities, Morioka, Hanaki and Moriguchi (eds), United Nations University Press, 2011, ISBN 978-92-808-1182-7

potential reduction of GHG emissions made possible by such partnerships and describe images and visions of the desired societies that would result from them.

The purpose of this chapter is to investigate possible options for designing regional energy and resource-circulation systems by means of partnerships between urban and rural areas. For this purpose, we first executed fieldwork in selected pilot areas in Asian countries and constructed regional partnership models. The research result is summarized as a multi-beneficial option that realizes the multiple benefits of low GHG emissions, pollution prevention and social development based on regional urban-rural partnerships. In this chapter, we focus on a proposed modelling framework for material and energy circulation in a particular area. This framework evaluates the potential and availability of partnerships by using "what-if" analysis. As a case study, we describe regional urban-rural partnership options using the Zhejiang area of China as an example.

4-1-2 The role of regional urban-rural partnership in constructing circular systems

The percentage of humans living in urban areas has increased. As of 2008, more than half the world's population, or 3.3 billion people, are said to live in urban areas (UN Population Fund, 2007). However, internationally the distinction between urban and rural areas has yet to be clearly defined. Examples of criteria include the population size of a locality, population density, distance between built-up areas, predominant economic activity, legal or administrative boundaries, etc. (UN Department of Economic and Social Affairs, 2007).

Table 4.1.1 summarizes the general characteristics of urban and rural areas and provides corresponding examples of possible urban-rural partnerships based on these criteria, referring in part to FAO (1995). In the process of composing the table, we came to define "urban-rural partnership" as the appropriate bilateral flows and circulation of materials, energy, information, money and people, which contributed to the following results:

- disparity adjustment and equitable distribution of wealth
- "win-win" situations making full use of each characteristic
- coexistence with mutually embedded structures; that is, urban functions in rural areas and rural functions in urban areas
- cooperative conservation of ecosystem services, primarily in rural areas.

We here propose a sector conjunction model and a spatial conjunction model for use in modelling urban-rural partnerships towards a sustainable

Table 4.1.1 Major characteristics of urban and rural areas, and examples of urban-rural partnership

Item	Urban	Rural	Examples of partnership
Population size in locality	Large and growing	Small and dwindling (growth in peri-urban area)	Population optimization
Population density	High density (DID in Japan)*	Excessive population decline	Decentralization of population and government Living in two areas
Predominant type of economic activity	Industry and commerce (secondary and tertiary sector)	Agriculture, forestry and fisheries (primary sector)	Agriculture, commerce and industry symbiosis Industrialization in rural area Urban agriculture and horticulture
Job and income	Mass influx of rural population Relatively high income	Lack of labour for primary sector Relatively low income	Socio-economic support mechanisms for disparity adjustment Bolstering of local finance
Medical welfare	Large centralized complexes	Home care and community welfare Inadequate healthcare service	Community-based healthcare and regional medical plan Utilizing traditional herbal medicine
Trend of education	Indoor and information-oriented with intensive study programmes	Outdoor and practical type involving physical activity	Mix and exchange programmes
Tourism resources	Historical and cultural sites	Landscape and natural sites	Eco-tourism, green tourism and intercity travel
Information	Centralization and overabundance of information	Inadequate information technology infrastructure	Bridge digital divide Enhancement of information sharing
Geomorphic characteristics	Plain field, coastal area	Intermediate and mountainous area	Land use according to land features Good access and transport optimization

Water use and management	For human and industrial use	For irrigation and agricultural produce processing	Water storage for both energy and irrigation Water management in watershed areas Afforestation programme
Foods	Fast foods and various foods from all over the world	Slow-cooked foods and local dishes from nature	Promotion of credit and markets for locally produced food Consideration of food mileage
Predominant biotic resources (biomass)	Food waste and sewage sludge	Crops, livestock, wood and aquatic biomass	Maintenance and optimum utilization by regional circulation Reuse of treated waste biomass on peri-urban agricultural lands
Man-made resources	High-density, high-rise buildings, industrial areas, and (peri-)urban infrastructure	Low density Expressways, power plants	Urban mining Effective utilization of existing infrastructure

Note: DID stands for densely inhabited district. When a research zone with high population density (around 4,000 per km^2 by census) is adjacent to another high-density research zone, and the total area encompasses a population of more than 5,000, the total zone is defined as a DID.

society. The sector conjunction model is produced by combining more than two economic activity sectors in a confined area to create technological innovation and socio-economic development. In contrast, the spatial conjunction model aims at maximizing the resource utilization potential of particular areas by integrating the activities of adjacent land parcels in those areas, thereby contributing to regional development.

4-1-3 Modelling regional urban-rural partnership

In this section, in order to clarify the properties of the pilot model areas, we propose a regional urban-rural partnership modelling method that integrates the regional data of the pilot areas into a common framework. Specifically, we developed two analytical tools to evaluate the resource-circulation system under the regional urban-rural partnership option, based on the stocks and flows of energy and materials.

Stock and flow accounts

This analytical tool is based on material flow accounting and analysis (MFA). MFA is a comprehensive and systematic assessment methodology that examines the stocks and flows of materials and substances within a defined system over a set period of time (Brunner and Rechberger, 2003; Ayres and Ayres, 1998, 1999; National Research Council, 2004; Hoekstra, 2005). MFA is an important tool of industrial ecology (Ayres and Ayres, 2002). It is used to investigate the material metabolism of anthropogenic systems (Baccini and Brunner, 1991) and calculate physical indicators of sustainability (Bringezu, 1997). It is also used to formulate policies for improving resource and environmental management as well as recycling and waste management (Moriguchi, 1999). MFA is essentially concerned with the interface between the anthroposphere and the natural environment.

We modified MFA as an analytical tool to evaluate the regional sustainability of an urban-rural partnership. This tool models the inputs, outputs and economic activities in the flows of energy and materials needed to satisfy the requirements of each sector in an area by describing the linear relations between inputs and outputs. Meanwhile, natural capital, artificial capital and land resources are accounted as stock. By distinguishing between flows of biotic resources and those of fossil fuel, and between flows within and beyond the region, this tool calculates the demand-and-supply balance of energy and materials (such as substitution from consumption of fossil fuel to regional cycles of renewable resources) as well as increases in food and energy self-sufficiency resulting from the regional urban-rural partnership. The stock and flow accounts tool consists of six factors.

- Definition of "system boundaries".
- Classification of "sectors" that are subdivisions in an economic system of the region.
- Estimation of "resources" that produce products accounted as flow.
- Setting of "product and by-product(s)" that are grown or produced by each sector.
- Clarification of the amount of "demands" for resources input in each sector.
- Assessing environmental loads caused by "emissions and wastes" from each sector.

Figure 4.1.1 shows the format of the stock and flow account used in this study. This account table consists of economy, demands, input, output and stock accounts. It is further described as follows.

- *Economy:* a user describes the economic activities (production value, number of employees) and the amount of products by inputting the corresponding figures in each sector. The sum of production value and number of employees is shown in the right edge of each sector cell. The user then marks the industrial type (primary, secondary or tertiary sector) and calculates the population balance (composition ratio of urban and rural population).
- *Demands by use:* the table calculates the demand for resources as the result of the economic activities. By distinguishing between the flow of renewable resources and that of fossil fuel, transition from consumption of fossil fuel to regional cycles of renewable resources is estimated.
- *Input:* the sum of the demand clearly distinguishes between flows within and flows beyond the region, and the input flows of each sector are then calculated. This allows the user to assess the inter-industry relationship within the region and the dependence on resources from outside the region.
- *Output:* environmental indicators are formulated in accordance with assessments based on GHG emissions and ecosystem carbon fixation. In addition, environmental waste stream emissions (solid, liquid, gas) by each sector are estimated.
- *Stock:* natural and man-made capital related to the flows of regional biomass. Natural capital is expressed by the size of the land required to support the biomass consumed within the region. A constraint results when the consumption is greater than the equivalent regional capacity. Man-made capital is represented by the biomass processing equipment and facilities. When man-made capital becomes obsolete, it is treated as waste under the economy cells.

Table 4.1.2 provides examples of the stocks and flows used in the case study.

Section	Category	Item	i	Unit	Sector: Production	Conversion	Consumption	D sposal	Industrial structure — Gross produce/employee: Primary	Secondary	Tertiary	Population — Total: Urban	Rural	Land use: Classification	Indicators: GHG emissions	Carbon fix
Economy	Activity	Production value		[Sum]								-	-	-	-	-
Economy	Activity	Employee		[Pop.]											-	-
Economy	Product	Main product	i	[WT]			-	-	-	-	-	-	-	-	-	-
Economy	Product	Waste							-	-	-	-	-	-	-	-
Demands by use	Intermediate commodity	Biotic resources / Fossil fuel	i	[WT]			-	-	-	-	-	-	-	-	-	-
Demands by use	Foods	Biotic resources	i	[WT]	-	-		-	-	-	-	-	-	-	-	-
Demands by use	Final energy	Biotic resources / Fossil fuel / Electricity	i	[WT]					-	-	-	-	-	-	-	-
Demands by use		...			-	-	-	-	-	-	-	-	-	-	-	-
Input	Material	Product (within)	i	[WT]		-	-	-	-	-	-	-	-		-	-
Input	Material	Product (beyond)	i	[WT]		-	-	-	-	-	-	-	-		-	-
Input	Water	Water (within)	i	[WT]		-	-	-	-	-	-	-	-		-	-
Input	Water	Water (beyond)	i	[WT]		-	-	-	-	-	-	-	-		-	-
Input	Land	Land resource	i	[Area]		-	-	-	-	-	-	-	-	-	-	-
Stock	Man-made capital	Biomass conversion tech.	i	[-]	-	-	-		-	-	-	-	-	-	-	-
Stock	Man-made capital	Inverse manufacturing	i	[-]	-	-	-		-	-	-	-	-	-	-	-
Output		GHG emissions (from energy consumption)		[CO$_2$]					-	-	-	-	-	-		-
Output		Carbon fixation by ecosystems		[CO$_2$]	-	-	-	-	-	-	-	-	-		-	
Output		...			-	-	-	-	-	-	-	-	-	-	-	-

Figure 4.1.1 Basic format of stock and flow accounts

Table 4.1.2 Accounting items of stock and flow in case study

Item	Coverage
Flow	
System boundary	Zhejiang province
Sector	Agricultural, forestry and fisheries, industry, service, construction, biomass, disposal, household
Resource	Biotic resources, fossil fuels
Product and by-product(s)	Edible crops, livestock, forest products, fisheries, petroleum refinery products, processed foods, fibre yarns and fabrics, plywood and woodchip, wooden products and furniture, paper, chemicals, construction, electricity, bioenergy, waste biomass, plantation biomass
Demands	Intermediate commodity – raw materials, fuels for electricity and gas; commodity consumed – foods, final energy, waste and drainage treatment, land resources
Emissions and waste	Greenhouse gas emissions
Stock	
Natural capital	Land resources
Man-made capital	Biomass conversion equipment, end-of-pipe disposal equipment

Causal model of regional urban-rural partnership

We also developed a causal model of regional urban-rural partnerships using a life-cycle simulator (Umeda, Nonomura and Tomiyama, 2000). As shown in Figure 4.1.2, this simulator models a network of processes and then runs a simulation based on discrete event simulation technique. Figure 4.1.3 shows the process editor of the life-cycle simulator. The description of each process is defined by using the process editor, which consists of given parameter, input parameter, output parameter and procedure.

- *Given parameter:* constant representing the property of each process.
- *Input parameter:* parameter inputted from the upstream processes of the life cycle.
- *Output parameter:* parameter calculated according to the expression described by procedure.
- *Procedure:* description of the relation expression between the parameters.

The simulation calculates temporal changes of parameter values in the process network according to the parametric dependency of the process network by evaluating procedures. These describe the relationship between inputs and outputs in each process as the process behaviour. The parametric dependency is automatically derived by the system from the process definitions. By describing a process as a node, then linking

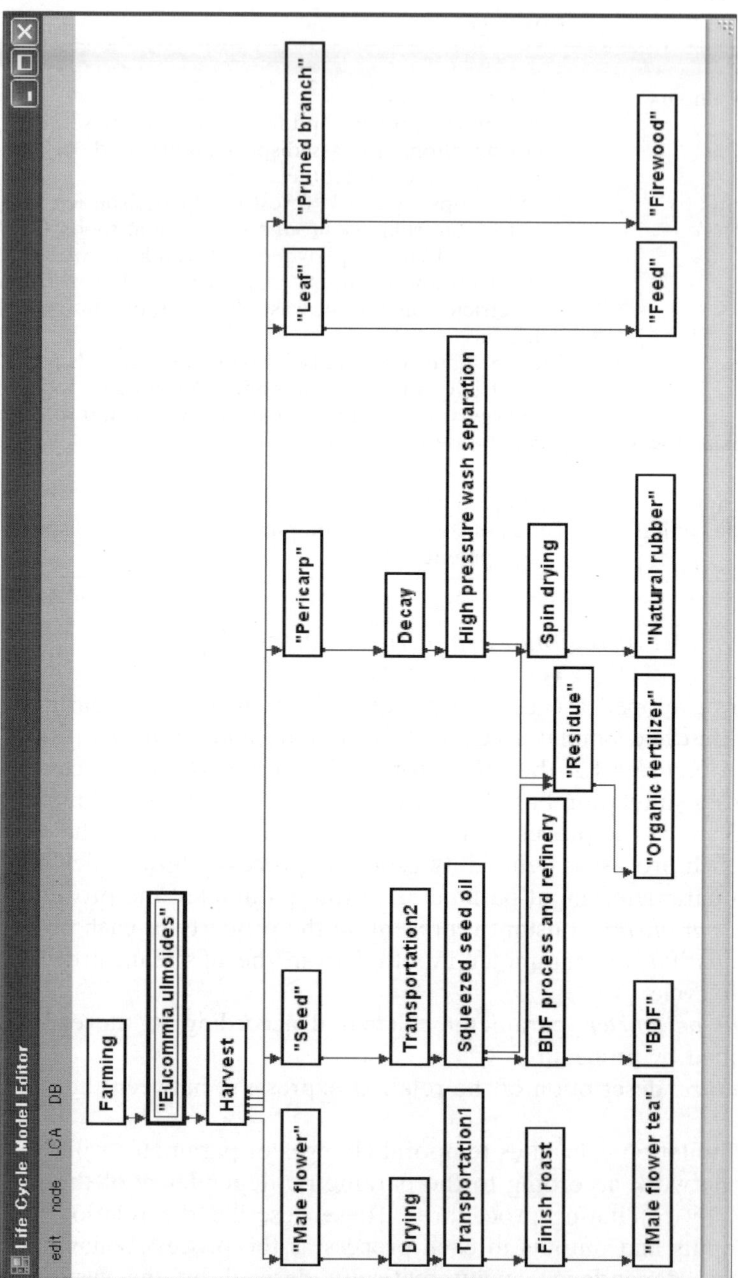

Figure 4.1.2 Life-cycle model editor

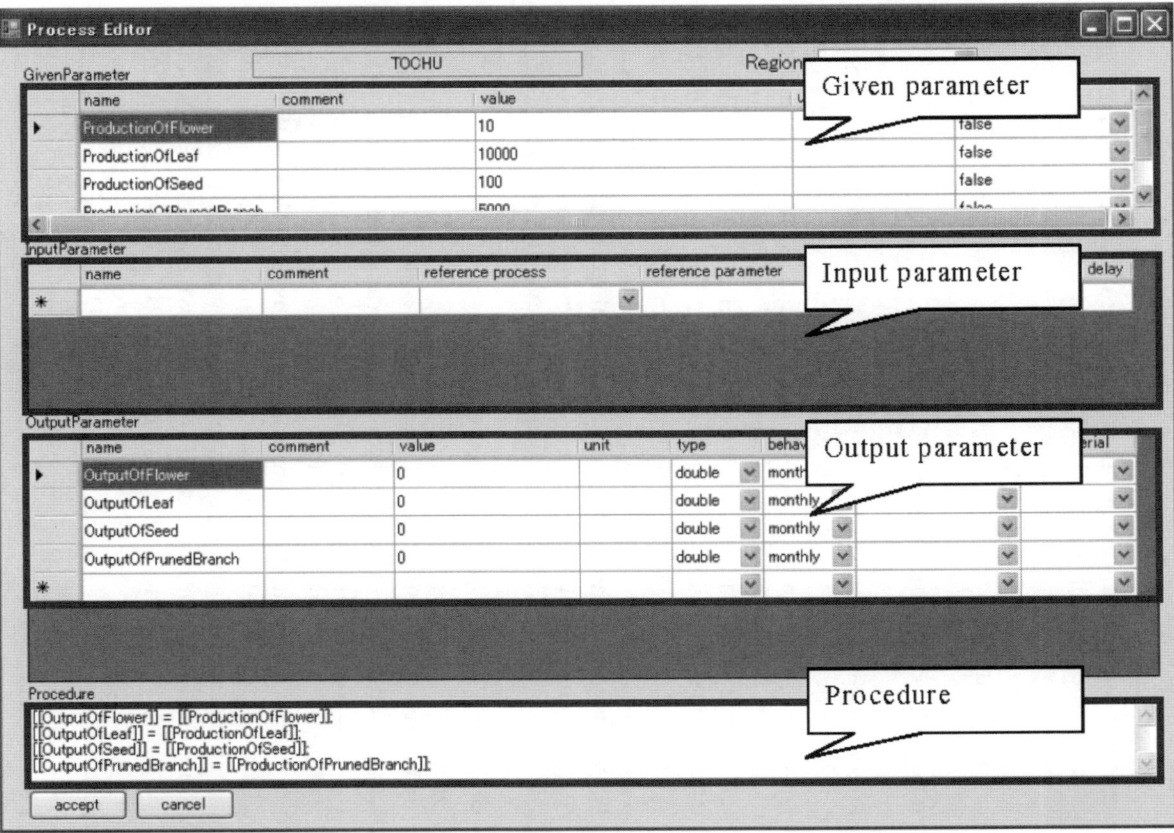

Figure 4.1.3 Process editor of life-cycle simulator

the processes and describing the input-output properties of processes as procedures, we can achieve detailed models and dynamic simulations. The synergy effects (e.g. a pilot model of a partnership that realizes GHG emissions reduction, soil and water conservation and job creation) and the constraint requirements (e.g. demand for natural resources, land area, water etc.) of the partnership can be quantified.

4-1-4 Case study

Application to Zhejiang province

Zhejiang is an eastern coastal province of China. The north of the province is just south of the Yangtze River delta. The province covers an area of 101,800 km^2 and has a population of approximately 46.29 million people. It is rich in forest resources, which cover 66,900 km^2 and account for 65.7 per cent of the total area. In the primary sector, the breakdown of production values (in billion yuan) is agriculture 52.57, forestry 5.57, livestock 11.17 and fisheries 23.02 (2006). Agriculture is the largest primary sector. In the coastal areas, chemical industries, notably chemical fibres, have been developed. The production value of fibre fabrics and textiles is the largest in the industry sector and accounts for 19.8 per cent of the total industrial output (Zhejiang Provincial Bureau of Statistics, 2007).

Describing possible options towards 2030

We created two future possible options for Zhejiang province – an industrial development (ID) option and an urban-rural partnership (UR) option. The base year is 2006, and both options cover the three decades to fiscal year 2030. The supply-demand balance and GHG emissions resulting from energy consumption were calculated by completing the values for the three operational variables of industry growth rate, and land-use rate and biomass utilization rate in the biomass conversion sector.

ID is a so-called business-as-usual option, in which industrial development continues along the present trend. In the UR option, the industry growth rate of the primary sector increased more than in the ID option, and the land-use and biomass utilization rates in the biomass conversion sector increased as well. In this study, production of organic feeds, a methane fermentation system, bioethanol production and gasification power generation were selected as biomass conversion processes. Organic feeds are created by composting any kind of food waste produced in urban areas, and are supplied to the livestock sector in rural areas. Methane gas is then produced from livestock, human and kitchen waste, and the gas is used in place of gasoline. Materials for bioethanol production are thinned wood, waste wood from lumbering projects, clipped branches and waterweed. Generating electricity by gasification power generation uses biomass feedstocks from rice straw and husks, sewage sludge, sludge from septic tanks and burnable wastes such as discarded paper, fabric and wood.

The calculation results of the demand-supply balance of energy in the options, given in "tonnes of oil equivalent" (toe), are shown in Figure 4.1.4. The final energy demands increased by 108.67 million toe (in the ID option), and from 64.46 million toe in 2006 to 109.04 million toe (UR option) in 2030. In the UR option, 17.14 million toe of biomass, 83.6 per cent of the biomass production within the region, was converted to energy. This broke down as 2.54 million toe of methane gas, 3.18 million toe of bioethanol and 2.41 million toe of electricity from gasification power generation. As a result, it was estimated that 7.5 per cent of the final energy consumption requirements could be covered by the four selected biomass energy technologies. The potential GHG emission reduction resulting from the introduction of biomass energy technologies was estimated at 25.31 million tonnes of CO_2, which represents 5.7 per cent of the total GHG emissions resulting from the overall energy consumption. Replacement of fossil fuel by biomass energy, especially from waste biomass exclusively, was limited.

Table 4.1.3 shows the results of changes to economic activities and self-sufficiency rates. In the UR option, the production value per employee in the primary sector increased to 60,161 yuan per capita in 2030, which is approximately 140 per cent of the amount obtained by the ID option. The self-sufficiency rate for food and wood in the UR option increased drastically in comparison to the ID option.

It can be seen that this method of combining stock and flow accounts with causal models by using life-cycle simulation allows us to model the state of economic activities and material flows in a region, and design the resource circulations of energy and materials based on an urban-rural partnership. Furthermore, these tools enable evaluation of synergy effects, constraint requirements and the potential for and availability of the partnerships.

4-1-5 Conclusions

This chapter proposed the concept of regional urban-rural partnerships by focusing on designing regional circulations of energy and materials and the construction of circular systems as methods towards developing a sustainable society. It also proposed a framework for modelling such

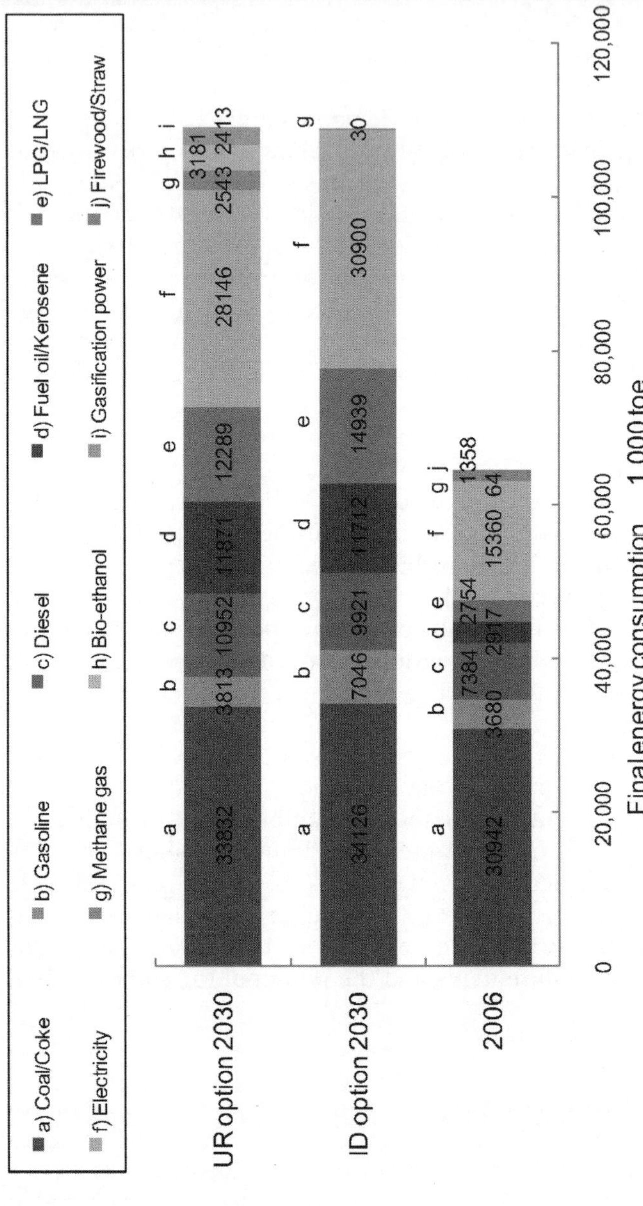

Figure 4.1.4 Calculation results of the demand-supply balance of energy

198

Table 4.1.3 Changes in amounts of economic activities and self-sufficiency rate

Item	2006	2030	
		ID option	UR option
Economic activity			
Production value (billion yuan)	1,574.3	7,286.6	7,064.8
Industrial type (%)	5.9, 54.1, 40.1	2.3, 56.1, 41.6	4.1, 51.9, 41.0
Population (1,000)	46,290	51,330	51,330
Self-sufficiency rate			
Energy (%)	0.1	0.0	7.5
Food (%)	118.4	103.7	134.1
Feeds (%)	9.5	8.3	10.2
Wood (%)	30.3	8.3	47.2

Note: In the "industrial type" item, the values indicate the rate of primary, secondary and tertiary sector from left to right.

partnerships. First, the characteristics of urban and rural areas and the potential urban-rural partnerships were generally defined. Second, in order to evaluate the effects of urban-rural partnerships on regional sustainability, two analytical tools were developed. To verify the advantages of those tools, a case study utilizing options set in Zhejiang province, China, was illustrated. In this case study, the supply-demand balance and reduction of GHG emissions by utilization of biomass resources were estimated.

Future work includes covering urban-rural partnerships other than "maintenance and optimum utilization of the biotic resources by regional circulations", in order to evaluate the patterns and effects of relationships between stakeholders and the changes in people's lifestyles, so that we can include them in future visions aiming towards a sustainable society.

We believe that, by clarifying the synergy effects of urban-rural symbiosis, we will be able to predict how the resulting symbiosis could be multi-beneficial to the creation of a sustainable society.

Acknowledgements

This work was supported by the Global Environment Research Fund (Hc-084: Ecodesign of Low Carbon Society Based on Regional Partnership between Urban and Rural Areas) of the Ministry of the Environment, Japan.

REFERENCES

Ayres, R. U. and L. W. Ayres (1998) *Accounting for Resources, 1: Economy-wide Applications of Mass-balance Principles to Materials and Waste*. Cheltenham and Northampton, MA: Edward Elgar Publishing.

———— (1999) *Accounting for Resources, 2: The Life Cycles of Materials*. Cheltenham and Northampton, MA: Edward Elgar Publishing.

———— (2002) *A Handbook of Industrial Ecology*. Cheltenham and Northampton, MA: Edward Elgar Publishing.

Baccini, P. and P. H. Brunner (1991) *Metabolism of the Anthroposphere*. Berlin: Springer-Verlag.

Bringezu, S. (1997) "Accounting for the Physical Basis of National Economies: Material Flow Indicators", in B. Molden and S. Billharz (eds) *SCOPE 58: Sustainability Indicators*. Chichester: John Wiley & Sons, pp. 170–180.

Brunner, P. H. and H. Rechberger (2003) *Practical Handbook of Material Flow Analysis*. Boca Raton, FL: CRC Press.

FAO (1995) *Planning for Sustainable Use of Land Resources: Towards a New Approach*. Rome: Food and Agriculture Organization.

Hoekstra, R. (2005) *Economic Growth, Material Flows and the Environment: New Applications of Structural Decomposition Analysis and Physical Input-Output Tables*. Cheltenham and Northampton, MA: Edward Elgar Publishing.

Moriguchi, Y. (1999) "Recycling and Waste Management from the Viewpoint of Material Flow Accounting", *Journal of Material Cycles and Waste Management* 1, pp. 2–9.

National Research Council (2004) *Materials Count: The Case for Material Flows Analysis*. Washington, DC: National Academies Press.

Umeda, Y., A. Nonomura and T. Tomiyama (2000) "Study on Life-cycle Design for the Post Mass Production Paradigm", *Artificial Intelligence for Engineering Design, Analysis and Manufacturing* 14(2), pp. 149–161.

UN Department of Economic and Social Affairs (2007) *World Urbanization Prospects: The 2007 Revision*. New York: United Nations.

UN Population Fund (2007) *State of World Population 2007: Unleashing the Potential of Urban Growth*. New York: United Nations.

Zhejiang Provincial Bureau of Statistics (2007) *Zhejiang Statistical Yearbook 2007*. Beijing: China Statistics Press.

4-2

A mosaic model for increasing stability of independence in food, biomass and energy

Mitsuru Osaki, Nobuyuki Tsuji, Toshiki Sato and Noriyuki Tanaka

4-2-1 Introduction

Biological production ecosystems need to be structured into three different categories, and reviewed based on the economic and natural characteristics of each category: large-scale production ecosystems; natural symbiotic production ecosystems; and conservation ecosystems (see Figure 4.2.1). In particular, Type 2 plays a central role in the cyclical community-linking model, and is a particularly important production ecosystem category in Asia. Type 3 requires sound preservation of the surrounding environment. Although Type 1 was important in the twentieth century, it is Type 2 that will be forced to play the central role in the twenty-first century. In this chapter we will show that the circulating community-linking model is critically important to achieving this.

Type 1 has been growing, with low-cost fossil fuel and "continental plains" as the basic criteria. However, these criteria are in fact turning into limiting factors in the twenty-first century. Heavy use of fossil fuel has brought global warming, which is becoming a contributing factor in climate change. This has led to a demand for drastic reduction in CO_2 emissions by 2050, making it difficult to use fossil fuels. Meanwhile, Type 1 has developed mainly in continental plains, which are characterized by relatively low soil fertility and a capability to increase crop productivity drastically through heavy fertilization. However, an enormous amount of energy is required for atmospheric nitrogen fixation. Due to depletion and restriction of use of low-cost oil resources, soaring prices for nitrogen

Establishing a resource-circulating society in Asia: Challenges and opportunities, Morioka, Hanaki and Moriguchi (eds), United Nations University Press, 2011, ISBN 978-92-808-1182-7

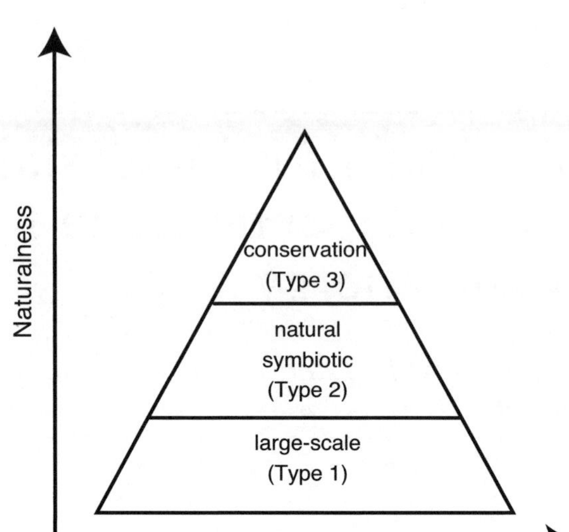

Figure 4.2.1 Triangular model of biological production ecosystems from economic and naturalness aspects

fertilizer are inevitable. With the depletion of phosphorus resources, heavy application of phosphate fertilizer is also becoming difficult. Additionally, rainfall is relatively low on the continental plains, making the use of large-sized equipment possible. However, increasing climate change stemming from global warming widely alters rainfall patterns. If rainfall is low, the effects of a drought are huge, while heavy rainfall limits the usage of large equipment for harvesting and cultivation. Furthermore, Type 1 has been conducted without giving much thought to ecosystem conservation. The aggregated soil structure is collapsing, making the soil prone to runoff and decreasing the soil-forming layer. An advantage in the twentieth century, large-scale production ecosystems are starting to become liabilities in this century.

Figure 4.2.2 shows a model of biological production ecosystems in terms of ecosystem function and sustainability. Judging by limited low-cost energy resources, climate change and the vulnerability of the environment, the balance between ecosystem function and sustainability for large-scale production ecosystems in the twenty-first century will probably be greatly destabilized. Of particular importance within the conservation ecosystem are the swamps and peatlands that spread over tropical regions. Here large natural ecosystems have been conserved due to relatively slow development, because agricultural use would be difficult even if these lands were developed. These ecosystems exist in the islands of

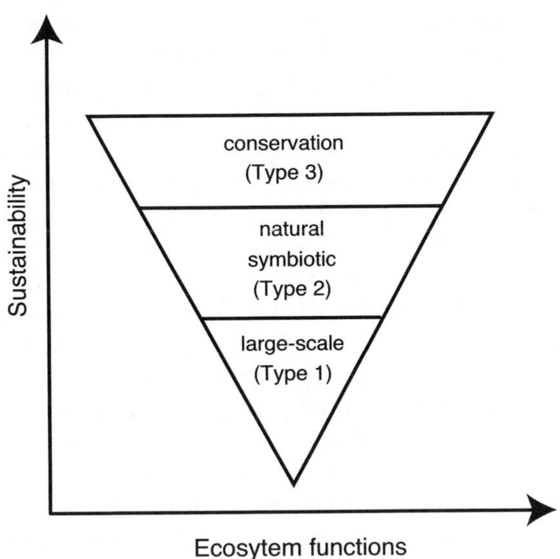

Figure 4.2.2 Triangular model of biological production ecosystems from ecosystem function and sustainability aspects

Southeastern Asia, the Amazon region and Central Africa, and are under development pressure due to depletion of lumber and demand for agricultural land. However, the impact on the global environment of developing these ecosystems is far greater than that of the traditional development of tropical rainforests, as large amounts of carbon have been accumulated in soil rather than in forests. The soil in these ecosystems has accumulated approximately 100 Gt carbon. Calculated simply, destruction of 1 per cent of this land would release 1 Gt of soil carbon, equivalent to 10 per cent of carbon released from fossil fuel. In reality, development is proceeding at a faster pace than this, and is beginning to impact on the global environment in an extremely severe manner.

4-2-2 Food production in Hokkaido

While the food self-sufficiency rate of Japan as a nation fluctuates at a level below 40 per cent based on calories, Hokkaido's rate is nearly 200 per cent (MAFF, 2009). Only five Japanese prefectures have food self-sufficiency rates higher that 100 per cent, with Hokkaido the highest at 195 per cent, Aomori 118 per cent, Iwate 105 per cent, Akita 174 per cent and Yamagata 132 per cent (all in 2006).

Although Hokkaido is sometimes called the "food production base" of Japan, the reality may be quite different. For example, 75 per cent of the livestock feed is imported (Manda, 2003), the fishing industry depends on large amounts of oil and both rice and crop farming depend on chemical fertilizers and large-sized farming equipment that uses huge amounts of oil. These facts tell us that Hokkaido's food production cannot stand on its own as a closed and independent system. For this reason, increases in prices of oil and imported feed crops, such as those that occurred in 2008, promptly led to a crisis. Protected horticulture and other energy-input agriculture are directly affected by increased prices of crude oil. Additionally, massive quantities of electricity are used to keep food-stock at comfortable temperatures. Thus production and storage depend heavily on crude oil, rendering sustainability impossible. The negative characteristics of agriculture in Hokkaido nowadays stem from its North-American-style monoculture, large-input production system and large agricultural production bases. These are relics of a past policy of increasing food production. As tools for efficiency, large scale and monoculture may be considered as two sides of the same coin, assuming the input is also large. If that is true, one could say that agriculture today is the process of converting fossil fuel to food (Saito, 2009). The energy spent in farming rice, Japan's diet staple, in 1990 is estimated to have increased an average of about five times since 1960 (although the land productivity has increased by about 1.3 times). The output energy/input energy rate was 2.5 in 1960, but had changed to about 0.7 in 1990, scoring below 1.0 (Sato, 2005). This vividly shows how dependent Japan's rice production has become on oil.

Thus agriculture in Japan, and similarly in Hokkaido, has become dependent on oil. It is feared that the present agricultural, forestry and fisheries systems of Japan's northern region might be very vulnerable to future peak oil prices (Amano, 2008).

4-2-3 Biomass energy

Biomass and its stored amount

As a renewable energy source, biomass is attracting attention as a means of preparing for the depletion of fossil fuels.

We present an overview of the potential for biomass energy in Hokkaido. Sato et al. (2009) estimated the biomass energy amounts for each of three Hokkaido regions: Kamikawa, Tokachi and Abashiri (see Figure 4.2.3). Wood-based and agricultural biomass energy sources occupy about 90 per cent of the entire Kamikawa region, where agricultural

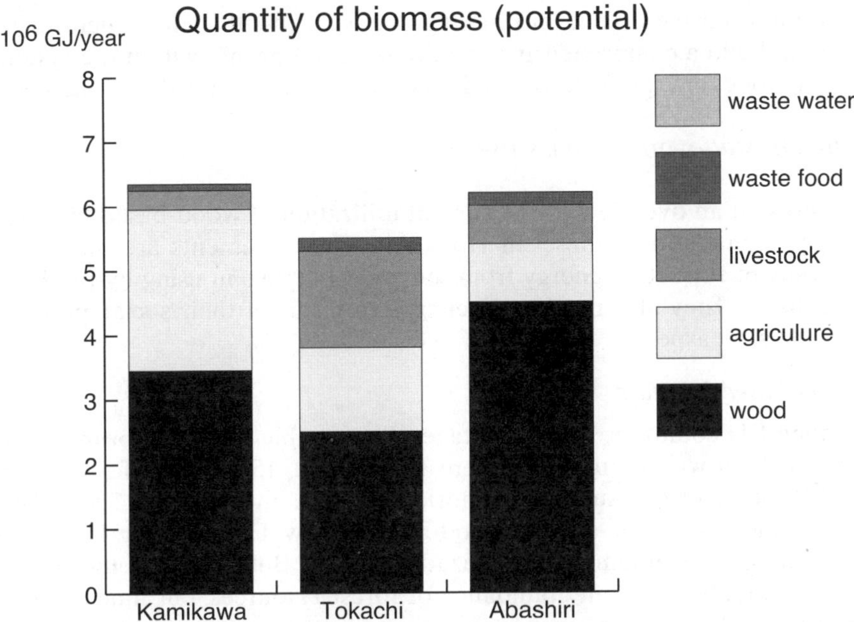

Figure 4.2.3 Biomass energy in three regions in Hokkaido (stored amount)

biomass energy accounts for a larger percentage than in other regions. This is because Kamikawa mainly produces rice, and reflects the combustion energy of rice by-products, rice straw and rice husks. Livestock, wood-based and agricultural biomass energy sources occupy over 95 per cent of the Tokachi region, where the biomass energy through livestock manure is significantly greater compared to other regions. Wood-based, agricultural and livestock biomass energy sources occupy 98 per cent of Abashiri, with wood-based biomass energy in particular playing a greater role than in other regions. This study found that the characteristics of the agricultural, livestock and forestry industries of a region determine the core of the biomass energy sources, and supplement the energy amount of each biomass. We estimated that each region in this study had about the same amounts of stored biomass energy.

As we have seen, we can calculate the stored biomass amounts for each region. However, we must consider here the fact that these amounts are values that have, as a supposition, the current production system for the agricultural, livestock, forestry and fisheries industries and their processing industries. In other words, it may be said that this stored biomass energy is calculated from cases where food production depends on materials from outside the region, such as fossil fuels, chemical fertilizers and imported feed. Thus, in thinking about a self-sufficient structure, we need to build a comprehensive and cyclical relationship within the system among food, energy, fertilizer and feed (as well as the residents' income).

Current status on biomass use

We present an overview of the current utilization of wood-based biomass, biogas plants and biodiesel in Hokkaido. These elements are important not only in extracting energy from the cycle, but also in using by-products (fertilizer). They also need maintenance in terms of their social, political and physical aspects.

Wood-based biomass

Among EU countries, the percentage of renewable energy in primary energy in 1999 was about 20 per cent for Finland, 15 per cent for Sweden and 10 per cent for Austria (Ohmori, Hasegawa and Nemoto, 2001). This renewable energy is mainly wood-based (New Energy and Industrial Technology Development Organization, 2006). Behind the achievement of such numbers lies an abundance of forest resources, but much of it is thanks to the physical development of regional heating systems (heat supply) and social systems such as carbon taxes (to be used for renewable energy). In Japan, most energy is supplied in the form of electricity. Since Hokkaido has a high demand for heating and warming (household heating and snow melting, for example), district heat supply (the use of heat produced in electricity generation – combined heat and power, or CHP) should be considered as one of the options. Although there are increasing numbers of wood-based pellet factories in many regions of Hokkaido, sluggish growth in the demand for pellets remains an unresolved issue.

About 70 per cent of Hokkaido is covered by forest (roughly the same as Japan as a whole). But the current situation is discouraging: in every region of Hokkaido, 5 per cent or less of the total production output is forestry. Given this, the town of Shimokawa in Hokkaido is using forestry to revitalize its economy by building a "green infrastructure". The town divided its forests into 50 ha sections, and logged one of the sections. It is planning to plant trees afterwards, and harvest them again in 60 years. Since 1989 the town's forestry cooperative has hired 43 new employees who have either come back from big cities to live and work in their native town or have been attracted to this town, as well as new local college graduates. Heating of hot (or cold) springs by wood chips is well known. Noticing the willow trees that grow as much as 3 metres (9.8 feet) a year, the town is considering using these as fuel for biomass boilers. Besides these measures, efforts to build a green infrastructure are ongoing in both physical and political/social aspects, including acquisition of a lumber processing certificate (FSC), forestry education for high school students and subsidies for houses built with local lumber. In addition, a carbon-offset system is gradually being built using the plentiful forests.

A traditional Japanese wood-based biomass is charcoal, which is one of the symbols of *satoyama*, a mountain bordering a village. It is not surprising that charcoal has been used as a snow-melting agent. Lately, however, other uses of charcoal, such as a soil conditioner (called Biochar), have been attracting attention. The porosity of charcoal makes it a good habitat for many microorganisms, which change the quality of the soil.

Biogas plants

Hokkaido has about 23 biogas plants (Association for Organic Waste Resources Recycling Systems, 2006). At these plants, livestock manure and food scraps are fermented to generate methane gas. This is then burned to generate electricity and hot water. An average livestock farmer in Hokkaido keeps about 100 cows. Processing their waste is a limiting factor in family-run farming. Most importantly, the prime benefit for adopting a biogas plant is concerned not with energy, but odour. Decomposition of organic matter reduces its odour. Generation of gas leaves a residue (digestive fluids), which is used as a fertilizer (liquid manure). However, the fertilizer is distributed only twice a year, which necessitates large storage tanks for the digestive fluids. Without large tanks, the fluids have to be processed for discharge. But this in turn necessitates facilities and energy for processing. It goes without saying that rice paddies and upland fields on which to spread the fertilizer are also necessary. Securing these tanks and fields is a big issue in using biogas. Because much of the fertilizer is imported, the fields for spreading it are often too small. In addition, equipment (slurry spreaders) is needed because the fertilizer must be distributed intensively within a certain amount of time.

Construction of a biogas plant for processing the waste of about 100 cows would cost between ¥50 million and ¥100 million (ibid.). The electricity generated is about 200 kWh/day, and, unlike in Germany, electric power companies in Japan buy it at a low price – hardly a profitable situation. Although electricity companies are required by RPS (Renewable Portfolio Standard) to buy a certain percentage of renewable energy, their current motivation to purchase is not high. In reality, successful fermentation requires professional skills, and it is very difficult for individual family farmers to do. Several livestock farmers could cooperate to build a large-size biogas plant. In this case, however, issues in transportation costs (purchasing of vehicles, labour costs and freeze-proofing, for example) would stand in the way. Another issue is the low power generation efficiency. Because of this, ways of using the gas to obtain heat and hot water without generating electricity (small livestock are vulnerable to the cold) are under consideration.

Biodiesel

The city of Takikawa and the town of Toyokoro in Hokkaido extract plant oil from rapeseed, while the town of Hokuryu, also in Hokkaido, extracts it from sunflower seeds. These municipalities make biodiesel from this oil after it has been used for frying tempura, in an effort to re-vitalize their neighbourhoods. While many towns in Hokkaido make bio-diesel by recovering used cooking oil, Toyokoro has a plant that operates one of the largest continuous production lines (batch processing is typ-ical) in Hokkaido. In this plant, the plant-oil extraction section is located next to the used-oil processing section. Rape and sunflower seeds also function as part of a rotational system, and their flowers attract tourists. Oil cake contains high-quality protein, making it suitable for feed and fertilizer. The process of making biodiesel also produces glycerin. Com-bustion of this by-product to generate heat is under consideration.

4-2-4 The composite biological production system and its governance

Towards food and energy self-sufficiency in Hokkaido

Energy flows and material cycles are important factors in considering re-gional energy and food self-supply systems (see Figure 4.2.4). We envi-sion that paddy, upland and feed fields, livestock raising, forests and residents should be the categories involved in these systems. An impor-tant element in a composite biological production system is the interac-tion of material and energy among the categories. For example, paddy, upland and feed fields can supply the residents' food, as well as rice straw and pasture grass as feed items, and rice straw and wheat straw as bio-mass fuels. Conversely, livestock and residents can supply fertilizer to paddy, upland and feed fields. Thus interrelationships among the catego-ries establish the material cycle and energy flow, leading to the continu-ing independence of the composite biological production system.

For example, as Figure 4.2.5 shows, the three Hokkaido regions with the highest production outputs in agriculture, livestock, forestry and fish-eries are Kamikawa (¥135 billion), Tokachi (¥255 billion) and Abashiri (¥230 billion). Positioned as a rice and upland-farming region, Kamikawa is active in rice paddy (25 per cent) and upland farming such as onions (52 per cent). With active livestock raising (46 per cent), mainly for dairy

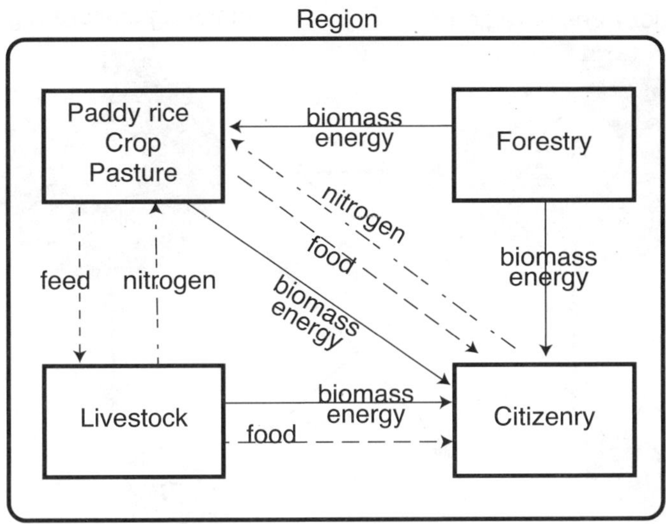

Figure 4.2.4 Concept of material cycling and energy

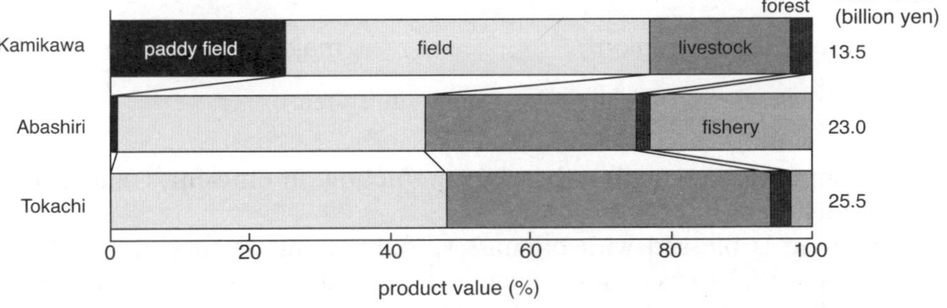

Figure 4.2.5 Production value at three regions in Hokkaido

products, and upland farming such as wheat and sugar beet (48 per cent), Tokachi can be called an upland-farming and livestock-raising region. In addition to livestock raising (30 per cent) and upland farming (44 per cent), Abashiri is active in fisheries (23 per cent), so it can be considered an upland-farming, livestock-raising and fisheries region. Thus different regional characteristics in the agricultural, livestock, forestry and fisheries industries may dictate the calories obtained from and energy spent on food production, while the biomass obtained from by-products displays regional characteristics. Each region must build a self-sufficient structure for the agricultural, livestock, forestry and fisheries industries, food processing, natural energy sources and residents' food and energy needs, while supplying each other with materials and energy that cannot

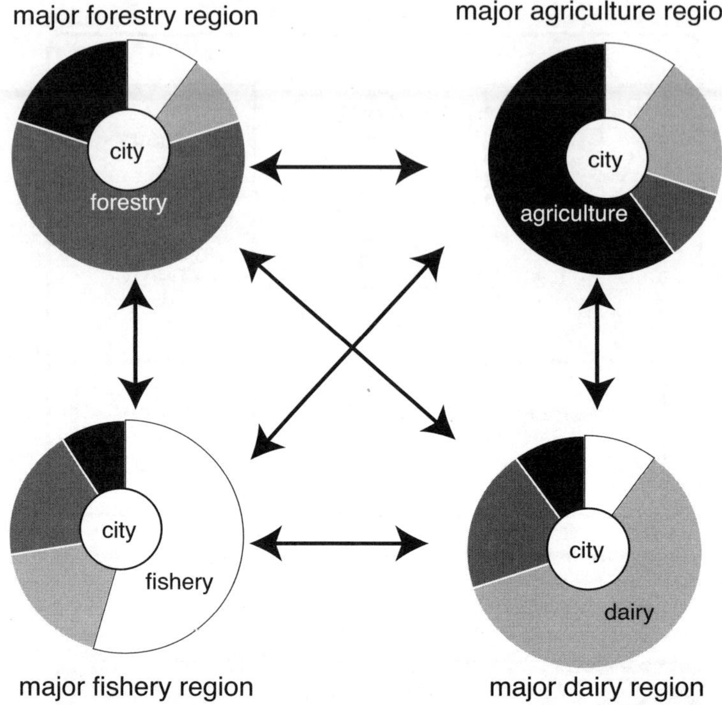

Figure 4.2.6 Composite system

be self-supported in-region, thereby completing an efficient, comprehensive model.

Hokkaido is blessed with biomass resources, and as such it may hold hidden potential for self-sufficiency in food and energy. To translate this into reality, we must build a self-sufficient model for food and energy from the spatial relationship with cities in terms of regional characteristics in the agricultural, livestock, forestry and fisheries industries, using Hokkaido as a prototype, to express the image of a society that does not depend on fossil fuels. In order to do this, it is necessary to categorize the main regions for agriculture, livestock, forestry and fisheries in Hokkaido, as in Figure 4.2.6, and assess their characteristic food and energy potentials. It is also necessary to assess Hokkaido's comprehensive and multiple potentials from the complementary relationships among the regions.

What is a sustainable biological production area?

For a sustainable northern region biological production system, Saito (2009) proposes "a composite system that combines available industrial modules, while sustaining the region's characteristics", adding that a compact design created through the governance of regional industries led by a governmental organization stabilizes the system. Osaki (2008) proposes "a sustainable composite biological production system that incorporates a renewable energy production system" by setting up modules for agriculture, livestock, forestry and fisheries. These two proposals are key to the region's food and energy self-sufficiency. One must examine the spatial association based on material cycles between the comprehensive agricultural, livestock, forestry and fisheries industries on the one hand, and regional cities on the other.

To build a self-sufficient and stable region or agriculture using natural, renewable energy sources (including biomass energy) and organic fertilizer cycles, it is crucial to design social and agricultural systems that take advantage of regional characteristics. To achieve this, it is first necessary to analyse a relationship between various biological production industries located at random within the region. Then the region should be recorrelated in detail towards a streamlined and sustained regional system, comprising interdependent networks. Agriculture, forestry and fisheries industries, which cannot hope for size expansion like manufacturing industry, should plan sustained stabilization of production through diversification of this network structure. It is also important to remember that systems such as this make sense when transport costs are small thanks to the proximity of the constituent industries (compact size).

In any case, these systems are not conceived within a single industry; rather, a governmental organization should take the lead in promoting compact systems through the governance of regional industries. These systems are at the opposite end of the spectrum to large-scale monoculture farming, livestock bases or large factories. And it is the correlations addressed above that have the effect of saving energy and materials while stabilizing the entire system as a network. The biological production area model is a composite system that combines available industrial modules (including small-sized energy plants) while taking advantage of regional characteristics. This model should be used to achieve a society that is low in carbon use and cyclical in nature.

The composite biological production system and the governance process

We have discussed the importance of the composite biological production system. To put this system into practice, the governance process becomes even more important. We structured the residents' awareness of sustainability in the city of Furano, Hokkaido (Motoda et al., 2009). In addition, Figure 4.2.7 shows our governance process model for the adoption of a

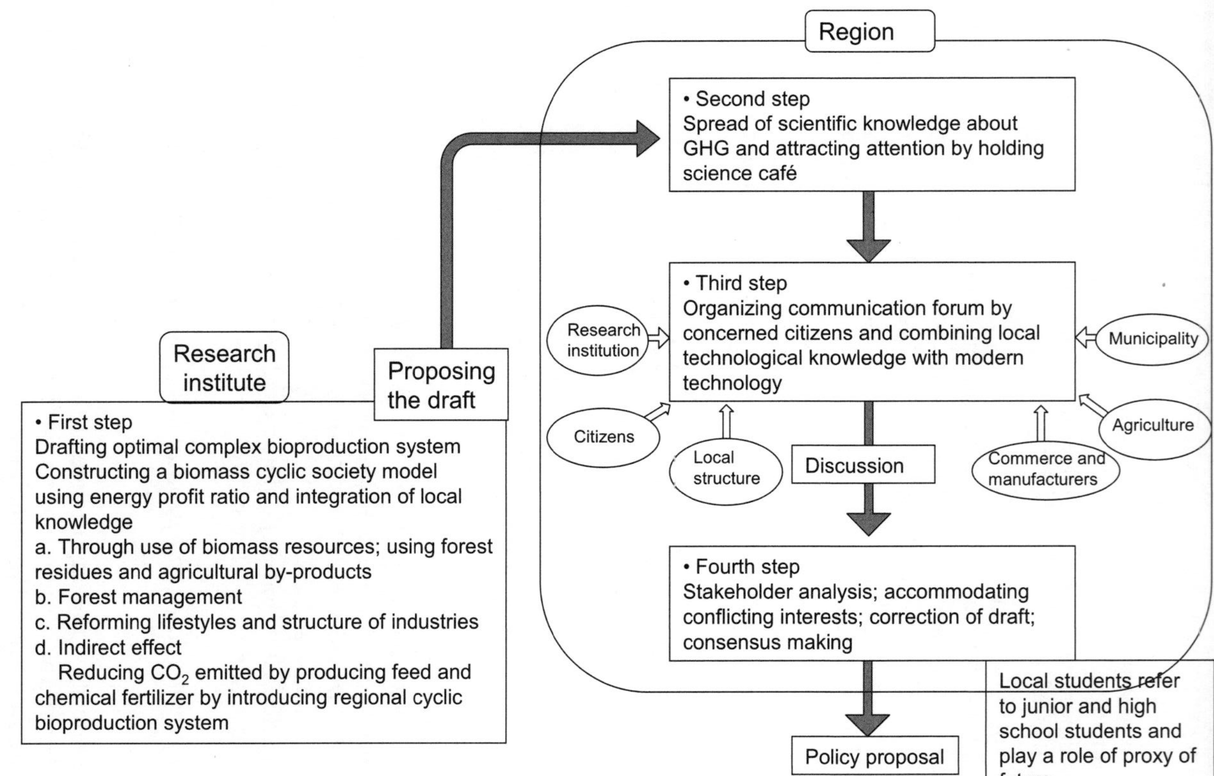

Figure 4.2.7 Strategic model for problem solution

new energy form in Furano. This model consists of four phases. Firstly, we present an optimal composite biological production system for solving the technical issues through building a model for an efficient biomass-cycle society, or learning the residents' practical knowledge of biomass use and integrating that with the latest biomass technology. Secondly, based on the biomass-cycle society model, we address the residents and other stakeholders who will be impacted by the implementation of this system, by using scientific and technological communication methods such as periodic science cafés, while creating opportunities for sharing thoughts on the composite biological production system. Thirdly, we hold a scenario workshop to discuss solutions for social issues caused by resident-led implementation of the composite biological production system. At this time, it is important to reclaim the biomass uses handed down through generations in that region, and add those uses to the modern biomass technology to create a plan that blends old and new technologies. Lastly, we analyse how this plan impacts each demographic of regional residents (stakeholder analysis), and work towards agreement on this plan based on this analysis.

If problems arise in any of these four phases, we provide feedback on the issue and make decisions in an iterative process. This enables the creation of an efficient policy.

4-2-5 Scenario of mosaic model in rural areas

Optimizing energy, food, feed and fertilizer in the rural area mosaic model

In modern agriculture, forced management of the ecosystem has been the objective. This method, however, is on the brink of being incapacitated by energy problems and deterioration of the environment. Recently, a millennium assessment report, as part of its ecosystem services, proposed an ecosystem management plan based on the adaptive mosaic model (Millennium Ecosystem Assessment, 2005). We now discuss the possibility of building a cyclical region-linking model based on the adaptive mosaic model. Basically, a composite production method is required for building a cyclical model. We have studied the feasibility of rural area mosaic models by simple mathematical modelling using field data obtained from Furano (Tsuji and Sato, 2010). The city's population is 25,000 and the main industries are agriculture and tourism. Furano produces many agricultural products: rice, wheat, onions, carrots, dairy products etc. As food, feed, fertilizer and energy sufficiency rates depend on land use assigned to these products, we tried to get an optimal solution: to maximize the

Table 4.2.1 Result of mathematical model

	Sufficient rate (%)				Allocation rate (%)			
Case	Energy	Food	Feed	Fertilizer	Rice	Pasture	Willow	r (%)
A	11	208	100	100	18	82		50
B	100	100	100	100	12	26	62	80

Note: Sufficient rate, allocation rate and r are shown in cases where willow is not planted (A) and planted (B), respectively. The parameter, r, is the income ratio; that is (income in the optimal land use)/(income in the current land use).

energy self-sufficiency rate such that food, feed and fertilizer self-sufficiency rates are over 100 per cent. However, as our result contained a low energy self-sufficiency rate (see Table 4.2.1), we planted virtual willows in our model. The result did not allocate any fields to onions (the highest-income product), only to willow, rice, wheat and cows (pasture), as cows and rice provide not only food but also feed and fertilizer. In this case we got 100 per cent self-sufficiency rates for food, feed, fertilizer and energy, and the farmers could receive at least 85 per cent of their previous income. Thus it can be concluded that the mosaic model is essential for establishing food, feed, fertilizer and energy independence in rural areas.

New functions of farms

Interaction with nature (Type 3: conservation ecosystem in Figure 4.2.1) and humans in rural areas (Type 2: natural symbiotic production ecosystem in Figure 4.2.1) is essential for establishing sustainable ecosystems. The concept of *satoyama* also captures the way humans (*sato*) and nature (*yama*) interact with each other. Tsunahide Shidei, a forest ecologist, studied material cycles – production, consumption and decomposition of organic matter. He defined *satoyama* as "a forest where fertilizer required for farmland is obtained" (Mori, 2001). In recent years the term has been interpreted more broadly, sometimes causing confusion. To differentiate the two uses, we use *satoyama* to mean "farm forest", as Shidei says, while expressing the *satoyama* that has recently been used and interpreted extensively as Satoyama. We define Satoyama as the aggregate of interactions between humans and nature. Under the concept of Satoyama, stabilization of ecosystems is explored through the interrelationships, cycles or coexistence of different ecosystems, such as nature-humans and forest-humans-sea. Within the relationship between humans and nature, the relationships of city-humans and city-nature are also important. Without the involvement of city citizens, it is difficult to preserve Satoyama. Until this point, economic efficiency has been pursued by forcibly accumulating material and human resources in cities. It has become clear that, in this way, sustainably protecting the surrounding ecosystems is difficult. It is very difficult to build a physical cyclical system between city and humans, or between city and nature. However, thinking about the Satoyama concept as including the city system will lead us to realize the importance of building a cyclical system for "the human heart". The creation of opportunities for composite Satoyama such as ecotourism, green tourism, agri-tourism and sustainable tourism (tourism and recreation), education on the environment and nature, nature conservation, intergenerational interactions and proposition of lifestyles (educational), long-term stays in natural environments, rehabilitation and animal therapy (therapeutic) and building partnerships between different entities such as governments and citizens, and participation in an environmental preservation events (volunteering), is also important (Osaki, 2007).

The agricultural, forestry and livestock industries are currently required not only to produce food, as they have in the past, but also to perform functions such as producing energy, cleaning up waste and driving the material cycle, assisting city dwellers with health improvements, efforts to go back to nature and storing water and carbon in the soil. It is extremely difficult to preserve the current ecosystem in monoculture cropping with large-scale equipment and large amounts of pesticides and fertilizers. We would say that the only solution for now is to build a cyclical region-linking model based on the adaptive mosaic. To do this we need to build, around the conservation ecosystems, a comprehensive ecosystem management system, through preserving environment activities, including a mechanism for reducing the absorption and release of CO_2 through the CDM (clean development mechanism) and REDD (reducing emissions from deforestation and degradation in developing countries) and a mechanism for conserving biodiversity. This will allow the local residents to make a living by conserving the ecosystems not suited for farming. Meanwhile, regions with arable land must achieve self-sufficient status by optimizing the natural renewable energies and material cycles through cyclical region linking (the city-farm link, the conservation ecosystem-farm link). In this chapter, we broadly interpreted this type of cyclical region linking city-farm-nature and called it the Satoyama system. Satoyama production ecosystems are typically located in the monsoon regions of Asia.

Broadening this concept even more, we can consider the Himalayan-Tibetan Plateau a *yama*, and its glacier a huge dam, with the glacier's melt supplying massive amounts of water and forming the Indus, Ganges, Brahmaputra, Salween, Mekong, Yangtze and Yellow Rivers. Suppose that the living spheres of people along these rivers are *sato*, we can say that a huge Satoyama (mega-Satoyama) is formed around the Himalayas.

This mega-Satoyama ecosystem has always produced the highest outputs. For this reason, 40 per cent of the world's population still lives in this region, with diverse natural environments, cultures, ethnic groups and languages. In the twentieth century this diverse (mega-)Satoyama production ecosystem was severely hit by the oil-dependent production system that pursued large scale, efficiency and uniformity. However, the Satoyama ecosystem should have significant meaning in the twenty-first century. At the very least, the collapse of this conventional ecosystem would lead to a significantly severe situation in such a populous region. The oil-dependent production ecosystem shows a trend for destabilization of the ecosystem itself, and for in-region processing of surplus agricultural products. This means we can say that it is time for the Satoyama production ecosystem, with its new theory, to contribute to not only the stabilization of regions but also the sustainability of global ecosystems. The Satoyama concept comprehensively studies the diverse interactions between humans and nature in an attempt to build a new social and living foundation. It will become an important concept for human culture and society in the twenty-first century (ibid.).

Acknowledgements

We would like to thank Furano, Date and Obihiro cities and Shimokawa, Bekkai and Ashoro towns for kindly agreeing to be interviewed. This work was supported by MEXT through Special Coordination Funds for Promoting Science and Technology, and the Global Environment Research Fund (Hc-084) of the Ministry of the Environment, Japan.

REFERENCES

Amano, Osamu (2008) *Energy after Oil Peak – Investigation of Resource Efficiency Use from Viewpoint of EPR (Energy Profit Ratio)*. Tokyo: Aichi Press (in Japanese).

Association for Organic Waste Resources Recycling Systems (2006) *Technology and System in Biogas*. Tokyo: Ohm-sya (in Japanese).

MAFF (2009) "Supply and Demand Table, 2006", Ministry of Agriculture, Forestry and Fisheries; available at www.maff.go.jp/j/zyukyu/zikyu_ritu/pdf/ws.pdf (in Japanese).

Manda, Tomiharu (2003) "What We Have to Do for Diffusion and Establishment of Grassland Farming", *Grass and Seed* August, pp. 1–5 (in Japanese).

Millennium Ecosystem Assessment (2005) *Ecosystems & Human Well-being: Synthesis*. Washington, DC: Island Press.

Mori, Mayumi (2001) *A Person in Forest. Tsunahide Shidei's Ninety Years.* Tokyo: Syoubun-sya (in Japanese).

Motoda, Yuka, Yasuhiko Kudo, Hideaki Shiroyama, Hironori Kato and Nobuyuki Tsuji (2009) "Regional Sustainability and the Structure of Issues Recognized by Relevant Actors: A Case of Furano City, Hokkaido", *Shakai gijutsu ronbunshu* 6, pp. 124–146 (in Japanese).

New Energy and Industrial Technology Development Organization (2006) "Overseas Report No. 983"; available at www.nedo.go.jp/library/index.html#database (in Japanese).

Omori, Ryota, Akihiro Hasegawa and Masahiro Nemoto (2001) "Perspective of Bio-energy Usage and Trend", *Kagaku Gijyutsu Douko*, December, National Institute of Science and Technology Policy; available at www.nistep.go.jp/achiev/ftx/jpn/stfc/stt009j/feature2.html (in Japanese).

Osaki, Mitsuru (2007) "Satoyama Concept Integrating Biological Production Ecology and Local Society", in Hiroshi Komiyama (ed.) *Challenge to Sustainability Science.* Tokyo: Iwanami-syoten (in Japanese).

———— (2008) "The Key for Recovering Food Self-sufficiency Rate", *Kita-kara Minami-kara* 331, pp. 16–20 (in Japanese).

Saito, Yutaka (2009) "The Perspective on Sustainable Northern Biosphere", *Energy Shigen* 30(2), pp. 39–43 (in Japanese).

Sato, Toshiki (2005) "The Actual State and Problems of Investing Energy in Rice Produce – On Investing Electrical Energy Analysis", *Bulletin of Hiroshima Prefectural University* 16(2), pp. 15–26 (in Japanese).

Sato, Toshiki, Nobuyuki Tsuji, Noriyuki Tanaka and Mitsuru Osaki (2009) "Biomass Potentials and Self-sufficiency Rate Analysis Considering the Primary Industry in Hokkaido, Japan", report on construction of harmonious social integrated model, Japan-China Cooperating Study Project, Ritsumeikan University, Kyoto, pp. 63–70.

Tsuji, Nobuyuki and Toshiki Sato (2010) "Analysis of Energy, Food, Fertilizer and Feed: Self-sufficiency Potentials of Furano City, Hokkaido, Japan", in Osaki Mitsuru, Ken'ichi Nakagami and Ademola Brimoh (eds) *Designing Our Future: Perspectives on Bioproduction, Ecosystems and Humanity.* Tokyo: United Nations University Press.

4-3

Regional sustainability-oriented agricultural technology and biomass circulation system development

Youji Nitta, Hiroyuki Ohta and Tasuku Kato

4-3-1 Introduction

Human activities have strongly affected the Earth's biogeochemical cycles through food and energy production. The most prominent influence is the incessant release into the atmosphere of enormous amounts of carbon trapped by prehistoric ecosystems (i.e. fossil fuels) and modern-day vegetation, caused by fossil-fuel burning and forest clearing, respectively (Houghton et al., 2001). The main cause for concern about increasing levels of carbon dioxide (CO_2) in the atmosphere is its role as a greenhouse gas (GHG). Before the rapid increase in the conversion of fossil fuels to CO_2, which occurred with the advent of the industrial era, the global carbon cycle comprised two major biological processes, photosynthesis accompanying fixation of CO_2 and its reciprocal process – mineralization – resulting in the liberation of CO_2 from organic carbon. Since then, CO_2 emissions resulting from the burning of fossil fuels have increased, and currently account for 4–5 per cent of the total biological contribution to atmospheric CO_2 (King et al., 2003). From a global perspective, the share of the anthropogenic contribution is small (4–5 per cent), but the values vary greatly at a regional level. This is particularly apparent when one considers urban and industrialized areas where the degree of uncoupling of CO_2 emissions compared to CO_2 fixation is large (Figure 4.3.1). Consequently, regional-level scenarios must be considered when looking at balances in carbon cycling.

Human impacts on the nitrogen cycle are considered severe because they have caused a marked increase in the amount of biologically avail-

Establishing a resource-circulating society in Asia: Challenges and opportunities, Morioka, Hanaki and Moriguchi (eds), United Nations University Press, 2011, ISBN 978-92-808-1182-7

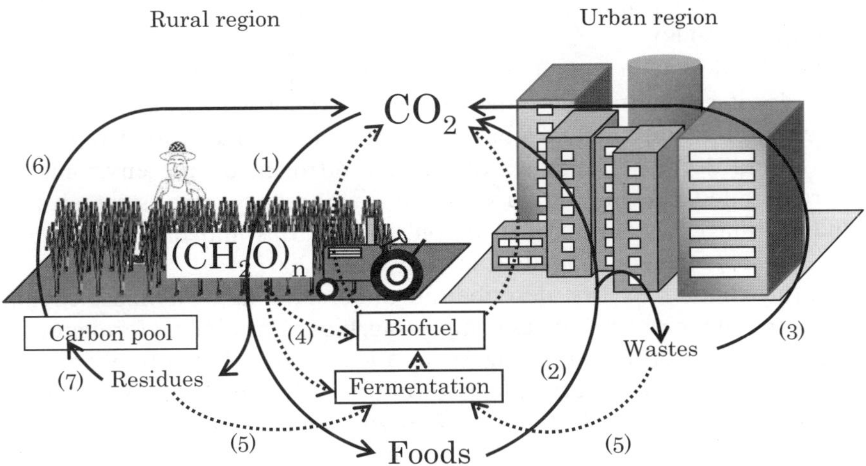

Figure 4.3.1 A simplified model for agriculture-based and fossil-fuel-independent carbon cycling in rural-urban linked societies
Note: In conventional carbon cycling, agriculture (1) has a central role in supplying food (carbohydrate [$(CH_2O)_n$]). This food is mainly consumed in the city and it is here that carbon is converted to carbon dioxide (CO_2) by respiration and through waste (2, 3). When considering fossil fuel-independent societies, agriculture must play another role; that is, the production of biofuels (alcohol and seed oil) (4). City and agricultural waste can also be used for biofuel production (5). Agricultural soils are both a major sink (1) and source (6) of carbon. Therefore, sustainable agricultural practices (7), such as no-till farming and cover cropping, are necessary to control the amount of atmospheric carbon.

able nitrogen (or "reactive nitrogen" when toxic to living things) in such forms as ammonia (NH_3), nitrogen oxides (NO_x, $= NO + NO_2$), nitrous oxide (N_2O) and nitrate (NO_3^-): atmospheric nitrogen (N_2) is unusable by all eukaryotic organisms. The main reason for the manufacture of NH_3 and NO_3^- is their use as fertilizers to increase food production. However, often more chemical fertilizers and animal wastes (organic fertilizer) are added to agricultural lands than the plants need. Consequently, only a fraction of the nitrogen applied to soil is actually taken up by crops and the rest moves freely through the environment, seriously affecting air, land, freshwater resources and oceans, as well as human health (e.g. Mulholland et al., 2008). Another major source of reactive nitrogen in the environment has been the inadvertent production of NO_x from burning coal, oil and natural gas (Galloway et al., 2008). Excess NO_x in the air increases levels of toxic ozone (smog) in the lower atmosphere and causes acid rain, which is harmful to plants and decreases the pH in soils, lakes and streams. In addition, N_2O, a non-CO_2 GHG, is an intermediate of microbial denitrification and a by-product of microbial nitrification in the soil. Agricultural production on well-drained soils with high rates of nitrogen fertilizer application results in large fluxes of soil N_2O and NO (Bouwman, 1998).

When a shift to sustainable carbon and nitrogen cycling is considered, the role of agriculture becomes apparent. Along with food production, agricultural activity includes biofuel production, sequestration of carbon in soil and decreased impacts of reactive nitrogen on the environment. More detailed information on sustainable soil management strategies, including tillage systems, crop rotation, cover crops and manure application, was reported by Komatsuzaki and Ohta (2007).

In this chapter we first describe our understanding of biomass circulation through measures such as composting, biogas-producing fermentation and the use of fermentation digests at a local scale. Recently, abandoned farms have become a serious agricultural problem in Japan. In response to this issue, we propose the use of sweet sorghum, an energy crop, and specifically examine its cultivation on abandoned farmlands. The circulation of biofuels and biomass produced from sweet sorghum is assessed from the perspective of regional sustainability.

4-3-2 Promotion of material circulation efficiency in local areas

For sustainable nitrogen circulation, the effective utilization of biomass as an "organic resource" is promoted. Herein, biomass refers to livestock wastes, residuals from agricultural areas, such as straw and tree bark, and food process and kitchen wastes in urban areas (Figure 4.3.2). In Japan, livestock wastes are often disposed of in earthen storage ponds. However, the nitrogen and phosphorus in these wastes gradually leach into the environment and degrade water quality in rivers and lakes (Kato, Kuroda and Nakasone, 2009). Crops produced in rural areas are consumed in urban areas, where the subsequent disposal of leftover food has become a social problem.

Biomass is useful for various purposes. Composting, methane fermentation and anaerobic digestion are among the most popular methods of using biomass. In modern agriculture, especially since the development of chemical fertilizers, overfertilized areas have emerged in many countries. Overfertilization has had adverse impacts on natural environments (Pierzynski, Sims and Vance, 1994: 77–78). For example, continuous application of chemical fertilizers to tea plantations in Japan has decreased soil pH, making them acidic; NO_3^- concentrations in discharged water are extremely high (Nakasone, Kuroda and Kato, 2002). If the use of compost and digested liquid that is the by-product of methane fermentation was promoted, and if implementation of these measures was sufficient, it would be possible to solve such fertilizer overuse problems.

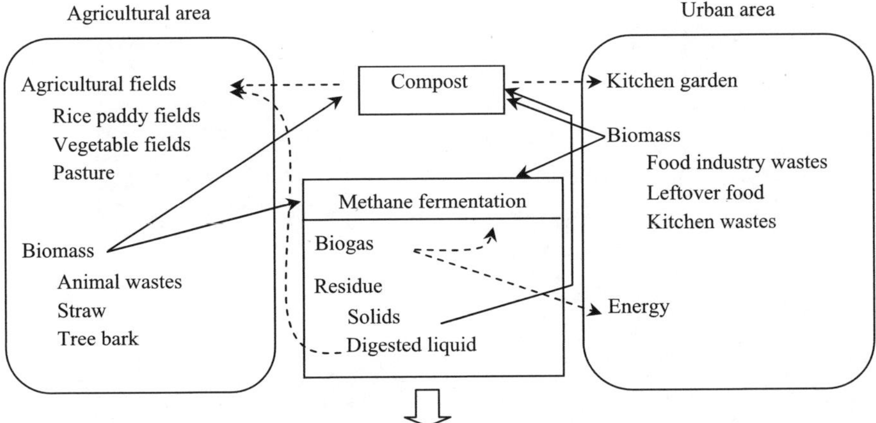

Figure 4.3.2 Biomass cycle between rural and urban areas through composting and methane fermentation

The effective use of this organic waste biomass will promote a low-carbon society, adequate nitrogen circulation and improvement of water environments. Better biomass utilization will contribute to harmonization between the environment and human society in urban and agricultural areas.

Composting

Compost is a mixture of biodegradable organic matter such as animal wastes, straw and tree bark that is accumulated or mixed and decomposed by thermophilic bacteria (JIE, 2008). Compost contains less nitrogen than chemical fertilizers; rather, the primary objective of compost application is to supplement soil organics. Thus some loss of nitrogen through volatilization and percolation to soils occurs during composting. Compost is effective for supporting the carbon cycle, but it is not very effective for the nitrogen cycle (ibid.). Along with its usage in commercial agriculture, compost has recently been used in kitchen gardens by residents who are aware of problems related to health and the environment.

Methane fermentation (anaerobic digestion)

Methane fermentation, or anaerobic digestion, is a complex microbial process in which organic compounds are degraded into biogases, or methane and carbon dioxide, by various anaerobic bacteria (ibid.; Plate 4.3.1(a)). Biomass sources for methane production have been reported in

Plate 4.3.1 (a) Methane fermentation test plant, (b) bucketful of digested liquid, (c) pot test of Komatsuna (*Brassica rapa* var. *peruviridis*) with digested liquid
Note: Please see page 432 for colour versions of these images.

the literature (Gunaseelan, 1997). Because methane is useful as an energy source, the reuse of biomass through methane fermentation is more economical than composting. The resultant energy is usually used for the maintenance of methane fermentation facilities and surplus energy is sold to power companies for use in urban areas.

Application of digested liquid to agricultural land

The residues remaining after methane fermentation are digested liquid (Plate 4.3.1(b)) and solid wastes, which are rich in nitrogen and phosphorus, respectively (Liedi, Bombardiere and Chatfield, 2006). Sewage treatment facilities need to treat such residues before they can be released into rivers, where they would otherwise have adverse effects on the environment. Recently, it has been proposed that digested liquids could be applied as liquid fertilizer in agricultural areas.

The ratio of nitrogen in the digested liquid varies according to the raw material used for methane fermentation and the fermentation conditions. The digested liquids typically have high nitrogen concentrations (0.2–0.5 per cent), the major forms of which are ammonium nitrogen and organic nitrogen. Studies (i.e. ibid.) have shown that the digested liquid is useful as a fertilizer and plants such as vegetables, rice and other agricultural crops grow as well in pastures fertilized with digested liquids as crops treated with chemical fertilizers (Plate 4.3.1(c)).

Because digested liquids are heavy, their transportation from a methane fermentation facility to agricultural fields, application methods on farmland and the storage of digested liquid during the off-season are all issues that must be resolved. Other problems include odour reduction during application near residential areas, removal of impurities that could interfere with plant growth (e.g. other plant seeds, heavy metals, flocculants) and NO_x gas production in agricultural fields. These problems are expected to be resolved through further research.

4-3-3 Local use of biomass in Japan

Problems of farm cultivation in Japan

Abandoned farm areas in Japan exceed 280,000 ha (MAFF, 2009), which is equivalent to the entire area of Kanagawa prefecture. This increase of abandoned farms is attributable to several reasons: shortage of labour because of an ageing population (45 per cent) and social factors (11.4 per cent); low farm productivity (12.8 per cent); and unfavourable farming conditions (9.8 per cent) (MAFF, 2007: 1–10).

The Ministry of Agriculture, Forestry and Fisheries (MAFF) provides support for the improvement and cancellation planning of abandoned farms, including assistance with basic maintenance of agricultural equipment and facilities, companies participating in agriculture, joint farm management, practical use as allotments and increased production of fodder and silage and/or pasturage. However, given that the social infrastructure necessary for supporting agricultural activities is missing, no effective solution to the problem of farm abandonment has been found. In addition, administration of such programmes on a national scale is difficult. An action plan should therefore be developed that considers the interaction between environmental conditions and the local community, as well as local and national governments.

Local use of biomass in Japan

Use of local areas for biomass production must be addressed as an alternative for agricultural activities. Biomass use has been addressed at the national level in the form of the Biomass Japan comprehensive strategy (adopted at a cabinet meeting in December 2002). This strategy promotes the use of biomass technology to develop fuel in rural areas within the context of the points below:
• ethanol production using domestically grown agricultural products, such as sugarcane and other crops

- introduction of inexpensive agricultural product supply techniques through cooperative stakeholder systems
- development and introduction of agricultural products that produce large quantities of biomass
- effective ethanol production techniques from wood biomass
- development of low-cost production techniques.

Several local governments and companies are currently undertaking projects incorporating these aims; bioethanol production is currently being undertaken in Tokachi, Tomakomai, Niigata, Osaka, Ie-jima Island and Miyako-jima Island.

In the Tokachi region of Hokkaido, bioethanol production is being conducted through cooperation of local governments, Japan Agriculture (JA) and a new company. This collaboration uses sugar beet and sub-standard wheat as feedstock; production capacity is currently around 15 ML (megalitres) a year. In Tomakomai, Hokkaido, rice is used for ethanol production. The venture is managed by the local government and a private brewer, and has an annual production capacity of approximately 15 ML. A venture in Niigata consisting of JA and the National Agricultural Research Center Hokuriku also uses rice for ethanol production and has an annual capacity of around 1 ML.

In Osaka, local governments and private companies use wood biomass (construction lumber, small pieces of wood, pruned branches), wastepaper and food residues for bioethanol production and also to produce electric power and lignin pellets. Improvements in recycling rates of wood biomass are their primary focus.

On Miyako-jima Island in Okinawa prefecture, four ministries (Economy, Trade and Industry; Environment; MAFF; and Land, Infrastructure and Transport) along with the Cabinet Office have jointly undertaken a cooperative initiative designated as "bioethanol island design". The plant produces bioethanol from sugarcane, and it is expected that the approximately 24 ML that will be produced a year will be sufficient to meet the E3 (a gasoline mixture that is 3 per cent bioethanol) needs of 50,000 inhabitants on the islands. On Ie-jima Island in Okinawa prefecture, a private brewery and the National Agricultural Research Center for Kyushu Okinawa Region also jointly manage a plant producing bioethanol from sugarcane. In recent years, MAFF has also proposed the establishment of a "biomass town design".

Why choose biofuel crops?

In recent years, production of bioethanol derived from sugarcane and corn has increased remarkably in North and South America. Approximately 19,500 megagallons of bioethanol were produced worldwide in

2009, with approximately 70 per cent of that produced in the United States and Brazil (Renewable Fuels Association, 2010). However, a serious dilemma has arisen because the crops used to produce this bioethanol could be devoted to human food production.

Prices for domestic animal feed have increased because silage crops are now being used for bioethanol production. In the United States more than 20 per cent of all corn crops are used for bioethanol production, leading to higher prices, particularly for cattle feed. Furthermore, rising prices in soybeans reflect a shift in cultivation for biodiesel feedstock.

It is therefore important that a shift is made towards using non-food crops as biofuel feedstock. At the Hokkaido Toya-ko Lake summit in July 2008, then Japanese Prime Minister Fukuda, acting as chairperson, emphasized that the development and choice of "third crops" are necessary for biofuel crops that do not compete with food and economic production.

4-3-4 "On-site" biofuel production and material recycling in local areas

Potential of sweet sorghum for use in biofuel production

It is therefore necessary to select biofuel crops that do not compete with food production. Moreover, in Japan, "on-site models (small scale/dispersion type)" for biofuel crop cultivation in various areas are recommended, whereas conventional energy supply systems are "large-scale/concentrated type". Local development is advantageous in terms of crop cultivation, fuel production, circulation and environmental and economic evaluation, in collaboration with local governments and companies. In other words, a "local production for local consumption" system of biofuel production is sought. In this chapter, a model example for the application of sweet sorghum is introduced (Plate 4.3.2; Table 4.3.1).

Sweet sorghum (*Sorghum bicolor* Moench) produces many sugars in its stem (Kamiyama et al., 2008; Nitta et al., 2008). Because sweet sorghum is grown in widely diverse areas, including northern Japan, it offers the potential to produce great amounts of biofuel (ethanol) without adversely influencing the food-crop economy. Additionally, it has been reported to have a high ability to absorb nutrients from soil, including excess nitrogen and phosphorus, which would otherwise adversely influence the surrounding environment. We investigated the sugar yield potential of sweet sorghum to evaluate its biofuel productivity. Subsequently, we also assessed the plant's potential for use in bioremediation.

Plate 4.3.2 Sweet sorghum (var. FS902) cultivated at Ibaraki University, Japan (36°02′10″N, 140°12′43″E), in the suburbs of the Tokyo metropolitan area. The height of the bar is 4 m (October 2008)
Note: Please see page 433 for a colour version of this image.

Three varieties are common in Ibaraki prefecture in Japan: FS501 (Ko-tobun sorghum), FS902 (big sugar sorghum) and KCS105 (super sugar). Experiments were conducted in a field at Ibaraki University, Japan (36°02′10″N, 140°12′43″E), which is in a temperate zone approximately 50 km northeast of Tokyo. Sowing took place on 30 June 2007. Row and hill spacing were, respectively, 80 cm and 15 cm. Slow-release (coated) fertilizer was applied at the rate of 9 g/m^2 of N, P_2O_5 and K_2O. Subsequently, quick-acting fertilizers were applied at the rate of 3 g/m^2 of N, P_2O_5 and K_2O as a basal dressing (treatment A), and supplemental dressing at 45 days after sowing (treatment B), respectively. Above-ground portions were harvested at 102–153 days after sowing. For estimation of bioethanol yields, we adopted six formulae based on previous reports. Plate 4.3.2 shows a photograph of sweet sorghum grown in 2008. The plant height reached more than 4 m approximately four months after sowing.

Table 4.3.2 shows some of the growth characteristics and stem sugar contents. The shoot fresh weight was 537 g (FS501/B) to 929 g (FS902/B)/plant, which was equivalent to 44,750–77,416 kg/ha. The plant height was lowest in FS501/B (292 cm) and highest in FS902/A (486 cm). The brix value and stem sugar contents were 14.0–16.2 per cent and 67.5–122.0 g/plant, and sugar yields were 5,607 kg/ha for FS501/B and 10,221 kg/ha

Table 4.3.1 Comparison between sweet sorghum and sugarcane

	Growth period	Growth area	Shoot weight	Sugar yield	Ethanol yield
Sweet sorghum (var. FS902)	<4 months	Tropical and cold districts (in Japan almost the whole area)	71–77 tonnes/ha	8.7–10.1 tonnes/ha	3.5–4.5 tonnes/ha (4.4–5.7 kL/ha)
Sugarcane	12–18 months	Tropical zone/subtropical zone	60–90 tonnes/ha	–	3.1–5.5 tonnes/ha (4.0–7.0 kL/ha)

Source: Kamiyama et al. (2008).

Table 4.3.2 Growth characteristics and stem sugar contents in different sorghum varieties

Variety/ treatment	Harvest (days after sowing)	Shoot						Stem sugar content	
		Fresh weight (g/plant)	Fresh weight (kg/ha)	Dry weight (g/plant)	Water content (g/plant)	Plant length (cm)	Brix (%)	(g/plant)	(kg/ha)
FS501/A	22 November (145)	558d	46,500	137c	421d	289d	15.4a	76.4d	6,378
FS501/B	22 November (145)	537d	44,750	124c	413d	292d	14.0b	67.5d	5,607
FS902/A	26 November (149)	852ab	71,000	288a	565b	486a	15.9a	106.4b	8,901
FS902/B	26 November (149)	929a	77,416	294a	635a	480a	16.2a	122.0a	10,221
KCS105/A	22 November (145)	811bc	67,583	325a	487c	352b	15.9a	92.4c	7,669
KCS105/B	22 November (145)	718c	59,833	220b	497c	322c	15.3a	89.9c	7,487
LSD0.05	–	100	–	52	65	17	1.1	11.8	–

Note: Values including the same letter are not significantly different at the 5 per cent level according to Fisher's LSD test.

Table 4.3.3 Theoretical ethanol yield (L/ha)

Formula	KCS105		FS902		FS501	
	A	B	A	B	A	B
Equation 1	4,236.00	4,133.24	4,917.28	5642.59	3,522.57	3,095.49
Equation 2	5,470.95	4,839.28	5,748.19	6260.80	3,760.04	3,621.13
Equation 3 (538 g ethanol/kg sucrose)	3,555.58	3,194.14	4,071.30	4393.90	2,454.54	2,270.59
Equation 3 (700 g ethanol/kg sucrose)	4,625.55	4,155.34	5,296.47	5716.14	3,193.18	2,953.87
Equation 4 (0.052 g ethanol/g total fresh weight)	2,809.77	2,485.36	2,952.16	3215.43	1,931.08	1,859.74
Formula 4 (0.084 g ethanol/g total fresh weight)	4,504.82	3,984.70	4,733.10	5155.19	3,096.04	2,981.66

Notes:
Equation 1: Ethanol production (L/ha) = total sugar content (%) × 6.5 (a conversion factor) × 0.85 (the process efficiency) × total fresh weight (t/ha) (Lipinsky and Kresovich, 1982).
Equation 2: Ethanol production (L/ha) = 0.081 × total fresh weight (kg/ha) (Pari and Ragno, 1998).
Equation 3: Ethanol production (L/ha) = 64.8–84.3 × total fresh weight (t/ha) × percentage of stem in total fresh weight (%) (Soldatos and Chatzidaki, 1999).
Equation 4: Ethanol production (g/ha) = 5.2–8.4 × (total fresh weight (g/ha) ÷ 100) (Mamma et al., 1996).

for FS902/B, respectively. For the bioethanol yield estimation, we used the four formulae portrayed in Table 4.3.3 (Lipinsky and Kresovich, 1982; Pari and Ragno, 1998; Soldatos and Chatzidaki, 1999; Mamma et al., 1996).

In equations 3 and 4, 538 and 700 g ethanol/kg sucrose, 0.052 and 0.084 g ethanol/g total fresh weight were used, respectively. The bioethanol yield was highest in FS902, followed by KCS105 and FS501. In FS902 the bioethanol yield was 2,952–6,261 L/ha using six formulae. Bioethanol yields for KCS105 and FS501 were estimated to be 2,810–5,471 L/ha and 1,860–3,621 L/ha, respectively. The results show that estimated bioethanol yields were highest for FS902 (6,261 L/ha), and lowest in the other three varieties and treatments (1,860 L/ha).

The results of this study revealed that harvesting should be done after allowing a sufficient time to pass after heading, and plants were high and had large above-ground biomass, which would be an important consideration for higher sugar production. Ethanol production was estimated to be approximately 5 tonnes/ha.

In Tokyo suburbs, non-agricultural and idle land has increased considerably recently. In these areas and on farms, nitrogen accumulation is becoming a serious problem. Sweet sorghum has great potential not only to act as a biofuel crop but also to prevent nitrogen leaching in these areas.

Selecting the appropriate cultivar or variety, fertilizer application and culture management is important, and careful attention should be paid to weather conditions, harvesting dates and plant lengths of each variety. Above-ground biomass differs markedly among varieties and treatments, which implies that nutrient absorbance from soil also varies depending on the physiological characteristics of each variety.

Material recycling of sweet sorghum in local areas

Sweet sorghum, which was introduced into Japan in 1877 (Goto and Nakamura, 2000: 175–177), is thus considered highly suited for use as a biofuel crop because its bioethanol production potential is high. Sugar production using this species was initially attempted because the sugar concentration of juice from pulverized stems is high. However, cheap sugarcane imports from Taiwan and the higher quality of sugar from sugarcane meant that sweet sorghum came to be used as animal fodder. Indeed, the residual substances after juice extraction from sweet sorghum have been used extensively as animal feed (Smith, 1987). Other rational uses of sweet sorghum residues include biofuel and paper production, and sorghum grain is used for *baijiu* (spirits) in China. Furthermore, similar species of sweet sorghum are commonly used as a soil improvement material.

Consequently, in addition to bioethanol production, almost all parts of sweet sorghum are useful. Bioresource circulation systems accompanying biofuel production in local communities and the establishment of sustainable farm systems and renewable energy production are expected in the future.

4-3-5 Conclusion

The Industrial Revolution initiated the current era of mass production and mass consumption, creating the conditions that underpin the present disruptions of Earth's biogeochemical cycles. This collapse has manifested itself as disruption of food and energy production and disruption of the balance of carbon and nitrogen cycles. It is impossible to restore these balances in a timely fashion on a global basis. Nevertheless, agriculture presents a promising means of returning nutrient cycles to their original levels. Development of appropriate farming techniques, establishment and development of a sustainable society and material circulation all represent a departure from the extensive disruption of Earth's biogeochemical cycles. Such innovation on a local level will guide humanity to a global sustainable society. Improved understanding of ecology and the environment in agricultural and agronomic fields is therefore necessary.

In Asian countries, municipal and industrial wastes cause environmental or hazardous problems around extremely large cities. Moreover, in rural areas energy demand is increasing because of agricultural modernization. In these countries, because fertilizer and energy for agricultural areas are imported from abroad, environmentally destructive impacts occur in both municipal and rural areas. Consequently, energy production from biomass or organic waste can be expected to improve the demand-supply balance of energy, especially in rural areas. On the other hand, there is the possibility of competition between food production and energy crops. Furthermore, because plantation agriculture has caused degradation of forests and other natural environments, as well as poverty problems in diminished agro-forest areas, it is difficult to produce bioethanol by merely switching food production as the United States has accomplished with corn, or by using other strategies as Asian rural areas have done.

Global energy resources are supplied mainly by fossil fuels such as oil, coal and natural gas, in addition to atomic energy. In the case of oil, extraction technologies have improved remarkably, but present oil-field resources will be exhausted in 42 years if consumption rates continue along their present trends (BP, 2009). Moreover, natural gas is expected to be exhausted in 60 years (ibid.). Consequently, the quantities of these fossil fuels are extremely limited.

Atomic energy efforts also face quantitative limitations of available uranium. Some critics are quick to point out safety and stability issues. In addition, the problem of waste storage looms large in this crowded world. Thus the constant use and supply of atomic energy cannot be expected to expand throughout the world either now or in the near future. Consequently, it is necessary to push forward anew to achieve more effective utilization of limited energy resources.

What is a stable, safe and sustainable energy resource? The only solution is to use a renewable energy source such as biomass, wind or sunlight. Of those, biomass resources offer numerous important advantages in terms of storage, transportation and conversion to gas and liquids, in addition to being CO_2 neutral and offering the capability of local production and consumption.

The most reliable energy resources remain fossil fuels. However, from a mid- to long-term perspective, the promotion of renewable energy resources used together with fossil fuels is necessary. Furthermore, also in the long term, it is promising that the establishment of renewable energy systems includes production, distribution and usage within local areas. In this chapter, composting technology, methane fermentation, digestive liquids for fertilizer and bioethanol from sweet sorghum were introduced for use in a future recycling society. Furthermore, these technologies are available for application as a small-scale and diffuse allocation system, meaning that the environmental impact will be less than that of a large-scale, centralized system.

Currently, renewable energy presents many attractive options for consumers. Among them, biomass can produce huge amounts of various materials in Asia. Moreover, as described in this chapter, sustainable systems can be established in local areas to benefit local society. In Asian communities, biomass, as a promising choice for renewable energy, is expected to be promoted and studied further for improved effectiveness and sustainability.

REFERENCES

Bouwman, A. F. (1998) "Environmental Science: Nitrogen Oxides and Tropical Agriculture", *Nature* 392, pp. 866–867.

BP (2009) *Statistical Review of World Energy June 2009*. London: BP.

Galloway, James N., Alan R. Townsend, Jan W. Erisman, Mateete Bekunda, Zucong Cai, John R. Freney, Luiz A. Martinelli, Sybil P. Seitzinger and Mark A. Sutton (2008) "Transformation of the Nitrogen Cycle: Recent Trends, Questions, and Potential Solutions", *Science* 320, pp. 889–892.

Goto, Y. and S. Nakamura (2000) *Crop II – Upland Crop*. Tokyo: Japan Agricultural Development and Extension Association.

Gunaseelan, V. N. (1997) "Anaerobic Digestion of Biomass for Methane Production: A Review", *Biomass and Bioenergy* 13(1/2), pp. 83–114.

Houghton, John T., Yihui Ding, David J. Griggs, Maria Noguer, Paul J. van der Linden, Dai Xiaosu, Kathy Maskell and Catherine A. Johnson (eds) (2001) *Climate Change 2001: The Scientific Basis*, contribution of Working Group I to Third Assessment Report of Intergovernmental Panel on Climate Change. Cambridge: Cambridge University Press.

JIE (2008) *The Asian Biomass Handbook*. Tokyo: Japan Institute of Energy, pp. 120–144.

Kamiyama, A., Y. Nitta, T. Matsuda, S. Nakamura, Y. Goto, E. Inoue, K. Narisawa, Y. Kurusu, H. Ohta, S. Chonan, A. Toyoda, T. Kato, H. Kobayashi, M. Komatsuzaki and T. Sato (2008) "Sweet Sorghum Cultivation as a Biofuel Crop in the Suburbs of Tokyo Metropolitan Area", in *Abstracts of Fifth International Crop Science Congress & Exhibition*, Jeju, 13–18 April. Jeju: Congress Organizing Committee, p. 234.

Kato, T., H. Kuroda and H. Nakasone (2009) "Runoff Characteristics of Nutrients from an Agricultural Watershed with Intensive Livestock Production", *Journal of Hydrology* 368(1/4), pp. 79–87.

King, Gary M., David Kirchman, Abigail A. Salyers, William Schlesinger and James M. Tiedje (2003) "Global Environmental Change – Microbial Contributions, Microbial Solutions", public affairs report, American Society for Microbiology; available at www.asm.org/Policy/index.asp?bid=6004.

Komatsuzaki, Masakazu and Hiroyuki Ohta (2007) "Soil Management Practices for Sustainable Agro-ecosystems", *Sustainability Science* 2, pp. 103–120.

Liedi, B. E., J. Bombardiere and J. M. Chatfield (2006) "Fertilizer Potential of Liquid and Solid Effluent from Thermophilic Anaerobic Digestion of Poultry Waste", *Water Science & Technology* 53, pp. 69–79.

Lipinsky, E. S. and S. Kresovich (1982) "Sugar Crops as a Solar Energy Converter", *Cellular and Molecular Life Science* 38(1), pp. 13–18.

Mamma, D., D. Koulias, G. Fountoukidis, D. Kekos and G. J. Macris (1996) "Simultaneous Saccharification and Fermentation of Carbohydrates by a Mixed Microbial Culture", *Process Biochemistry* 31, pp. 377–381.

MAFF (2007) *The Present Conditions and a Problem of the Cultivation Abandonment of Farms*. Tokyo: Ministry of Agriculture, Forestry and Fisheries.

——— (2009) "To Maintain Irreplaceable Farmland – Promotion Guide for Usage of Abandoned Farm Areas"; available at www.maff.go.jp/j/nousin/tikei/houkiti/index.html.

Mulholland, Patrick J., Ashley M. Helton, Geoffrey C. Poole, Robert O. Hall Jr, Stephen K. Hamilton, Bruce J. Peterson, Jennifer L. Tank, Linda R. Ashkenas, Lee W. Cooper, Clifford N. Dahm, Walter K. Dodds, Stuart E. G. Findlay, Stanley V. Gregory, Nancy B. Grimm, Sherri L. Johnson, William H. McDowell, Judy L. Meyer, H. Maurice Valett, Jackson R. Webster, Clay P. Arango, Jake J. Beaulieu, Melody J. Bernot, Amy J. Burgin, Chelsea L. Crenshaw, Laura T. Johnson, B. R. Niederlehner, Jonathan M. O'Brien, Jody D. Potter, Richard W. Sheibley, Daniel J. Sobota and Suzanne M. Thomas (2008) "Stream Denitrification across Biomes and Its Response to Anthropogenic Nitrate Loading", *Nature* 452, pp. 202–205.

Nakasone, H., H. Kuroda and T. Kato (2002) "Causes of Animal Extinction in Small Irrigation Reservoirs in Japan and Requirements for Future Reestablishment", *Lakes & Reservoirs: Research & Management* 7(1), pp. 49–54.

Nitta, Y., A. Kamiyama, T. Matsuda, S. Nakamura, Y. Goto, E. Inoue, K. Narisawa, Y. Kurusu, H. Ohta, S. Chonan, A. Toyoda, T. Kato, H. Kobayashi, M. Komatsuzaki and T. Sato (2008) "Sweet Sorghum Cultivation as Biofuel Crop in Ibaraki Prefecture", *Japanese Journal of Crop Science* 77(Extra 1), pp. 90–91.

Pari, D. and I. Ragno (1998) "Biomass Crop Energy Balance", in H. Kopertx, T. Weber, W. Palz, P. Chartier and G. L. Ferrero (eds) *Proceedings of Tenth European Conference on Biomass for Energy and Industry*, Wurzburg, 8–11 June. Wurzburg: Organizing Committee, pp. 819–823.

Pierzynski, G. M., J. T. Sims and G. F. Vance (1994) *Soils and Environmental Quality*. Boca Raton, FL: CRC Press.

Renewable Fuels Association (2010) "2010 Ethanol Industry Outlook: Climate of Opportunity"; available at www.ethanolrfa.org/page/-/objects/pdf/outlook/RFAoutlook2010_fin.pdf?nocdn=1.

Smith, G. A. (1987) "Evaluation of Sweet Sorghum for Fermentable Sugar Production Potential", *Crop Science* 27, pp. 788–793.

Soldatos, P. and M. Chatzidaki (1999) "Economic Evaluation of Biofuel Production in Greece. The Case of Ethanol", *Proceedings of AgEnergy* 99(2), pp. 973–980.

4-4

Resource-circulating society and water security

Ken'ichi Nakagami, Hironori Hamasaki and Myat Nwe Khin

4-4-1 Introduction

A vital policy issue related to ensuring the viability of urban activities and the formation of a resource-circulating society is to secure sustainable water resources in metropolitan areas. One of the paradigm shifts involved in global, social and human systems is the movement towards achieving global sustainability and the development of resource-circulating societies. In Japan, the promotion of sustainable management of urban environments has been an established policy since the promulgation of the Basic Environment Law (1993) and the Fundamental Law for Establishing a Sound Material-Cycle Society (2000). Considering basin areas as functional land units within the context of developing a resource-circulating society, the primary aim of a basin management plan is the combined protection of water resources in urban and rural areas. The significance of developing a resource-circulating society is being considered in cases where integrated water resources management plans have been established as the primary method for environmental management. This chapter deals with the relationship between the sustainability of water resources and water security, and advocates the creation of a concept for ensuring water supplies to metropolitan areas.

Establishing a resource-circulating society in Asia: Challenges and opportunities, Morioka, Hanaki and Moriguchi (eds), United Nations University Press, 2011, ISBN 978-92-808-1182-7

4-4-2 Resource-circulating society and water resources environment

Since the enactment of the River Law in 1895, which set forth the basic concept of water resources environment management in Japan, the integration of resource management and environmental protection for rivers has proceeded with only a few revisions. In land use and urban development, the issue of river management is central in cities, rather than on the periphery, and the optimal management of water resources is a vital consideration in the development of a resource-circulating society. Water is a fundamental and vital resource for agriculture and industry. Especially in Asia, as the economy and population grow, so too will the demand for water, while the inefficiencies in water use are serious. Constructing a resource-circulating society, water use will be required to be much more efficient (ADB/IGES, 2008: 30–35).

Water, one of the necessities of life, is in a condition of crisis in many areas of the world. In such areas, water quantity and quality have reached dangerous levels, characterized by the phenomena of floods and droughts resulting from the impact of global warming, as well as acid rain and desertification. Because recent typhoons and other adverse weather phenomena have exceeded previous events in both scale and frequency, it is clear that urgent efforts are required in the mitigation of, and adaptation to, climate change.

Since the twentieth century, technology has evolved to assist with the conservation of water resources and other environmental issues. Because the ongoing water crisis is one of the most pressing issues of the twenty-first century, it is necessary to create a new socio-economic framework along with an international network to promote water security as a comprehensive and strategic necessity. The preservation of water resources and environmental security in urban areas is a fundamental aspect of a resource-circulating society.

Actions towards the formation of a resource-circulating society should be based on the conservation and regeneration of natural environments, improvements to living environments and provisions against waste and for mitigating global warming. As a result of the land and industrial policies adopted after the Second World War, both urbanization and depopulation in Japan accelerated and local water environments have become degraded. Numerous river ecosystems have been destroyed by excessive and improper waste disposal, land reclamation and the addition of excess concrete reinforcements. The phenomena of "red tides" resulting from eutrophication (such as that which occurred in Lake Biwa) and ecosystem destruction due to algal blooms (as has occurred in Lake Kasumigaura) are becoming increasingly frequent in lakes in Japan. At the seaside, pollution and the loss of natural coastal environments as a result of anthropogenic activities (such as along the shorelines of Tokyo and Osaka Bays) can be seen as a nationwide trend. Given the severely degraded status of the nation's water resources, it will be impossible to resolve extant problems merely by implementing conventional policies, such as decreasing water pollution loads and better observance of environmental water standards.

4-4-3 Water cycles and basin areas

Population increases in recent years have altered the network and distribution of rivers, watercourses, undeveloped land and land use. These changes affect the cycling of water and other substances (e.g. nutrients), ecosystems and land use, sometimes resulting in floods, water scarcity, etc. The substance cycle can be considered in terms of water quality as determined by the relation between pollutant loads and the water cycle, water quality in closed watersheds, eutrophication and other factors. In order to regenerate basin areas, management plans considering basins and urban areas in harmony with nature are now required in most major developed countries.

The scope of environmental considerations that need to be adopted by basin management plans should extend to cover the entire basin. The factors and elements to be taken into consideration can be categorized in accordance with the framework of environmental resources (Table 4.4.1).

- *Biophysical elements* (ecological environmental resources): e.g. water, air, soils, terrestrial life, aquatic life.
- *Economic elements* (productive activity-oriented environmental resources): e.g. primary, secondary and tertiary industries.
- *Urban elements* (urban activity-oriented environmental resources): e.g. urban space and urban social overhead capital.
- *Socio-cultural elements* (socio-cultural environmental resources): e.g. population, health, education, cultural assets and social organizations.

The main issues in the regeneration of basin areas are environmental conservation (including cultural scenery), reviving local areas (sustainability of economy) and harmonious achievement of both in addition to the protection and recovery of water cycles and river basin ecosystems.

4-4-4 Security of water resources and integrated water resource management

Water security is deeply related to considerations of the sustainability of water resources, environmental development and international

Table 4.4.1 Environmental resources framework

Environmental resources (ERs) / Environmental management	Environmental improvement	Environmental conservation	Environmental creation
Natural/ ecological ERs	Natural disasters Soil pollution	Biosphere Natural landscape	Environmental carrying capacity
Production activity-oriented ERs	Air pollution Water pollution Wastes	Lithosphere Water-sphere Atmosphere	Local energy
Urban activity-oriented ERs	Noise, vibration Odour Land subsidence	Spatial organization	Aesthetic resources
Socio-cultural ERs	Neighbourhood pollution	Historical and cultural resources	Amenities and services

environmental cooperation. The concept of water security is currently being formulated in line with security concepts in sectors other than traditional defence and diplomacy; it is defined as the "foundational and institutional maintenance of water resources and environmental security in urban areas". This indicates that arguments related to water issues have entered areas that are not sufficiently well understood from hydrological or "human beings and water culture" perspectives.

Severe water resource conditions have been reported in the Asia-Pacific region in recent years, including floods, droughts, water pollution, soil erosion, destruction of mangrove areas and groundwater pollution. Indeed, the greatest environmental problems of the region in the twenty-first century are urban and water-related. Not only are water shortages likely to continue in the metropolitan areas of the region, but fewer people will have access to safe water. Taken together, these issues have contributed to water security becoming an important issue in large Asian cities. One of the outcomes of the First Asia-Pacific Water Summit held in December 2007 was the "Message from Beppu". This was the chair's summation of the event, and it emphasized that protection from water disasters and water sanitation are deeply related to climate change. Among the goals set forth at the event was that the number of persons in the Asia-Pacific region who do not have access to safe drinking water and water-related sanitation facilities should be reduced by half by 2015, and to zero by 2025. The message emphasized that these targets should be realized within the context of water security, in spite of problems such as population growth, expense and required infrastructure.

The water systems that support both human life and production activities have improved constantly over time and been adapted to local areas. Water supply systems have changed, from the oldest method, where users drew water directly from wells or rivers, to modern systems that provide potable water within the comfortable surroundings of city life. Sewerage systems have evolved into fundamental infrastructures that are necessary for securing the safety of cities by enhancing sanitation and facilitating rainwater drainage. Irrigation systems have histories spanning thousands of years. They evolved in response to local conditions and have facilitated a continuous and sustainable supply of farm products. Modern cities have been made possible by the constant improvements to these social infrastructures over time.

Even so, many urban water environments are deteriorating and urban water security in some areas is more severe than ever before. Water security is defined as the "foundational and institutional maintenance of water resources environmental security in urban areas". The severity of the situation is exacerbated by difficulties associated with the financial and technical maintenance of social infrastructures and the serious damage to water resource environments resulting from climate change. This highlights the need not only to implement sustainable urban development but also to ensure water security by emphasizing the importance of fundamental and institutional maintenance of water infrastructure in urban areas. Water security in cities means securing hope for the future as well as pursuing solutions to current severe conditions and avoiding future threats.

Sustainability of water resources should be reflected in actual systems, based upon efficient and effective water resource management. Urban water security depends on urban conditions. Cities in Asia can be categorized as city areas centred on agriculture, city areas centred on industry and city areas based on sustainable society. The actions required by cities in order to secure water security are as follows:
- resolve existing water resource environment problems
- plan the future water resources environment
- ensure sustainability of the water resources environment.

To gain an understanding of these characteristics, it is necessary to consider the water security factors of each urban area. The process employed for establishing water security factors in urban areas is as follows.
- *Determination of urban areas based on water use and social system.* Urban areas are categorized as farm-centred societies, industrial-urban societies and sustainable societies. Since water usage differs between

Asian societies, the water resources environment must reflect those differences. Urban areas of local agricultural societies are areas where water use is centred on traditional agricultural use. Urban areas of industrial-urban societies are areas where water use is centred on industries and their associated services. Urban areas of sustainable societies are areas where use of water resources is centred on assuring sustainability in both urban growth and water use.

- *Setting standards for the use of water resources in each urban area.* The ordinal level (O) standard reflects a water resources environment under normal conditions. The emergency level (E) standard reflects a water resource environment that has been degraded from present conditions. The climate change level (C) standard reflects the water resources environment in situations where natural, social and institutional foundations have been structurally altered by climate change.

- *In each urban area, and for each water resources environment standard*, three factors are identified as components of water security: nature and ecosystems; technical and scientific characteristics; and society and culture. When focusing on sustainable societies in urban areas, additional factors are introduced: the quantity of water necessary for life; water quality; effectiveness of data collection; equity; efficiency; and incentives for improvement.

- *Distribution of water security factors in urban areas.* Nature and local ecosystems include land, ecology, rivers, lakes, forests; weather (climate change); and water balance (hydrological cycle, underground water). Technical and scientific characteristics cover planning (urban planning, environmental planning, water quality management); water systems (supply and demand, flood control, water quality management); and technology innovations (technology standards, management, evolution). Social and cultural factors include the economy (economic and industrial policy); finance (financial and monetary policy); and human development (education system, training programmes).

Using these factors, the status of urban water security can be evaluated at ordinal, emergency and climate change levels. It is necessary to construct an evaluation system for water security and diagnose the level of water security in urban areas. Based on the water security level, it may be necessary to consider mitigation and adaptation actions for dealing with the impact of climate change on water resources in urban areas. Table 4.4.2 shows the essential elements of integrated water resources management; it covers all the elements of the present water crisis and can be used by water resources management institutions to solve related problems.

Table 4.4.2 Elements of integrated water resource management

- Water resources: water quantity and quality, water balance, water cycle
- Integrated issues: sustainability, human rights, global warming
- Governance: basin integration, public participation, partnership
- Standard from the viewpoint of demands: accountability, transparency, equity, efficiency
- Interdisciplinary fields: technology, law, economics, political science

4-4-5 Constructing an integrated water resource infrastructure and developing a resource-circulating society in Yangon

Myanmar is the largest country on the mainland of Southeast Asia. It has a land area of approximately 677,000 km^2 and is divided into seven divisions and seven administrative states. Yangon, the former capital of the Union of Myanmar, is highly urbanized and had a city population of approximately 5 million in 2004.

The water basin characteristics in Myanmar are quite variable due to the differences in physiographic features. The principal watercourses flowing in Myanmar comprise four major rivers, the Ayeyarwady, Sittaung, Thanlwin and Bago, and their major tributaries. All rivers, except the Thanlwin, start within Myanmar territory and can be considered as national water assets. Their drainage area is spread widely over the country, amounting to 1,082 km^3 of water volume per annum from a drainage area of about 738,230 km^2. The estimated groundwater potential in Myanmar is about 495 km^3 in eight principal river basins.

As an agro-based country, the agricultural sector in Myanmar accounts for 90 per cent of water use while industry and domestic use is about 10 per cent. The total utilization of the nation's water resources is only about 5 per cent of the potential. It is clear that the physical potential for further development of water resources in Myanmar is quite substantial (Water Environment Partnership in Asia, 2009)

Stratigraphically, there are 11 different types of aquifers in Myanmar. Depending on their lithology and depositional environments, groundwater from those aquifers has disparities in quality and quantity. Groundwater from alluvial and Irrawaddian aquifers is more portable for both irrigation and domestic use. However, in the water-scarce regions, groundwater from Peguan, Eocene and plateau limestone aquifers is extracted for domestic use.

The former capital city, Yangon, is located 34 km inland from the mouth of the Yangon River. It is bounded by the Hlaing and Yangon

Rivers in the west, Pazundaung and Ngamoe Yeik Creeks in the east and northeast and Bago River in the southeast. Regardless of the abundance of water, concerns over the sustainability of water supply and protection of water quality have become important issues due to the influence of natural saline water intrusion and tidal effects of groundwater downstream of Yangon. Water resources for supplying the city are obtained further inland from the urban areas. Furthermore, there are many threats to water resources in Yangon. One of the most important is pollution in river water. Much of the city's river pollution is associated with urbanization.

With the increasing population and enhanced need of water for economic activities, there is pressure on extraction of groundwater in Yangon. This is accentuated by poor sanitation facilities, as there is an inherent risk in using shallow groundwater without the monitoring of pathogens. Control and management of groundwater are therefore necessary to ensure its safety. Unrestricted groundwater extraction could result in land subsidence and salt-water intrusion. To ensure recharge of groundwater aquifers, surface water has to be managed in cycle with the groundwater in an integrated way.

There are nine industrial estates developed within the city boundary; most are located near the rivers so as to be accessible by both motor vehicles and cargo ships. Although economically advantageous, locating these estates along and near the rivers increased the potential for environmental degradation. The government is already concerned that some factories are causing water pollution, and has taken measures to ensure that effluents are not discharged unless they are pre-treated to make them relatively free from pollutants. Some factories have been illegally discharging untreated wastewater into nearby rivers, including paper mills, textile mills with bleaching and dyeing facilities, tapioca starch factories, leather tanneries and breweries. In some areas agricultural pesticides have greatly increased water pollution.

As regards domestic sources of river pollution, wastewater discharge from household sources is one contributor. The centralized sewerage system covers only the central city area; many buildings in Yangon still rely on septic tanks to store waste, and pour-flush latrines and open-pit systems are used in suburban areas. The centralized sewerage network was constructed in 1888, and was designed to handle the human excreta of the 40,000 residents of the city at that time. The population of downtown Yangon today is approximately 350,000. The volume of untreated wastewater discharged from domestic sources and industrial effluent and pollution loads are both projected to increase with the urbanization and expansion of the city. In considering what services to include in a city, wastewater facilities are essential, being directly linked to public health and environmental security. A new wastewater treatment plant was constructed in 2004, and has reduced pollution to some extent. Nonetheless, constructing sewage disposal infrastructure is still an urgent issue in Yangon.

Untreated domestic wastewater and industrial effluent often flow into the sea with little or no provision to pipe them far enough out to sea to protect the beaches and inshore waters, thereby posing a major health risk. Furthermore, pollution from cities can also negatively impact on coastal fisheries and livelihoods, creating serious health problems in downstream settlements and reducing the usability of water.

Pathogenic bacteria and viruses are found in untreated sewage and effluent from industrial wastewater, storm-water runoff and leaching from open waste dumpsites. Increases in pathogen levels in water bodies are directly proportional to density of population. Hence the levels of pathogens found in streams and lakes are related to the concentration of people in cities. This is particularly true when wastewater is not treated.

The level of pathogens is measured by a variant of either dissolved oxygen (DO), biochemical oxygen demand (BOD) and/or chemical oxygen demand (COD). BOD measures the load of biodegradable organic substances and COD measures the chemical degradability of nearly all water-soluble organics. The higher the BOD or COD measure, the greater the oxygen needed to break down material in the water and the higher the level of organic pollution. In a sample with a fixed supply of oxygen, it is possible to measure the amount of oxygen consumed over a period of time (usually five days). The level of BOD in Yangon River is higher than the acceptable limit set for surface water of 20 mg/lit. Thus the river pollution, particularly biological/nutrient levels, remains an important environmental security concern in Yangon. U Khin Maung Win, managing director of Myanmar Water Engineering and Products, agreed that "in some areas, ailments like diarrhea occur due to a lack of sanitary systems and people are still unaware" (Win and San, 2004).

Many rivers and canals in the central part of the city play a role in the natural drainage system in Yangon. The drainage channels are covered with concrete slabs, some of which are broken or missing. The system was built more than 120 years ago during the British colonial period. An overloaded and faulty drainage network, filling up of drainage canals, lack of proper drain cleaning and the need for residents to make a bigger effort to follow regulations against littering have contributed to waterlogging in the city. An official said the creeks in Yangon are gradually narrowing because of the accumulation of sediment; the width of some creeks had narrowed by half to about 10 feet (Wai, 2005). Many areas of the city are subject to seasonal flooding, so there are also city-wide water-related challenges.

Wetlands are formed by the seasonal flooding of the rivers during the monsoon and after the floods subside, especially downstream. These wetlands provide a habitat for many aquatic and bird species and improve the overall landscape aesthetically. Freshwater lakes are also of substantial economic importance. There are more than 100 natural or man-made reservoirs throughout the country and six reservoirs/lakes in Yangon, providing drinking water and water for agriculture. However, many of these aquatic ecosystems are under pressure from settlement, economic development and overuse. The river systems are widely disturbed by sediment.

The mission statement of the water sector states its purpose as relating "to the establishment of a beneficial framework and effective mechanism for managing, developing and protecting water and related resources in an environmentally and economically sound manner in order to meet the needs of the people of Myanmar". However, there is no single law covering all aspects of water resources. The Ministry of Forestry was originally responsible for the rehabilitation and conservation of forests and watersheds, especially in rural areas. The National Commission for Environmental Affairs (NCEA), which was formed in 1990, has subsequently assumed responsibility for all environmental matters. To establish sound policies in the utilization of water, land, forests, minerals, marine resources and other natural resources for conserving the environment and preventing its degradation, the government of Myanmar adopted the national environmental policy in December 1994.

The Irrigation Department and Water Resources Utilization Department are responsible for river water quality testing and studies for new water development projects. The Environmental Conservation Committee was set up in 2004 for conservation purposes. Nevertheless, no regular water tests have been conducted for any of the streams and rivers in Myanmar. Furthermore, the Yangon City Development Committee has enacted regulations to control the systematic disposal of sewerage from households, commercial activities and factories. Emission standards for water and air pollution were formulated as part of a ministerial standing order issued by the Ministry of Industry, but these refer only to wastes generated by industrial activities. There is no specific national law or regulation on sewerage system management in Myanmar. The NCEA has therefore initiated the drafting of a framework Myanmar Environmental Protection Law. However, the specific contents of this order cannot be fully implemented. There has also been no discussion regarding environmental pollution control management in annual meetings or official reports.

While infrastructural improvements are being implemented, the problems of water quality management in Myanmar involve numerous legal issues that must be addressed. The existing institutional mechanism and legal authority for the control of industrial and domestic effluents and water pollution are ambiguous. Responsibility is fragmented among many agencies at low levels in the bureaucratic hierarchy. Thus the roles and responsibilities of various government agencies as they relate to specific activities in water pollution control need to be clarified. There is an urgent need for additional legislation or decrees to ensure proper management. The legal framework (i.e. laws, ordinances, regulations, sanctions for non-compliance) covering pollution control and waste management should define the responsibilities of each organization in implementing relevant laws and the procedures by which the responsible agencies should carry out their functions. Meeting the urban environmental challenges with regard to pollution control is a shared task with actions taken by a host of stakeholders, including national and local governments, non-governmental organizations, communities, the private sector and international agencies. Therefore higher political commitment and priority need to be assigned to the water resources sector along with appropriate support, including adequate financial and human resources.

The most important elements in forming a resource-circulating society in Myanmar include the need for the following:

- national consistency in methods for setting goals, objectives and standards
- a clear and explicit administrative process and responsibilities for the water sector
- accountability and matching of administrative structures
- involvement of stakeholders in definitions of goals, development of plans and implementation of strategies
- grasping opportunities for harnessing market forces to water quality management tasks
- developing water quality criteria/guidelines
- developing waste treatment facilities.

4-4-6 Conclusion

The expansion of modern urban areas into the basin areas of Asia has resulted in drastic changes that must be understood from the viewpoint of sustainability of the water resources environment and water security in urban areas. As such, the need to build resource-circulating societies is becoming critical.

Acknowledgements

This work was funded by Grant-in-Aid for Scientific Research B, Ministry of Education, Culture, Science and Technology, "Water Resources & Environmental Impact Evaluation by Climate Change and Integrated Water Resources Management", representative researcher Ken'ichi Nakagami (Ritsumeikan University).

REFERENCES

ADB/IGES (2008) *Toward Resource-Efficient Economies in Asia and the Pacific.* Manila: Asian Development Bank/Institute for Global Environmental Strategies.

Wai, Phyo Myint (2005) "Drains Under Pressure", *Myanmar Times Weekly Review*, 11–17 July; available at www.myanmar.gov.mm/myanmartimes/no274/MyanmarTimes14-274/n015.htm.

Water Environment Partnership in Asia (2009) "State of Water Environmental Issues – Myanmar"; available at www.wepa-db.net/policies/state/myanmar/myanmar.htm.

Win, M. T. and M. M. San (2004) "Yangon's Sanitation System Must Be Overhauled: Experts", *Myanmar Times*, 4–10 October; available at www.myanmar.com/myanmartimes/MyanmarTimes12-236/023.htm.

4-5

Development of biomass recycling on the urban fringe: A case study in Nonthaburi province, Thailand

Ai Hiramatsu, Yuji Hara and Keisuke Hanaki

4-5-1 Biomass circulation in urban-rural fringe areas

The urban-rural fringe area is the border between urban land use and rural areas. Mixed urban-rural land use is common in large Asian cities situated on deltaic lowlands in the humid monsoonal climate zone (McGee, 1991). Before urbanization, such lowlands were intensively cultivated, primarily to grow rice, which supported a considerable rural population and for which infrastructure such as irrigation canals and pathways between paddies was developed. Due to scarcity of funds and a lack of plans for developing new urban infrastructure, this rural infrastructure is directly converted during urban development. Irrigation canals become drainage routes for urban wastewater, and rural pathways become paved urban roads. Because the original rural population is not completely displaced, this reuse of rural infrastructure has resulted in a broad mosaic of urban and rural land uses in expanding urban-rural fringe areas (Hara, Takeuchi and Okubo, 2005).

Although this urban-rural land-use mixture has produced several urban environmental problems, it does have several associated advantages. Current urban planning measures, which are of Western origin and designed to separate urban and rural areas, do not adapt well to Asian cities. Instead, it is more practical to accept the inherent Asian urban-rural land-use mixture, and develop planning measures that maximize and minimize the associated advantages and disadvantages, respectively (Yokohari et al., 2000).

Establishing a resource-circulating society in Asia: Challenges and opportunities, Morioka, Hanaki and Moriguchi (eds), United Nations University Press, 2011, ISBN 978-92-808-1182-7

Biomass utilization is one of the most promising advantages of mixed urban and rural land uses. Because of the spatial contiguity between urban and rural areas, the cost and energy requirements of delivering compost of urban organic waste origin to farmlands can be lower. Moreover, fresh vegetables produced by farms using such compost can be consumed by the residents of the adjacent urban settlements. Such urban bioresource circulation can efficiently contribute to the establishment of a resource-circulating society (Takeuchi and Hara, 2006).

However, in reality the supply of compost often exceeds the demand (Furutani et al., 2009). The amount of waste discharged from urban areas is considerably in excess of what is needed to make compost for agricultural use in the surrounding rural areas. Another constraint is the cost of transport. Because compost has a lower price than the same weight or volume of vegetables, it is not economically viable to transport it long distances. A situation has therefore arisen in which there is an imbalance in the exchange of biomass, and this needs to be addressed.

4-5-2 Nitrogen balance in urban-rural fringe areas in Nonthaburi province, Thailand

Case study is an effective way to reveal the balance between compost supply from urban activities and nitrogen demands in agriculture in urban fringe areas. Previous studies dealing with urban-rural bioresource circulation systems have been conceptual and theoretical, and thus provide only limited usable information and indicators regarding biomass utilization. This is, in part, because of spatial-scale gaps between material flow analysis (MFA) studies and land-use studies. MFA research relies primarily on statistical data based on administrative boundaries, which do not reflect detailed urban-rural land-use patterns (Haberl et al., 2004). In contrast, land-use studies typically use existing maps as well as aerial and satellite images to analyse spatiotemporal patterns of land use. However, such studies give little consideration to variable material flows accompanying land-use changes. Furthermore, in developing Asian cities reliable statistical data for MFA studies and imagery for land-use map preparation are often unavailable. This makes it difficult to conduct comprehensive studies on urban-rural land uses and bioresource flows (Kojima, 2008).

In considering the ideal concept of urban-rural harmonization along with the lack of actual field information, we conducted a field case study in the urban-rural fringe area of the Bangkok metropolitan region (BMR) in Thailand, focusing on the spatial scale at which the actual mosaic of urban and rural land uses could be distinguished, and examined the associated spatial patterns of land use and existing bioresource flows between them. In this chapter we evaluate the potential amount of compost that might be produced from organic wastes and utilized in farmlands instead of the current fertilizer input. Finally, we discuss spatial-scale matching between the urban-rural land-use mosaic and the increased biomass flow, as well as possible indicators to create more detailed scenarios for the development of Asian urban-rural resource-circulating societies.

Study area

The BMR is a typical fast-growing Asian urban region with a broad fringe area comprising a mosaic of urban and rural land uses (Hara, Takeuchi and Okubo, 2005). Our study area was in Nonthaburi province (Figure 4.5.1), where urbanization is proceeding rapidly. The population

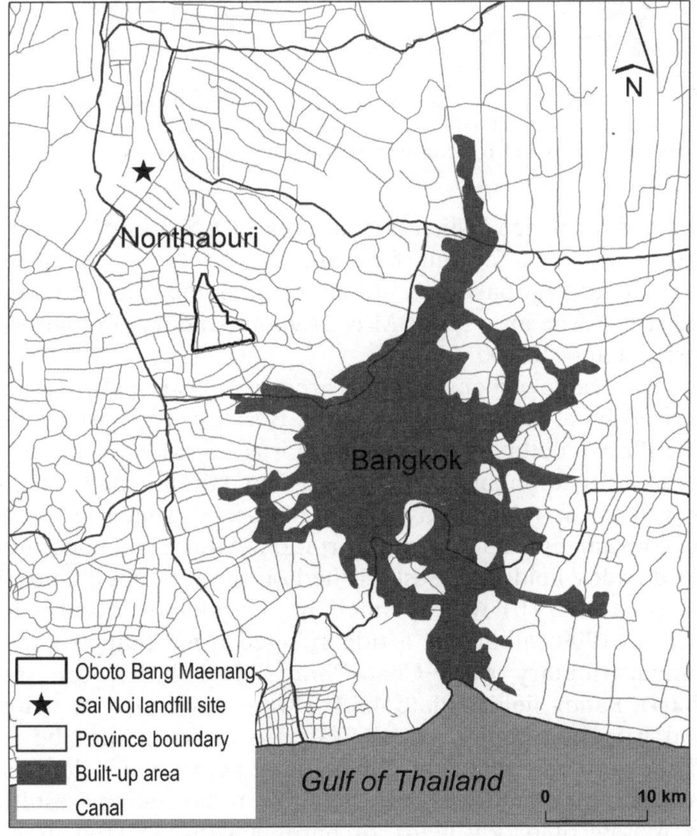

Figure 4.5.1 Case study area

Plate 4.5.1 Typical features of the study area: (a) paddy field, (b) orchards and gardens, (c) canal transport, (d) garbage collection truck
Note: Please see page 434 for colour versions of these images.

of Nonthaburi province, which has an area of 622.3 km^2, was 986,000 in 2006. The study area for our field survey was Oboto Bang Maenang (OBM), in the central part of Nonthaburi (an *oboto* is a local administrative subdistrict). The area of OBM is 21.9 km^2, and its population in 2007 was approximately 18,000.

Before it became urbanized, this area was historically agrarian and characterized by a dense canal network. Because it is part of the extensive Chao Phraya delta, canal excavation was necessary to provide irrigation for rice cultivation and fill for house foundations (made of excavated soil), as well as for water transport (Plate 4.5.1c), which in the past was the most convenient mode of transportation. After canal construction, orchards and paddy fields were established on the reclaimed land. In OBM orchards (Plate 4.5.1b) were planted in a poldered, raised-bed system (Molle et al., 1999) alongside a tide-affected canal that was formerly a natural main tributary of the Chao Phraya (Tachakitkachorn and Shigemura, 2004). Paddy fields (Plate 4.5.1a) were developed as strips beside excavated irrigation canals, whose water level could thus be managed (Hara, Thaitakoo and Takeuchi, 2008). These agrarian developments continued to influence land-use patterns after urbanization, resulting in a complex mosaic of paddy fields, orchards and urban land uses (Figure 4.5.2).

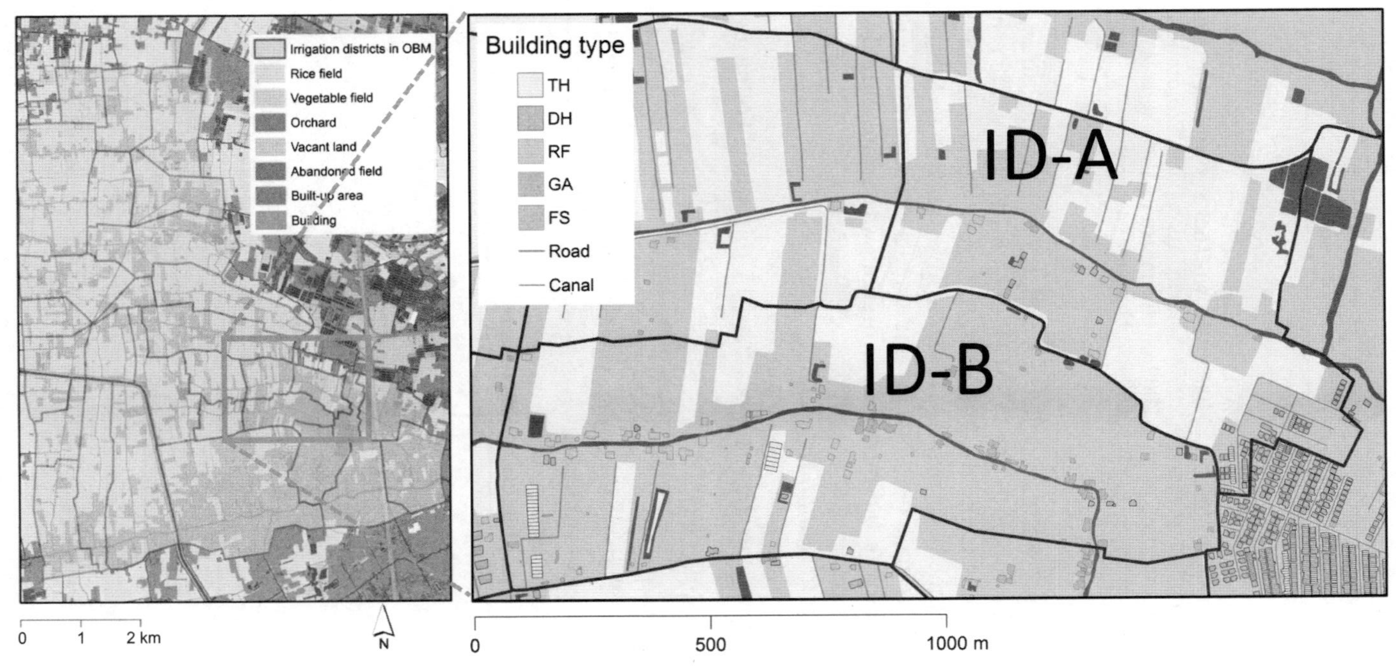

Figure 4.5.2 Current land-use patterns in irrigation districts in OBM (a) and sample districts ID-A and ID-B (b)

Table 4.5.1 Data sources

Data source	Year	Reference
Digital vector map	2003	Department of Public Works and Town & Country Planning, Thailand
Digital vector map	2007	Hiramatsu et al. (2009)
1:25000 colour aerial photos	2002	Royal Thai Survey Department
ALOS PRISM satellite imagery	2007	Japan Aerospace Exploration Agency
Waste generation amount	2009	Hiramatsu et al. (2009)
Nutrient flow via canal	2009	Honda et al. (2010)

Municipal solid waste is collected and transported in three garbage trucks owned and operated by OBM (Plate 4.5.1d). The waste is currently transferred directly to the Sai Noi landfill (Figure 4.5.1), which is the only landfill in Nonthaburi province (Hiramatsu et al., 2009). Most valuable materials such as glass bottles, cans and metals are separated and sold to private sector buyers, but most of the organic wastes are buried.

Data sources and spatial analysis

Table 4.5.1 shows the data sources used in this study. Following Honda et al. (2010), we considered an irrigation district to be the basic minimum spatial unit for bioresource circulation, calculated on a nitrogen basis via irrigation water. An irrigation district is an area of farmland irrigated and drained by the same canal section (Figure 4.5.3). Because OBM is in the

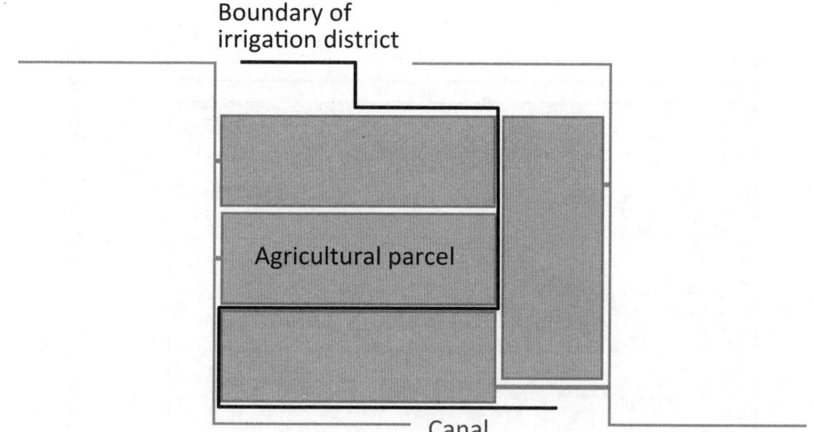

Figure 4.5.3 Definition of an irrigation district

lower part of the Chao Phraya delta, where the average gradient is 0.006/1000 (JICA, 1985), each farm parcel generally has only one water gate. Traditionally, water-level fluctuations caused by tides were used to irrigate and drain the fields; petrol-powered pumps are currently used (Hara, Takeuchi and Okubo, 2005). Hence we used the irrigation district as the basic spatial unit in our analysis of bioresource flow. We identified irrigation districts in OBM for the current canal configuration by interpreting aerial photographs and ALOS PRISM satellite imagery (Table 4.5.1) with ground truthing (Figure 4.5.2a).

In this study we used the data on amounts of household waste generation reported by Hiramatsu et al. (2009), and also conducted elemental analyses at the Environmental Center of Rajabhat Suan Dusit University (Table 4.5.2). Sampling was done by house type using the house-type categories of the digital base maps (Table 4.5.1). We used the average nitrogen content of sampled waste generated by each house type in our calculations.

Our study focused on two sample irrigation districts, ID-A and ID-B, along two canals (Figure 4.5.2b) in which the current nutrient flow was studied by Honda et al. (2010). We first calculated the total nitrogen amount generated by household waste within ID-A and ID-B in 2003 and 2007 using the following formula:

$$V = \sum_{k=1}^{n} \left(X_k \times Y_k \times Z_k \right)$$

V: total nitrogen content of waste generated by all households
X_k: nitrogen content of waste generated by one person by house type
Y_k: average household population by house type
Z_k: total number of households by house type
k: house type

We then calculated the potential nitrogen content of compost made from the waste using the following N-loss formula (Kirchmann, 1985):

$$\text{N-loss ratio} = 0.559031 - 0.01108 \times \text{C/N ratio}$$

where the C/N ratio was estimated from the waste sample elemental test results.

We estimated the compost demand by farmlands in 2003 and 2007 by multiplying the areas of paddy fields and orchards (calculated with GIS) by the input data (per square metre) reported by Honda et al. (2010).

Table 4.5.2 Household waste generation units

House type (defined by Hiramatsu et al., 2009)		Abbreviation	Waste generation amount (kg/day/person)	Average nitrogen content (%)	Average carbon content (%)	Average no. of persons per household
Urban	Town house	TH	0.54	4.5	42.5	2.39
	Detached house	DH	0.54	4.0	48.9	2.16
	Food shop	FS	1.11	3.6	28.2	3.16
Rural	Rice farmer's house	RF	0.30	4.8	41.2	3.53
	Gardener's house	GA	0.61	4.1	40.5	3.53

Due to its slow-acting nature, all of the nitrogen needed for cultivation cannot realistically be supplied by compost alone, so in this study we assumed that just half of the needed nitrogen would be supplied by compost. Next, we compared the supply in compost with demand for nitrogen in 2003 and 2007 within ID-A and ID-B. Finally, we calculated population densities that balanced the nitrogen supply and demand in ID-A and ID-B by comparing the results between 2003 and 2007. In the same way, we calculated the compost supply-demand balance for each irrigation district and visualized it using GIS.

Estimated results

Figure 4.5.4 shows the nitrogen-basis supply-demand balance between household waste generation and fertilizer input for farmlands in relation to population density in ID-A and ID-B. The balancing point between the nitrogen supply in compost and the nitrogen demand of farmlands was approximately 1,200 persons/km^2 for ID-A and 1,400 persons/km^2 for ID-B. These densities correspond to a residential area to total area ratio of 9 per cent for ID-A and 10 per cent for ID-B. Figure 4.5.5 shows the supply-demand balance for each irrigation district; only a few irrigation districts faced an oversupply of compost of household-waste origin at the development density of 2007.

These results support our view that it is possible to develop an efficient bioresource circulation system between spatially adjoining urban and rural areas on the fringes of large Asian cities, where a highly variable mosaic of urban and rural land uses exists. We propose that planners should put more emphasis on density-control measures that consider bioresource circulation within an irrigation district (Figure 4.5.5) rather than just drawing arbitrary land-use zoning lines (Figure 4.5.6). To this end, the division between agricultural and urban planning in governmental bodies must be bridged, and studies should take an interdisciplinary approach.

4-5-3 Promotion of biomass-circulation systems in fringes

The previous section showed that nitrogen from urban activities can be effectively used in agricultural areas. However, establishment of solid waste management and a biomass-circulation system is necessary to realize this. As urban-rural fringe areas usually change rapidly, establishment of such a system is difficult, but is the key to success. Both physical and social systems need to be established.

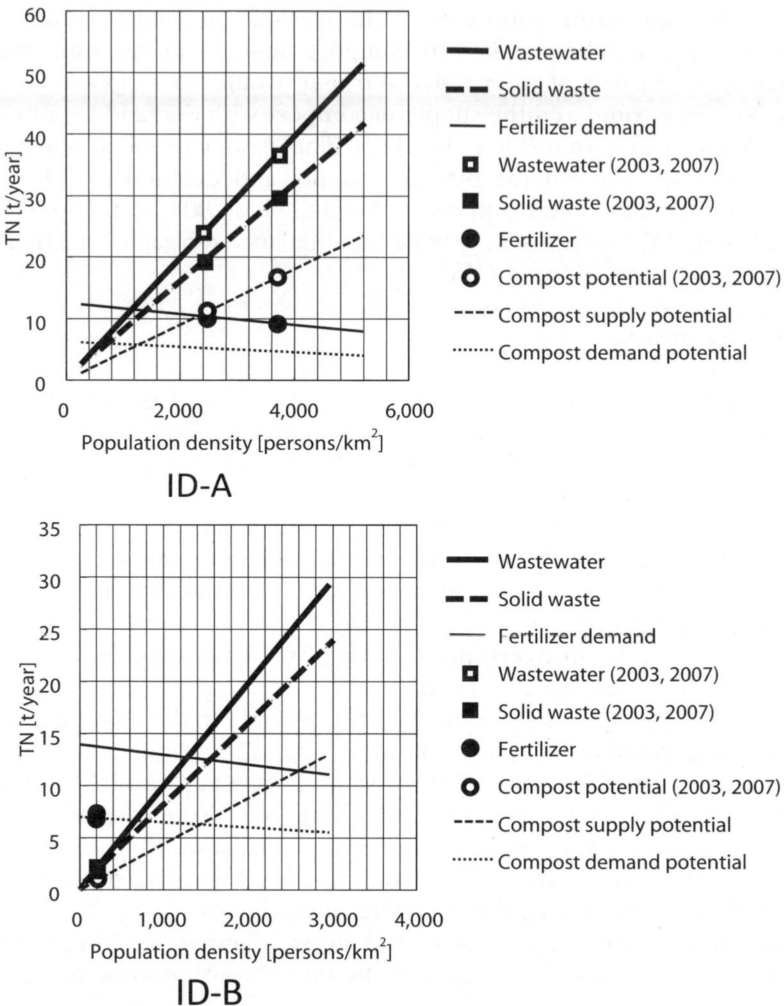

Figure 4.5.4 Nitrogen-basis supply and demand balance between household waste generation and fertilizer input to farmlands in relation to population density in ID-A and ID-B

Solid waste collection systems are not well established in this case-study area. Domestic solid waste collection for town houses, apartments and food shops was 100 per cent, but for detached houses was only 64 per cent (Hiramatsu et al., 2009). Satisfactory sanitary conditions have not yet been established.

Public awareness is also essential to promote a biomass-circulation system. Less than 33 per cent of residents of Nonthaburi knew the fate of

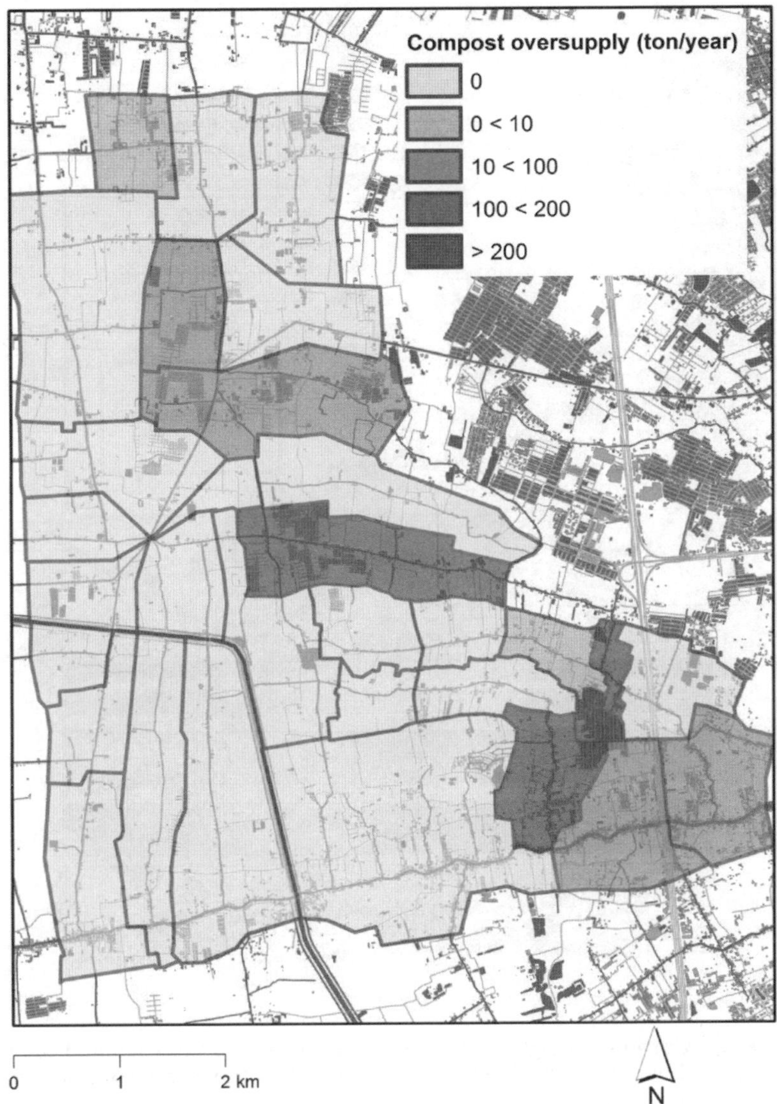

Figure 4.5.5 Map of OBM showing compost oversupply in the irrigation districts

their solid waste, but 80 per cent of households separated glass bottles and similar materials to sell them to private buyers (ibid.). Organizing people's behaviour and giving incentives are needed to enhance the circulation.

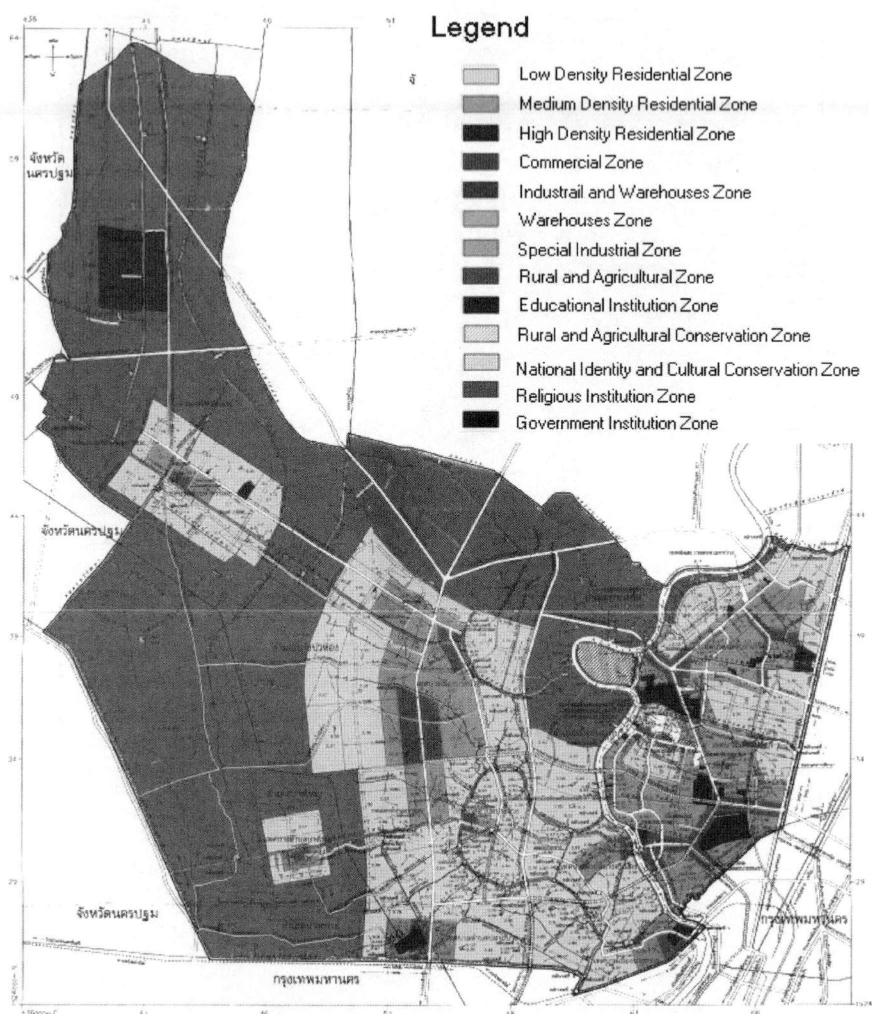

Figure 4.5.6 Current zoning map of Nonthaburi province showing land-use planning, which is based on the existing road network without any consideration of irrigation districts
Note: Please see page 428 for a colour version of this figure.

REFERENCES

Furutani, Takashi, Yuji Hara, Akinobu Murakami, Armando M. Palijon and Makoto Yokohari (2009) "Organic Waste Management and the Potential of Its Local Recycle Use in the Suburbs of Metro Manila", *Landscape Research Japan* 72, pp. 719–722 (in Japanese with English abstract).

Haberl, Helmut, Marina Fischer-Kowalskia, Fridolin Krausmanna, Helga Weisza and Verena Winiwarter (2004) "Progress Towards Sustainability? What the Conceptual Framework of Material and Energy Flow Accounting (MEFA) Can Offer", *Land Use Policy* 21, pp. 199–213.

Hara, Yuji, Kazuhiko Takeuchi and Satoru Okubo (2005) "Urbanization Linked with Past Agricultural Land-use Patterns in the Urban Fringe of a Deltaic Asian Megacity: A Case Study in Bangkok", *Landscape and Urban Planning* 73, pp. 16–28.

Hara, Yuji, Danai Thaitakoo and Kazuhiko Takeuchi (2008) "Landform Transformation on the Urban Fringe of Bangkok: The Need to Review Land-use Planning Processes with Consideration of the Flow of Fill Materials to Developing Areas", *Landscape and Urban Planning* 84, pp. 74–91.

Hiramatsu, Ai, Yuji Hara, Makiko Sekiyama, Ryo Honda and Chart Chiemchaisri (2009) "Municipal Solid Waste Flow and Waste Generation Characteristics in an Urban-Rural Fringe Area in Thailand", *Waste Management & Research* 27, pp. 951–960.

Honda, Ryo, Yuji Hara, Makiko Sekiyama and Ai Hiramatsu (2010) "Impacts of Housing Development on Nutrients Flow along Canals in a Peri-urban Area of Bangkok, Thailand", *Water Science and Technology* 61(4), pp. 1073–1080.

JICA (1985) *Master Plan on Flood Protection/Drainage Project in Eastern Suburban Bangkok*. Tokyo: Japan International Cooperation Agency.

Kirchmann, Holger (1985) "Losses, Plant Uptake and Utilization of Manure Nitrogen during a Production Cycle", *Acta Agriculture Scandinavica* Supplement 24.

Kojima, Michikazu (ed.) (2008) *Recycling in Asia*. Chiba: JETRO (in Japanese).

McGee, Terry G. (1991) "The Emergence of Desakota Regions in Asia: Expanding a Hypothesis", in N. Ginsburg, B. Koppel and T. G. McGee (eds) *The Extended Metropolis: Settlement Transition in Asia*. Honolulu: University of Hawaii Press, pp. 3–25.

Molle, François, Chusak Sutthi, Jesda Keawkulaya and Roongnapa Korpraditskul (1999) "Water Management in Raised Bed Systems: A Case Study from the Chao Phraya Delta, Thailand", *Agricultural Water Management* 39, pp. 1–17.

Tachakitkachorn, Terdsak and Tsutomu Shigemura (2004) "Spatial Structure and Transformation Process of Waterside Dwelling in Khlong Bangkoknoi Waterway Network: Case study of the Waterside Village in WatSakyai and WatJumpa Canal", *Memoirs of the Graduate School of Science and Technology, Kobe University* 22A, pp. 45–55.

Takeuchi, Kazuhiko and Yuji Hara (2006) "Recycling-Oriented Society and Urban-Rural Sustainability in Asian Megacities", *Journal of Rural Planning Association Japan* 25, pp. 201–205 (in Japanese with English abstract).

Yokohari, Makoto, Kazuhiko Takeuchi, Takashi Watanabe and Shigehiro Yokota (2000) "Beyond Greenbelts and Zoning: A New Planning Concept for the Environment of Asian Megacities", *Landscape and Urban Planning* 47, pp. 159–171.

5

Biotic resource utilization and technology development

5-1

Potential of bioethanol production from rice in Thailand – Scenarios based on fuel, feed and food priority strategy

Shinya Yokoyama, Kiyotaka Saga and Toshiaki Iida

5-1-1 Estimation of the potential of ethanol production from rice

At present, the average rice yield in non-irrigated fields in Thailand is 2.6 tonnes per hectare (t/ha). Since the average yield in Japan is 5.3 t/ha, with advanced irrigation, sufficient fertilizer application and high-yield rice planting, it is expected that the same yields could be achieved in Thailand.

We assumed that 434 L (litres) of ethanol can be produced from 1 tonne of rice, 300 L from 1 tonne of rice straw and 264 L from 1 tonne of rice husk, respectively. Ultimately, 792 L of ethanol could be produced from 1 tonne of rice, as seen in Table 5.1.1.

5-1-2 Improvement of rice yield by irrigation

First, the yield of rice planted during the rainy and dry seasons should be clarified. Statistics from the Thai Office of Agricultural Economics (www. oae.go.th) show that the yields of rice planted during the rainy season on irrigated and non-irrigated fields are 2.6 t/ha and 1.6 t/ha, respectively. During the dry season the yield is 3.6 t/ha irrespective of irrigation. Thus it is assumed that the yield of rice planted during the rainy season increases by a factor of 1.6 by irrigation, but that rice planted during the dry season is not affected by irrigation provided that sufficient water is

Establishing a resource-circulating society in Asia: Challenges and opportunities, Morioka, Hanaki and Moriguchi (eds), United Nations University Press, 2011, ISBN 978-92-808-1182-7

Table 5.1.1 Ethanol production from different parts of rice plant

Rice	1.0 t	434 L
Rice straw	1.0 t	300 L
Rice husk	0.22 t	58 L
Whole crop	2.22 t	792 L

Note: The ratios of rice straw and rice husk to rice are 1:1:22 on a dry basis (Ogawa, Takeuchi and Katayama, 1988). For rice, starch content is 87 per cent, hydrolysis efficiency 95 per cent and fermentation efficiency 90 per cent. For rice straw, cellulose and hemicellulose are 43 per cent and 25 per cent. For rice husk, cellulose and hemicellulose are 35 per cent and 25 per cent (NAS, 1989).

supplied to the fields to grow the rice. We can thus safely assume that irrigation has a negligible effect on the yield of rice planted during the dry season.

Increase in available harvesting area by irrigation

The harvested area of rice in Thailand is approximately 9 million ha, and approximately 25 per cent of this is irrigated. This proportion increased by 5 per cent per year from 1981 until 1985, then remained constant for the next 20 years. This is primarily because the price of rice decreased as consumption fell, so there was no need to increase production. However, in order to produce bioethanol, the yield of rice should be increased by irrigation.

Potential of proportion of irrigated land for rice production

It is important to identify the best region in Thailand for improvement by irrigation. The proportion of irrigated land in the northeastern region is approximately 10 per cent, which is significantly less than in other regions. Furthermore, the rice yield in this region is just 1.6 t/ha, which is considerably below the yield of 2.6 t/ha in the central plains. However, as shown in Figure 5.1.1, the rice-harvesting area in the northeastern region provides more than 50 per cent of Thailand's total rice production. It therefore appears feasible to increase the proportion of irrigated land in this region.

Next, we considered the potential amount of land to be earmarked for irrigation. According to the literature (Boonlue, 2005), the proportion of irrigated land in the northeastern region could be increased from 10 per cent to 40 per cent, which would mean that the overall proportion of irrigated land in Thailand could be raised to 50 per cent.

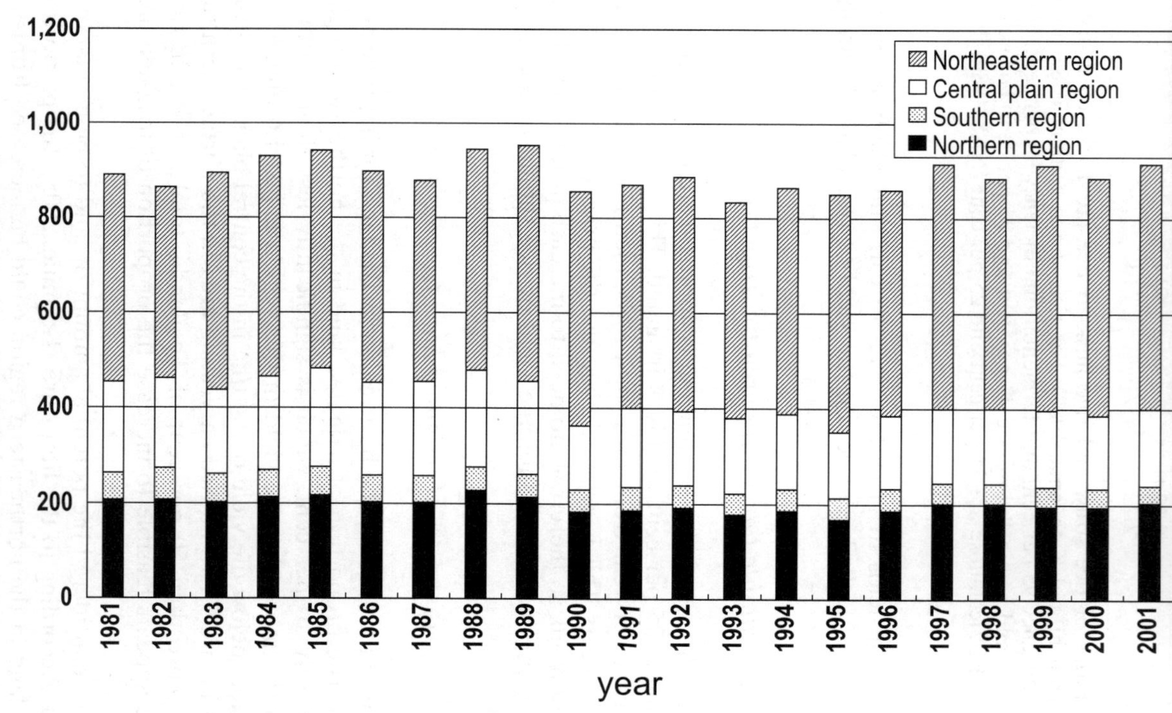

Figure 5.1.1 Annual changes in rice yields per region (rainy season)

5-1-3 The effect of chemical fertilizer application on rice yield

The effect of fertilizer application on rice yield is also important. We examined fertilizer application in Thailand and Japan based on available statistical data and clarified the relationship between fertilizer application and rice yield. From these data, we extrapolated the rice yield that could be obtained in Thailand by using the same level of fertilizer application as in Japan.

Fertilizer application for rice production in Thailand

The rate of fertilizer application for rice production in Thailand at present is less than 20 kg/ha. In Japan, fertilizer application was 120 kg/ha in the late 1980s; this has now decreased to 70 kg/ha (Figure 5.1.2). Fertilizer application in Thailand therefore appears insufficient since it is less than one-third of that used in Japan. Figure 5.1.3 shows the annual variation in chemical fertilizer application in Thailand (Office of Agricultural Economics, 1982, 1990, 1997).

Relationship between chemical fertilizer application and rice yield

First, we analysed the relationship between chemical fertilizer application and rice yield for irrigated fields in Japan. A comparison from the 1940s

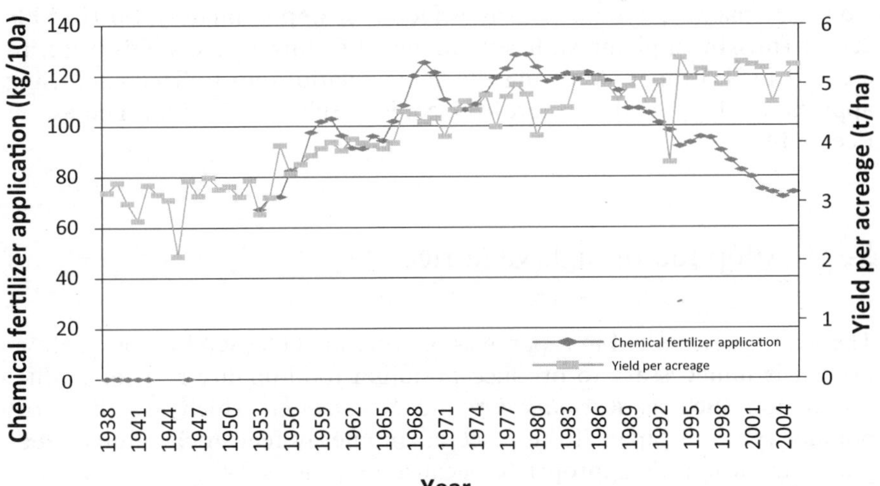

Figure 5.1.2 Annual change of chemical fertilizer application and rice yield in Japan over time

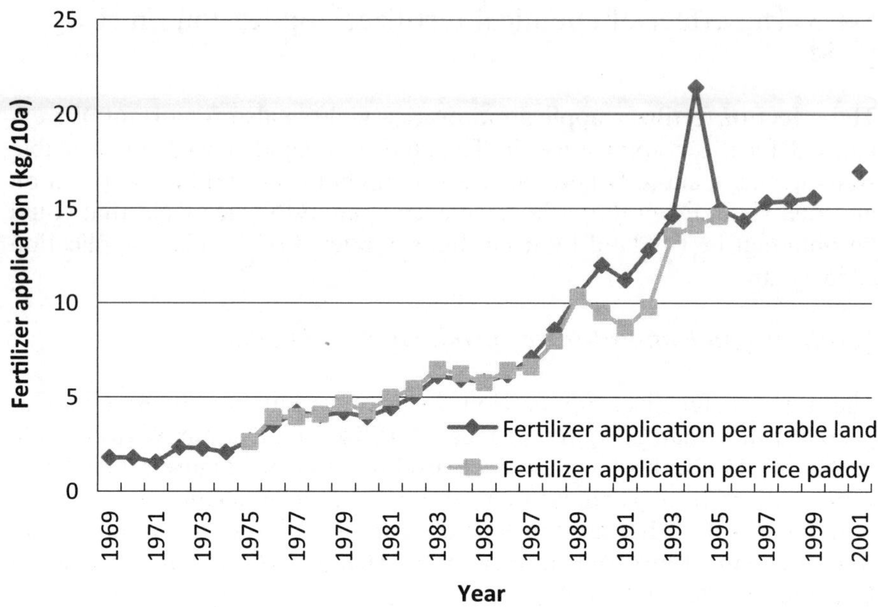

Figure 5.1.3 Annual change in fertilizer application

to the late 1980s shows that yields increased from 3.2 t/ha to 5 t/ha, a factor of approximately 1.6. Similarly, the rice yield for dry fields increased from 1.3 t/ha to 2.1 t/ha, also by a factor of approximately 1.6 (MAFF, 2006). Thus, by applying sufficient chemical fertilizer, rice yields were increased by 1.6 times. Applying the same relationship to Thailand, using approximately 70 kg/ha of fertilizer could result in a 1.6-fold increase in rice yield.

5-1-4 Adoption of high-yield rice

The average rice yield in Japan was 5.3 t/ha in 2006 (MAFF, 2007). However, it is unnecessary to produce premium food-quality rice for biofuel production such as *Koshihikakri* and *Sasanishiki*, which are the most popular types in Japan. To use rice as an energy feedstock, animal-feed-grade rice would be appropriate because its yield is 8–9 t/ha, or 1.7 times that of ordinary rice. It is assumed that the rice yield in Thailand could be increased by 1.7 times by using this high-yield rice type. Both irrigation and increased fertilizer application are indispensable.

Table 5.1.2 Estimated rice consumption and demand in 2008 and 2050

Year	Rice consumption (kg/capita/y)	Population	Export and others (t)	Demand (t)
2008	160	63,000,000	11,540,000	21,620,000
2050	80	62,000,000	11,540,000	16,500,000

Estimation of rice demand in Thailand

In Thailand the annual consumption of rice for food, including that destined for export, is 21.62 million tonnes. With respect to rice production, Kawashima, Shindo and Hori (2007) pointed out that it is closely linked with GDP. According to them, it increases with a rise in GDP up to US$1,000, but decreases beyond that number. So it is expected that the per capita consumption of rice will change from 160 kg/y to 80 kg/y in 2050 if this trend is applied to Thailand (Table 5.1.2). According to the UN FAO statistics on world population, the birth rate of Thailand was 1.93 in the period 2000–2005; however, UN projections show it decreasing to 1.35. If this low projection is applied, the population in Thailand will decrease slightly from 63 million to 62 million by 2050. The total consumption of rice (including food, feed and exports) is therefore likely to decrease from 21.62 to 16.5 million tonnes by 2050. Even if rice production remains at current levels, rice surpluses will increase as consumption decreases, and the surplus could eventually be used for ethanol production.

Estimation of the demand for rice as feed

At present, corn is the only cereal grain used for livestock feed in Thailand. However, the demand for cereal grain as feed is expected to increase if the demand for meat production increases in line with changing consumption patterns. If this happens, it will be necessary to clarify the grain quantities that will be needed to meet the rising demand. For our estimates, the intake of protein is based on Kawashima, Shindo and Hori (2007) and MAFF data. The protein content of meat and eggs is assumed to be 18 per cent and 13 per cent, respectively, and the lowest projected population in 2050 is used.

With regard to the ratio of feed to meat (the amount of feed needed to produce 1 kg of meat), the figures reported by Kawashima, Shindo and Hori (ibid.) and the estimates for Japan in 2050 are used. It is not feasible to use a simple extrapolation, as the amount of meat produced will be too small to satisfy consumer demand in 2050 using the present feed ratio.

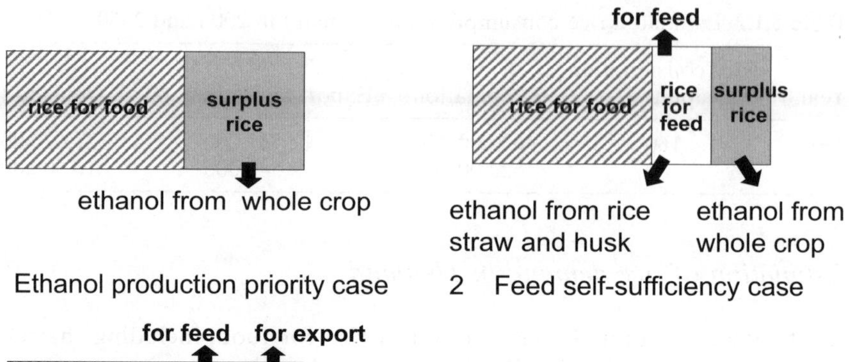

1   Ethanol production priority case

2   Feed self-sufficiency case

3   Food priority case

Figure 5.1.4 Outline of the three cultivation cases used in the study

5-1-5 Scenarios

As shown in Figure 5.1.4, three cases for ethanol production from rice are considered. In all three cases, it is assumed that rice production for food demand is maintained and that the straw and husks of rice grown for food are not used for ethanol production.

Case 1 places a priority on ethanol production. In this case, the entire rice crop is converted to ethanol, except for rice needed for food. Case 2 places priority on feed self-sufficiency. In this case, rice production in excess of food requirements is used as livestock feed, and the straw and husks of the livestock-feed rice in addition to surplus rice are used for ethanol production. Case 3 places priority on food production. In this case, the surplus rice is stockpiled for export or emergency use, and only the straw and husks of livestock feed and surplus rice are converted to ethanol. As mentioned above, the straw and husks of rice reserved for food are not converted to ethanol.

For each case, the following were identified to clarify the potential of ethanol production:

- *consumption of rice:* data from the present and 2050
- *proportion of irrigated land:* present data (25 per cent) and 2050 (50 per cent)
- *chemical fertilizer application:* present data (20 kg/ha/y) and 2050 (70 kg/ha/y)
- *adoption of high-yield rice:* present data and 2050 (1.7 times higher).

Using these assumed conditions, 16 scenarios (2^4) are obtained, but the following are excluded.

- The scenario in which no countermeasures are taken, because no ethanol is produced from rice.
- In the food priority case, high-yield rice is not planted.
- In the animal feed self-sufficiency case, all feed for livestock is produced from domestic corn.

5-1-6 Results

The potential ethanol production for each scenario is shown in Figure 5.1.5 for the case in which priority is placed on ethanol production. The maximum potential ethanol production is 32.44 million kL and the minimum is 4.06 million kL. In the two scenarios of increased chemical

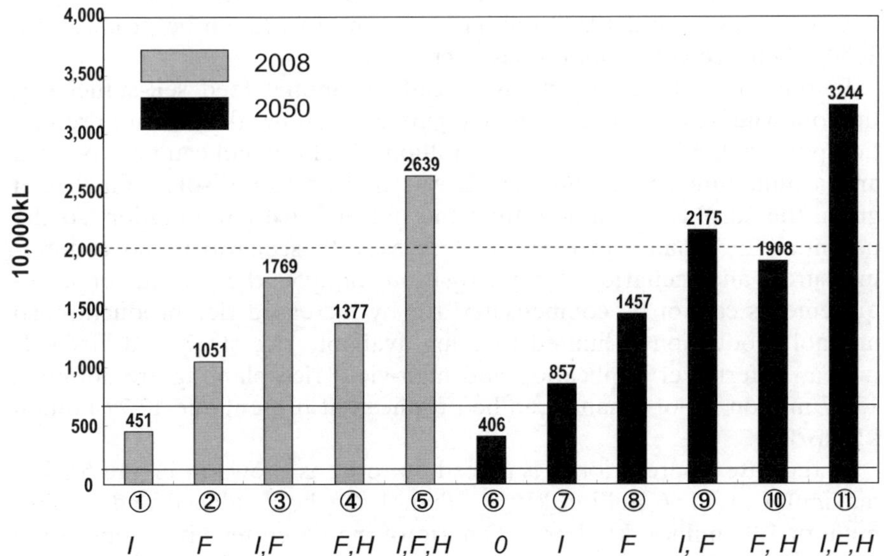

Figure 5.1.5 Scenarios for the ethanol priority case

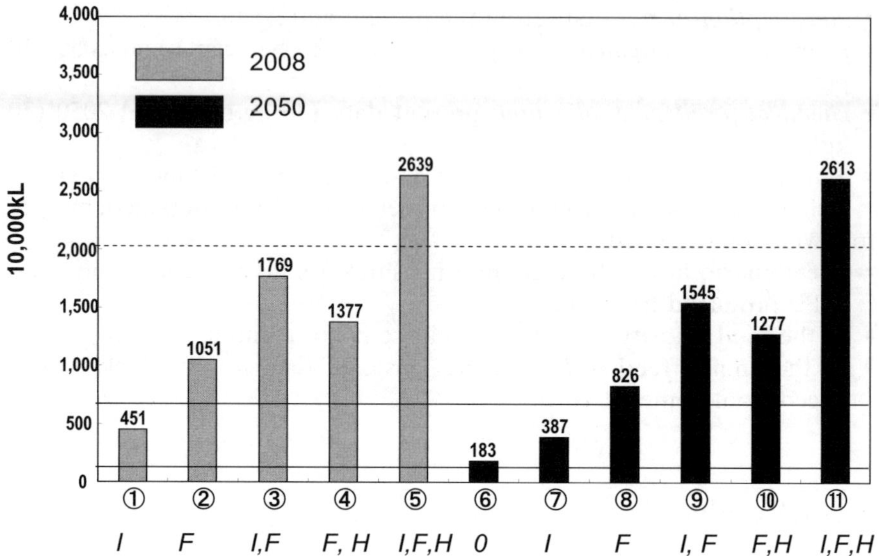

Figure 5.1.6 Scenarios for the livestock feed self-sufficiency case

fertilizer application and high-yield rice planting, which could be achieved relatively quickly, 13.77 million kL of ethanol (scenario 4) can be produced at present and 19.08 million kL (scenario 10) can be produced in 2050, when rice consumption has decreased.

In the case where priority is placed on animal feed self-sufficiency, the following results are obtained. Figure 5.1.6 shows the ethanol production potential. A maximum of 26.4 million kL of ethanol can be produced and a minimum 1.83 million kL. If rice is used as the sole animal feed grain, the surplus rice is less than the present rice consumption, so the potential for ethanol production decreases. In scenario 6 (no countermeasures) and scenario 7 (only irrigation) in 2050, the gain in cereal requirements cannot be compensated for by increased rice production, so ethanol production is limited to using available rice straw and husks. If increased fertilizer application and high-yield rice planting are adopted, 13.77 million kL of ethanol can be produced at present and 12.77 million kL in 2050.

In the case where priority is placed on food, as shown in Figure 5.1.7, a maximum of 14.66 million kL of ethanol can be produced and a minimum of 1.83 million kL. For a scenario of increased fertilizer application combined with high-yield rice planting, 6.22 million kL could be produced at present and 8.62 million kL in 2050.

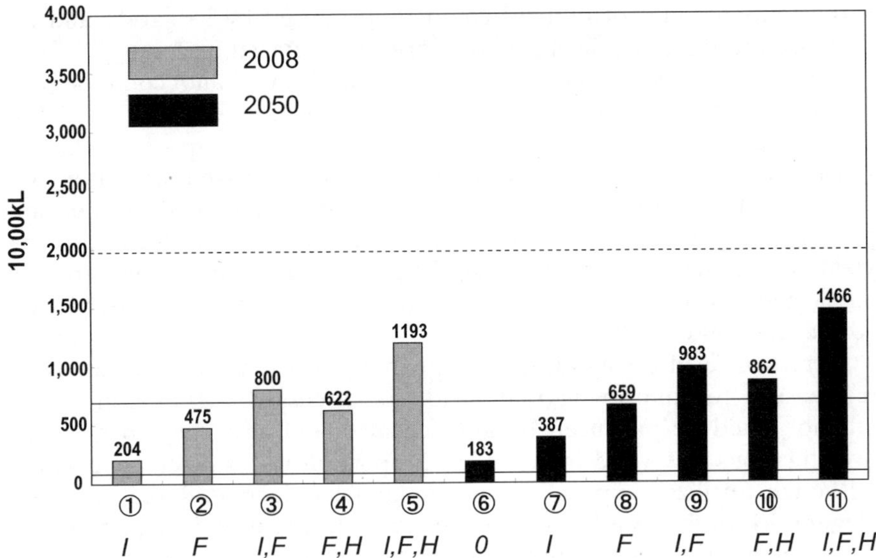

Figure 5.1.7 Scenarios of the food priority case

5-1-7 Discussion

The Thai government decided that E10 should be produced in the country using biomass by 2011. Petrol consumption in Thailand is 11 million kL and the ethanol equivalent of E10 is 1.1 million kL (http://sugar.lin.go.jp/jp/japan/fromalic/fa_0705a.htm). Lines A, B, and C in Figures 5.1.5–5.1.7 represent 1.1, 7.1 and 20 million kL of ethanol, respectively.

As shown in Figures 5.1.5–5.1.7, the 1.1 million kL target of the Thai government could be achieved by any scenario; ethanol production is greater than that indicated by Line A in every scenario. In 2006 the Japanese government decided that the target for ethanol production should be 6 million kL of E10. This is difficult to achieve in terms of the available resources, maturity of ethanol production from cellulosic materials and infrastructure.

One of the plausible options is to import ethanol from Thailand, with the initial technology transfer and funding provided by Japan. If this were possible, 7.1 million kL of bioethanol would be needed in accordance with environmental requirements on the Japanese side and economic benefits on the Thai side. The above results show that:

- 7.1 million kL of ethanol can be realized by increased fertilizer application if the priority is placed on bioethanol production and feed self-sufficiency

- the same amount of ethanol could be produced by irrigation and increased fertilizer application if the priority is placed on food
- excluding the food priority case, 20 million kL of ethanol could be produced by irrigation, increased fertilizer application and high-yield rice planting.

The effects of the three countermeasures (improved irrigation, increased fertilizer application and the adoption of high-yield rice) on improving rice yield are discussed. Irrigation is very effective for improving yield and the Irrigation Department of the Thai government has strongly advocated improvements to the irrigation infrastructure in order to increase rice yields in the long term.

Increased fertilizer application appears to be the most efficient countermeasure for improving rice yield. As discussed, 1.1 million kL of ethanol could be produced by any scenario, and according to previous investigations rice yield increases in proportion to fertilizer application. Although fertilizer application in Thailand has increased year on year (Figure 5.1.3), the rate is 20 kg/ha, lower than that used in Japan (70 kg/ha). Increased fertilizer application is expected to improve rice yields considerably.

Recently, the production of bioethanol has been increasing in Thailand, where it is produced primarily from cassava and molasses. If the demand for bioethanol increases, the area required for planting cassava may affect the area dedicated to other crops. However, shifting bioethanol production to rice will not adversely affect the areas dedicated to rice agriculture because the total area of rice fields (10.2 million ha) is unlikely to change. Thus if either the population or rice consumption per capita decreases, a number of rice production areas will become surplus (4.29 million ha). If this excess land is neglected, it will become degraded and cause negative environmental effects. Bioethanol production from rice can prevent such problems while offering benefits in terms of rice production, development of the bioethanol industry, job creation, preservation of the landscape, prevention of soil erosion and cultivation of water resources.

If irrigation is to be realized, considerable funds are needed for agricultural civil engineering and maintenance. In addition, great efforts will be required to manage social factors such as water governance in order to distribute the irrigation water to farmers impartially. For fertilizer application and high-yield rice adoption, it is expected that chemical fertilizer and high-yield rice will be applied if the benefit exceeds the costs. Although Japan is aiming at 6 million kL of E10 in the future, it seems quite difficult to supply this amount from domestic biomass resources because fallow land is limited and technology for the production of bioethanol from lignocellulosic materials is still immature. Under such circumstances, it is plausible that Japan and Thailand collaborate to make use of surplus arable land for bioethanol production and export. This scheme is basically applicable to Southeast Asian countries where there is marginal land for the production of biofuels.

5-1-8 Summary

In this study, we estimated the potential of bioethanol production from rice in Thailand. As in Japan, the Thai population and per capita rice consumption are expected to decrease in future. If this trend continues, surplus arable land will become available. If irrigation, fertilizer application and high-yield rice were used on this surplus land, rice production could be substantially increased. We tried to utilize the expected surplus land or surplus rice in harmony with food and energy security. Based on this idea, three scenarios are examined: case 1 prioritizes ethanol production, case 2 prioritizes feed self-sufficiency and case 3 prioritizes food production. According to estimates based on the above assumptions, 1.1 million kL of bioethanol, which is the E10 equivalent of the national target set by the Thai government, could be produced in each of the three cases. In case 3, E10 would be possible by improved irrigation and increased fertilizer application. In cases 1 and 2, 20 million kL of bioethanol could be produced by improved irrigation, increased fertilizer application and adoption of high-yield rice. For comparative purposes, estimates were also made for 2050.

REFERENCES

Boonlue, Chatchai (2005) "The Present Condition of Water Resources Development in Northeastern Region of Thailand", in *Proceedings of the International Symposium on Sustainable Development in the Mekong River Basin*, Ho Chi Minh City, 6–7 October; available at http://iirc.ipb.ac.id/jspui/bitstream/123456789/28609/1/b361.pdf, pp. 133–142.

Kawashima, H., J. Shindo and M. Hori (2007) "Energy Crops Production Using Surplus Paddy Areas in South East Asia", *Journal of Environmental Science* 20(4), pp. 279–289.

MAFF (2006) *Statistics 1: Production of Rice and Wheat*. Tokyo: Ministry of Agriculture, Forestry and Fisheries.

——— (2007) *Statistics 2: Crop Statistics*. Tokyo: Ministry of Agriculture, Forestry and Fisheries.

NAS (1989) *Alcohol Fuels; Options for Developing Countries*. Washington, DC: National Academies Press.

Office of Agricultural Economics (1982) *Agricultural Statistics of Thailand 1981/82*. Bangkok: Government of Thailand.

——— (1990) *Agricultural Statistics of Thailand 1989/90*. Bangkok: Government of Thailand.

——— (1997) *Agricultural Statistics of Thailand 1996/97*. Bangkok: Government of Thailand.

Ogawa, K., Y. Takeuchi and M. Katayama (1988) "Hokkaido no Bokusouchi ni okeru Baiomasu Seisanryou oyobi Sakumotsu niyoru Mukiseibun Kyuushu-uryou", *Hokkaido Noushi Kennpo* 149, pp. 57–91.

United Nations (2004) *World Population Prospects: The 2004 Revision*. New York: UN Department of Economic and Social Affairs.

World Bank (2005) *World Development Indicators*. Washington, DC: World Bank.

5-2

Systematic design of multiple-benefit biomass utilization: A practical example of Eucommia biomass use in rural China

Takashi Machimura, Akio Kobayashi and Yoshihisa Nakazawa

5-2-1 Why establish new biomass industries in rural Asia?

Many Asian nations have grown rapidly over recent decades, overcoming severe economic and political crises. Common national policies towards industrialization have unquestionably helped many developing Asian nations to achieve economic prosperity. Mass-production industries supporting this economic growth require intensive resource investment in the form of collateral, material, energy, labour and information. Closely linked to this is the progress of urbanization, which is associated with the process of adapting to social structural change brought about by industrialization. Urbanization is further accelerated by the growth of the service sector and public investments in the infrastructure that supports both industry and urban residents. However, from a negative perspective, rapid and excessive industrialization and urbanization have aggravated numerous issues such as overpopulation and environmental degradation in urban areas. These influences also extend into rural areas and to issues related to disparities in economic prosperity and living standards, emigration to urban areas, the decline in agriculture and the cohesiveness of local communities, all of which are potential hazards to stable and balanced national development.

The transfer of industry to rural areas is a common policy that attempts to solve issues associated with urban environmental decline and disparity in living standards. However, the transfer of conventional resource-intensive industries merely relocates these urban issues to rural areas.

Establishing a resource-circulating society in Asia: Challenges and opportunities, Morioka, Hanaki and Moriguchi (eds), United Nations University Press, 2011, ISBN 978-92-808-1182-7

The distance from resources to market, less-stringent institutional controls and lower technology levels may exacerbate some of the adverse environmental burdens. Furthermore, rural residents and societies may not enjoy sufficient returns from the capital held by organizations outside the region, and the economic divide between industrial workers and farmers may increase within the region. Thus a rural economy promotion policy based on industry transfer is not the best choice given the many associated negative effects.

There is an alternative policy, which involves the establishment of new rural biomass-use industries. A variety of advanced rural industries once prospered in numerous regions of Asia before the modern age, producing high-quality and high-value products such as silk, textiles, dyes, furniture and other goods. These industries, which utilized local biomass resources and stimulated the rural economy, have become increasingly scarce and been replaced by plastic mass-production equivalents. Recently, however, local biomass utilization is being re-evaluated from the perspective of carbon neutrality. Technological progress in facilitating improvements and cultivation and product refinement are also extending the potential of biomass utilization. This may result in the development of new biomass products with unique functions and value that can return economic benefits to the farmers who supply the biomass material, and to the local community. This chapter considers new biomass utility industries in Asian rural regions that have attempted to maximize the benefits for the environment, rural economy, society and welfare of residents.

5-2-2 Biomass-using technologies adaptable to rural Asia

Biodiesel fuel

Biodiesel fuel (BDF) not only has the advantage of being carbon neutral, but also has low NO_x and diesel particle emissions. As a result, such fuels are currently experiencing increased levels of worldwide production and consumption. A variety of oils can be used as raw materials for BDF, including vegetable oils from crops such as soybeans, cotton, rapeseed and sunflowers, animal fats from livestock and other waste oils. In urban areas, waste cooking oil from households, restaurants and food factories is collected and recycled to produce BDF, which is often used to fuel public buses and government automobiles. In rural areas, where the supply of waste oil is generally insufficient to maintain a stable and competitive BDF supply in markets, virgin vegetable oil from crops must be used instead. But this diversion of resources could be in direct conflict with the demand for food.

However, there is another vegetable oil resource that has the potential to be adapted to rural Asian BDF production – tree-seed oil. For example, fruit trees belonging to the genus *Zanthoxylum* (*Z. bungeanum, Z. piperitum* etc.) grow in a wide range of areas across Asia. The fruit of these trees is used in spice production and for medicinal purposes in China and other countries. But only the skin of the *Zanthoxylum* fruit is used for spice production, and the seed is normally disposed of as industrial waste. Annual *Zanthoxylum* seed waste reaches up to 20,000 tonnes in China. This is notable because a *Zanthoxylum* seed contains approximately 30 per cent oil, which can be used for BDF feedstock. *Melia azedarach, Ligustrum lucidum* and maple (*Acer* spp.) trees grow rapidly after planting, and are often used for the reforestation of degraded land. Some of these species switch from vegetative growth to reproductive growth when they are approximately 10 years old, at which time seed production begins to exceed woody biomass production. Such trees provide seed oil in high yields and, more importantly, are not subject to any potential conflicts with food production.

The BDF production process using tree-seed oil is similar to that for waste oil, but requires an additional pre-processing step to remove gum and free fatty acids from the crude seed oil. Both continuous and batch processes are applicable to tree-seed oil BDF refineries. However, production plant capacity is the single most important criterion governing the potential adaptability of tree-seed oil. Larger continuous-process BDF plants have several advantages when using urban waste oil or cultivated vegetable oil, due to easy availability and stable supplies, with the current largest plant capacity exceeding 100 tonnes per day. BDF production costs using waste oil are presently approximately US$1 per litre, and material resources account for one-third of the total cost. In contrast, in the case of tree-seed oil, resources are generally extensively available in wide and remote areas that are far from the centre of processing and demand. This means that feedstock costs will increase due to the longer collection distances and larger yard capacities needed to store sufficient quantities of tree seeds for running large-capacity BDF plants. Thus BDF production systems suitable for using tree-seed oil in Asia are normally designed as small batch-process systems for output of 100 litres per day, built on the rear of trucks so they can be driven to wherever seed supplies are present. Tree-seed oil BDF production is currently limited to laboratories, and the commercial success of pilot plants has yet to be reported. Developing compact, cheap and easy-to-use systems is the key engineering objective for realizing the true potential of tree-seed oil BDF.

Other resource plants and utilization technologies

Polyploid plants have evolved naturally, but selective breeding in laboratories can produce them by inducing cell division under the existence of colchicines. Poplars are often used for reforestation and desert protection, and in energy and pulpwood plantations where the species is valued due to its properties of rapid growth and tolerance against drought and cold. Triploid ($3n$) poplars produced by crossbreeding wild species ($2n$) and $4n$ mutations have high productivity and grow twice as rapidly as wild-type plants. In addition, the crossbred trees have higher tolerance to pests, drought and cold than wild types, and can grow up to 20 m tall and 20 cm in breast-height diameter in just five years. The triploid poplars can be reproduced by grafting: the trees do not have reproductive organs and thus do not spread seeds by wind dispersal. This is important because genetically modified plants must be handled safely to prevent introgression with wild species. Triploid poplars contain only non-modified natural genomes, and so are not controlled by the Cartagena Protocol on Biosafety.

According to FAO statistics, China became the world's second-largest citrus-producing country in 2007 and harvests approximately 20 million tonnes of citrus fruit a year. Citrus food processing is an important industry in rural China, where significant amounts of the harvested citrus fruit are peeled and canned, or squeezed to make juice. Limonene and higher fatty acids can be extracted from the peeled citrus fruit skin and are mixed in detergents as supplements. Limonene, as an organic solvent, is also used to dissolve foamed sterol for recycling purposes. Currently, after thermal cracking of its C-C (carbon-carbon) bonds, application of limonene as a fine chemical material and as an agent in refinery processes is being researched.

China is also one of the world's largest grape producers and harvested approximately 6.5 million tonnes in 2007. Grape seeds removed at wineries and juice factories are squeezed to produce seed oil for foods and cosmetics. Furthermore, grape seeds contain medically effective ingredients such as tannins, polyphenols, polyunsaturated fatty acids and compounds. Of these, proanthocyanidin has significant antioxidant, anti-cancer and skin-whitening effects. The Ningxia Hui autonomous region near the middle reaches of the Yellow River is a well-known grape-harvesting area. A chemical company established in Ningxia succeeded in improving proanthocyanidin productivity by introducing supercritical fluid-extraction technology imported from Germany.

5-2-3 Systematic design of biomass utilities

A system framework for biomass use

Figure 5.2.1 shows a sample framework of a biomass-utility system. General industrial production systems normally consist solely of factory processes: importing materials from and exporting wastes to external systems. Feedstock supply and waste capacity are restrictive conditions determined by the external system, and only those processes undertaken within the factory are considered during product design. In contrast, biomass-use

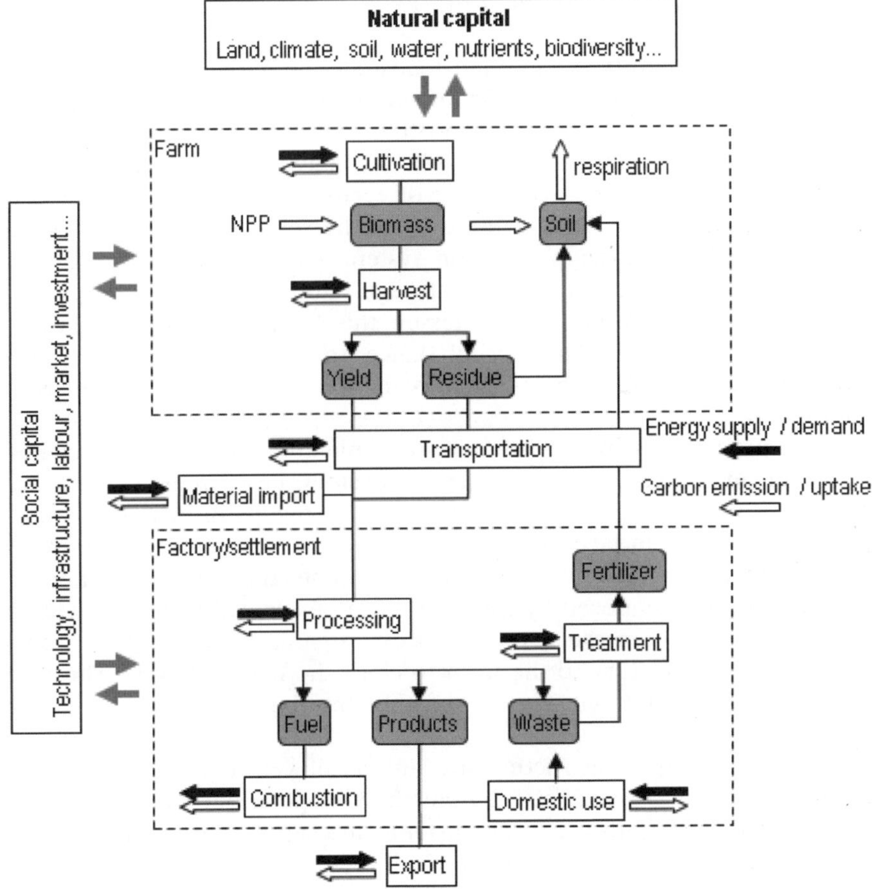

Figure 5.2.1 General structure of the biomass-use system

systems incorporate material suppliers, i.e. farms, into the overall system. The majority of biomass factory waste is organic, and is preferably recycled and returned to the farm as organic fertilizer to decrease pollution and promote crop growth. Thus the two components of factory and farm are closely connected and should be designed as a single system. Common methodologies within system engineering schemes, such as systems analysis, flow analysis, linear and non-linear planning, optimization techniques, etc., are readily applicable to the design and optimization of systems for biomass use. However, there are also several aspects that are unique to the design of biomass-use systems, and these are presented below.

Aspects of biomass-use system design

The type and quantity of supplied feedstock, i.e. farm crops and yields, are affected by the characteristics of the natural environment, including climate, soil, topography, water and other factors. This means that feedstock supply and quality are not stable and may vary between years and locations. Moreover, the availability of feedstock is usually highly seasonal, being most abundant at the time of the relatively short harvesting periods, which decreases production system availability (operating time per year) or increases the cost of storage. Utilizing multiple crops and producing multiple products can lessen this feedstock supply volatility and reduce the supply-demand imbalance. In addition, mixed-crop production is also preferable for increased biodiversity and plant disease control.

Large processing capacity is more profitable due to improved efficiency. However, in the case of a biomass-use system, large areas of land are needed to produce sufficient feedstock, which results in increased transportation costs from farm to factory. Since the water content of biomass is generally high relative to its usable ingredients, the unit cost and environmental burden imposed by transportation per constituent mass will be high. Furthermore, in the reverse process, organic waste must be transported from the factory to the farm to close the material cycle. Thus the overall transportation mileage becomes the limiting factor of biomass-use system capacity.

Technology and infrastructure are not, as of yet, highly developed in many parts of rural Asia. For example, the voltage and frequency of commercial electricity grids are often unstable and supply is often interrupted due to insufficient capacity and poor facility management. System robustness is indispensable in factory processes, and delicate technologies such as clean-room processes, multistage continuous processes and intelligent systems are difficult to implement. In addition, industrial water of a sufficiently high quality is not available except in recently developed industrial parks. This is also true for waste treatment facilities. Consequently, recycling water and waste within the system is preferable.

While natural conditions affect biomass-use system performance (as stated above) in terms of land area, soil, water, nutrients, pollinators, etc., and by controlling climate, nature is also a form of capital that is invested in the biomass-use enterprise. Indeed, biomass production depends largely on natural capital. To make production sustainable, maintenance and return on investment must be considered in order to ensure that over-exploitation of soil, water and biomass is avoided. Similarly, local rural communities, as social capital investing money, labour, infrastructure and institutional support, must be maintained and must profit equally.

5-2-4 Practical example of a new biomass-use system combined with the "grain for green" policy in Henan, China

Model region

In 2009 a pilot project for a new biomass-use industry was established in Zhuyang township, Lingbao city, in Henan province, China. The project is a joint venture between a local agro-forestry corporation and a Japanese engineering company, and is supported by local governments and universities in China and Japan. It is located at the southeastern end of the Loess Plateau, where the climate is temperate inner-continental monsoon, with mean annual air temperature and precipitation of 12.9°C and 650 mm, respectively. The soils of the region consist of thick loess sediment, which has an extremely high erosion potential, and annual soil loss by water and wind is up to 200 tonnes per hectare (Ritsema, 2003). Coupled with water scarcity and desertification, degradation of the land is considered the most serious environmental threat in the region. Furthermore, steep gullies hinder productive farming and the development of land for residential, economic or transportation purposes. Agricultural productivity is approximately half that of southeast China and farmer incomes are low.

In an attempt to prevent soil degradation and desertification due to crop production and grazing on steep slopes, the government of China instituted the "grain for green" policy in 1999, which encouraged residents of the area to abandon farming and grazing, and promoted forestation on these steep slopes. In Lingbao approximately 10 per cent of the area has been converted to woodland or fruit plantations. Funded by the "grain for green" policy, a local agro-forestry corporate launched a Eucommia plantation in 1998, and has since extended the project area to 1,400 hectares, planting 1.2 million trees. Male flowers for tea were once the main harvest product from the Eucommia plantation. However, recently seed harvesting has increased in order to produce new products, described in detail in the following section.

Eucommia – A multi resource plant

Eucommia (*Eucommia ulmoides*), known as *duzhong* in Chinese or hardy rubber tree, is a tall, deciduous, broad-leaf species whose natural habitat is limited to central China, but which has now been widely introduced in Europe, Japan and other countries as a medicinal tree. Its bark, leaves and roots contain pharmacologically active compounds and have been considered "top-grade medicines" since ancient times – as described in *Shen Nong's Herbal Classic*, which was written around 300 BC (Ma and Su, 2007). There are a variety of traditional uses for the Eucommia tree. Powder extracted from the leaf and bark is used in liver and kidney medicines, while tea made from the leaves and male flowers provides health benefits, such as decreased blood pressure. Edible oil, which contains much α-linolenic acid, is found in the seeds, and improved egg productivity has been observed in laying hens fed Eucommia leaves.

Eucommia is also known to contain natural rubber in the seed shell, leaves, bark and other parts of the plant. Eucommia rubber is a trans-form polyisoprene and has a different configuration from the cis-form rubber harvested from tropical rubber trees (*Hevea brasiliensis*). Although Eucommia rubber is less elastic than cis-type rubbers, it has other valuable properties such as high durability, thermoplasticity, high electric insulation capability and acid and alkali resistance. The product is used in earthquake-resistant construction, aqua regia containers, etc. In recent decades studies have progressed on techniques for molecular and material property analysis and gene manipulation to control the productivities of specific organs and the molecular number of extracts. Industrial treatment systems and refining methods have also been improved (Nakazawa et al., 2009).

An environmentally sound multipurpose biomass-use system

Our pilot project used trans-rubber extracted from Eucommia fruit shells as its primary product. The entire biomass production system, from cultivation to waste treatment, was designed with due regard to both social restrictions and environmental performance.

Much of the natural rubber presently on the market is supplied by commercial plantations in tropical Asia. However, such plantations have caused considerable forest area loss over the last century (UNEP, 2001:

12). Latex is tapped from the tree stem, but frequent tapping and over-exploitation of latex damages the trees and decreases productivity, necessitating plantation renewal approximately every 20 years. In contrast, Eucommia rubber is derived from harvested fruit shells and harvesting does not damage the trees. This results in an exceptionally long harvest lifespan for the trees – currently estimated at more than 100 years – which significantly reduces land degradation resulting from plantation renewal. Eucommia plantations can be established on abandoned farmland, contributing to an increase in the wooded area in this semi-arid region.

Eucommia rubber accumulates in the tree's laticifer cells, where it forms a complex polyisoprene fibre with a diameter of approximately 2 μm and a length of approximately 1 cm. Organic solvents are generally used to break down the laticifer cells for rubber extraction. However, this method introduces the risk of environmental pollution, along with high energy and resource consumption. We used a newly developed method in our pilot factory, involving putrefaction of the Eucommia fruit shells with wood-decaying fungi, followed by a wash-separation step to extract the rubber. This method only requires the time for decay and the water and electricity needed to power the high-pressure washer. Since Eucommia fruit is harvested once a year in autumn, the long shell decay process also has the effect of smoothing feedstock supply. Wastewater is stored in sedimentation ponds, and is either reused or used for irrigation. Additionally, the separated sediments are dried and used as organic fertilizer.

Other parts of Eucommia trees can also be used as by-products. Male trees are planted among female trees for pollination, and their flowers are picked to make male flower tea. Following shell removal, the seeds are squeezed to extract oil. While Eucommia seed oil is edible and can be used for dietary supplements, in the pilot factory it is used to produce BDF, as this was considered preferable given the prevailing supplement market conditions. Leaf harvesting has a limited effect on fruit production, and harvested leaves can be used for livestock feed. Pruned branches can be used for firewood, and the process residues from rubber and BDF can be used for organic fertilizer. Figure 5.2.2 illustrates the material and process flow of our Eucommia biomass-use system. The system is designed to balance sustainable plant growth and product yield, and to ensure that all residues are recycled within the system.

Environmental and socio-economic co-benefits

The Eucommia biomass system in Lingbao went into operation in 2009, and its productivity and environmental performance are as yet unreported. Environmental and socio-economic benefits provided by the enterprise will be discussed here based on the system design and available

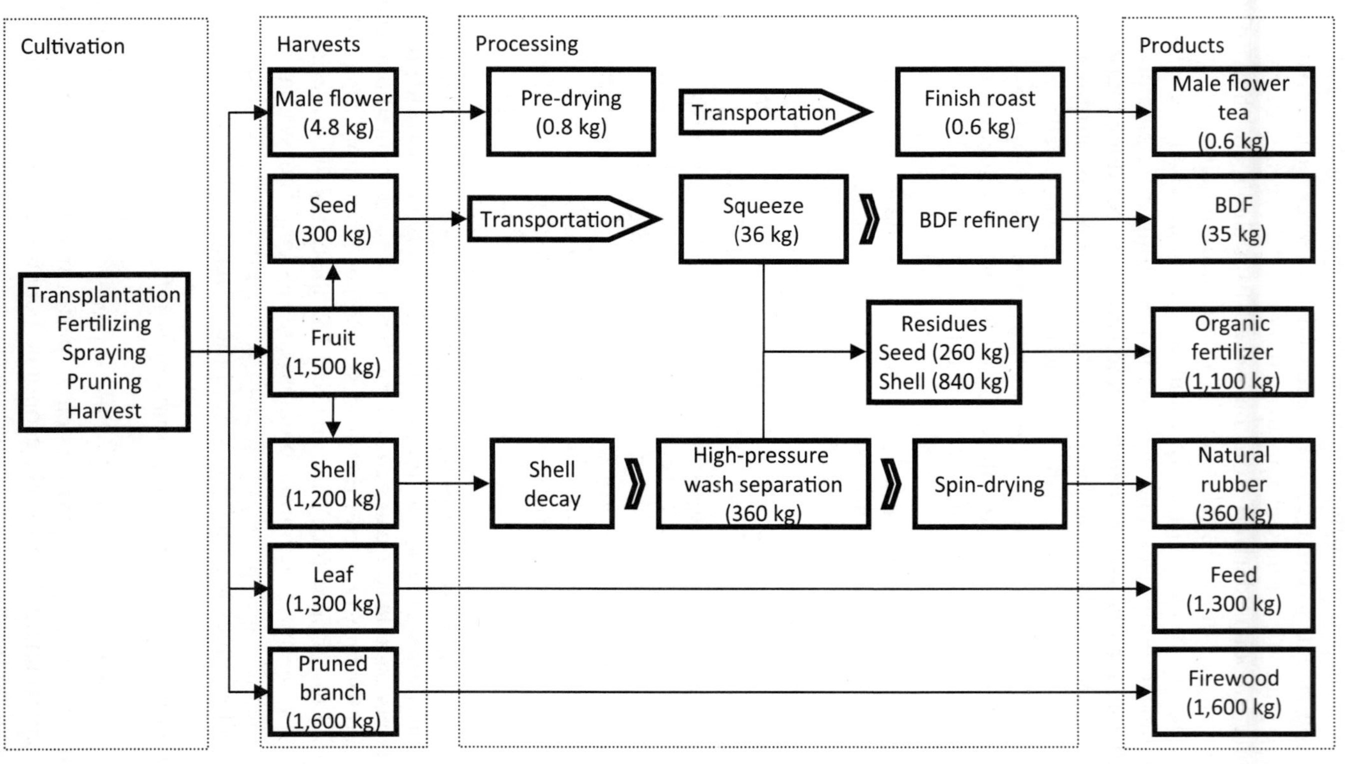

Figure 5.2.2 Material mass per hectare land area and process flow in the Eucommia biomass-use system established in Lingbao, Henan province, China

scientific knowledge. To clarify the advantages associated with using Eucommia, performance of this biomass system will be compared with two alternative land-use plans: maize crops (farmed before the introduction of the "grain for green" policy), and the introduction of black locust (*Robinia pseudoacacia*) plantations for timber production, which is another common practice following farm abandonment in the Loess Plateau.

Reduction in CO_2 emission

The most important environmental benefit associated with using biomass is related to reductions in CO_2 emissions. The reductions are measured by comparing the total CO_2 emissions for fossil-based products to those of biomass products that provide the same value (heat value or functional value). Emissions from fossil-fuel-based products include those associated with their production and consumption. However, since biomass is a renewable resource, the CO_2 emissions from biomass associated with consumption can be excluded, which means that only the emissions generated during the production process need to be considered. The pilot system uses male Eucommia flowers, fruit, leaves and pruned branches to produce male flower tea, BDF, natural rubber and feed. It also provides firewood and organic fertilizer as by-products (see Figure 5.2.2). Of these products, BDF, rubber and firewood can be used as substitutes for fossil-fuel resources. Table 5.2.1 summarizes the CO_2 emissions and reductions achieved through the cultivation of maize, black locust and Eucommia. CO_2 emissions during the cultivation stage are considerably larger for maize, which consumes significant amounts of farm chemicals and fertilizer, while the Eucommia system is the only one that emits CO_2 during the processing stages of producing male flower tea, BDF and natural rubber. Total anthropogenic CO_2 emissions are largest for maize production. BDF from Eucommia and the solid fuels produced from various residues can be used as alternative fuels, so the CO_2 reductions were evaluated by using oil-equivalent heat values.

The maize stem provides the largest volume of alternative fuel per hectare, and consequently the largest CO_2 reduction, but that reduction cannot compensate for the outsized emissions produced during cultivation. CO_2 reductions obtained for Eucommia rubber were measured based on the CO_2 emissions associated with production of the petroleum-based styrene-butadiene rubber (SBR) it is intended to replace. Note that 1 kg of SBR emits 1.5 kg CO_2 during production and 2.4 kg of CO_2 when combusted after disposal. The emission from burnt Eucommia rubber is not taken into consideration because it is regarded as "carbon neutral". As a result, the Eucommia biomass system showed the largest reduction in CO_2 emissions due to the balance between the high fossil resources substitution effect and the relatively low amount of associated emissions.

Table 5.2.1 CO$_2$ emission in biomass cultivation and product processing, and CO$_2$ reduction by substituting for fossil resources in maize crop production, black locust plantation and Eucommia biomass-use system (kg CO$_2$ per hectare per year)

Harvest and product (mass in kg)	Maize crop production		Black locust plantation		Eucommia biomass use					
		Stem	Trunk	Branch	Male flower		Fruit	Leaf	Pruned branch	Residue
	Grain (6,800)	Household fuel (4,100)	Timber (1,300)	Firewood (770)	Tea (1)	BDF (35)	Rubber (360)	Feed (1,300)	Firewood (1,600)	Organic fertilizer (1,104)
CO$_2$ emission										
Cultivation		+6,621		+59				+214		
Processing	0	0	0	0	+3	+18	+262	0	0	0
Total		+6,621		+59				+497		
CO$_2$ reduction	0	−4,400	0	−917	0	−91	−1,404	−2,998	−2,000	0
Total		−4,400		−953				−3,495		
CO$_2$ balance		+2,221		−894				−2,998		

In addition, Eucommia is associated with another aspect of low-carbon performance: ecosystem carbon balance, which is a measure of how much carbon plants and soils gain or lose. Plants absorb atmospheric CO_2 by photosynthesis and store it as carbon in their tissues. Net annual carbon fixation by plants per unit of land area is defined as net primary production (NPP). Part of a plant's fixed carbon is transferred to the soil as plant litter (dead biomass such as leaf fall), which is decomposed by soil organisms (insects, earthworms, fungi, bacteria, etc.). Heterotrophic respiration results in CO_2 emissions by organisms decomposing soil organic matter. The natural carbon balance in an ecosystem is represented by the difference between NPP and heterotrophic respiration, and is referred to as net ecosystem production (NEP). Anthropogenic carbon motion occurs in farms and plantations through harvesting and the application of organic fertilizers. The total carbon balance in an ecosystem, including anthropogenic motion, is defined as net biome production (NBP). Table 5.2.2 shows the carbon balance for a maize farm, a black locust plantation and a Eucommia plantation, estimated using measurements and literature data for plant growth. The popular RothC soil carbon turnover model (Coleman and Jenkinson, 1999) and farm management practice research were also used. The values obtained for the plantations are for trees aged 13 years old. Note that a system's carbon balance is dynamic and changes according to both plant growth and variations in the organic carbon content of the soil. Cultivated maize has the largest NPP, but its NBP is zero because the ecosystem carbon balance has reached equilibrium. Similarly, when considering carbon loss due to future deforestation, the NBP for the black locust plantation is almost zero. The Eucommia plantation showed the largest ecosystem carbon accumulation. By considering both CO_2 reduction of products and ecosystem carbon sequestration, the Eucommia plantation has a carbon reduction potential of approximately 12 tonnes of CO_2 per hectare per year. The details of this evaluation are reported in Machimura et al. (2009).

Soil conservation

Another environmental benefit of the pilot biomass-use system is soil conservation. The severity of soil erosion by rain depends on factors such as the soil erosion potential, rainfall intensity, topography and land use. The revised universal soil loss equation (RUSLE; Renard et al., 1997) shown below is commonly used to predict annual amounts of soil erosion:

$$A = R\ K\ L\ S\ P\ C$$

Table 5.2.2 Ecosystem carbon balance of maize farm, black locust plantation and Eucommia plantation, including anthropogenic carbon movement (harvest and fertilizing), in tonnes of carbon per hectare per year

	Maize farm	Black locust plantation	Eucommia plantation
NPP	+8.6	+2.8	+6.7
	(+31.5)	(+10.3)	(+24.6)
Heterotrophic respiration	−5.0	−2.1	−2.2
	(−18.3)	(−7.7)	(−8.1)
NEP	+3.6	+0.7	+4.5
	(+13.2)	(+2.6)	(+16.5)
Harvest	−6.3	−0.9	−2.6
Organic fertilizer	+2.7	0.0	+0.6
NBP	0.0	−0.2	+2.5
	(0.0)	(−0.7)	(+9.2)

Note: Tonnes of CO_2 per hectare per year are in parentheses. The positive and negative numbers denote carbon gain and loss of the ecosystems, respectively.

288

Plate 5.2.1 Soil erosion observation plot installed at the Eucommia plantation
Note: Please see page 433 for a colour version of this image.

where A is annual soil erosion per hectare, and R, K, L, S, P and C are rainfall kinetic energy, soil erodibility, slope length, slope steepness, conservation practice and vegetation cover, respectively. Land-use change has been shown to have the most marked effect on factor C, and some studies have considered the C factor for various land-use types on the Loess Plateau (e.g. Fu et al., 2005; Jabbar and Chen, 2005; Wang, Yang and Liu, 2009). Generally, the C factor associated with cropland areas is large compared to forest areas, which can be as much as one or two orders smaller. For sparse woodland or orchard, the C factor is more than half that of cropland. Although the C factor for Eucommia plantations is currently being investigated (Plate 5.2.1), it is believed to be either similar to, or better than, that of woodland, implying that Eucommia has relatively higher stem density than ordinary orchards or woodlands in this region. Wind erosion is also a serious concern on the Loess Plateau, and wind-blown soil dust affects transportation and human health, especially in winter and spring when the surface soil of cropland is exposed and susceptible to being moved by strong winds. Yellow sand dust travels great distances, often reaching as far as Japan. Eucommia plantations can decrease wind erosion through covering the soil surface with debris and the windbreak effects of dense branches and twigs. Reports from farmers living in the region have highlighted the decreased occurrence of sand-storms since the plantations were introduced.

Socio-economic benefits

This pilot biomass project is expected to provide a variety of socio-economic as well as environmental benefits. The Chinese government is promoting the "grain for green" policy by compensating farmers who abandon their farms. However, these payments end after five years in cases where an economic forest (e.g. a fruit plantation) is planted, or after eight years for ecological forest (the payment period is recently being considered for extension). Thus farmers may be left without em-ployment and income once the period of compensation comes to an end. Once full production begins approximately one year after project com-mencement, our pilot plant has the potential to create 40,000 work-days for Eucommia cultivation and farm management, and an additional 9,000 work-days in the processing factory. The factory could potentially ship 720 tonnes of natural rubber, 70 tonnes of BDF and 2.5 tonnes of male flower tea a year. The potential economic land productivity of the Eucom-mia biomass system (measured as product sales per land area) is similar to that of a conventional crop farm in the township and higher than the "grain for green" compensation. Furthermore, gross economic productiv-ity per unit of labour of the Eucommia system is far higher than that of crop farming, and consequently it helps increase farmers' income. The pilot enterprise also improved roads for the transport of feedstock and products, thus providing residents in the surrounding settlements with safer access to the centre of the township. Thus the pilot Eucommia biomass-use system could make an important contribution to the local economy and overall development in the society.

The Eucommia pilot enterprise as an Asian resource-circulation model

The Eucommia biomass pilot enterprise developed in Henan is consid-ered as a model of resource circulation in rural Asia. Rapid motorization in Asian newly developing economies pushes demand for rubber and other chemical materials up; remarkably, China accounted for a quarter of world rubber consumption in 2008. Eucommia rubber can substitute transpolyisoprene materials refined from petroleum oil. One must clarify the life-cycle carbon inventory of Eucommia rubber from cultivation to waste treatment for environmentally sound industries that require life-cycle analysis of ingredients. Effective traditional material-circulation systems exist in rural Asia, in which farm, animal and household wastes are recycled locally for feed, fertilizer and energy. Transfer of resource-dependent industries to rural areas causes an intensive material flow that far exceeds the capacity of the local circulation systems and may spoil them. The Eucommia pilot enterprise utilizes only locally produced biomass resources and all wastes from cultivation and processes are properly recycled within the region, forming a local material circulation.

A wise and sustainable use of natural capital in industries in which local biomass production and processes are managed systematically is indispensable to switch rural Asian economies from backwardness to progress in this age of globalization. In addition, it is preferable to incorporate a variety of co-benefits for the regional environment, residents and society when introducing a biomass industry, to support its permanence and economic success.

5-2-5 The age of "green gold"

As the conclusion to this chapter, we foretell an age of "green gold". Modern human history can be summarized by the continued trend towards industrialization, urbanization and globalization, in which "black gold" (fossil fuels) and "real gold" (key currencies) have ruled the world, but have also caused considerable environmental and social issues. However, we now find ourselves at the beginning of the age of "green gold" (biomass), in which the wise and sustainable use of biomass can overcome the environmental problems caused by the previous world order and lead to improvements in human welfare. With this will come an increase in the value of rural Asia, which produces a variety of "green gold" from the rich diversity of its natural resources and rural cultures. This new concept of biomass utility, and the practical examples we have presented here, will assist in pointing the way towards this age.

To conclude, we present a mandala of high-order biomass utility, excluding the very traditional utilities such as food, timber and generic fibre (Figure 5.2.3). A "mandala" normally refers to a chart that interprets the world of the Buddha with unique abilities and missions. Many of the products shown in the figure are indispensable for human life and can be used as substitutes for products derived from "black gold". Not only will they enable us to survive the threats posed by fossil-fuel use, but through committed technological progress the world of biomass can be developed to offer greater variety, increased safety and overall added value to people and their local regions. The promise of biomass can be realized by understanding and believing in the power of "green gold".

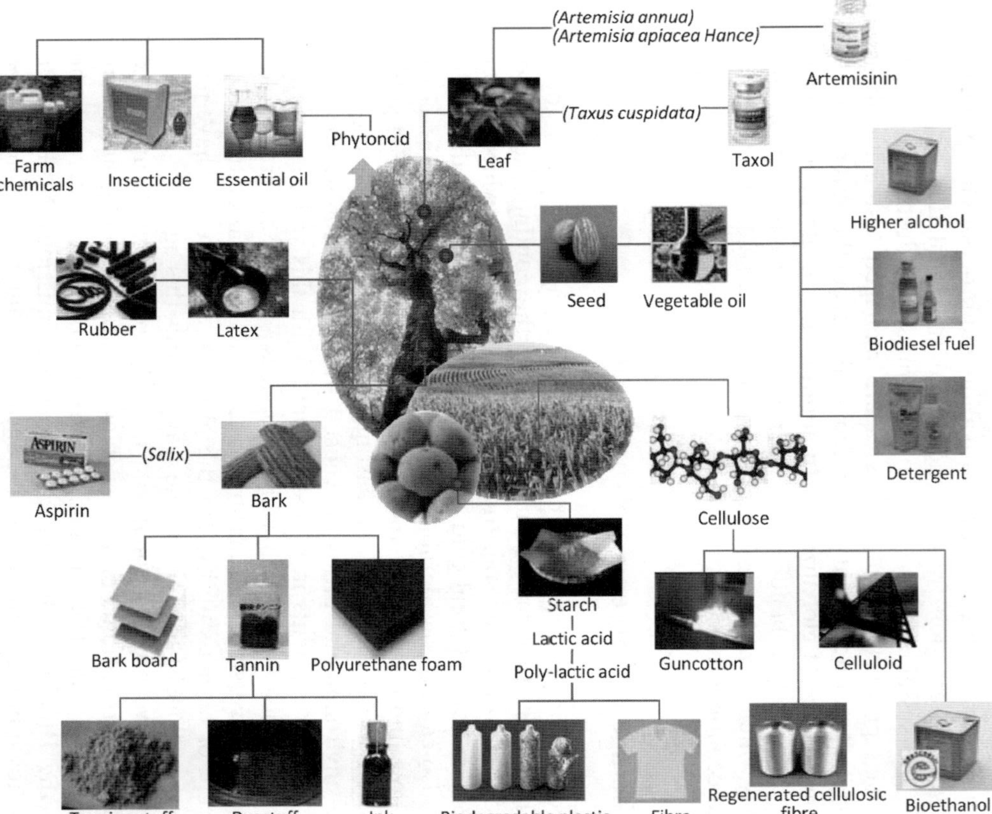

Figure 5.2.3 The mandala of high-order plant biomass utility
Notes: 1. Thousands of plant species including trees, crops, grasses, and seaweed provide us with a greater range of valuable and indispensable materials than mineral and fossil-based resources do.
2. Please see page 429 for a colour version of this figure.

REFERENCES

Coleman, K. and D. S. Jenkinson (1999) *RothC-26.3 A Model for the Turnover of Carbon in Soil. Model Description and Windows User Guide. November 1999 Issue.* Harpenden: IACR.

Fu, B. J., W. W. Zhao, L. D. Chen, Q. J. Zhang, Y. H. Lu, H. Gulinck and J. Poesen (2005) "Assessment of Soil Erosion at Large Watershed Scale Using RUSLE and GIS: A Case Study in the Loess Plateau of China", *Land Degradation & Development* 16, pp. 73–85.

Jabbar, M. T. and X. Chen (2005) "Soil Degradation Risk Prediction Integrating RUSLE with Geo-information Techniques: The Case of Northern Shaanxi Province in China", *American Journal of Applied Science* 2, pp. 550–556.

Ma, X. and Y. Su (2007) "A Brief Introduction to the Resource and Utilization of *Eucommia ulmoides* in China", in *International Symposium on Eucommia ulmoides*, Vol. 1. Tokyo: Japanese Society of Eucommia, pp. 7–10.

Machimura, T., T. Sada, A. Kobayashi, Y. Nakazawa, K. Gyokusen, M. Tsutsumi, K. Hidani, K. Tsuda and Y. Su (2009) "High Order Biomass Utility of Grain-for-Green Plantation in China and Its Carbon Reduction Potential: A Case Study of a Eucommia Plantation in Henan Province", *Environmental Systems Research* 37, pp. 467–475 (in Japanese with English summary).

Nakazawa, Y., T. Bamba, T. Takeda, H. Uefuji, Y. Harada, X. Li, R. Chen, S. Inoue, M. Tutumi, T. Shimizu, Y.-Q. Su, K. Gyokusen, E. Fukusaki and A. Kobayashi (2009) "Production of Eucommia Rubber from *Eucommia ulmoides* Oliv. (Hardy Rubber Tree)", *Plant Biotechnology* 26, pp. 71–79.

Renard, K. G., G. R. Foster, G. A. Weesies, D. K. McCool and D. C. Yoder (1997) *Predicting Soil Erosion by Water – A Guide to Conservation Planning with the Revised Universal Soil Loss Equation (RUSLE)*, Agriculture Handbook No. 703. Washington, DC: US Government Printing Office.

Ritsema, C. J. (2003) "Introduction: Soil Erosion and Participatory Land Use Planning on the Loess Plateau in China", *Catena* 54, pp. 1–5.

UNEP (2001) *Asia-Pacific Environment Outlook 2*. Pathumthani: UNEP RRC.

Wang, B., Q. Yang and Z. Liu (2009) "Effect of Conversion of Farmland to Forest or Grassland on Soil Erosion Intensity Changes in Yanhe River Basin, Loess Plateau of China", *Frontiers of Forestry in China* 4, pp. 68–74.

5-3

Redesign of the urban venous circulatory system

Keisuke Hanaki

5-3-1 Introduction

Urban activity is often expressed as an analogy to the circulatory system in the human body (Figure 5.3.1). Various kinds of virgin materials, energy and water are supplied to an urban area to maintain human activities and society. This supply side can be thought of as an arterial system. At the same time, food, paper, plastic and other materials become solid waste after use, wastewater is generated and the consumption of energy causes global warming through the emission of carbon dioxide. Proper management of these compounds through a venous circulatory system is essential to protect the environment and maintain human activity.

Traditionally, end-of-pipe technologies have been used to treat wastewater and remove sulphur oxide from flue gases. These technologies remove pollutants before they are discharged to the environment, and have dramatically improved air and water quality in developed countries. Although people may have originally thought that such end-of-pipe technologies could solve most of the pollution problems in urban areas, we now recognize that waste, resource and climate change issues cannot be solved by using these technologies alone.

Materials should be used repeatedly, and when that is not possible, they should be used in a cascading manner. Although material reuse and recycling are essential, conversion of waste materials to energy sources is also an effective way to reduce the environmental burden caused by

Establishing a resource-circulating society in Asia: Challenges and opportunities, Morioka, Hanaki and Moriguchi (eds), United Nations University Press, 2011, ISBN 978-92-808-1182-7

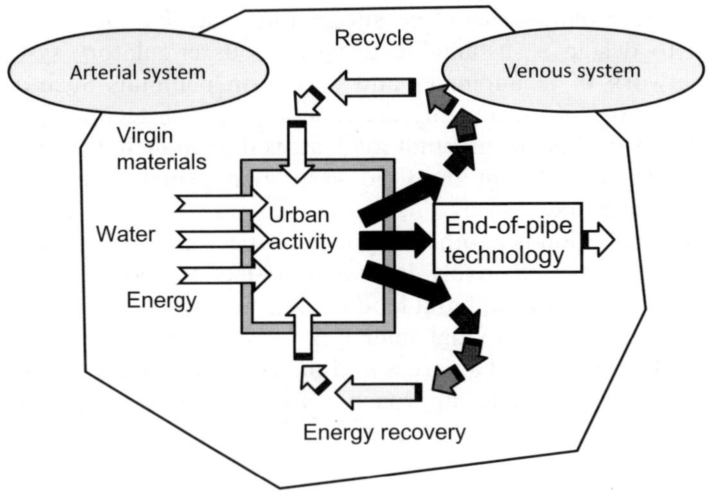

Figure 5.3.1 Urban arterial and venous systems

urban activities. Essentially, a move from a linear material flow to a circular system is required.

Waste materials produced in urban areas represent potential resources. The effective use of biomass generated from such waste is discussed in this chapter. Because the carbon in biomass originates from atmospheric carbon dioxide, carbon dioxide emitted through the combustion or biodegradation of biomass is not considered to be an anthropogenic emission of carbon dioxide. In other words, biomass is a carbon-neutral fuel.

Biomass in urban areas typically includes various types of solid waste and sewage sludge. Wastewater treatment and other technologies are used to reduce the environmental burden of these urban wastes, but other possible outcomes exist, such as converting them to usable resources or energy.

There are many end-of-pipe technologies for the treatment of sewage, sewage sludge and solid waste. However, each technology has been developed and applied in a discrete manner. For example, anaerobic digestion, which produces biogas, has been used for more than half a century to treat sewage sludge, but only recently has it been used to treat solid wastes.

In addition, the management of sewage and sewage sludge, solid waste and energy supply has been planned and implemented independently in most cities. Although there are some overlapping functions, the potential benefits of an integrated management system have mostly been ignored.

To manage urban wastes more successfully and live more sustainably, we need to design a sustainable urban venous circulatory system that uses a network of technologies and long-term planning. Such a system has the potential of maximizing the function of each technology and reducing the overall environmental load, as well as reducing costs. The link between sewage treatment and solid waste management is an example of this type of network.

Spatial distribution is another important aspect in biomass use in urban areas. Biomass is a relatively low-value-added compound. This means that the cost and environmental load from transportation of biomass may be a practical barrier. Spatial matching between biomass supplies and processing factories in urban areas and the surrounding agricultural areas is important. A systematic approach considering characteristics of biomass, relevance of technology, location and cost is critical.

5-3-2 Types of biomass and their utilization

Types of biomass

The wide variety of human activities produces a corresponding wide variety of organic wastes. Although there are different ways to categorize them, a typical classification is based on water content (Figure 5.3.2). In

DRY ↑ ... ↓ WET			
Wood waste	Municipal	Parks, street trees, golf courses, garden waste
	Industrial	Wood processing industries (thinned trees) Construction waste, agricultural waste (wood)
Paper waste	Municipal	Paper (households/offices)
	Industrial	Paper processing industries Information and communication sectors (newspapers)
Food waste	Municipal	Food waste (households/restaurants/supermarkets/schools/hotels)
	Industrial	Food processing industries Agricultural waste (vegetables)
Sludge	Municipal	Sewage sludge, human waste, sludge from digesters
	Industrial	Organic sludge, animal waste

Figure 5.3.2 Types of organic waste in urban areas

this classification wood and paper are considered dry, sludge is wet and food waste is in between.

Sewage is also biomass, but it is not included in Figure 5.3.2 because its direct use as biomass is not common. Instead, sewage sludge, which is produced during sewage treatment, is included in the figure. A disadvantage of wastewater (sewage) as a resource is that, although its organic content is high from the viewpoint of water pollution, it is very low as an organic material. The typical concentration of organic matter in raw sewage is about 100 mg/L, or about 0.01 per cent on a weight basis. Sewage sludge produced during wastewater treatment, however, has a 1 per cent organic content.

Human excreta used to be applied as fertilizer in agricultural areas in Japan until about 100 years ago, but this resulted in health problems, such as parasites. A modern practice of human excreta use now primarily found in Europe is source separation. Urine and faeces are separated at the toilet. Because urine contains no infectious microorganisms, it can be used as fertilizer.

A major source of biomass in urban areas is waste generated by households, shops, restaurants, schools, hotels and industries. The value of municipal solid waste as a resource depends on its homogeneity. If paper, food and other wastes are separated, they can be treated by applying different technologies, but treatments are much more limited if the wastes are mixed. Proper separation therefore increases the value of solid waste. However, in practice such separation depends not only on technical issues but also on the perceptions of citizens and hygiene issues.

The amount and characteristics of industrial wastes vary considerably among factories. Although constituents and biodegradability can vary, they tend to have fairly constant characteristics and the source is easily identified, which are advantages over household food waste. High-quality waste can be used as animal feedstock, and compost is also a common product from such industrial waste. Some food wastes are also suitable for methane production.

Utilization technologies

There are several ways of using biomass as an energy source or for other purposes (Table 5.3.1). Direct combustion of biomass as fuel is the most primitive but effective way to obtain energy. Because a low water content is beneficial, wood and paper are the most suitable biomasses for this use. Biomass used for household cooking and heating, which is still done in developing countries, is an example. Such traditional in-house burning of biomass can cause indoor air pollution, however, and is not realistic in a contemporary urban area. A solid waste incineration plant is a much

Table 5.3.1 Suitability of resource or energy recovery from various biomasses

	Direct burning	Biogas production	Compost
Wood	Suitable	Not possible	Not possible
Paper	Suitable	Not possible	Possible
Food	Need energy input	Suitable	Suitable
Sludge	Need energy input	Good	Possible

larger and more advanced example of technology used for heat supply. Moreover, modern plants use technology to reduce or eliminate typical air pollutants, such as NO_x and dioxins. There is a problem of mismatched distribution of source and demand because such plants are often located in suburban areas, which have a lower demand for heat. Using the heat from combustion to generate electricity solves the spatial discrepancy problem, but there is an energy loss of about 80 per cent during power generation.

The combustion of food and sludge requires a fuel input because of their high water content. In spite of this disadvantage, combustion of these materials is actually done to sanitize and treat them safely. The fossil fuel consumed to burn these biodegradable wastes does emit carbon dioxide, but if these wastes are landfilled an even larger amount of greenhouse gas (methane) would eventually be released into the atmosphere.

The most typical and established process of conversion of wet biomass is biogas production. This technology has long been used for sludge digestion in the sewage treatment process and for farm-scale biogas production in rural areas in Asian countries, such as China and India. The produced biogas contains methane and carbon dioxide. Methane is the major constituent of natural gas, and this biogas has a high fuel value after the carbon dioxide and other trace gases are removed. Biogas is utilized for local heating as well as to produce electricity by gas-powered generators. It can be mixed with natural gas in city gas supplies. The biogas production process is described in more detail in the next section.

In addition to its uses in producing energy, biomass can be used as a resource. For example, urban waste can be used to produce compost. Composting is an aerobic microbiological conversion process from biodegradable organic matters to more stable residual organic matters with nutrients. All biodegradable compounds and paper can be used as source material. The composting process usually requires an energy input, but the product is used as a replacement for chemical fertilizer, which also requires energy in its production process.

Conversion to fuel is another option to solve the problem of unmatched distribution of supply and demand. Bioethanol, biodiesel and bio-oil can be produced from sewage sludge and solid waste. Solid waste can also be converted to solid fuel as refuse-derived fuel, and sewage sludge can similarly be converted to charcoal.

Biogas production

Biogas is produced by an anaerobic microbial process used to treat sewage sludge and animal waste. The main function has been to stabilize organic matters and reduce the volume of waste. The energy recovery has been an additional benefit.

If methane is released to the atmosphere, it adds to the greenhouse effect; if it is collected and used as fuel, it can be used as a substitute for a fossil fuel. Hence the recovery of methane is essential from the viewpoint of greenhouse gas control. Unfortunately, methane is released in poorly managed biogas plants.

In the microbial process, a consortium of bacteria converts many types of biodegradable organic matter to methane under anaerobic conditions. The process usually proceeds in a liquid condition and is divided into an acid production stage and a methane production stage (Figure 5.3.3). The process has great advantages in terms of treating waste and recovering energy, and it requires a small energy input, unlike aerobic treatments. It can treat a wide variety of organic matters, including sewage sludge, food waste and animal manure, and convert the waste into a relatively clean source of energy (methane).

Although the process has significant advantages, it also has disadvantages. It is a slow process requiring a long retention time, which in turn means that a large facility and a large amount of land are required. This is a critical problem in high-density urban areas.

During the process, the digester is usually heated to 35–55°C to enhance the reaction in temperate climates. The retention time is tens of days long in this temperature range, but it could be more than 100 days without heating. Thus heating is essential, which substantially decreases the advantage of this process in terms of energy recovery. The energy for

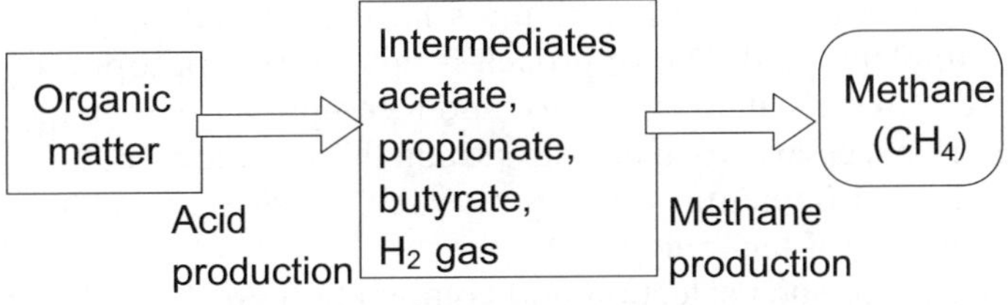

Figure 5.3.3 Biogas production process

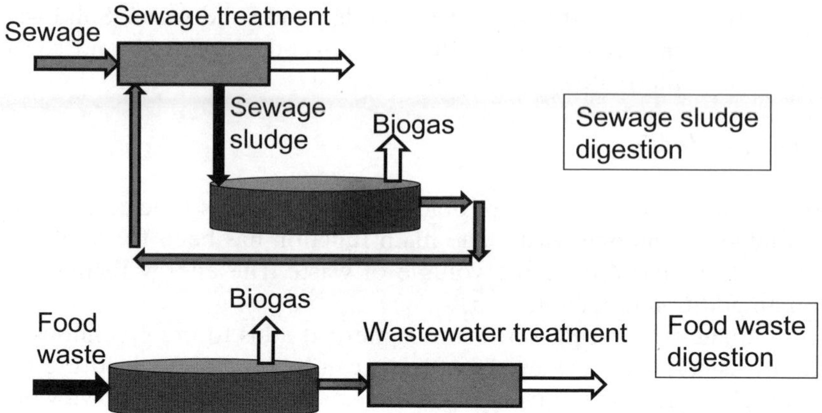

Figure 5.3.4 Biogas production from sewage sludge and food waste

heating is generally proportional to the treated volume of waste. The amount of methane produced is proportional to the amount of organic matter in the wastes. Because of these two facts, wastes with high organic concentrations are more advantageous than those with low concentrations. In fact, a large fraction of the methane produced is utilized for heating in sewage sludge digestion. Food waste has a larger energy recovery potential in this regard because it has a much higher organic concentration than sewage sludge.

Another disadvantage of a biogas plant is the need to treat wastewater from the biogas reactor (Figure 5.3.4). The concentration of organic matter in the effluent from the reactor exceeds the allowable standards for untreated discharge. Hence a wastewater treatment facility needs to be constructed alongside a biogas plant. Sewage sludge digestion has an advantage because the effluent from the anaerobic process is easily returned to the sewage treatment process.

A systematic approach in urban biomass utilization

Various technologies for using biomass have been independently developed and implemented. This approach is not always appropriate in a sustainable resource-circulating society, and a comprehensive and systematic approach is necessary to increase sustainability. Material flow balance and overall environmental loading must be considered in the selection and combination of technologies.

The criteria for such selection and combination are a good balance between supply and demand, reasonable cost and low overall environmental loading. The balance between supply and demand is critical in material recycling, such as composting. Matching demand and supply in the case of composting is a problem in a large city that has little agricultural activity and thus low demand for fertilizer. There have been many cases where large amounts of compost from sewage sludge or domestic solid waste facilities remained unsold. The supply and demand balance is influenced by many factors; for example, availability of compost from agricultural materials decreases the demand for compost from sewage sludge.

Cost is, of course, an important factor, but the implementation of technology should not be denied solely because of high current costs. Costs change with the development of technology and with mass production. The cost of fossil fuels influences the relative cost of new technology. In fact, cost alone cannot explain the actual implementation of various expensive technologies, such as photovoltaic cells.

Knowledge of overall environmental loading is necessary to evaluate the venous circulatory system. Life-cycle assessment (LCA) is a commonly used and effective tool for judging overall environmental loading. LCA could prove useful in comparing the different options of biomass management, but applying it to this kind of resource recovery is more complicated than using it with a standard manufacturing process. Figure 5.3.5 shows an example of an LCA evaluation of the composting process. When compost is produced from waste, environmental loading occurs during the process, but loading from the production of chemical fertilizers and waste disposal is avoided. To estimate the reduction in environmental loading, one must estimate what would happen in the absence of compost production and compare the two scenarios. In this case, without recycling, an equivalent amount of chemical fertilizer would have to be produced and any waste would go to landfill, both of which create environmental

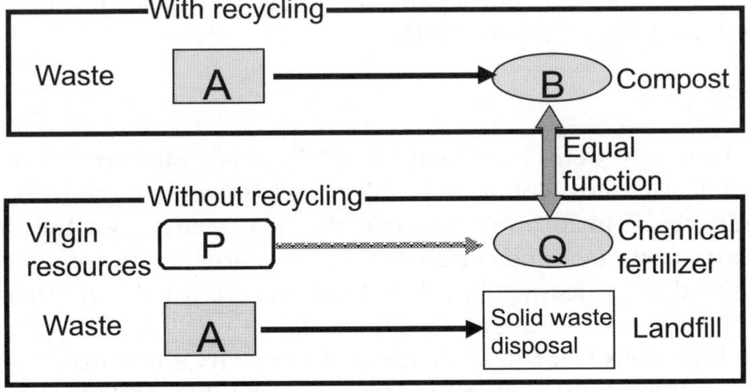

Figure 5.3.5 Life-cycle assessment of resource recovery

loading. The reduction in loading is thus the difference (e.g. in carbon dioxide emissions) between the two scenarios.

5-3-3 Energy recovery from sewage sludge and solid waste

Potential

The potential amount of energy that can be recovered from sewage sludge and solid waste can be calculated on the basis of their energy contents. An approximate evaluation of the Japanese case is shown below. Incineration is assumed for solid waste and methane fermentation is assumed for sewage sludge and kitchen waste.

One person discharges about 300 L per day of sewage, which flows into the sewage treatment plant. Sewage sludge is formed during the treatment process. Based on statistics from the Japan Sewage Works Association (2006) and several assumptions on degradation rate of sludge, the approximate amount of sewage sludge is 15 kg dry solid/year/person and its energy content is 0.3 GJ/year/person. Kroiss (2004) reported that per person annual sludge production ranges from 7 to 50 kg and is typically about 40 kg dry solid/year/person in large-scale treatment plants in Europe.

Amounts of municipal solid waste generated in 2005 in Japan and Korea are 400 and 380 kg per person per year, respectively, whereas the OECD average value is 580 kg per person per year (OECD, 2008). The energy content of solid waste in Japan is about 10 MJ/kg (Japan Environmental Sanitation Center, 1999). Therefore, the annual potential energy recovery is about 4 GJ/year/person in Japan, or more than 10 times greater than the potential energy recovery for sewage sludge.

For comparison, per person energy consumption in the commercial, office and residential sector in Japan was about 33 GJ/year in 2007 (Energy Data and Modelling Center, 2009).

Spatial context

District heating systems used heat from solid waste incineration or biogas combustion. The most common problem of a waste-heat recovery system is the difference in location between the heat source and the demand. Wastewater treatment and solid waste incineration plants are typical heat sources for district heating, but their locations are usually in urban fringe areas or by the waterfront, as shown for the 23 wards of Tokyo in Figure 5.3.6. A high density of heat demand is necessary for a district heating system, but the locations of the heat sources in Tokyo are not close to the high-demand area.

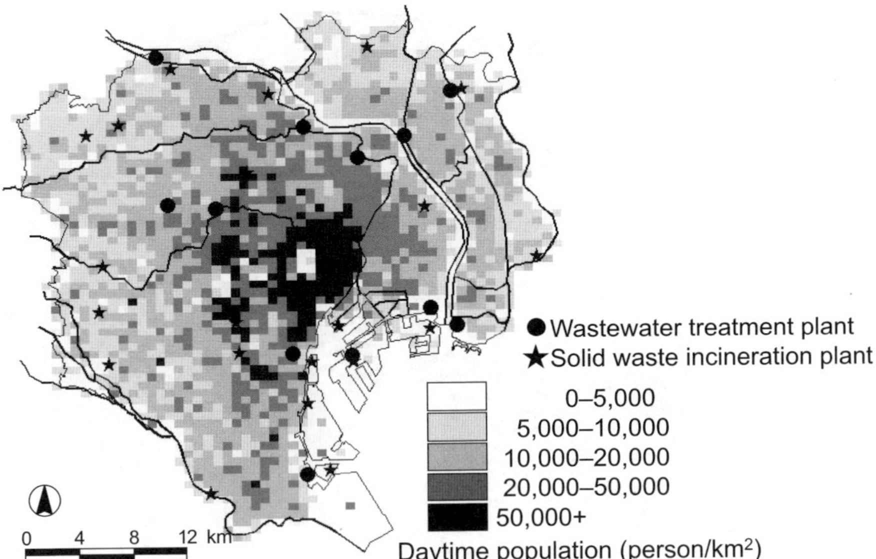

Figure 5.3.6 Distribution of daytime population and source of waste heat in Tokyo

A geographical information system (GIS) is an effective tool to assess the efficiency of a district heating system with heat recovery. In Figure 5.3.7 a district heating system serves an office building, commercial premises and apartments but not detached houses. GIS can identify target buildings within a certain distance from the heat supply source, and heat demand can then be calculated. Such simulation at design stage helps evaluation of energy-saving effects, though data availability and rapid future development are barriers to applying this method in fast-growing cities.

5-3-4 Co-digestion of sewage sludge and food waste

If food waste can be transported to the anaerobic digester in a sewage treatment plant, co-digestion of sewage sludge and food waste in the plant could have several advantages (Figure 5.3.8). The energy balance of the sludge digester would be greatly improved with the addition of food waste because the concentration of organic material is much higher in this waste. In addition, it would no longer be necessary to build a treatment facility for effluent from an anaerobic digester (Figure 5.3.4). A third benefit is improved incineration of solid waste. Food waste is not

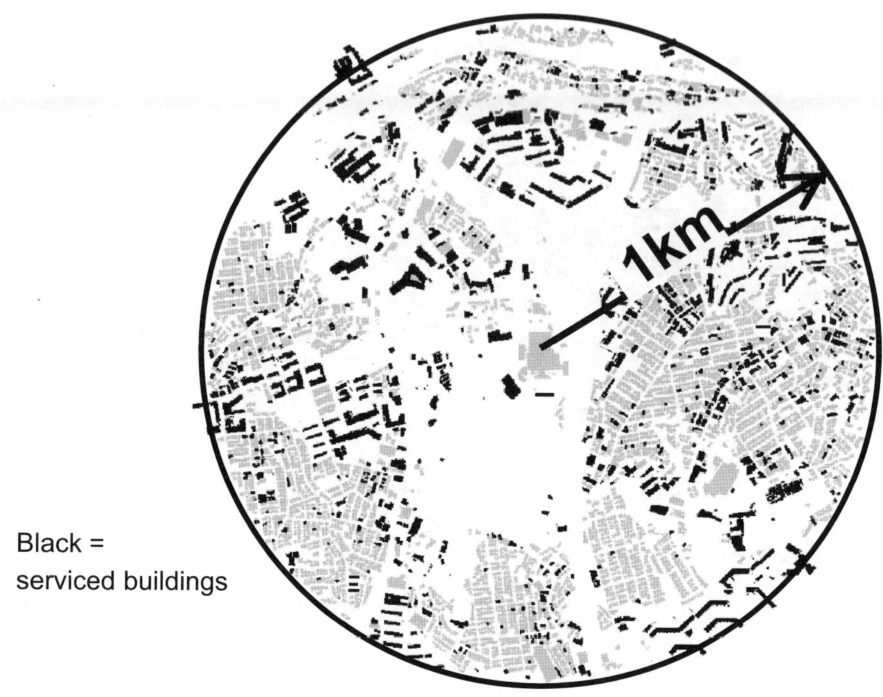

Figure 5.3.7 Heating demand around the solid waste incineration plant

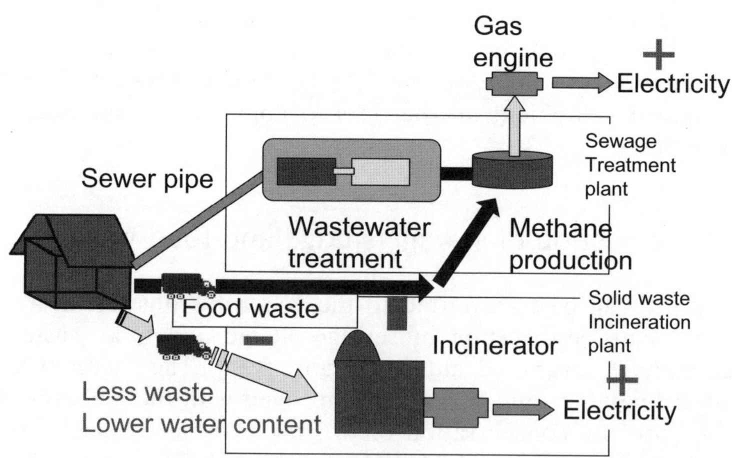

Figure 5.3.8 Co-digestion of sewage sludge and food waste

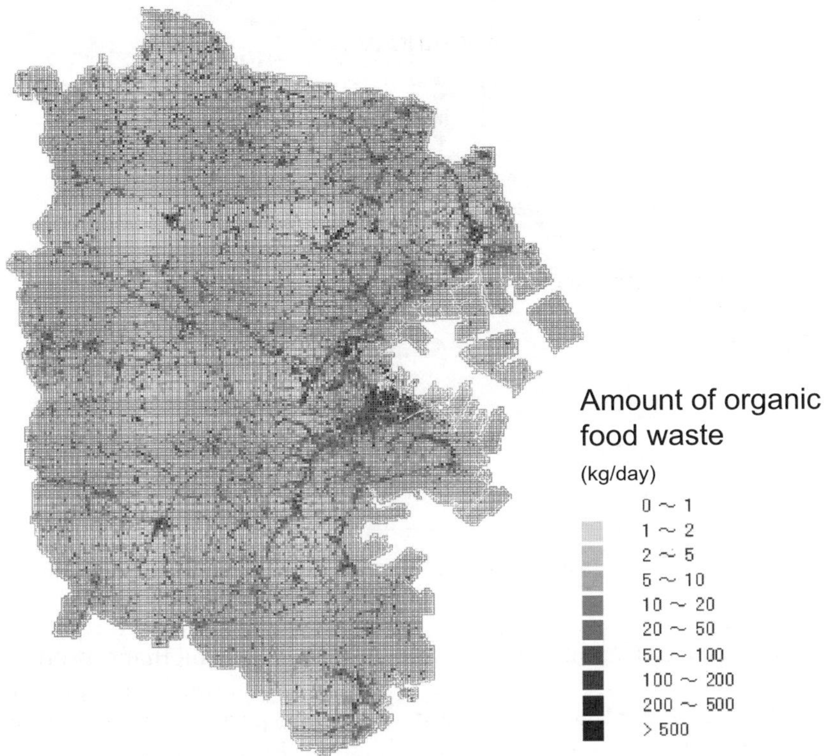

Figure 5.3.9 Distribution of food waste generation from the business sector in Yokohama city, Japan

suitable for incineration, and eliminating it from municipal solid wastes will increase the relatively low heating value of the waste. This results in an increase in the overall amount of heating energy despite a decrease in the total amount of solid waste incinerated.

Separation and collection are a barrier to such a diversion of food waste. Accepting food waste from industries or restaurants would be easier. Restaurants, hotels and other public facilities, which are encouraged to recycle their food waste, are widely distributed throughout urban areas, and often have a high density in commercial areas. The distribution of such food waste sources can be estimated using a GIS. Figure 5.3.9 shows an example of one such estimation for Yokohama city, Japan (author's data).

The scheme can be modified through the use of an in-sink garbage disposal system (Figure 5.3.10). With this system, food waste can be discharged into the sewer from each house and treated at the sewage

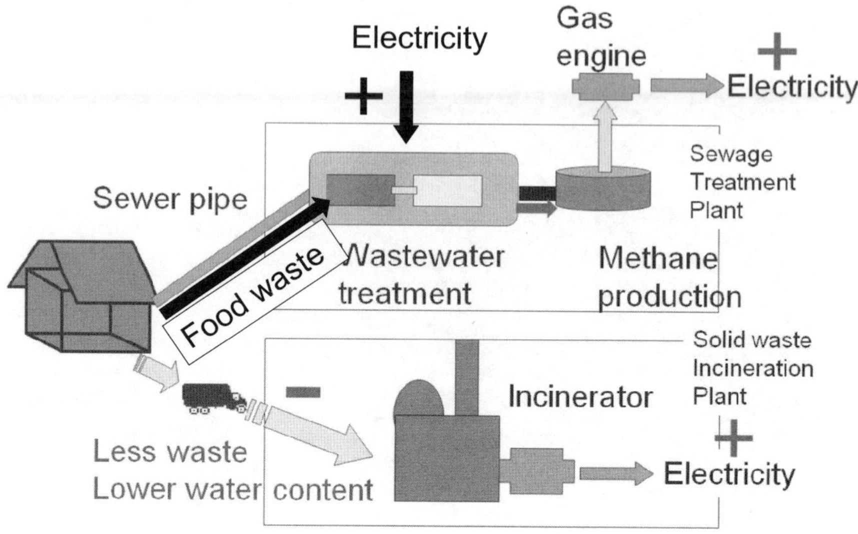

Figure 5.3.10 In-sink garbage disposal system and energy recovery

treatment plant. The amounts of sewage sludge and methane produced both increase because of the food waste in the sewage. However, the methane increase is lower in this system because part of the food waste is degraded in the wastewater treatment system. Furthermore, energy consumption in the wastewater treatment stage increases because of the increased load. From the viewpoint of energy recovery, this is not the best option, but it is a more feasible option in terms of collecting food waste from households.

5-3-5 Link to forestry and agriculture

Urban activity is supported by agricultural and forest products. In addition to supplying commercial goods, forests and farms assimilate some of the impacts of urban areas on the environment. The flow of material, including biomass, should be enhanced between urban areas and forested and agricultural areas.

Agricultural waste, which usually contains waste from livestock and crop residues, tends to be treated within agricultural areas. But this waste could possibly be combined with urban biomass.

Forests are a natural source of wood biomass. In addition to traditional biomass uses of forest products, fast-growing trees could be planted to achieve higher production of wood biomass and enhance the capacity of biomass use. Biomass pellets can be used as a source of fuel and are more easily transported than other biomass options. They also avoid causing indoor air pollution, but the spatial location problem still exists.

Compost typically flows from urban to forested and agricultural areas. However, this flow is limited and usually much smaller than the material flow from agricultural to urban areas. Agricultural demand for urban compost is a limiting factor in its production.

5-3-6 Tailored technology implementation in Asian cities

Technologies mentioned in the previous sections can be implemented into any city. However, the suitability of each technology depends on local factors. Organic waste containing food is suitable for biogas production. The organic content of municipal solid waste in developing Asian cities is high (40–70 per cent) (Asian Development Bank and Institute for Global Environmental Strategies, 2008), whereas the value is low in Japanese cities. Such high organic content makes the biogas process more feasible. Incineration is a reasonable option to recover heat from solid waste containing much paper. A cold climate makes this option more attractive. Each city needs a strategy to utilize biomass in the most suitable manner.

REFERENCES

Asian Development Bank and Institute for Global Environmental Strategies (2008) *Toward Resource-Efficient Economies in Asia and the Pacific*. Manila and Hayama: ADB/IGES.

Energy Data and Modelling Center (2009) *EDMC Handbook of Energy & Economic Statistics in Japan*. Tokyo: Energy Conservation Center, Institute of Energy Economics.

Japan Environmental Sanitation Center (1999) "Trends of Lower Calorific Value"; available at www.jesc.or.jp/environmentS/study/fact/img/06_fact6p.pdf.

Japan Sewage Works Association (2006) *Sewage Works Statistics (FY2004)*. Tokyo: Japan Sewage Works Association (in Japanese).

Kawakami, Yumi, Toshiya Aramaki and Keisuke Hanaki (2008) "CO_2 Reduction Potential in Japan by Utilizing Heat from Waste Incineration Plants for District Heating and Cooling Systems", *Environmental Systems Research* 36, pp. 87–95.

Kroiss, H. (2004) "What is the Potential for Utilizing the Resources in Sludge?", *Water Science and Technology* 49(10), pp. 1–10.

OECD (2008) "OECD Environmental Data Compendium 2006–2008: Waste"; available at www.oecd.org.

5-4

Renewable fuel supply by sewage sludge pyrolysis technology towards a sustainable society

Noboru Yoshida, Tohru Morioka and Yugo Yamamoto

5-4-1 Relationship between Asia and sewage sludge with pyrolysis technology from biomass utilization perspectives

This chapter focuses on sewage sludge to discuss biotic resources in Asia. Sewage sludge is a waste biomass resource that is closely related to future Asian socio-economic development; it is also suitable for use in a variety of technologies for biotic resources based on recent experiments in Japan.

Waste-derived biotic resources and Asian socio-economic development

When we think about biotic resource utilization in Asia, we should take Asia's high growth and diverse socio-economic activities into consideration. Population is a basic indicator, and is closely related to environmental pressure. According to medium-range UN estimates, the population in Asia will reach 4.9 billion by 2030, with China and India having a large share (United Nations, 2008). In these countries, the percentage of people living in urban areas is increasing at an astounding rate. For example, the urban population of China was 17.4 per cent in 1970, rising to 35.8 per cent in 2000. The United Nations (2007) predicts that the proportion of urban population in China will reach 60.3 per cent and 72.9 per cent in 2030 and 2050, respectively. This population concentration in cities is putting serious pressure on urban environments: water pollution caused

Establishing a resource-circulating society in Asia: Challenges and opportunities, Morioka, Hanaki and Moriguchi (eds), United Nations University Press, 2011, ISBN 978-92-808-1182-7

by residential wastewater, air pollution caused by numbers of automobiles, waste disposal problems and so on. On the other hand, the population concentration generates great amounts of waste biomass such as urban garbage and sewage sludge (Khajuria, Yamamoto and Morioka, 2008). According to a report by the Central Research Institute of Electric Power Industry, total biomass from waste materials in Asia is estimated to be around 1.2 billion tonnes (Iuchi, 2006). This biomass is generated stably and intensively, as it is treated in environmental infrastructures such as municipal waste disposal plants and sewage treatment plants. Japan's Ministry of Environment (2006) estimates that the Asian environmental business market potential will reach US$134–164 billion in 2020, with China having a two-thirds share. The MOE also estimates that municipal waste disposal and sewage treatment have great potential in China's future environmental business market. Most developed countries have built environmental infrastructures based on the so-called end-of-pipe principle. However, in a future sustainable Asia, environmental infrastructure must play a role in using waste-derived biotic resources based on a "cleaner production" and "zero-emission" approach (Morioka, Yoshida and Yamamoto, 2003).

Variety of technologies to utilize biotic resources

Another perspective is the role of technology development in biotic resource utilization. In general, biotic resources have versatile applications, known as 5F (food, feed, fertilizer, fibre and fuel) or 7F (5F plus feedstock and fine chemicals) (Yukawa, 2001). There are two main branches of conversion technology: microbial and physicochemical. Microorganisms are good at converting miscellaneous waste into useful material by processes such as alcoholic fermentation. Physicochemical processes are suitable for mass conversion and production with expeditious reactions, like gasification. Given the versatility and diversity of biotic resources, efficient cascade systems should be built up using various utilization technologies. While waste power generation is a main way of garbage utilization, various sludge-to-fuel technologies have been developed in Japan on the basis of roadmaps for biomass utilization. NEDO (2004) drew up a technology roadmap for biomass energy in 2004. The Ministry of Environment (2008) established core countermeasure technologies of biomass energy aiming to realize a low-carbon society towards 2050. Pyrolysis is identified as a representative technology in these roadmaps. Biomass utilization technologies have a close relationship with industrial technologies. For example, gasification and Fischer-Tropsch, which are typical pyrolysis processes, are derived from the coal industry, a major player in China. These industrial technologies can be converted and applied in biomass utilization in a future Asian sustainable society, as demonstrated in various eco-industrial parks in Japan (Morioka et al., 2005).

5-4-2 Low-carbon society and sludge-to-fuel movement – Japan's experiment

Sewage works are an indispensable component of city infrastructures, as they are essential for healthy and hygienic living. However, they also produce a significant amount of sludge through the wastewater treatment process. In Japan, approximately 2.2 million tonnes of dried sludge were generated in 2005. To reduce the volume of landfill disposal, a material-recycling programme has recently been adopted for sewage sludge. In 2005 the amount of sewage sludge recycling approached 70 per cent, primarily for material recycling. However, in terms of energy utilization, the energy recovery from sewage sludge covers only 7 per cent of the total recycled amount.

Currently, the recycling policy for sewage sludge is changing. As shown in Figure 5.4.1, greenhouse gas (GHG) emissions from sewage plants in 2004 equaled 7 million tonnes of CO_2. This is 0.5 per cent of Japan's total CO_2 emissions, and the rate of increase is more than 50 per cent from the standard recommended by the 1990 Kyoto Protocol. In a target based on the Kyoto Protocol, the Japanese government announced plans to increase the use of sewage sludge energy to 29 per cent by 2012.

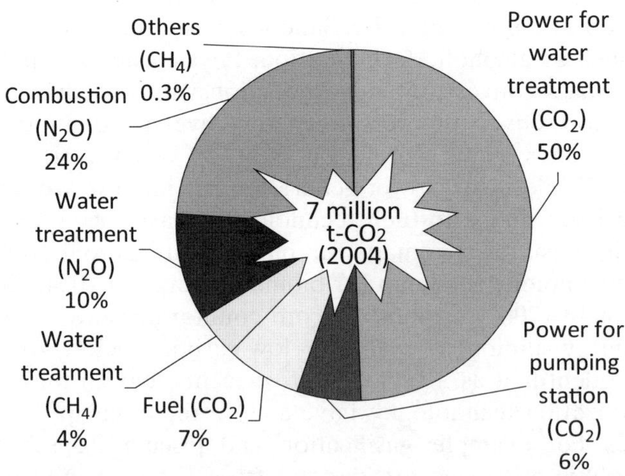

Figure 5.4.1 Greenhouse gas emissions from sewage works in Japan, 2004

5-4-3 Sludge-to-energy conversion technologies

Conversion technologies of biomass to energy are divided into the two main branches of microbial and physicochemical processes. Fast pyrolysis can even utilize digested sludge as a residue of the microbial process.

Microbial and physicochemical conversion processes

In recent years, biorefinery technologies have been widely applied to use biomass as energy and other industrial resources. Figure 5.4.2 shows the technical innovations in both the microbial and physicochemical processes that enable the conversion of biomass into various fuels. Most of these technologies, such as methane fermentation and gasification, can also be applied to sewage sludge.

As represented by the activated sludge process, microbial functions play crucial roles in environmental infrastructure. The microbial process can generate such useful fuels as bioethanol and biodiesel oils. However, microorganisms also simultaneously release a residual by-product called sludge in the energy conversion process. Additionally, the quality of the fuel required differs depending on the intended use. While internal combustion engines, such as those used in automobiles, require light oil, heavy oil is sufficient for direct combustion facilities such as boilers. Using both superior and inferior components is important when employing biomass as an energy resource.

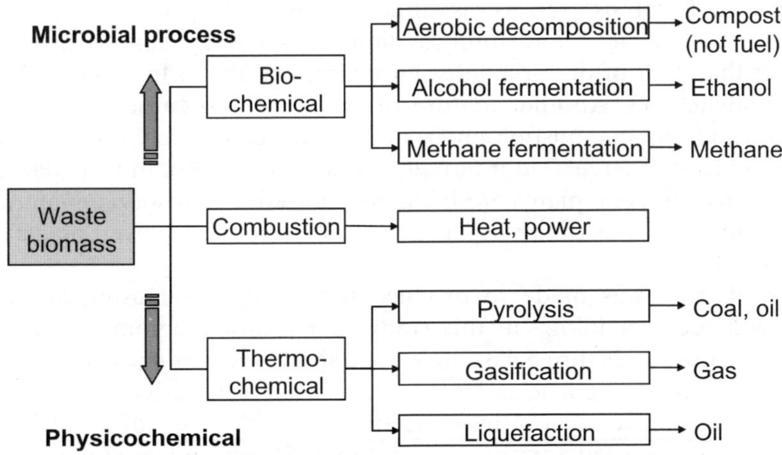

Figure 5.4.2 Conversion technologies of biomass to energy

Sludge-to-fuel utilization in Japan

Examples of sludge-to-fuel utilization can be found in Japan. One sewage water treatment facility in Tokyo has subcontracted a private company sponsored by an electricity provider. The company produces carbonized fuel using dewatered sewage sludge and a carbonization furnace. The carbonized sludge is used as a coal substitute for power generation. Carbonized sludge is easy to transport, but its yield is poor and its use is limited to coal-burning facilities such as power plants.

Methane fermentation is another sludge-to-fuel technology that uses microbial decomposition activity. The methane concentration of biogas is usually around 60 per cent, but with advanced purification technology can be increased to 98 per cent, enabling this purified gas to be used for city buses. Biogas is not easy to transport, so it is currently limited to on-site use. If it is to be transported by city gas pipelines, high purification is required.

Dried sludge with granulation and fried sludge from waste cooking oil are other sludge-derived fuels that are used by paper factories and coal-burning power plants.

Pilot test of sludge-to-oil conversion

Fast pyrolysis is a furnace process in which organic materials are rapidly heated to 450–600°C at normal atmospheric pressure in the absence of air. Under these conditions, organic vapours, permanent gases and charcoal are produced. The vapours are condensed to produce pyrolysis oil. In general, 50–75 weight per cent of the feedstock is converted into pyrolysis oil. Pyrolysis transforms difficult-to-handle biomass of different natures into a clean and uniform liquid. Its energy density is usually higher than that of the original solid material, which offers important logistic advantages. Another feature of this advanced furnace is that the gasification and combustion environments are completely separated and the fluid sand is circulated internally (Xiao et al., 2009). In Canada, commercial pyrolysis oil plants are being introduced. The resource material is woodchips and the pyrolysis oil produced is sold to power plants and metal refiners.

An attempt was made to produce fast-pyrolysis oil using advanced fluidized-bed technology in this study, and a flow diagram of the pilot plant is shown in Figure 5.4.3. Table 5.4.1 shows the test parameters. After being ground into particles less than 2 mm in size, dried and digested sludge was constantly fed into the furnace at the rate of 1.0–1.5 kg/h. Silica sand was used for the bed material. Steam and preheated air at

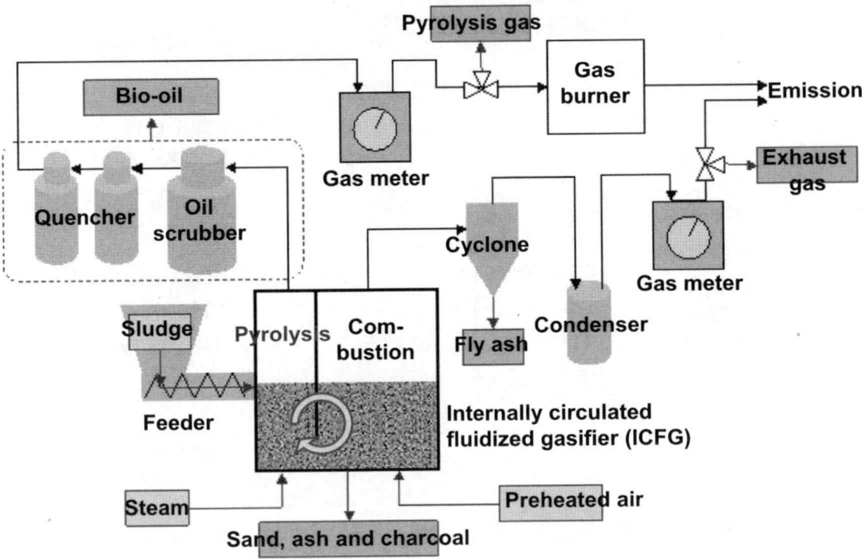

Figure 5.4.3 Flow diagram of the fast-pyrolysis sludge-oil pilot plant

Table 5.4.1 Parameters examined during fast-pyrolysis sludge-oil pilot test

Parameter	Unit	Value
Feed rate	kg/h	0.5–1.2
Total steam	mL/min	7.2–13.3
Steam temperature	°C	503–566
Air for fluidization	NL/min	20–33
Air temperature	°C	350–403
Gasification-bed temperature	°C	508–599
Gasification-freeboard temperature	°C	498–558
Combustion-bed temperature	°C	584–686
Combustion-freeboard temperature	°C	606–706

500–600°C were supplied from the bottom of the furnace. The reaction time is approximately one second.

Figure 5.4.4 shows the energy balance of the pyrolysis oil production, obtained from the pilot test data. The results indicate that pyrolysis oil can be generated without external energy resources. Note that approximately two-thirds of the previously produced oil was used for drying the dewatered sludge. If available, the utilization of other waste heat effectively increases the oil yield.

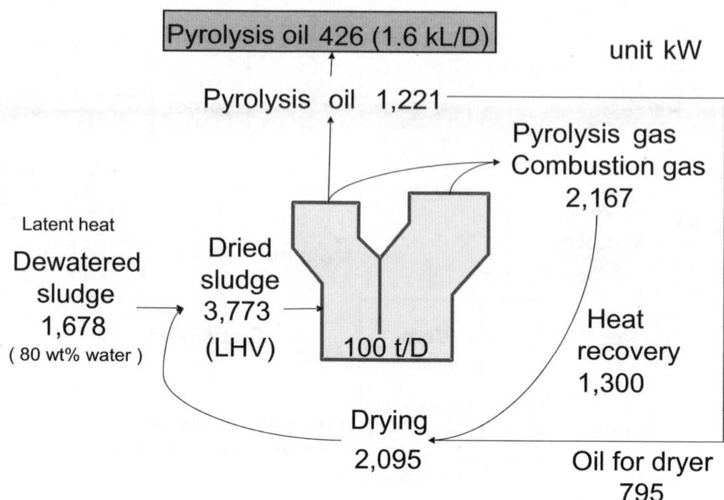

Figure 5.4.4 Energy balance of pyrolysis sludge-oil production

Characteristics of sludge-derived pyrolysis oil

Table 5.4.2 shows the characteristics of pyrolysis oil. A high concentration of oxygen is recognized in comparison with diesel and heavy oil. Oxygen tends to stimulate polymerization and high viscosity, so pyrolysis oil should be employed before polymerization.

Nitrogen content, which causes air pollution if facilities do not have nitrogen oxide removal equipment, is also a disadvantage of using bio-oil.

Table 5.4.2 Characteristics of pyrolysis sludge oil

		Bio-oil 2007	Bio-oil 2008	Diesel oil	Heavy oil
Ultimate analysis	C	40.4	50.6	86.6	84
(weight %, dry	H	4.39	7.61	13.3	12
and ash free)	N	8.64	9.71	0.0065	0–0.5
	S	1.00	2.30	0.1	3
	O	45.3	29.54	0.01	1
Viscosity (50°C, cSt*)		0.985	–	2.1	<20–25
Density (15°C)		1.03	–	0.82	0.85–0.94
Flash point (°C)		≥80	≥80	54	70~150
Fluid point (°C)		–8	–	–28	0~10
High heating value (MJ/kg)		11.4	20.2	45.5	42~46.2

*Centistokes

The production of low-nitrogen sludge oil, which is an aggressively pursued breakthrough, is currently being attempted using catalysis.

5-4-4 Life-cycle CO_2 of sludge-to-fuel technologies

The life-cycle GHG emissions of fast-pyrolysis oil, in terms of CO_2, were compared with methane fermentation, high-temperature incineration and conventional incineration.

System boundary and parameters for calculating $LCCO_2$

Figure 5.4.5 illustrates the system boundary for calculating life-cycle CO_2 ($LCCO_2$). The major factors in life-cycle GHG emissions are the energy and resource use during plant construction and operation, including the chemical substances and maintenance parts required for sludge treatment, fuel use during the transportation of dewatered sludge, demolition of obsolete facilities and the release of CH_4 and N_2O during water treatment and sludge combustion.

The parameters for calculating $LCCO_2$ are shown in Table 5.4.3. Regarding flocculants for water treatment, the CO_2 emission intensity parameter for flocculants such as poly-aluminium chlorite (PAC) was estimated as the intensity per unit of the gross product multiplied by the unit prices of the flocculants. Each intensity was obtained using data from the National Institute for Environmental Studies (2002).

Comparison of $LCCO_2$ among conversion technologies

As indicated in Figure 5.4.6, when compared to conventional incineration, pyrolysis sludge oil can reduce the life-cycle GHGs by 60 per cent. The operation stage is dominant in terms of the reduction of GHG emission (Figure 5.4.7). Since fast-pyrolysis oil is produced in a completely anoxic environment, the process can significantly reduce N_2O production. High-temperature incineration also contributes to the reduction of $LCCO_2$ compared with conventional incineration, although heavy oil is required to increase the temperature. For methane fermentation, the effect of power generation using digested gas was cancelled by the energy consumption required during the digestion and disposal of the digested sludge.

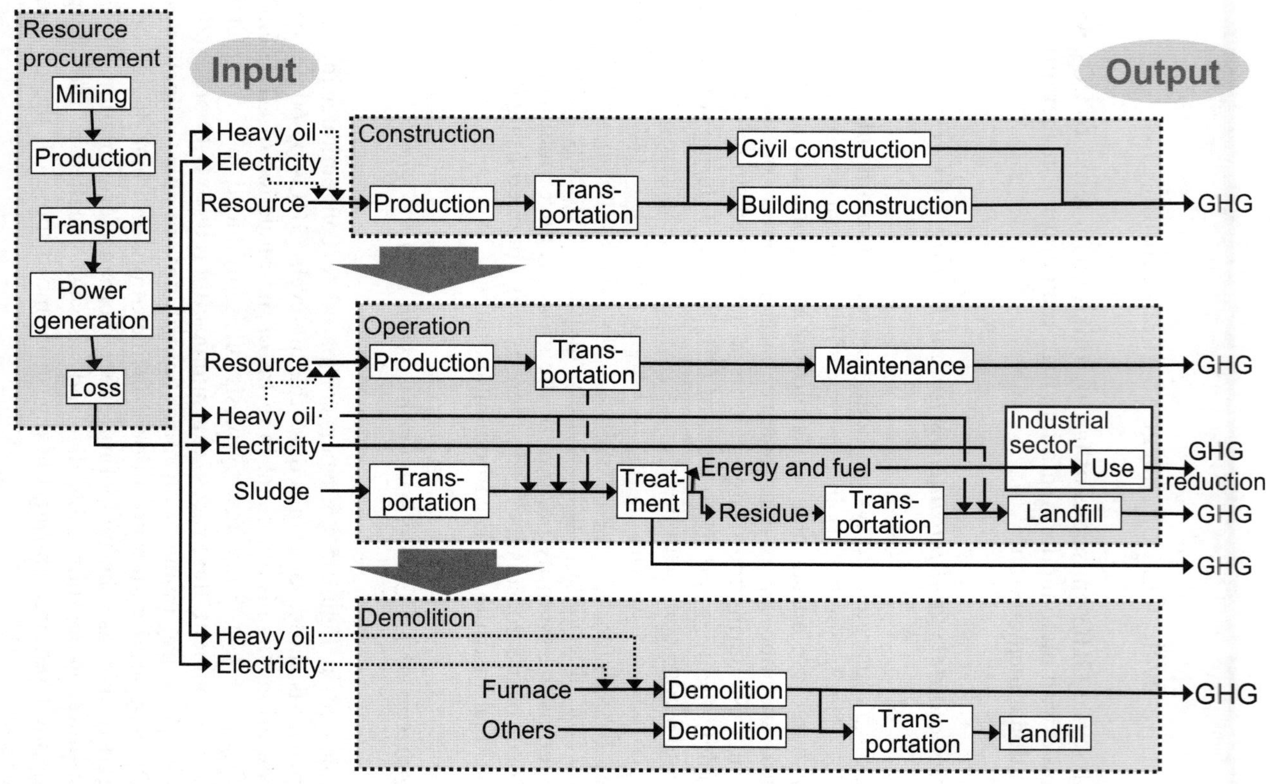

Figure 5.4.5 System boundary of LCCO$_2$ in sludge-to-fuel conversion

Table 5.4.3 Parameters of $LCCO_2$ in sludge-to-fuel conversion

Parameter	Unit	Value
Electricity	$t\text{-}CO_2/MWh$	0.378
Heavy oil	$t\text{-}CO_2/GJ$	0.0693
Sodium hypochlorite	$t\text{-}CO_2/t$	0.191
Polymeric flocculant	$t\text{-}CO_2/t$	2.94
Poly-aluminium chlorite (PAC)	$t\text{-}CO_2/t$	0.405
Caustic soda	$t\text{-}CO_2/m^3$	0.754
Water (industrial)	$t\text{-}CO_2/m^3$	1.08E-04
Electricity use for landfills	MWh/t	0.03068
Heavy oil use for landfills	KL/t	0.0024
CO_2 from landfill	$t\text{-}CO_2/ash\ t$	0.0368
CH_4 (water treatment)	$t\text{-}CH_4/m^3$	8.8E-07
N_2O (water treatment)	$t\text{-}N_2O/m^3$	1.6E-07
N_2O (sludge incineration)	$t\text{-}N_2O/t$	1.80E-03
Maintenance	$t\text{-}CO_2/Myen$	1.98
Construction	$t\text{-}CO_2/Myen$	3.355

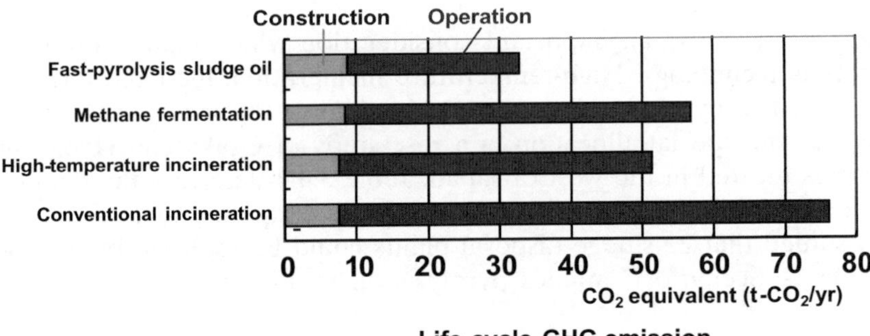

Figure 5.4.6 $LCCO_2$ in sludge-to-fuel conversion

5-4-5 Sludge pyrolysis oil implementation scenarios considering renewal and reconstruction of environmental infrastructure in Kansai region

Generally, engineering processes have advantages of scale. However, the current allocation of existing sludge incineration furnaces is not efficient in terms of exploiting the advantage of scale. Future scenarios should therefore be considered on the basis of renovation, scale and allocation.

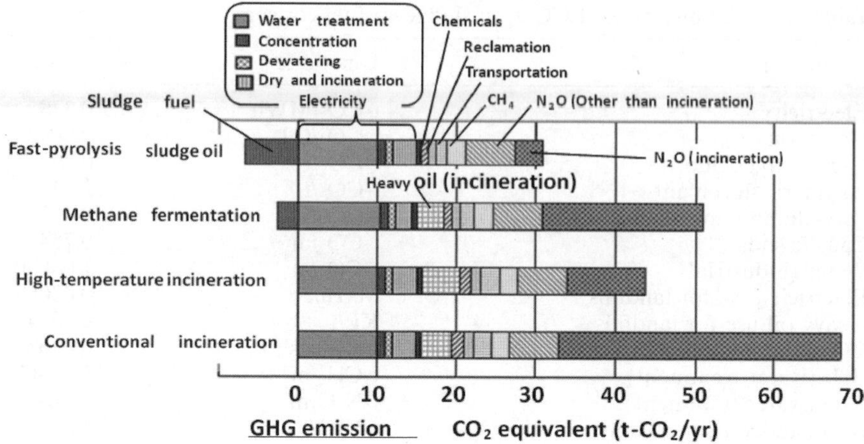

Figure 5.4.7 CO$_2$ in sludge-to-fuel conversion (operation stage)

Future renovation scenarios

Scale merit is also an important consideration when implementing fast-pyrolysis technology. High-temperature incineration, methane fermentation and fast-pyrolysis oil were examined from the viewpoints of plant renewal and special allocation in a case study of Osaka and Hyogo prefectures located in the west of Japan. Table 5.4.4 describes the details of each scenario. In scenarios A to F, sludge oil is applied to C, E and F. It is assumed that 22 sludge disposal plants could be replaced by pyrolysis oil plants. Scenario C applies pyrolysis oil to 13 large plants and high-

Table 5.4.4 Scenarios of sludge disposal/utilization

Scenario	Sludge plants	
	13 large plants (≥100 t/d)	9 small plants (<100 t/d)
A		HTI
B		MF + HTI
C	PO	HTI
D	HTI	TL
E	PO (13 plants)	TL
F	PO (reconsolidated 7 plants)	TL

HTI: high-temperature incineration
MF: methane fermentation
PO: pyrolysis oil
TL: sludge transport to large plants

temperature incineration to nine small plants. In scenario E nine small plants are demolished, and the sludge of those plants is delivered to 13 large plants where it is processed using fast pyrolysis. In scenario F, 13 large plants are consolidated into seven plants.

Geographical features in each scenario

A typical geographical distribution of sewage sludge plants in these scenarios is shown in Figure 5.4.8. As typically shown in scenarios E and F, small plants are located in suburbs and large plants are set in either coastal or urban areas. Apart from C, where pyrolysis oil conversion and high-temperature incineration are applied to existing large and small plants respectively, transportation of the dewatered sewage sludge is required in the other scenarios, while scale merit can be obtained for production of pyrolysis oil. Intensive pyrolysis oil conversion is applied to scenarios D and E, and further intensive conversion is implemented in scenario F. In the case of F, the plant consolidation requires significant amounts of dewatered sewage sludge to be transported to seven large-scale sludge-oil plants over distances varying from several miles to nearly 60 miles.

$LCCO_2$ with each scenario

Figure 5.4.9 shows the accumulated life-cycle GHG emission result for 2010–2034 in terms of CO_2. The accumulated GHG (CO_2 equivalent) from fast pyrolysis following radical plant consolidation (scenarios E and F) is around 50 per cent of that for high-temperature incineration under normal renovation schemes (BAU scenario), and around 70 per cent of that for methane fermentation and high-temperature incineration. Before our analysis, we were concerned about the increase in GHG emissions caused by the increased sludge transportation. However, since GHG emission due to sludge transportation is only 2–3 per cent, its influence on the total GHG amount is negligible.

Taken as a whole, increased fuel conversion efficiency due to drastic plant consolidation exceeded increased energy and material consumption resulting from plant renovation.

Effect of CO_2 emission credit

In contrast, the treatment cost of sewage sludge using pyrolysis increases nearly 10 per cent compared to conventional disposal. From the viewpoints of cost and effects, emission credits are thus an important future

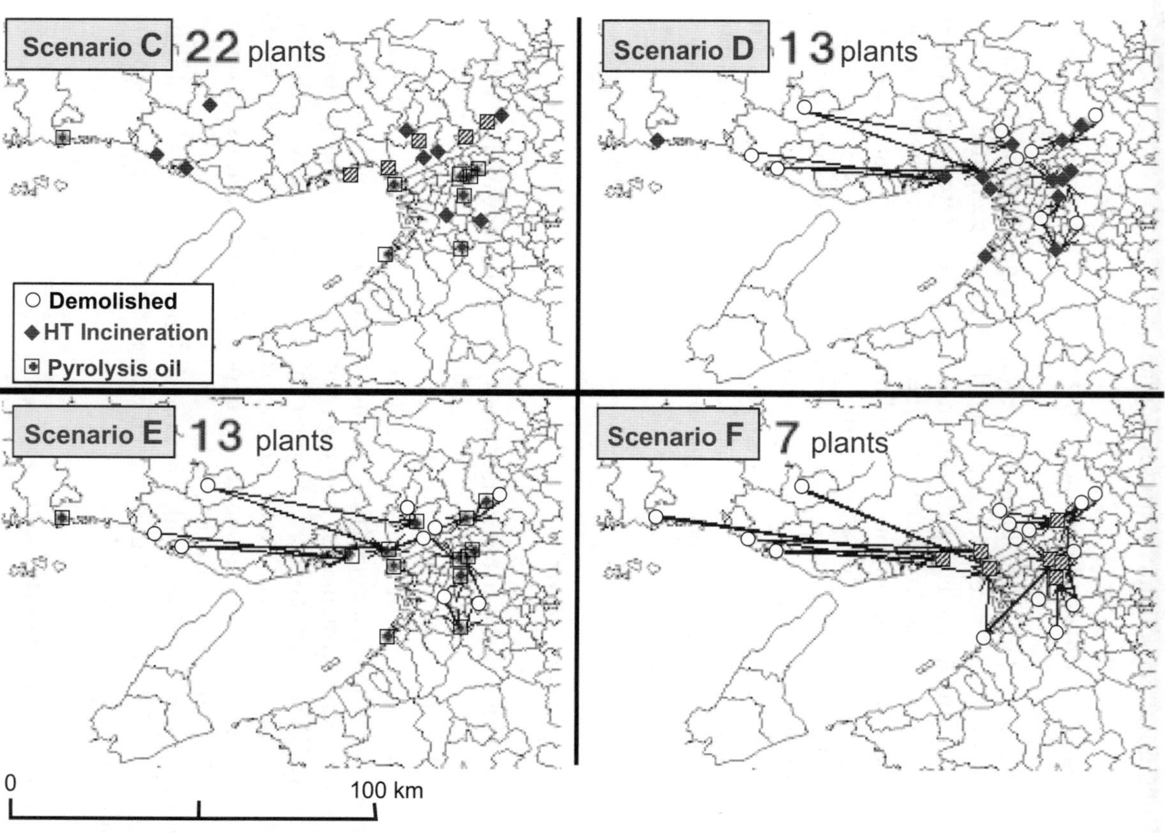

Figure 5.4.8 Spatial allocation of sewage sludge plants with scenarios

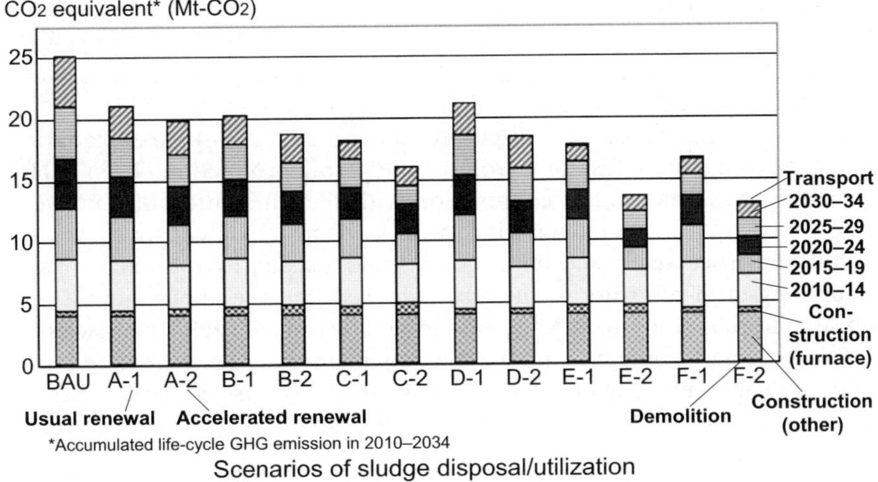

Figure 5.4.9 LC GHG with scenarios for sewage disposal/utilization

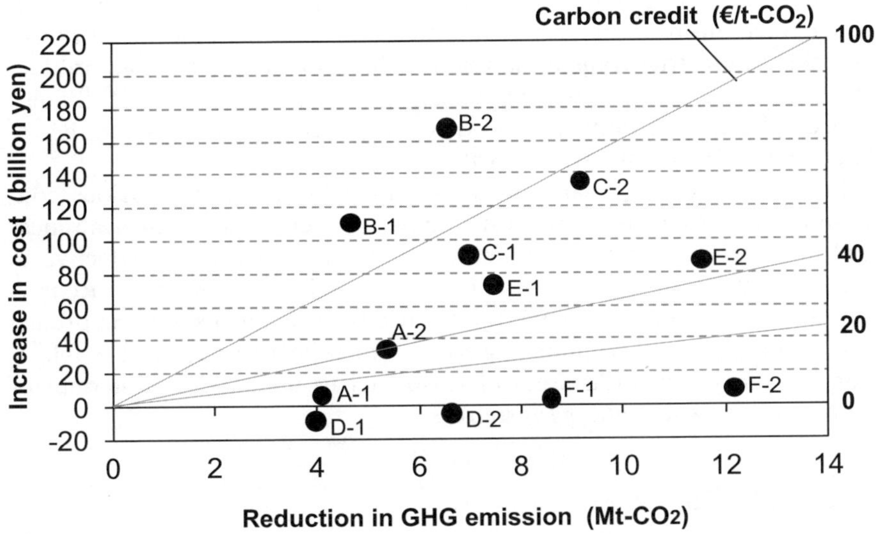

Figure 5.4.10 GHG reduction cost and effect of carbon credits

consideration. As shown in Figure 5.4.10, F is more reasonable than E, although their GHG reduction amounts are almost the same. Without emission credits, drastic plant consolidation, as seen in F, would be effective.

5-4-6 Conclusion

In this chapter, recent changes in the positional relationship of sewage policy and the technological feasibility of utilizing sewage sludge as a renewable energy source were discussed in conjunction with an explanation of an ongoing pilot test of pyrolysis sludge-oil production. Then GHG reduction was analysed in conjunction with the innovation of a conventional sewage sludge incineration process using advanced pyrolysis oil and other processes, based on life cycles and a scenario approach considering long-term renovation. The result showed that the application of pyrolysis oil technology to sewage sludge would reduce GHG emissions by more than half compared to the current incineration method, and that more sewage sludge would be utilized effectively as an input material during pyrolysis oil production. We also discussed the effect of CO_2 emission credits.

Towards a low-carbon sustainable society, technical innovations will increasingly take the lead in highly efficient energy conversion using biomass. Conventional and stable technologies like carbonization would be replaced by next-generation technologies such as gasification and pyrolysis. Such an innovation does not mean only technological change but also socio-industrial transformation, which covers a material and product chain of energy utilization including pre- and post-treatment technologies, combustion equipment, cascade energy-recovery systems and the related energy infrastructure renovations, etc.

In reality, technological innovations are adopted within various constraints, such as investment cost, regulations, environmental awareness and so on. Therefore appropriate policy instruments are also effective to accelerate renewable energy use. For example, in addition to the Renewable Portfolio Standard system for electricity in Japan, a similar approach will be proposed in an interim government report to impose an obligation on heavy industrial users of fossil fuel to use a certain amount of fuel from renewable energy resources.

REFERENCES

Iuchi, Masanao (2006) "Development of the Asian GIS Database and Current Issues of Energy Use", Central Research Institute of Electric Power Industry Report Y05030, CRIEPI, Tokyo (in Japanese).

Khajuria, A., Y. Yamamoto and T. Morioka (2008) "Solid Waste Management in Asian Countries: Problems and Issues", *Waste Management and the Environment* IV, pp. 643–653.

Ministry of Environment (2006) *Survey on Estimation of Potential Environmental Business Market Scale in Asian Major Countries*. Tokyo: MOE (in Japanese).

———— (2008) *Survey Report on Medium- and Longer-term Technological Strategy of Biomass Energy towards Low-carbon Society towards 2050*. Tokyo: MOE (in Japanese).

Morioka, T., N. Yoshida and Y. Yamamoto (2003) "Cycle-closing Product Chain Management with Appropriate Production Site Metabolism toward Zero Emission in an Industrial Machinery Corporation", *Clean Technology and Environmental Policy* 6, pp. 7–17.

Morioka, T., K. Tsunemi, Y. Yamamoto, H. Yabar, and N. Yoshida (2005) "Eco-efficiency of Advanced Loop-closing Systems for Vehicles and Household Appliances in Hyogo Eco-town", *Journal of Industrial Ecology* 9(4), pp. 205–221.

National Institute for Environmental Studies (2002) *Embodied Energy and Emission Intensity Data for Japan Using Input-Output Tables (3EID) Data Book*. Tsukuba: NIES (in Japanese).

NEDO (2004) *Survey on Establishment of Biomass Energy Technology Roadmap*. Kawasaki: New Energy and Industrial Technology Development Organization (in Japanese).

United Nations (2007) *World Urbanization Prospects: The 2007 Revision*. New York: United Nations.

———— (2008) *World Population Prospects: The 2008 Revision*. New York: United Nations.

Xiao, X., D. D. Le, K. Morishita, L. Li and T. Takarada (2009) "Development of Catalytic Tar Decomposition in an Internally Circulating Fluidized-bed Gasifier", in *Proceedings of the 20th International Conference on Fluidized Bed Combustion*. Beijing: Tsinghua University, pp. 747–753.

Yukawa, Hideaki (2001) *Technology of Biomass Energy*, CMC Technical Library 238. Tokyo: CMC Publishing.

6

Exploring opportunities for sustainable city-region design

6-1

Local initiatives and practices of policy and technology innovation towards a low-carbon society: Linking sustainable resource management to low-carbon policy

Tohru Morioka

6-1-1 Sustainable urban management: Promoting local resource-circulating actions and taking responsibility for hidden and virtual associated environmental burdens

Asia has experienced rapid economic growth and uneven urbanization in the last decades, and these trends will likely continue in the future. This has resulted in the emergence of megacities, particularly in developing countries. Of the 300 cities with a population of over 1 million people, around half are located in Asia, and of the 25 largest cities in the world, i.e. megacities, 14 are in Asia. In order to achieve a sustainable Asia we need to tackle three major megacity problems: urban population explosion, per capita resource consumption increase and higher environmental impact per resource use.

Even though megacities cover no more than 2 per cent of the Earth's land surface, they account for roughly 60–80 per cent of the resource consumption (directly and indirectly). Megacities consume 60 per cent of the water and 75 per cent of processed timber, and account for 75 per cent of anthropogenic CO_2 emissions. Furthermore, the consumption and emission estimations are only based on direct values. When we include the indirect consumption related to goods and services such as extracted resources, the amount of water, minerals and energy used during the manufacturing process and the land use associated with those activities, we understand that cities have a huge footprint on the environment. Cities and their surrounding areas or city-regions should consider the

Establishing a resource-circulating society in Asia: Challenges and opportunities, Morioka, Hanaki and Moriguchi (eds), United Nations University Press, 2011, ISBN 978-92-808-1182-7

following guides when taking the lead in terms of resource-circulating initiatives.

- Cities must minimize as much as possible their local environmental impacts associated with urban infrastructure, production systems, etc. For this purpose, while promoting zero-emission and recycling initiatives, cities should also pursue a transition to a low-carbon economy. Concrete aspects of low-carbon urban design are addressed in section 6.1.2.
- Cities must take responsibility for the indirect burden caused by their increasing demand for resources by minimizing their virtual burden: ecological, water and carbon footprints, etc. Cities must also develop policies that encourage the industrial sector to provide energy-efficient products and services, especially focusing innovation on products with high energy consumption in the use phase.
- When we extract underground resources there is concern that we are exceeding the carrying capacity, even with the use of renewable and/or efficient innovations like large-scale solar power generation, wind power or biomass energy and relying on eco-system services. The exploitation of nature without any consideration of rural communities and their culture also poses a risk. When we look for a symbiotic system with nature, we have to understand the cultural traditions and customs and incorporate this understanding in the concept of sustainable forests (Chapter 6-2).
- To minimize the environmental impacts associated with urban growth, we must put special focus on resource use efficiency. We also need to find equilibrium between centralized and decentralized urban design that prioritizes eco-efficient mobility, and improve efficiency in floor-space use in buildings. We must focus on the indirect burden associated with land use. One effective way to minimize the indirect environmental burden is to promote the design of compact cities and avoid large-scale infrastructure (Chapter 6-3).

6-1-2 Overview of local initiatives for low-carbon policy and practices

The IPCC Fourth Assessment Report estimated the CO_2 reduction potential by sectors and at different carbon tax options by the year 2030 using a bottom-up approach (Metz et al., 2007). Under the scenario that the carbon price is less than US\$50/t-CO_2, the building sector could reduce by around 5 Gt-CO_2/year by 2030. This mitigation potential is the highest of all sectors. By introducing economically feasible measures, OECD (Organisation for Economic Co-operation and Development) countries can cut down carbon emissions by 2 Gt-CO_2 in the building sector. Non-OECD countries, on the other hand, will face serious challenges when introducing a carbon tax. In any case, urban areas play a central role when looking for climate change mitigation potential.

Japan has launched city-level or local government collaboration programmes for environmental sustainability on several fronts. The most recent initiatives on environmental model cities are addressed in this chapter; other programmes include the Japan Network of the International Council on Local Environmental Initiatives (ICLEI), the Eco-city Council and the Special Task Committee for Assemblies of Large City Governments. These initiatives will contribute to reducing CO_2 emissions by changing priorities to low-carbon actions related to urban space renovation, town planning, infrastructure maintenance and traffic/energy/ logistic facilities.

Low-carbon societies envision the achievement of a sustainable modern world by altering the course of global climate change through mid-term programmes focused around 2020 and long-term scenarios for 2050. Through joint research, the Ministry of Environment and National Institute of Environmental Studies in Japan and the Department for Environment, Food and Rural Affairs, the Tyndall Centre on Climate Change and the Energy Research Centre in the United Kingdom have proposed different long-term scenarios towards a low-carbon society (LCS). Their modelling approaches, which were reviewed in the journal *Climate Policy* (Strachan, Foxon and Fujino, 2008), revealed that energy efficiency, consumer behaviour and selection of the best technologies for electricity generation play crucial roles in CO_2 emission reduction.

The Large Cities Climate Leadership Group, or C40, is a group of the world's leading cities committed to tackling climate change. These cities introduce policies that promote action programmes and seek the best practices to combat climate change. In this sense, achieving an LCS is one of the C40's central goals. Through this initiative, which started in London in 2005, cities pledge actions on climate change by setting greenhouse gas (GHG) emission reduction targets and implementing their action programmes and best practices in order to achieve their targets.

In both the Tokyo C40 Conference 2008 and the Seoul C40 Summit 2009, C40 leaders acknowledged the serious need to reduce GHG emissions by cities, which account for 75 per cent of global energy consumption and 75 per cent of global GHG emissions. The former mayor of London introduced a climate plan aiming to decrease CO_2 emissions by 60 per cent compared to 1990 baseline levels by 2025 (Mayor of London, 2007). As a member of C40, the metropolitan government of Tokyo proposed Tokyo Renewable Energy 2020 and its Climate Change Strategy 2020, which set a target of decreasing GHG emissions 25 per cent by 2020 (Tokyo Metropolitan Government, 2006, 2007).

Local initiatives by cities and local government associations, including the above-mentioned action plans, are shown in Figure 6.1.1. In Asia 12

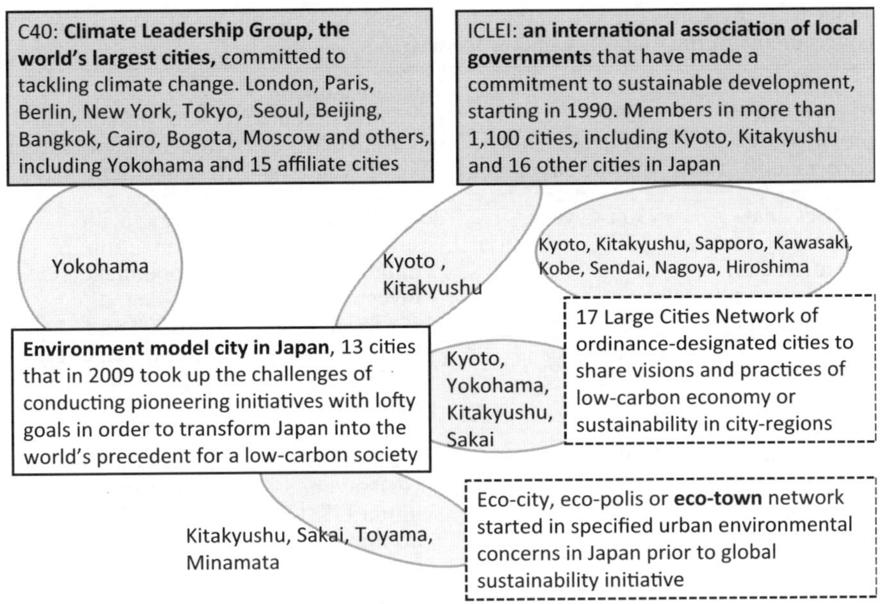

Figure 6.1.1 Typical city networks for low-carbon societies

cities participate in C40, while 121 cities of different population densities have joined the ICLEI initiative. In addition to Tokyo, 17 major Japanese cities (population 1 million or higher) have established local initiatives directed at establishing environmentally sustainable societies. The action plans of Yokohama, Kyoto, Kitakyushu and Sakai are pilot models of comprehensive city plans for low-carbon societies.

Japanese large cities have set carbon reduction targets for the years 2020 and 2050, similar to those of the C40 members. The most drastic initiatives among C40 members include the 60 per cent reduction by 2025 compared to 1990 levels set by London, and a 30 per cent reduction from 2007 levels by 2030 set by New York. Other cities have set CO_2 emission reduction targets that range from 25 to 50 per cent of 1990 levels in the 2020–2030 timeframe (Los Angeles, Toronto, Amsterdam, Rotterdam, etc.). There are also initiatives that set short-term emission reduction targets, such as pledges to effect 10–20 per cent reductions by 2010–2012 (Mexico City, Portland, Philadelphia, etc.).

C40 promotes and disseminates the best practices on its website (www.c40cities.org/ccap/). A summary of examples in terms of cost-benefits in monetary and energy/carbon volume is shown in Table 6.1.1. If these programmes are well designed and implemented, innovation in urban energy systems yields both CO_2 emission reduction and economic benefit even in the short term. However, the payback time at which the

Table 6.1.1 Cost-benefit estimates of best practices originally provided by city governments in the Clinton Climate Initiative

Best practices provided by city government	Carbon reduction, and volume saved	Benefits gained from investment in CBA (Cost Benefit Analysis)	Other practices and categories of carbon management
District heat-pump system, Amsterdam	730 t-C/year, 70% reduction	200,000 €/year saved, €25 million initial investment	Energy facility innovation in Copenhagen etc.
Tune-up boilers, Chicago	7,966 t-C/year, 12% gas saving	US$1.65 million/year saved, initial US$0.5 million investment	Retrofits and improvement in Houston etc.
Green building programme, Austin	15.9 Kt-C/year,	US$2.2 million/year saved, initial US$1.2 million investment	Regulation and monitoring in Melbourne etc.
Bus rapid transit system, Jakarta	120 Kt-C/year, 5% in modal shift	Fare of RP3,500 for 39 million annual passengers	Cost-effective mass transit system in Bogota etc.
Solar system and green lighting, San Francisco convention centre	1 Kt-C/year, 4.5 million kWh/year saved	US$0.6 million gain, US$8 million initial investment	Building code and installation in Heidelberg etc.
Intelligent road-lighting system, Oslo	1.4 Kt-C/year, 70% reduction in energy consumption	450,000 €/year saved, €12 million initial investment	LED, energy-efficient facilities innovation in London etc.

increasing net present value of discounted monetary flow (revenue or expenditure) become positive varies from 10 years (in the case of solar power systems) to 25 years (intelligent road lighting). Carbon pricing should shorten the payback time in the extended cost-benefit analysis.

The 17 large cities in Japan aim to achieve CO_2 emission reduction that ranges from 6 per cent below 1990 baseline levels by 2012 to 15–25 per cent below 1995 baseline levels by 2020. Actions to achieve these targets include policies for stimulating renewable energy supply and ecologically efficient facility management; smart mobility management towards low emissions, emphasizing user-friendly bicycle roads, transit malls and peaceful downtown locations; and establishing networks of green and blue corridors that will provide pleasant areas for citizens while supporting eco-system services.

The Japanese government, which tends to support city-level programmes facilitating the development of an LCS, has introduced three principles for achieving sustainable environmental model cities:

- minimization of CO_2 emissions from all sectors
- shifting from a mass-consumption society towards a quality of life (QoL) oriented society led by consumer choices based on the Mottainai spirit (Mottainai is a campaign launched in 2005 which strives for environmental conservation, effective use of our limited natural resources and efforts to prevent climate change)
- maintaining and managing the ecosystem services essential for an LCS.

In 2009 the Japanese government selected additional model cities as global environmental pioneers. This increased the total number of models to four large cities (population 1 million or more), a ward of Tokyo, four medium-sized cities and four small towns (Kantei, 2009). In Japanese cities affected by the East Asian monsoon warm climate, CO_2 emissions are in the range 2–3 t-CO_2/capita/year, except Tokyo business district and rural towns with mild and fairly temperate weather conditions. An examination of the network of city-level climate change actions revealed the need for government-led initiatives to promote the application and adoption of energy-saving and eco-efficient urban technologies, such as energy systems for combined heat and power, use of light-emitting diodes (LED) in lighting, solar power, fuel cells and storage batteries. The environmental model cities in Japan that have set carbon reduction goals for 2020 and 2050 also introduced typical pilot projects aimed at changing traditional urban systems into systems with low-carbon performance. The wide-ranging projects include mobility and transport infrastructure, waterworks, waste management, green and park systems and building and district management.

The CO_2 emissions from the industrial sector in urban areas, such as the steel industry in Kitakyushu, the petrochemical/machinery industry in Sakai city and the car manufacturing industry in Toyota, exceed 6 t-CO_2/capita/year, which accounts for up to three times the emission of commercial/residential cities. The Sakai model is a typical industrial innovation-oriented pilot, and intends to develop a new mega solar power plant and eco-industrial park producing liquid-crystal display and photovoltaic cells, and shift the mass-transport system to an LRT (light-rail transit) system. The greening industries programme of Sakai, where CO_2 emissions will peak in 2012, is expected to introduce an energy-saving urban grid management system and support zero-emission initiatives for manufacturers encouraging the mutual utilization of by-products, surplus energy, water and other resources in industrial zones.

Several EU cities in the C40 group have successfully launched profitable methane-recovery projects. In contrast, large Japanese cities have less to show in terms of quantitative GHG reduction through methane recovery as they tend to rely more on other technologies, such as biodiesel fuel or ethanol production using non-food biomass resources. The cities of Yokohama, Kyoto, Kitakyushu and Sakai have also organized collaborative councils for private-public partnerships and voluntary actions aimed at achieving the objectives of climate change plans, especially home energy management systems, eco-mobility and/or green purchasing of carbon-offset products or those with low carbon footprints.

6-1-3 Eco-model city environmental action programme: Outlook for Sakai, Japan

Japan's environmental model city initiative

Japan's prime minister and cabinet introduced the Environmental City Initiative through a series of pilot programmes (Kantei, 2008). In response, more than 80 city governments developed action plans, including mid- and long-term CO_2 emission reduction targets along with roadmaps for achieving these. With these plans, cities expect to revitalize both their QoL and economies under the umbrella of environmental technologies and social systems innovation. After a rigorous screening and peer-review process, six pilot cities and seven associate cities were selected in July 2008. Pilot city approval was assessed using a set of indicators and ranking systems, with the major indicators being:
* establishment of a serious carbon reduction goal
* assumption of leadership roles and realistic courses of action as eco-innovation pioneers
* community involvement and partnership among stakeholders towards goals that reflect the city's individual characteristics
* high feasibility and reasonable level of performance expected in plan implementation
* confirmed executive ability of city government and reasonable anticipation of continuity in planning, programming, performance and verification following actions.

Medium-term environmental actions of Sakai: Industrial sector commitment

Sakai (population 840,000), one of the selected cities, has a rich history that dates back to the Middle Ages. The city has industrial development along the coastal area, where steel, petrochemical and energy supply industries are located, and large-scale housing developments. Since industrial activities currently account for roughly 60 per cent of Sakai's CO_2 emissions, an agreement was negotiated between the local government and the industrial sector to reduce emissions using a framework with specific benchmarks. The city has also established a demand and supply management scheme for public transport that includes a new LRT network as part of a symbolic urban renovation project. The construction of large-scale solar power generation facilities and practices of symbiotic zero-emission policies in the industrial sector will yield renewable energy and resource-efficient products in the urban industrial zone. In addition, the city will develop urban blue and green corridors associated with restored parks and waterways to improve QoL.

Sakai adopted the motto "Cool City Sakai" to highlight its commitment to becoming a low-carbon city while promoting comfortable lifestyles and urban vitality. More specifically, the motto refers to decoupling urban metabolism from carbon emissions and a reduction in the urban heat-island effect resulting from waste heat generated by energy use. The basic strategies of the Cool City Sakai initiative are promoting a production and consumption system for environment-conscious industry that could produce renewable energy; guiding urban mobility and business activities while minimizing CO_2 emissions through use of the best available technologies and systems; and fostering sustainability in simple but spiritual lifestyles that promote improved QoL.

The Sakai CO_2 emissions plan includes a 10 per cent reduction as a medium-term target for 2030, and a 70 per cent reduction by 2050. The business-as-usual (BAU) scenario shows a 30 per cent increase in total CO_2 emissions due to increased activity in the petrochemical and solar/ TV panel manufacturing industries. However, the peak-out scenario states that CO_2 emissions will reach their highest level in 2012, with less than a 26 per cent increase at the maximum emission stage.

Based on the city's plan, CO_2 emissions will continue to increase slightly before peaking in 2012. By 2020 emissions will be cut by 15 per cent based on 2005 levels (Figure 6.1.2). This reduction will be achieved alongside sound economic growth and technology innovations in the electronic and electro-mechanic industries. Thus the Sakai initiative is regarded as industrial eco-reform that decouples carbon emissions from the manufacturing of eco-products. The Sakai environmental plan currently focuses on the three innovations, shown in Figure 6.1.3, which in turn encompass five strategic approaches.

- Stimulating business, community and governmental activity in consonance with global climate policies.
- Developing local medium-term environmental programmes and initiatives.

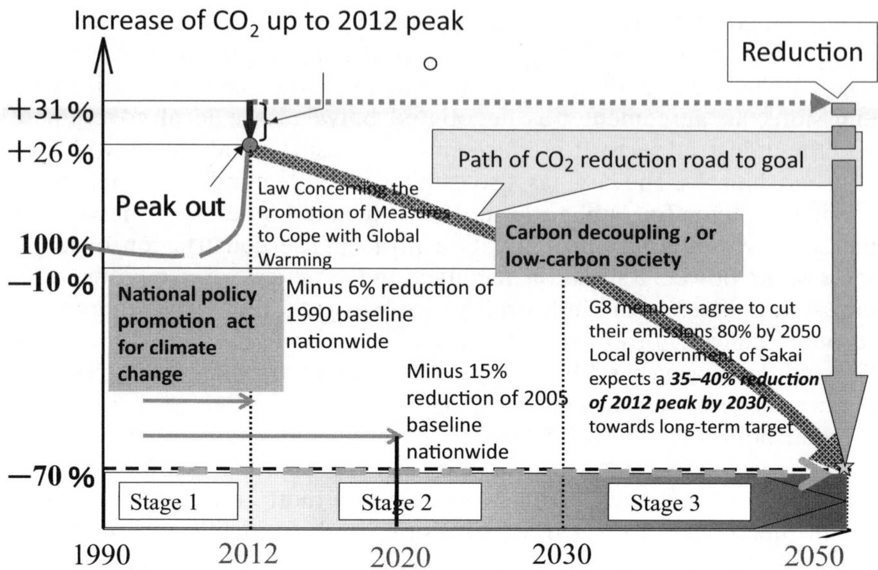

Figure 6.1.2 Outlook of mid-term CO$_2$ emissions and reductions in Sakai based on the "Sakai environment model city action plan, 2009"

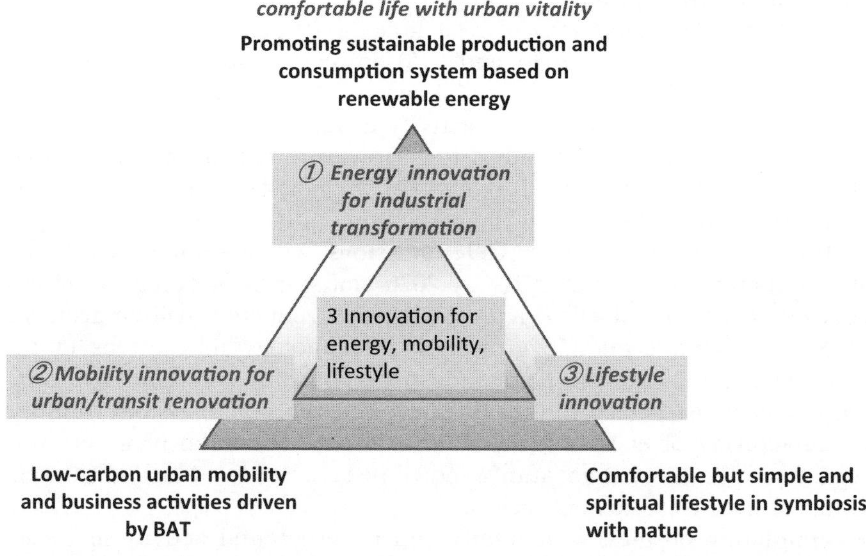

Figure 6.1.3 Three innovation modes for "Cool City Sakai" as part of the basic plan

334

- Encouraging industrial innovation in terms of renewable energy supply with production and consumption decoupled from CO_2 emissions.
- Changing mobility management through the promotion of bicycle and pedestrian programmes, and encouraging use of low-emission transport systems such as buses and trains within compact cities in harmony with nature.
- Promoting lifestyles that result in relatively low carbon emissions and encourage voluntary participation in resource-saving and conservation initiatives.

6-1-4 Eco-innovation of an industrial park aiming at carbon decoupling and green product life-cycle management

Encouraging industrial innovation in terms of renewable energy supply and eco-efficient production and consumption

District-wide collaboration for environmental innovation has been enhanced for product chains and processes with maximum eco-efficient production and corporate social responsibility. Initially, joint business alliances will establish a solar power supply system for local consumption and mutual utilization of surplus thermal energy and material by-products in the city's eco-industrial park, and through city-region business coalitions. Specifically, district facilities for energy grids with local electricity storage and control capacity have been installed to manage unexpected fluctuations in on-site renewable power/thermal supply potentials. These facilities are managed in consonance with a wider ICT-based system, which includes street lighting, traffic control, logistics, security, waterworks, waste treatment and the supply of welfare services.

The industrial innovation strategy of the eco-industrial zone will supply renewable energy and eco-efficient production systems in conjunction with non-toxic energy-saving products. These innovations are grouped into three frontier action plans.

- Energy supply sectors are expected to construct 10 MW solar power generation plants on a sanitary landfill site, an industrial park and industrial waste landfill, and networking distributed power generation devices will be installed on the roofs/walls of urban buildings within the regional electricity grid to provide an additional bottom-up type megawatt-class power supply system. Central government will subsidize between half and one-third of the construction cost of the first 10 MW solar power plant, which is estimated at around US$50 million in total.

- Local governments will provide incentives to core factories to manufacture solar cells, lithium-ion batteries or other energy-efficient electro-mechanical products, such as thermal exchangers, pumps and high-quality air conditioners, which are expected to be developed based on international standards. Manufacture will occur in eco-industrial parks associated with the zero-emission system, and will employ green labelling and incorporate a well-designed internal and external communication and certification system.
- Sakai is committed to providing its citizens with three benefits through the solar power system initiative: an environmentally sound energy supply, new job opportunities and new business opportunities related to component and materials supply industries.

The low-carbon city programme will also include solar power devices in the urban streetscape such as roadside bulletin boards, stand-alone clock towers, bus-stop stands, disaster prevention monitoring stations, tourist guide boards and vehicle-sharing e-ticketing facilities. The firms based in the eco-industrial park will use recycled water from sewage treatment plants and harness the large amounts of thermal energy discharged by heat pumps, chemical reactors and combined heat and power supply systems. The construction of additional public eco-infrastructure and corporate eco-efficient facilities may temporarily increase CO_2 emissions, direct material input and waste discharge, either directly or at the upstream side of the resource supply chain.

The temporal integration of the initial negative environmental effects derived from construction of energy-saving (resource-efficient) urban facilities and the time-variant discounted flow of saved energy (saved resources, or reduced carbon) within the same boundary could be implemented by averaging the extended cost-benefit analysis. In the case of export-oriented industries, the boundaries for evaluating the production and user stages are not compatible. This type of transboundary linkage is not considered in the Kyoto Protocol carbon management mechanisms.

Even if the new industrial estate was built as an eco-industrial park with the lowest possible emissions, the initial balance of waste discharge or CO_2 emissions would be higher on the manufacturing side of the environmental accounting sheet. Therefore, the long-term advantages of long-life products in the use stage, in terms of energy saving and other environmentally optimal performance outside the exporting countries, should be fairly assessed by the recipient country's carbon management authority. Actions to offset increased emissions in the exporting country by reduced emissions in importing countries will be determined to be reasonable when a common scientific basis is agreed regarding advanced carbon management criteria.

The accounting basis of this offset function is not yet certificated, but some innovative companies are trying to integrate their environmental policies in terms of combining environmental actions of eco-processing, servicing eco-products and eco-management. For example, an electric and electronic appliances corporation which launched eco-industrial factories in Sakai in 2009 states that the CO_2 reduction potential in the use phase and due to renewable energy supply originating from solar power will exceed the total CO_2 emission volume in all factories in its worldwide accounting system in 2010. Total sales amounted to US$11 billion a year and the total GHG emissions reached 1.7 million t-CO_2 in the firm's production stage in 2008. According to the corporation's estimations, in 2008 GHG reduction through customer use of PV (photovoltaic) cells was 1.02 million t-CO_2, with a further 0.95 million t-CO_2 through customer use of energy-saving products (Sharp Corporation, 2009).

As shown in Figure 6.1.4, the estimated CO_2 reduction achieved by solar power generation in the industrial zone in Sakai is not that big when compared with the expected volume of CO_2 reduction derived from

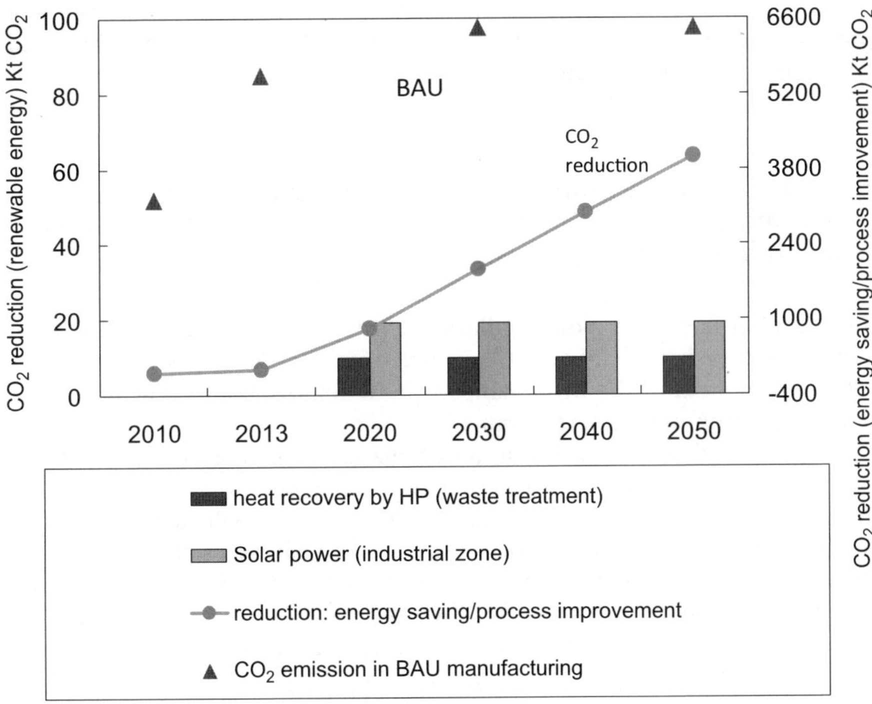

Figure 6.1.4 Performance of energy innovation in the industrial zone

process improvement in industrial plant operation or thermal energy recovery in manufacturing. Thermal recovery by municipal waste treatment techniques, many of which have been reported in C40, provides considerably larger CO_2 reductions in the Sakai case. The achievement of the goal in the Cool City programme depends on voluntary but socially responsible action. The effective amendment of the Industrial Energy-saving Act in national policy is expected to stimulate corporate sectors to follow the city mayor's target setting.

Carbon reduction in homes and small offices seems to be hard work in the environmental model cities in Japan. Sakai, as well as the other model cities, counts on reduction effects in rapid dissemination of solar power to private houses. The outlook for carbon reduction in households shown in Figure 6.1.5 indicates that distributed solar power to 100,000 houses should have a significant role by providing twice the volume of renewable energy supply in the planned two 10 MW solar power plants in the industrial zone in the Cool City programme. The local government has also stimulated refurbishing houses for effective insulation performance. The rapid increase of CO_2 reduction volume in the household sector from 2020 to 2030 is attributable to a wide variety of demand-side actions, such as replacement of energy-using products by energy-saving products, equipping individual/distributed solar power systems and changing lifestyles regarding energy use.

6-1-5 Changing mobility towards pedestrian and bicycle programmes and bus and train transport systems in compact cities in harmony with nature

Sakai's plan has three policy pillars regarding mobility: a medium-scale vehicle system for the city centre, priority for bicycle and pedestrian mobility and reform of the urban landscape to achieve compactness and enhanced environmental performance.

The LRT plan stands on a modernized tram system that expects to provide convenient mobility to citizens along 6.9 km of new track and 7.9 km of refurbished existing railway. This system will facilitate movement of increasing numbers of workers and visitors to the city centre, thus improving commerce. Since use of public transport accounts for a 7 per cent decline in individual CO_2 emissions, while private automobile use accounts for 30 per cent during intra-city travel, it is clear that adoption of this programme will result in a considerable reduction in CO_2 emissions.

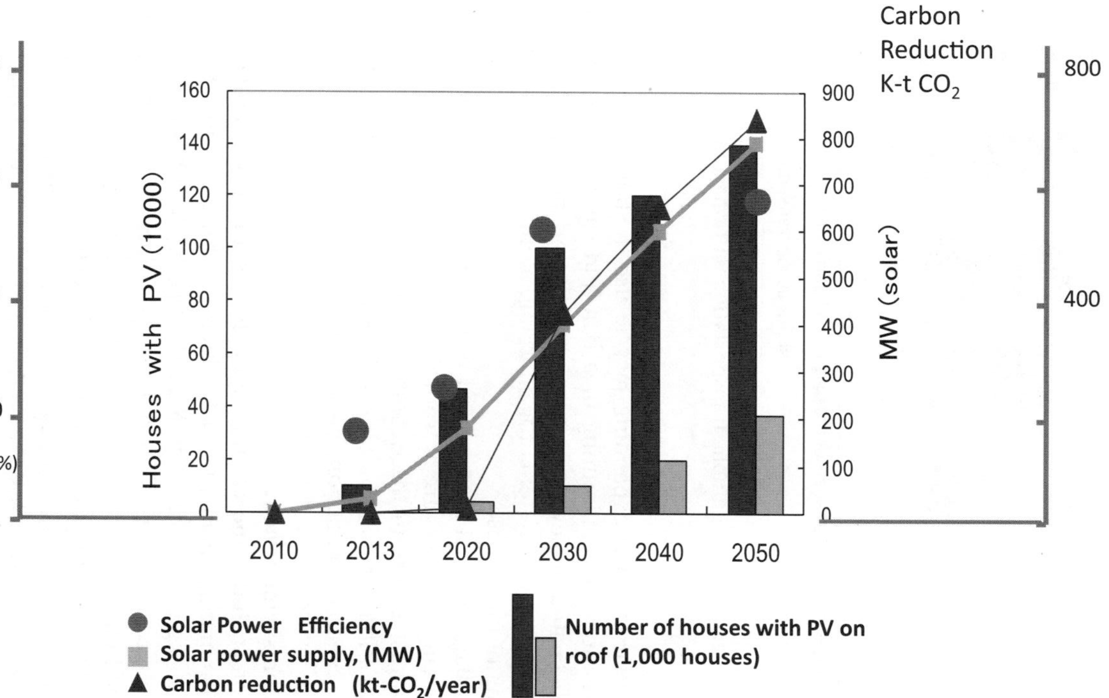

Figure 6.1.5 Performance of lifestyle innovation in terms of PV cells on buildings and changes to electricity use

Note: Please see page 430 for a colour version of this figure.

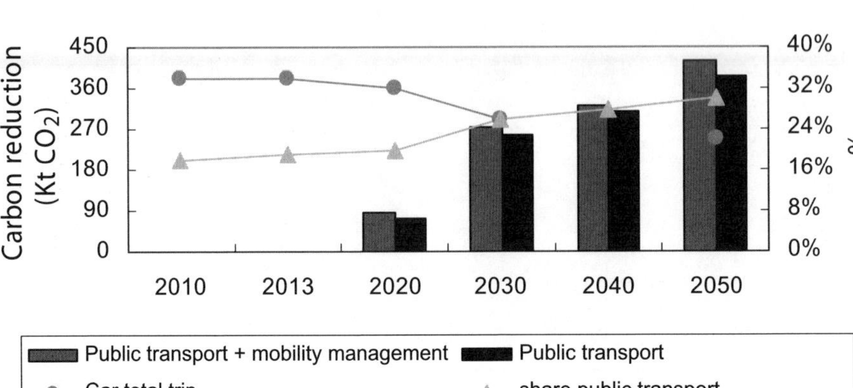

Figure 6.1.6 Performance of rising public transportation and smart mobility management

The second pillar involves expanding bicycle use in shopping areas as well as for recreation and commuting in urban and suburban areas. An ICT system will facilitate bicycle renting, sharing and parking that will include convenient transfer systems for charging, monitoring and carbon credit accounting of bicycle use.

In the third pillar, the local government will encourage stakeholders to install energy-saving devices, green roofs and solar-cell equipment on buildings and infrastructure in the downtown area. Stakeholders will assess the CO_2 emissions of their buildings throughout their entire life cycles, including resource extraction, construction and usage stages. The government will award prize certifications to building owners with the best CO_2 emission-saving practices.

The Sakai plan includes the carbon reduction of the LRT services in the total mobility management forecast, which is estimated to be 85 Kt/year (around 100 kg/capita/year) by 2020 (Figure 6.1.6). Other cities of the C40 group expect to return CO_2 reductions as high as 258 kg/capita/year through road taxes and automobile control in the case of the downtown district of Stockholm, Sweden, and 180 kg/capita/year through the promotion of bicycle use in Copenhagen, Denmark. Sakai intends to study the best practices of European cities and may adapt several of these, including integrated transport management and transportation guidelines during "no-driving days". Interestingly, a mixed policy of taxation and subsidy supported by ICT monitoring has yielded 6 per cent reduction of total CO_2 emissions in Seoul, Korea.

6-1-6 Policy integration in low-carbon initiatives of selected large cities in Japan

In Japan, 17 large cities have designed city-level climate policies that have been incorporated in local government charters, mayoral manifestos, environmental master plans, local climate change action plans and local ordinances related to building and/or energy policy. In each case, the cities framed three key projects in local climate policy: renewable energy supply with integrated facility management, smart mobility management with low emissions and the networking of blue and green corridors. In this sense, carbon management has become a new linking domain between policy formulation, comprehensive facility renovation and collaboration among stakeholders.

Frontier technologies promote best practices in energy-use applications in building development, followed by surveillance and reporting to authorities. Other best practices include local renewable energy quotas, local versions of carbon emission offsetting, a special floor-area ratio permits system for compact city nodes, grading of appliances in terms of carbon footprint, commendation and awards for good performance to enterprises for energy saving and tradable carbon reduction at local eco-points. Local carbon initiatives have also intensified policy integration between voluntary and regulatory instruments, short-term and long-term periods and supply side and demand side, as well as the financing and recipient sides.

Local energy, transport and greening plans are specified as major domains of local climate policy (Morioka, 2009), as shown in Figure 6.1.7. Local governments try to reform urban structure into compact cities by means of smart growth in suburban areas, strengthening activity intensity in urban core zones and managing sound mobility-based transport-oriented development. They aim at complete alternative urban energy policy, in terms of decoupling energy use and saving energy with carbon discharge in a new energy vision, eco-energy plan and/or eco-industrial park project. The third domain is greening city-regions through urban reforestation, revitalizing forest resources in biomass model towns and/or stimulating local production/consumption links with minimum food mileage.

In every domain, governments pay attention to raising environmental values, offering incentives to promote eco-action and supporting behavioural change, such as with an eco-points card system. They also expand participatory opportunity to develop cooperation through dialogue in town meetings, in parallel with strengthening the partnership with business associations. The 17 large cities are boosting community vitality by

Focus on three domains

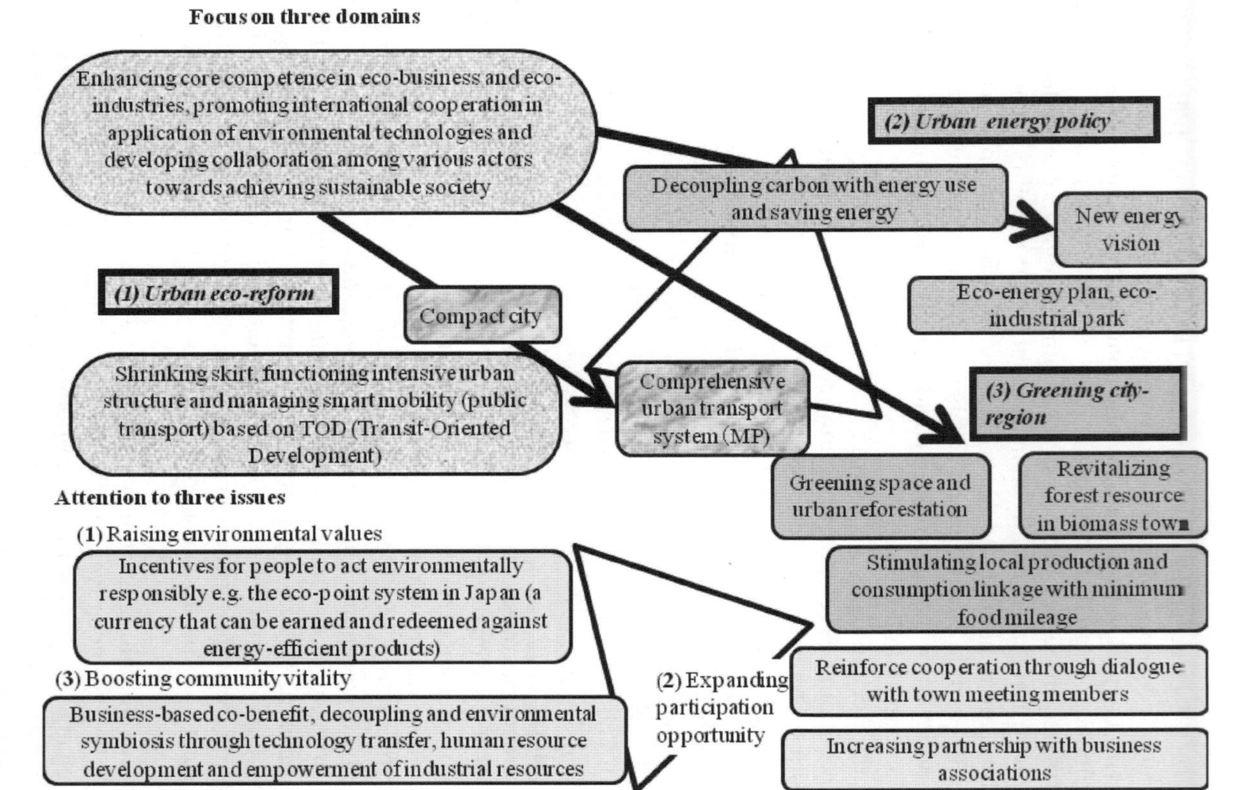

Figure 6.1.7 Strategies on climate change policy in 17 large cities in Japan

means of business innovation of eco-industries, human capacity development and empowerment of locally distinct industrial resources.

In local energy plans, as illustrated in Figure 6.1.8, the 17 cities emphasize matching renewable energy, recovered energy and high-efficiency energy mixes of electricity and heat with the full spectrum of energy demand (ibid.). Typical examples are a new user alliance for solar power supply, an area-wide town facility management scheme between users and suppliers, a steam and heat-recovery network in industrial zones, digested gas for combined power generation, heat-pump systems for buildings in riverfront zones, biofuel crop production in neighbouring rural areas for bioethanol manufacturing, home cooking-oil recovery for biodiesel supply to buses or garbage trucks, an eco-museum educational park for urban energy saving, special promotion areas for house and building energy management systems, energy audits and a saving consultation system for business profits and other collaboration schemes.

Greening and transport policies can provide double benefits for citizens. For example, since downtown green corridors provide open space, landscape and other amenity services, the use of air conditioning in summer should be reduced. The 17 large cities foster the construction of carbon-neutral buildings using wooden materials, and forest conservation programmes for watersheds which are also considered as carbon credit projects. The collaboration between urban stakeholders and relevant counterparts in forest areas to promote local timber purchasing, biomass-based (organic waste) power generation and other projects is considered an important pillar of local climate policies and resource-circulating policies. In the case of urban transport, the 17 cities have focused on measures beyond demand/supply management and include installing charging stations for electric vehicles in networked urban subcentres, construction of LRT systems in compact city centres and car-pool systems using hybrid automobiles in low-carbon cities.

As these practices are very ambitious, they share with the C40 member cities similar uncertainties in short-term cost performance and institutional barriers. However, C40 cities have already implemented cost-effective measures, including roadside or outdoor lighting systems using LED, building insulation improvement programmes and selected biomass-derived power generation programmes. In Japan the urban climate-related energy policy has integrated with regulatory enforcement such as the feed-in tariff system for electricity supply sectors beyond the voluntary action base, downtown traffic systems beyond road pricing for congestion and energy consumption quotas for large firms. Energy-saving or green technologies could be applied in other countries despite the high initial costs. The difficulty of disseminating urban eco-innovations most probably would be attributed to lack of political will.

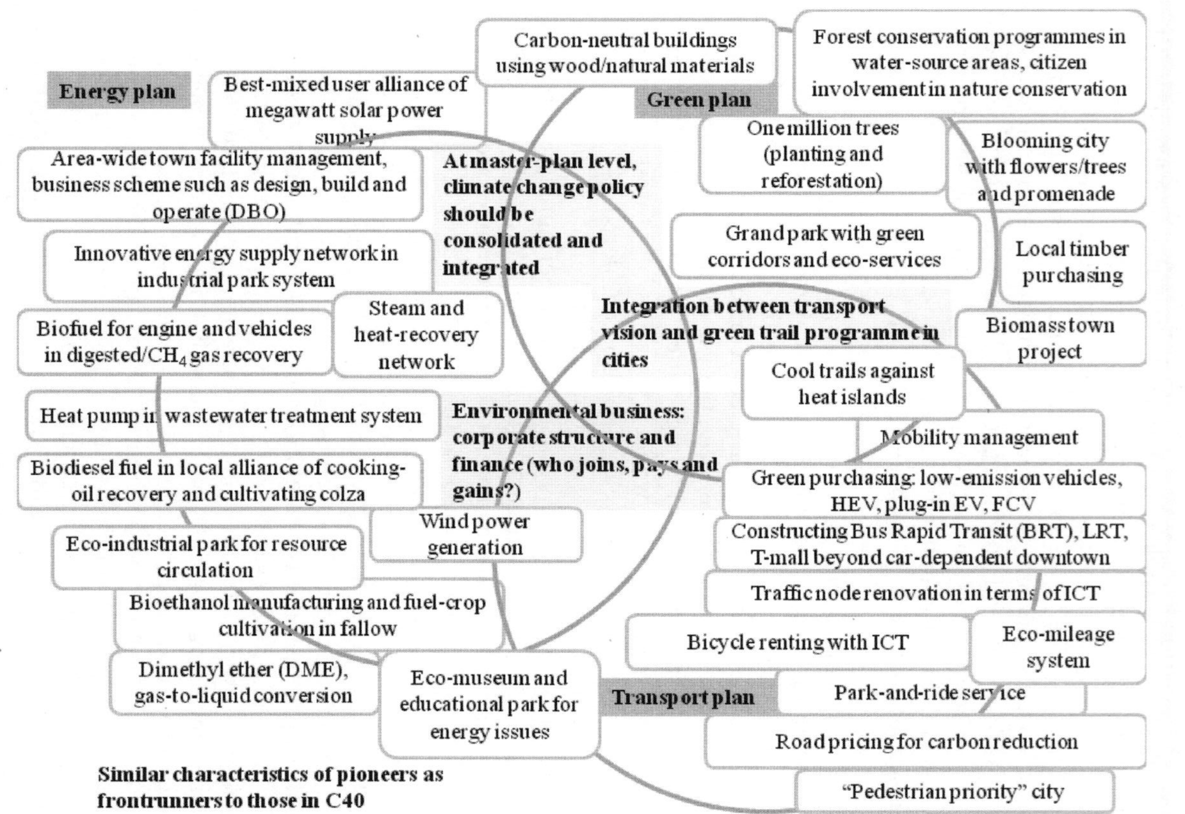

Figure 6.1.8 Policy domains in 17 cities: Energy, transport and greenery

6-1-7 Conclusions and recommendations

Cities, currently responsible for 75 per cent of global energy consumption and 75 per cent of global GHG emissions, are the key to stopping climate change. Since cities are centres of resource consumption and waste emissions, they are also very important for achieving resource-circulating systems. International initiatives in global carbon management like the C40 group have spread worldwide, showing the importance of climate policy at local level. Environment model cities like Sakai are challenged to reduce CO_2 emissions through energy innovation systems, while 17 large Japanese cities try to implement urban eco-reform, energy policy and greening of city-regions. The city networks in Asian countries promote local initiatives to design sustainable low-carbon cities with the aim of achieving a comfortable life with the lowest environmental impact. The experiences in the environment model city programmes in Japan may be considered pilots to promote eco-development in industrial cities.

Sharing experiences among initiative members and similar alliances through networking will speed up the results of these efforts globally. A performance-based model, which consists of setting a baseline, developing and implementing a local action plan and evaluating the results, is vital to estimate the progress. Alliances also enable the possibility of finacial cooperation, technology development and capacity building with developing countries where most megacities are located.

Amsterdam launched a smart city initiative as a collaboration between residents, business and government to promote a low-carbon city. The initiative includes projects like the smart meter, smart electric grid, smart building technologies and electric vehicles to reduce energy consumption dramatically in urban housing and commercial buildings and mobility services. This is the first EU initiative that strives to create an intelligent energy-offset city. The US Department of Energy is seeking alliances for a smart grid observatory in Arizona as a Green New Deal core project. Green innovation is moving beyond city boundaries in the global market, as can be seen by the example of the solar-cell market.

While German companies have been the main players in large-scale solar power plants (up to 50 MW), the US solar power business sector has reached an agreement with the Chinese government to build the world's largest solar power plant (2 GW) in Chinese Mongolia by 2019. The Japanese solar power sector, which has explored projects like the eco-industrial park in Sakai, is seeking to invest billions of dollars in a solar power project venture jointly with an Italian energy company in Italy and the African region. At the same time the Chinese solar cell sector has the advantage of low production costs.

The virtual environmental burdens from cradle to cradle, instead of cradle to grave, should be accounted and evaluated in terms of carbon footprint and total material requirement or a resource-based ecological rucksack. To address this challenge, the Bali Action Plan in 2008 proposed a new worldwide carbon management framework as a post-Kyoto mitigation mechanism. This introduced the measurement, reporting and verification (MRV) management tool as a verification standard. According to this tool, emission reduction activities in industrial city-regions should be verified and certified in terms of direct reductions and indirect embedded/virtual energy reduction associated with energy-using, energy-related and renewable energy supply products globally.

The Copenhagen Accord in 2009 agreed that the emission targets of developed countries (Annex I countries) and their financial help to developing countries will be measured, reported and verified according to specific guidelines. The accord also agreed that developing countries' actions will be subject to domestic MRV and the reports will be subject to international analysis. Finally, the accord establishes that developing countries receiving international support will be subject to international MRV according to the COP guidelines (Pew Center, 2009).

REFERENCES

Kantei (2008) "Integral Regional Revitalization"; available at www.kantei.go.jp/jp/singi/tiiki/ (in Japanese).
——— (2009) "Actions of Eco-Model Cities. Summary of the Initiatives of the 13 Selected Cities"; available at www.kantei.go.jp/jp/singi/tiiki/siryou/pdf/13EMCs.pdf (in Japanese).
Mayor of London (2007) "Action Today to Protect Tomorrow: The Mayor's Climate Change Action Plan", Greater London Authority, London.
Metz, B., O. R. Davidson, P. R. Bosch, R. Dave and L. A. Meyer (eds) (2007) *Climate Change 2007: Mitigation of Climate Change*, contribution of Working Group III to Fourth Assessment Report of Intergovernmental Panel on Climate Change. Cambridge: Cambridge University Press.
Morioka, T. (2009) "Attempt to Develop Urban Policies Towards Low-Societies in Large City Governments in Japan", *Journal of Urban Policy* 137, pp. 4–12 (in Japanese).
Pew Center (2009) *Fifteenth Session of the Conference of the Parties to the United Nations Framework Convention on Climate Change and Fifth Session of the Meeting of the Parties to the Kyoto Protocol*. Arlington, VA: Pew Center on Global Climate Change.
Sharp Corporation (2009) "Sharp Environmental and Social Report"; available at http://sharp-world.com/corporate/eco/csr_report/2009pdf/sharp_eall.pdf.
Strachan, N., T. Foxon and J. Fujino (2008) "Policy Implications from the Low-carbon Society (LCS) Modelling Project", *Climate Policy* 8, pp. 17–29.

Tokyo Metropolitan Government (2006) "Tokyo Renewable Energy Strategy: Create a Sustainable Future by Choosing Renewable Energy"; available at www.kankyo.metro.tokyo.jp/kouhou/english/pdf/TOKYO%20Climate%20Change%20Strategy%202007.6.1.pdf.
———— (2007) "Tokyo Climate Change Strategy: A Basic Policy for the 10-Year Project for a Carbon-minus Tokyo", TMG, Tokyo.

6-2

Building coexistence with nature in a low-carbon society: Initiatives for transition to a woody biomass society

Shuji Kurimoto

6-2-1 Low-carbon society and biomass

Switching to renewable energy

On 8 July 2008, the day before the end of the G8 Hokkaido Toyako summit, a declaration by leaders regarding global warming and other issues was adopted. This declaration indicated the long-term objective of reducing emissions of greenhouse gases (GHGs) by half by 2050. The following day a meeting of the leaders of 16 major GHG-emitting countries was held, including newly emerging countries such as China and India. The latter countries reacted, stating that the objective of at least a 50 per cent reduction in GHG emissions by 2050 was unacceptable, and a common numerical objective that included newly emerging countries could not be successfully established. However, in a joint statement announced after the meeting, the newly emerging countries recognized that they shared the long-term objective of reducing GHGs. In the leaders' declaration made at the G8 summit held in 2009 at L'Aquila in Italy, it was clearly stated that all nations of the world would reduce GHG emissions by 50 per cent, with the developed nations reducing them by 80 per cent, to keep the global temperature increase at 2°C or less since the time of the Industrial Revolution.

In the June prior to the Toyako summit, Japan's National Institute for Environmental Studies published its research findings on GHG reduction

Establishing a resource-circulating society in Asia: Challenges and opportunities, Morioka, Hanaki and Moriguchi (eds), United Nations University Press, 2011, ISBN 978-92-808-1182-7

scenarios for the target year of 2050 (Japan Low-Carbon Society Scenario Team, 2008). Japan's Ministry of Environment funded this research. The study concluded that 70 per cent reduction in GHGs was possible by 2050, and offered two scenarios. Scenario A was an urban model looking forward to the development of scientific techniques, while scenario B was a nature-oriented model urging reconsideration of mass consumer lifestyles. Both scenarios projected a reduction in primary energy consumption of around 60 per cent compared to 2000 levels. Both also suggested increasing the proportion of renewable energy sources such as biomass and solar power.

The amount of primary energy in Japan in 2050 is predicted to be 280 Mtoe (mega-tonnes of oil equivalent); detailed composition is about 15 Mtoe for coal, 45 Mtoe for oil, 80 Mtoe for gas, 45 Mtoe for biomass, 55 Mtoe for nuclear, 5 Mtoe for hydro and 35 Mtoe for solar and wind. Given Japan's current food self-sufficiency rate, which is about 40 per cent (Ministry of Agriculture, Forestry and Fisheries, 2009), even if agricultural residue is used, cultivation of bioenergy crops will be very difficult in the long term. We will be forced to rely on woody biomass in the short-term future at least. The New Energy and Industrial Technology Development Organization (2008) provides a guideline for municipalities making new energy plans. It can be expected that a sustainable production amount of woody biomass is 20.6 Mtoe, applying the following calculation:

$$A \times B \times C \times D \div E = 20.6 \text{ Mtoe}$$

A: amount of growth of forest per ha = 3.6 m^3/ha
B: weight of wood per m^3 = 500 kg/m^3
C: average calorific value per kg of tree = 19.2 MJ/kg
D: area of forests in Japan = 25 Mha
E: calorific value of oil per tonne = 4.19×10^4 MJ.

The figure of 20.6 Mtoe corresponds to about 45 per cent of the numerical value of the biomass in scenario B. The calculation is based upon the assumption that wood originating in forests will be first used as timber, paper, etc., and then reused as a source of energy later on.

If we assume, taking various efficiencies into consideration, that 70 per cent will be used, domestic woody biomass can supply about one-third of the total biomass energy. Moreover, the estimated forest growth is considerably lower than the reality. Thus woody biomass could significantly contribute to achieving a low-carbon society.

Forming consensus over use of woody biomass

Of the various kinds of renewable energy, solar power generation has reached a certain technical level and is at a stage where plans can be made to spread and promulgate it to citizens everywhere through economic policies, etc. Woody biomass is already used in the paper and timber industries as a resource and energy for power generation. Stoves and boilers using wooden pellets have started to become widespread. Woody biomass is a form of renewable energy that we can switch to immediately. The use of solar power and woody biomass (which utilize natural resources) is considered a realistic option for constructing a low-carbon society. However, since forests are home to multilayered ecosystem services, such as preservation of biodiversity and absorption of GHGs, the use of woody biomass requires careful planning to balance this use against other ecosystem services.

In the 1970s and 1980s many nature conservation activist groups worked to prevent development and preserve forests, so we can see the need to gain the understanding of the nature conservation movement in moving forward with the use of woody biomass. Japan's 67 per cent rate of forest coverage is second only to Finland, and this abundant forest exists even around large metropolitan areas. Up until the 1960s, residents of villages surrounding cities such as Kyoto came to the cities to sell charcoal, firewood and sometimes even agricultural products and flowers directly to city-dwellers. After the 1960s the use of oil pervaded the Japanese lifestyle, and this rural/urban interaction ceased and the forests grew more distant from the cities. Today, this distance only makes the use of biomass more difficult. Previously, produce and people flowed in a one-way movement from rural villages to urban areas, but we need to enrich both rural and urban lives by constructing a cyclical interaction between the two, enabling effective networks not only for biomass but also ecosystem services. To this end, we need to discuss initiatives for consensus formation for use of biomass, initially from the urban side. This chapter proposes an effective measure for forming consensus using a case study.

6-2-2 Stocks of woody biomass

Japan's forests

Until 1960 each rural village in Japan had its own forest, from which villagers would cut wood for use in their daily lives. Fuel forests were both broadleaf and pine. Broadleaf forest was normally logged at 20-year intervals. The cut stumps would then bud again and the forest would regenerate naturally in 20 years. If logging is continued regardless of regeneration periods, renewability drops and logging shifts over to pine forest. Since the renewability of pine is extremely poor, once all the forest is logged the land is bare, which increases the danger of landslides. It was a rule in rural villages to refrain from logging pine, but instead to utilize the pine needles and azalea shrubs. In the 90 short years from the demise of the Edo government (when Japan introduced Western civilization) through to 1960, Japan's population roughly tripled to 100 million people. Rural villagers started excessive logging, heedless of old rules, in order to maintain their lifestyles, and by 1960 the woodlands surrounding villages were becoming devastated. Village people used to live in observance of the first of Herman Daly's three rules (Daly, 1990) – that renewable resources such as fish, soil and groundwater must be used no faster than the rate at which they regenerate – but as populations have grown it has become impossible to observe this rule in some aspects.

In the 1960s the use of LP gas and oil stoves spread in rural areas, and logging of village fuel forests ceased. Some fuel forests were converted to timber forests. As Figure 6.2.1 shows, many timber forests were planted during the 1960s and 1970s. At present, coniferous trees in timber forests constitute around 40 per cent of all Japanese woodland. Some were planted as public works in devastated mountainous areas prone to landslides. The forests have recovered hand in hand with Japan's economic development. It could be argued that the switch from woody biomass to oil actually resurrected Japan's forests. Old-growth forest still remains on mountains far away from villages, but such forest is scarce in Japan, given the high population density. The majority of broadleaf forest is secondary forest that was originally fuel forest.

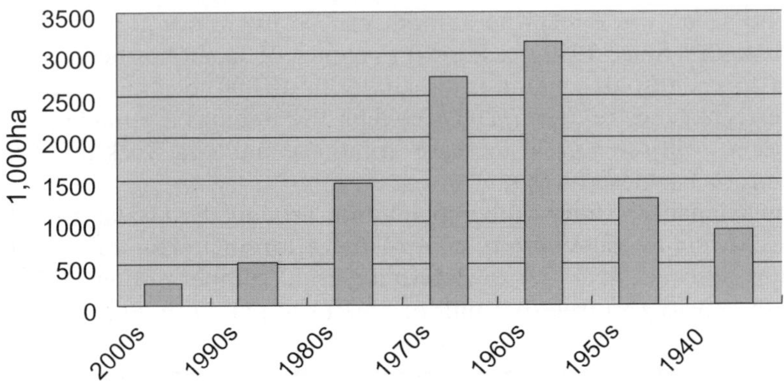

Figure 6.2.1 Forest planting by planning period

Table 6.2.1 Comparison of forest resources by year
Unit: thousand ha, million m^3

Year	Total		Planted forest		Natural forest and others	
	Area	Stock	Area	Stock	Area	Stock
2007	25,097	443,174	10,347	265,131	14,750	178,043
2002	25,121	404,012	10,361	233,804	14,760	170,208

Source: Forestry Agency of Japan (2009a, 2008).

Amount of growth of Japanese forests

According to the Forestry Agency of Japan (2008, 2009a), in the five years from 2002 to 2007 Japan's accumulated forest stock increased by 391.62 million m^3 (Table 6.2.1). Since Japan has around 25 million hectares of forest area (covering 67 per cent of the territory), this figure represents an increase of around 78 million m^3 per year. If we include the domestic lumber supply of around 20 million m^3 per year (Forestry Agency of Japan, 2009a), forest stock is growing by 98 million m^3 per year. As a very rough figure, if we assume an increase of 90 million m^3 per year, this represents 3.6 m^3 per hectare of forest growth, which is the official basic unit used when local authorities create new energy plans (New Energy and Industrial Technology Development Organization, 2008). Since the overall increase in forest of 90 million m^3 per year is roughly equal to the amount of timber Japan consumes, it can be argued that it has recovered to the point of self-sufficiency in timber supply.

In undertaking forest growth surveys, I have found that in some cases, depending on the forest, the amount can be five times greater that this 3.6 m^3 figure. Since 1999 the Forestry Agency of Japan has been conducting a forest resource monitoring survey in 16,000 locations nationwide (Forestry Agency of Japan, 2009b); when the findings are made public, I expect we will see a great increase in the accumulated stock and growth amount of Japanese forests.

For a Japanese cedar timber plantation around the Osaka area, I use the following average density control curve formula (Japan Forest Technology Association, 1999) to determine trunk timber volume (V) from growth density (N) trees per unit of area (1 ha) and top-level tree height (H):

$$V = (0.061977 \times H^{-1.351766} + 4725.2 \times H^{-2.823636} \div N)^{-1}$$

If timber volume can be calculated, then with measurement of tree age average yearly growth can be analysed. For example, if we apply this formula to 1,000 40-year old Japanese cedars with an upper height of 22 m, timber volume comes to 583 m^3. Over a 40-year period, this represents an average yearly growth of 14.5 m^3. In my experience, these figures are average for Japanese cedar timber in the Osaka area. Since these figures represent only trunk volume, the entire biomass including branches would be greater still. We have also prepared an average density control curve formula with different variables for broadleaf forest that was once fuel forest, such that timber volume and amount of growth can be analysed. The amount of trunk mass for broadleaf forest is less than for Japanese cedar, but as they are both temperate forest trees there should be no great difference in the average amount of biomass once they reach a certain age. From 1960 to the present Japan's forests have recovered, with resource reserves and growth amounts both increasing.

6-2-3 Resource-circulating society and coexistence with nature

Japan's stance on a resource-circulating society

An ecosystem implies the circulation of material among living organisms and groups of living organisms. A resource-circulating society is one in which humans, as part of an ecosystem, obtain material from groups of living organisms, and in doing so sustain the subsistence of other living organisms and groups of living organisms. This idea is not so peculiar; it was the traditional Japanese lifestyle, at least until 1960. Humanity has relied on forests for countless items: utensils, furniture, farming implements, agricultural fertilizer, livestock feed, household fuel, medical goods, houses, paper and more. Even when trees were logged, the forests would grow back. Most Japanese experienced how trees taken from the forest circulated throughout daily life, and must have been aware that a resource-circulating society involved not simply circulation of material but also circulation of life, including ecosystems. The Japanese term *mottainai* (or "wasteful") applies not only to material things, but also to how the very existence of those things means depriving the wilderness of life. We should take more note of this cautionary term, which describes respect for the wilderness while also taking life from it.

In building a resource-circulating society, we have to focus not only on the circulation of trees but also on the concept of circulation of life from the wild. When villagers logged forests, those forests recovered in around 20 years. Five years after logging, the area becomes grassy. Animals such as hares and insects gather there to graze, and wild flowers bloom. Golden eagles come, hunting the hares. Five years later, many different kinds of shrub grow thickly and roses bloom in spring. You can eat wild strawberries there, too. Ten years or so after logging, trees budding from cut stumps have grown large branches and all the pre-logging plants are present. Ten years later, the forest has recovered. Given 20-year logging intervals, the forest's diversity can be maintained (Figure 6.2.2).

A stone arrangement called Shumisen is placed in Japanese-style gardens. Shumisen is an imaginary mountain where the gods live in India; the idea was introduced from India to Japan with Buddhism through China and the Korean peninsula. The method of stone arrangement was described in *Sakuteiki*, a guide to garden making written 1,000 or more years ago. Thus the Japanese assumed that the spirit of gods stays in things such as trees, stone arrangements and statue/Jizou. In this way the Japanese have a particular affinity for trees and forests, despite less daily reliance on trees since the 1960s, so the commercial development of forests has not been easy. At the moment, forestry volunteer activities have been developed in every area, and links with forests are gaining strength.

Coexistence with nature

When forest vegetation shifts from deciduous to evergreen, the forest grows darker and other plants do not flourish. This is the current state of Japan's fuel forests. Scholars who recognize the value of natural old-growth forest and call for its protection have realized this fact, and started to advocate the protection of rural village forest. In order to protect these forests, I believe it is necessary to bring back the logging cycle, but biologists do not actually advocate logging. However, those living in rural villages know from experience that logging can bring new life to the forest and maintain its diversity: people have a long history of preserving forests by removing trees. Rural villagers are not consciously trying to live in harmony with nature; their living in harmony with nature is simply a consequence of daily life.

In lifestyles before 1960, human removal of trees from the forest led to an integration of materials and life, creating a resource-circulating society. Increases in population around 1960 started to cause devastation of forests due to over-logging, but in the following 50 years people worked hard to ensure that mountain forests recovered. A new biomass-using society must respect Daly's (1990) three rules and maintain an intelligent awareness of coexistence with nature. Previously, if we failed, we could always fall back on oil, but we must ready ourselves for the fact that if we fail in the future, there will be no oil. If we believe that human society has acquired the scientific techniques that civilization requires and is

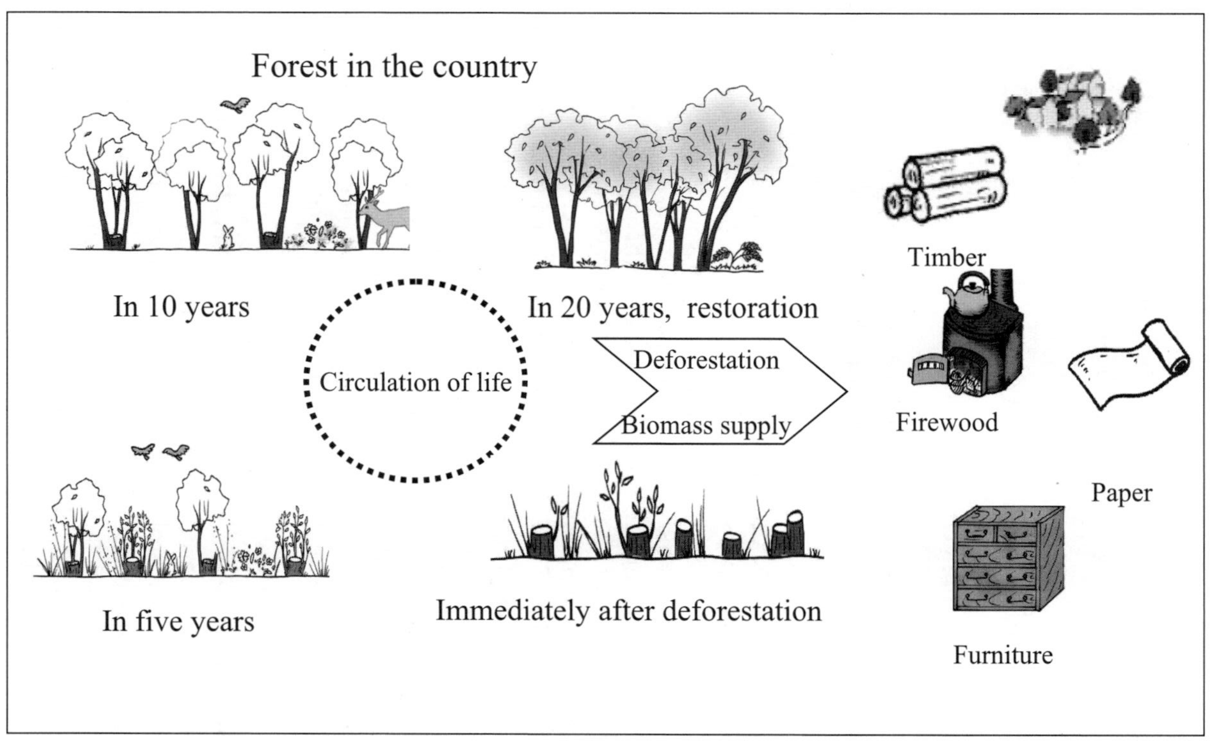

Figure 6.2.2 Forests and a resource-circulating society until 1960

capable of overcoming difficulties, then we should develop the technology to use woody biomass effectively, as well as techniques to assess and manage ecosystem services in combination with logging. Japanese society has a particularly long history of utilizing woody biomass, so if the support of citizens for logging forests can be gained, Japan should be able to develop these technologies and techniques.

6-2-4 Case study of eco-model cities

Purpose of analysing eco-model cities

Even if technologies are developed, humanity does not always display rational behaviour towards living organisms based on economic and scientific knowledge. The sight of majestic trees can make anyone hesitant about logging. For us to accept logging of forests, it is important for us to know our history of coexistence with nature, and then experience this. We must first accept in a physical or bodily sense the pain logging causes by depriving the wilderness of life, before we can experience the new life that grows there. This kind of forest activism allows us to reconsider carefully the very human impulse to offer thanks to the gods of the mountain. Just as in lifestyles of the past, a biomass-using society must first construct a resource-circulating society in coexistence with nature, which must be sustainable. Since our lifestyles no longer involve us removing trees from the forest, forest-based activities (such as forest volunteer activities) are one means to enable us to experience the new life that grows there. If we develop logging technology to dominate the forest with heavy machinery and log excessively, we will never successfully coexist with nature, and people will likely never agree to logging of the forests. If we truly hope to construct a biomass-using society, we need a smooth transition to such a society and must incorporate sustainable mechanisms for this into our society. I examine this idea using case studies of eco-model cities.

The Japanese government, in preparation for the Toyako summit, not only announced low-carbon society scenarios but also opened application for its eco-model city project. The government hopes that pioneering facilities from local authorities will lead the way to a low-carbon society, first within Japan and later across the world. Since local governments stood to obtain financial subsidies from the national government once selected as an eco-model city, 82 proposals were received. Local authorities based these applications on opinions of residents and regional environment factors in order to make proposals for the construction of low-carbon eco-model cities, working towards the year 2050. The total population across the 82 applicant cities was 33 million people: more than a quarter of Japan's entire population. Since the proposals were created independently by local authorities, it is believed that they accurately reflect the stance of Japan's citizens towards a low-carbon society. Accordingly, by analysing the 82 eco-model city proposals, I believe we can investigate the construction of forest activities that would assist the smooth transition to a biomass-using society and sustain a resource-circulating society in coexistence with nature. Essentially, biomass is not only biomass energy, but since the purpose of the eco-model city is to reduce greenhouse gases, my argument is developed along the lines of biomass energy.

Urban facilities connected to woody biomass energy

Forty-nine of the proposals touched on the idea of biomass energy as a long-term prospect leading up to 2050. Within the various categories of biomass energy, if we exclude agricultural residue and household waste processing, and limit the discussion to forest-derived woody biomass, there were 33 proposals. Of these, 25 projects outlined facilities for woody biomass energy to be tackled within the next five years. Of these 25, if we exclude simple project creation initiatives, such as for woody biomass projects, 18 proposals outlined concrete plans for initiatives. Of the 82 proposals, 21 per cent included concrete planning proposals related to woody biomass. These range from cities in excess of 1 million persons to towns of a few thousand. As can be seen in Table 6.2.2, these projects can be broken down into three main categories: proposals to promote the spread of woody biomass equipment, proposals for woody biomass supply facilities and proposals to integrate both the spread of equipment and supply facilities. Proposals to promote the spread of equipment were more common in larger cities, while proposals to integrate were more prevalent in smaller towns with larger forested areas (see www.kante.go.jp/jp/sing/tiiki/teiannaiyou.html).

As the table shows, proposals to promote the spread of equipment were the most common. The municipalities that made these proposals judged that pellet stoves and boilers would be effective in building a low-carbon society, and thus proposed initiatives for the spread of this equipment. Several municipalities already possess pellet production factories, and their promotion of the equipment-spreading initiative was also intended to support these factories. In the facility-supply and integration-oriented proposals, support for maintenance of forests and forestry was clearly viewed as a premise for building a low-carbon society. Projects to produce wood ethanol and coke emphasized experimental facilities for the validation phase; production had become the objective here, with projects for utilization falling by the wayside. In these projects, the raw

Table 6.2.2 Woody biomass projects in 18 eco-model cities

Type of proposals	No. of proposals	Overview
Promoting spread of equipment	10	Support for households to promote spread of pellet stoves, installing chip boilers or pellet boilers in public facilities, etc.
Supply facilities	4	Installation of pellet production and wood-based power generation facilities etc. Wood-based power generators can be either chip-burning or wood gas-burning types
Integration	4	3 projects involve installing pellet production facilities and pellet boilers simultaneously 1 project involves installing experimental facilities for wood-based bioethanol production combined with a wood boiler in a shared facility

material for this woody ethanol did not come from existing forest stocks, but rather from newly cultivated trees grown for raw wood.

Forest activism within the eco-model city proposals

Of the 18 proposals that listed concrete initiatives, eight planned for forest activism to assist a smooth transition to a woody-biomass-using society. All 82 proposals made provision for forest activism as one element within their environmental education activities; almost all municipalities with forests conduct such projects. Environmental education activities are important in building a woody-biomass-using society. However, since this chapter's hypothesis is that forest activism is necessary as a sustainable mechanism for a smooth transition to such a society, of these 18 proposals, I extracted and analysed the eight that specifically linked forest activism to the use of woody biomass. These eight proposals were all from small or mid-size municipalities; an overview can be found in Table 6.2.3.

Each of the eight proposals featured unique characteristics. One common element was some attempt to incorporate mechanisms to seek the support and understanding of people outside the forestry industry. Shimokawa, a mountain town with an extremely small population, plans to take urban children to the local forest, while the town of Isuhara has made plans in conjunction with urban corporations to call on company employees to act as forest volunteers. These plans are clearly attempts at interaction aimed at attracting residents of downstream urban areas to

Table 6.2.3 Forest activism of eight eco-model cities
(Population units: 10,000 persons)

Name of municipality	Pop.	Overview of forest activism
Shimokawa	0.3	The town commissions residents to cultivate trees as raw material for wood alcohol and coke The town has established the forest as a place where urban and rural children can interact with each other
Iitoyo	1	Raw materials for wood pellets are sourced from ex-fuel forest, and the town has created plans for sustainable use of forests in liaison with stakeholder institutions and groups
Toda	12	The city supports forest-thinning work by dispatching forest-thinning crews to affiliated cities Forest-thinning wood is chipped for use in woodchip-burning power generation
Suzu	2	The city has established a fund to cultivate its forestry industry, and is training forest volunteers The city holds enlightenment events aimed at promoting use of woody biomass
Yamanashi	4	The city conducts forest maintenance in conjunction with corporations Forest-thinning wood is used as raw material for paper The city plans to implement a sustainable support system for forest maintenance
Higashiomi	7	The city trains groups in coordinating effective use of forest resources, and provides opportunities for residents to participate in forest building
Isuhara	0.5	The town accepts volunteers through liaison with corporations The town cultivates new businesses utilizing forest resources in conjunction with corporations etc.

upstream forest areas. On the other hand, except for Shimokawa's plan for interaction among children, the proposed forest activism, such as forest-thinning work aimed at maintenance of timber forests, was all deeply connected with the forestry industry. These kinds of activities were proposed because timber forest was seen solely as raw material for woody biomass.

However, since timber forest is cultivated and managed for resources such as construction materials, the amount of residual material usable for

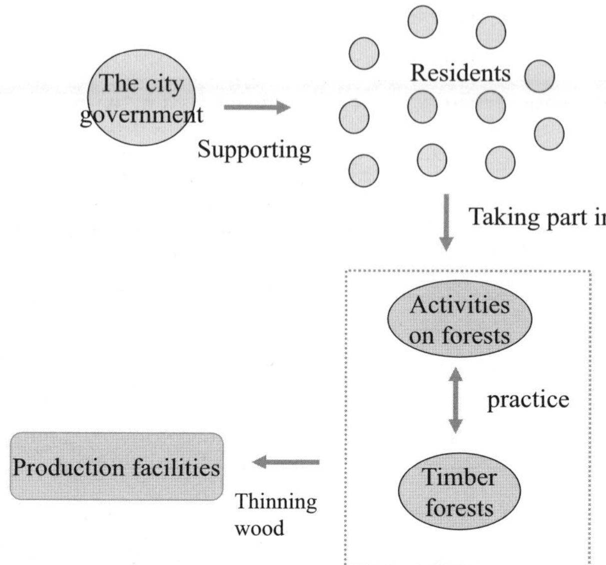

Figure 6.2.3 The forest activism framework within the eight proposals

biomass energy is limited. If our objective is truly to achieve a biomass-using society, the day must come when broadleaf forests (which are ex-fuel forests and known for their high diversity of living organisms) are logged again and used for their original purpose of providing fuel. This is why I hold that, in order to shift to a sustainable woody-biomass-using society, mechanisms are required to convince people of the benefits of a resource-circulating society based on coexistence with nature. Examining the forest activism framework within the eight proposals (Figure 6.2.3), I believe it is inadequate as a mechanism for shifting to and sustaining such a society. The town of Iitoyo clearly states that it seeks raw materials from fuel forest, which can be read as an understanding of the necessity of forest activism as a mechanism to promote the benefits of coexistence with nature. However, there are no concrete proposals indicated for this activity. Even so, at the current stage I believe these eight proposals are acceptable. If the objectives of forest activism are clear, it is easy for people to decide whether to participate or not, and to assess these activities for themselves.

Liaising between urban and rural areas

Aside from these proposals, there are also plans in huge metropolitan areas to support forest activism. For example, the city of Yokohama, with

3.64 million residents, has built a model for liaison between the urban area and rural villages, as well as promoting the use of wood pellets etc. in the city, and has plans to create mechanisms for supporting forest activism. However, since the details were not yet concrete, I did not analyse this proposal. I hope that in future Yokohama will construct mechanisms for direct support of forest activism. Kyoto, with a population of 1.47 million, also has plans to seek participation from corporations and volunteer groups in forest maintenance. These are the kinds of plans that Japan's major metropolises have for forest activism. As with the eight proposals examined earlier, they indicate that forests are sites for concrete projects; if these activities can commence, woody biomass as a renewable energy source would move from agricultural villages to cities, while people would move from cities to rural villages to undertake forest activism, enabling creation of a circulating system.

One unique attempt from among the eco-model city proposals was the case of Miyakojima Island, located on Japan's southernmost edge. The city of Miyakojima's plans involve reversing the disadvantage of its isolation by establishing wind and solar power generation. Miyakojima also plans to produce ethanol from the residue of sugarcane, its principal industry, and to construct a CO_2-free transport system using E100. It intends to review its agricultural industry to prevent pollution of the water required for daily life. With only 60,000 residents, the island sees 400,000 tourists yearly. The plan is first to achieve zero CO_2 emissions, in order to provide these tourists with the experience of island life amid abundant natural blessings. This high-quality natural island lifestyle will be positioned as the largest source of tourism, and the island plans to bring in urban residents and give them the opportunity to reconsider their lifestyles. The case of Miyakojima can offer some direction to rural mountain villages. Although these villages may not be blessed with much sunlight or wind power, they do possess forest-derived biomass resources. They may not have coral from the sea, but there is a diversity of life and living organisms in the forest.

6-2-5 Forest activism and deep ecology

The nature conservation movement in Japan

In order to construct a resource-circulating low-carbon society enabling coexistence with nature using biomass, we must accept the logging of forests. To this end, we must recognize the movements and activists that have protected the forests, and become convinced of the benefits of forest logging through our own forest activities. As repeatedly stated, forest activities are a mechanism for shifting to and sustaining a biomass-using society. In this section, I will reflect on the history of the nature conservation movement and activists who protected the forests.

Japan's most famous botanist, Makoto Numata, who served as head of the Nature Conservation Society of Japan (NACS-J), has described how the Japanese nature conservation movement started in 1949 with opposition to the development of power generation facilities at Ozegahara (Numata, 1994). In 1951 the NACS-J was organized from the Oze Conservation Alliance, and in 1954 the Ecological Society of Japan was formed. To protect the unspoiled nature of Ozegahara, Numata and others pressured the government to designate it a national park and specially protected zone, while also conducting nature conservation education. In this way, the Japanese nature conservation movement emerged as an opportunity for enlightening activities by academics, and came to target old-growth forests and unspoiled areas of high scientific value selected by scholars. More than 60 years prior to this, John Muir pressured the US government to designate Yosemite a national park, from which process Yosemite National Park was born. After this, Muir founded the Sierra Club and became involved in the nature conservation movement. As indicated on the Japanese Ministry of Environment website (www.env. go.jp) outlining the history of Japan's national parks, which also profiles Yellowstone in the United States, Japan's system of designating national parks closely follows the US system. I believe the biologists who took such interest in nature conservation were also influenced by the US nature conservation movement.

The influence of deep ecology

In the United States pollution became a serious issue in the 1960s, and the anti-pollution movement became far more active. Earth Day was established on 22 April 1970, and developed into a vast congregation of more than 20 million people across America taking a stance on pollution, nature conservation, poverty, population, nuclear weapons, etc. During this period, a movement emerged that was different from the conventional enlightened nature conservation movement. Stone's (1972) notion that trees should have equal legal standing with humans was introduced into Japan and immediately adopted by the nature conservation movement. Naess's (1973) concept of deep ecology, which stated that humanity and other living creatures are equal since they all simply constitute organisms inhabiting the Earth, also exerted a major influence on the US environmental movement. Devall and Sessions (1985) called for self-awareness to realize lifestyles valuing the idea that life is fundamentally equal, and sharply criticized modern societies in which high-tech civilization gives rise to centralized power, by which humanity is diminished. Nash (1989) suggested that the traditional US nature conservation movement was human-centric, in that it protected only the nature judged by humanity as having value. Although the deep ecology approach was criticized from social ecology perspectives as unable to stop the devastation of nature in Japan, which was carved up by society through the efforts of individuals, it was interpreted as a way of living that valued nature, and was accepted favourably. As Nash (1982) argues, wild areas in the Christian world were seen as inhabited by the Devil, and thus required development, but in Japanese Shinto wild areas were the dwelling places of the gods and thus deserved reverence, meaning that the deep ecology approach shares a strong affinity with the Japanese view of nature.

From movements to activism

In the same way as in the United States, activism developed after the 1960s from the anti-pollution movement. The first president of the Ecological Society of Japan, Iijima (1996), suggests that 1974 was the turning point in Japan for the pollution movement to incorporate the natural environment and become the environmental movement. Iijima suggests that the Tenjinzaki Trust was critical in this process, and identifies it as the first nature conservation movement to be based on the views of local residents rather than the enlightened activism of academics. Iijima also argues that for local residents fighting against a worsening living environment, pollution and destruction of nature are the same. When it was no longer necessary to gather fuel from forests, there was a strong tendency for forests to become subject to development. In the 1980s there were plans for development of golf courses and building sites across the nation, and in 1987 the government established the law known widely as the Resort Act to support these plans. However, residents living near the sites and urban residents affiliated with them opposed these developments. As Iijima indicates, although the pollution movement achieved certain outcomes and some visible improvements were made to the environment, nature still faced an ongoing crisis of devastation. The pollution activists also joined the nature conservation movement, which then became widespread across Japan. Starting from the 1970s, new nature conservation concepts such as the US and European deep ecology were introduced into the previous enlightenment-based approach, and diverse movements thus developed. As a result of this activism, the forests were protected.

After the Earth Summit of 1992, Japan's government made a major turnabout on nature conservation. Public works were obliged by law to take the natural environment into consideration. Since the nature conservation movement had a better grasp than the administration of the environmental information required to implement this obligation, the government needed to work in liaison with nature conservation groups. The Law on Promotion of Specified Non-Profit Activities enacted in 1998 was an opportunity for conservation groups in various regions to shift from being movements opposing environmental destruction to activism aimed at improving the regional environment. Some groups then shifted their efforts to the forests and commenced forest activism. Today, in order to preserve the natural environment of these regions, local authorities are offering active support for forest activism.

People are starting to build true-to-life inhabitable worlds in the forests, based on their bodily sensations or bodily knowledge and experience. I believe that living worlds based on vital systems and biomass-using societies represent the same kind of society. Despite this, looking at the history of the nature conservation movement, it might be thought that those playing a major role in forest activism are likely to express strong misgivings over logging, thus hindering the shift to using biomass. However, I do not believe so; I hold that forest activism can lead to a smooth transition to a biomass-using society.

6-2-6 Transition to a woody biomass society

Forest activism and the public

In order to realize a low-carbon society, international society and government have started to try to guide the lives of citizens following certain scenarios. We have had bitter experience of being conveniently mobilized in the name of the public good. Habermas (1990) discussed this, and explained how we must shift from an old conception of the public to a new citizen-oriented conception that emphasizes the agency of citizens. He argued that this transition would require volunteer activism independent of administrative or economic systems. I discussed earlier how the conception of forest activism in eco-model cities was inadequate but acceptable. This is because the purpose of this activism is clearly to cultivate and manage timber forest, so people can judge for themselves whether to participate or not. Actually, forest activism surrounding urban areas is not only intended to produce timber, but has diverse other objectives: sustaining biodiversity, nature observation, recreation, experiencing outdoor life and so on. Even if multilayered and diverse forest activism is provided, it may confuse those who are not used to this, making it difficult for them to decide whether to participate.

The multilayered objectives and interests in forest activism should spur exchange and interaction among activism groups sharing the same objectives and interests, which should lead to the formation of a community of regional forest activism groups. This community is necessary in order to establish a citizen-oriented conception of the public within our biomass-using society. If this community does not exist, forest activism groups will have to criticize or oppose overly convenient mobilization on their own. If there is such a community of forest activism groups, criticism or opposition should be able to be independently resolved through exchange and interaction among groups and group members. It follows that for a citizen-oriented conception of the public to be achieved within regional society, so that independently a biomass-using society is possible, local authorities must create policy initiatives to establish places and opportunities for the formation of a community of forest activism groups. An example of such an initiative follows.

Advanced case study for woody-biomass-using society

The Keihanshin area, centred on the cities of Kobe, Osaka and Kyoto, has a population around 18.64 million, which represents around 15 per cent of Japan's total. The city of Takatsuki is located within this area of concentrated population: it has 350,000 residents and forested land occupies close to 50 per cent of the city's area. There are often high expectations of ecosystem services for forests located within huge metropolitan areas, and many people take part in forest activism; some come by train from the city of Osaka to participate. Even in areas where urbanization is rapidly progressing, forests have been protected and maintained by the efforts of activists. Within the city's forests are groups whose objective is the protection of fuel forests, groups whose objective is simply encountering nature, those protecting precious flora and fauna or conducting environmental education, groups offering charcoal-burning demonstrations, those supporting the forestry industry and more.

Osaka Forest Owners' Association switched 40 per cent of fuel forest to timber forest in the 1960s and 1970s; at the time, residents' groups criticized it for making this switch. Today, the organization coordinates with the forest activism of local residents. It led the nation in establishing a residents' amateur forester system, which gives opportunities for local people to work alongside professional foresters after a certain period of education and training. The amateur foresters organize themselves independently, and support logging etc. to sustain biodiversity in response to requests from other forest activists. This kind of interaction between groups has formed a community of forest activism groups for Takatsuki. The groups are not only active in the forests; they also accumulate knowledge by inviting biology and forestry specialists to study sessions. By exchanging this knowledge among groups and through newsletters, it is conveyed not only within the community of groups but also to a wider audience of local residents. In the eco-model city case studies presented earlier, the local authorities of small to mid-sized towns in mountainous areas are planning biomass production facilities and building forest activism to support these plans. If we consider that in Takatsuki, with its concentrated population, people with diverse experience in nature conservation movements are practising forest activism, then we can also believe that if a system for acceptance was established in small and mid-sized towns, people from massive metropolitan areas such as Yokohama would participate in forest activism.

Towards formation of a community of forest activism groups

In the theory of symbolic interactionism proposed by Turner (1981) and others, which draws upon Blumer (1969), sharing an image of the future and friendly emotions are described as conditions for group behaviour working towards some objective. The leaders of forest activism, in addition to instrumental activities such as logging trees for the cultivation and management of timber forests or for biodiversity purposes, also emphasize symbolic activities such as fostering camaraderie and outlining visions of the future. If these symbolic activities are insufficient, there may be clashes of opinion at activist sites regarding the logging of trees. By establishing symposia and introductions to unified action by forest activism groups, and creating mutual interaction among groups through symbolic activities, forestry unions and local authorities are working to shift these groups away from opposition to mutually interactive efforts. As a result, these forest activism groups have come to form a community, and the oppositional scheme of "forestry industry versus nature conservation" has been converted to a scheme of mutual interaction. This conversion facilitates the policy initiatives of local authorities.

Nature conservation initiatives and forestry industry initiatives are successfully operating simultaneously without any conflict in the city of Takatsuki, working to promote forest conservation while tackling the use of woody biomass. Obtaining the approval of local residents and the municipal assembly assisted the establishment in 2000 of Japan's first forestry-association-managed pellet production factory. The forestry association has made the technology and management information relating to operating the pellet factory available to the public. This factory in Takatsuki can provide useful reference regarding the scale and management of pellet factories in the future creation of eco-model city proposals. There is no particular opposition to logging fuel forests for raw pellet material from forest activism groups. When the groups were informed that logging trees and cutting grass in the forest had led to the blooming of many beautiful wild lilies, group members went to see the lilies. Through these sorts of experiences, awareness of the necessity of regular logging to sustain the biodiversity of fuel forests is spreading among activism groups. The city of Takatsuki has established a public pellet boiler facility, and is providing support on the factory operations side. Residents have welcomed these efforts. It is clear that Takatsuki has used public funds to lead the nation in making the transition to a biomass-using society. This example demonstrates the need for a community composed of local authorities, forestry unions and forest activism groups on an equal basis in order to drive the transition to a biomass-using society. This community must be open to, and convey information about its activities to, local residents, as these are basic principles of the citizen-oriented conception of the public.

I have no objection to Lester Brown's (2008) Plan B, but his use of metaphors, such as constructing "wind power generators as rapidly as in time of war" demonstrates that he has more faith in powerful political leadership than the independence of residents. In a society in which people hold diverse values, where those concerned over the warming global environment come to rely solely on our political leadership, reconsideration of our lifestyles, which must accompany the shift to a low-carbon society, becomes very difficult. In Europe, the United States and Japan people have built up experience in civil society movements since the 1970s, and have learned techniques for resisting imposed conceptions of the public.

Asian countries, including Japan, have actively adopted a rational way of thinking which originates in Western societies in the course of their economic development. I propose that, with the help of such a way of thinking, low-carbon societies are promoted in cities that utilize woody biomasses by further enhancing the technologies related to this utilization. Nonetheless, people in rural communities have lived in close harmony with nature and acquired indigenous cultures and local customs. Forests, as the supplier of biomass, are usually situated in peri-urban or rural areas, serving the circulation of natural lives. We know that even the rational ways of thinking about nature are diverse, and local communities have deeply rooted views on nature. It is therefore essential to introduce mechanisms (like a community of forest activism groups) that allow the adjustment of multiple ways of thinking (Figure 6.2.4). In pluralistic and highly diverse societies with both Western and oriental ways of thinking, and urban and rural perspectives mixed together, it is indispensable to have a mechanism that effectively adjusts these mindsets and views, particularly when it comes to transforming to low-carbon societies, since the

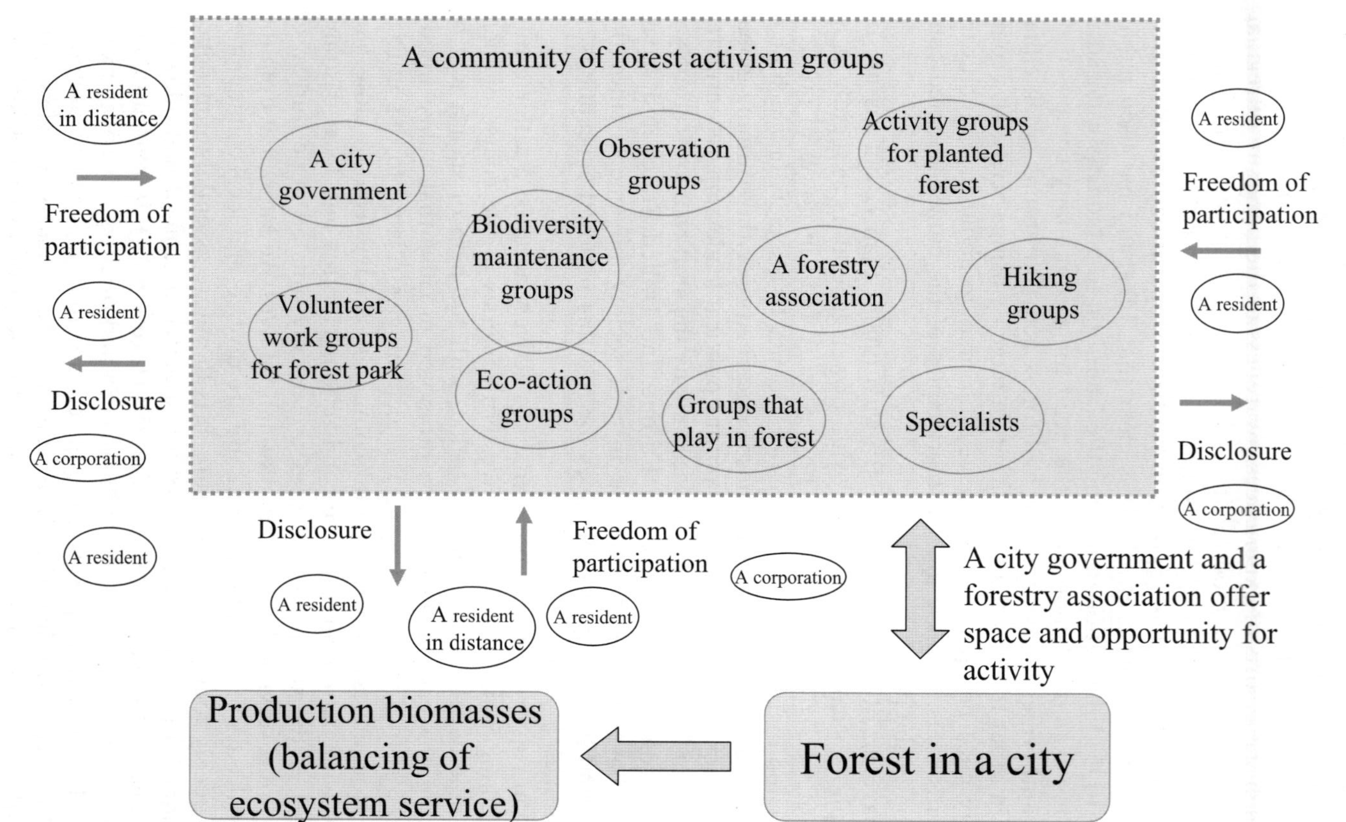

Figure 6.2.4 A mechanism such as a community of forest activism groups

transformation requires changes in people's lifestyles. A woody-biomass-using society would enable us to experience living in coexistence with nature within the constrained framework of life in the wild. By doing so, I believe we will gain the opportunity to reconsider our wasteful lifestyles. I would thus promote the transition to a society that uses the limited natural resource of forest-derived biomass.

REFERENCES

Blumer, Herbert (1969) *Symbolic Interactionism Perspective and Method*. Englewood Cliffs, NJ: Prentice-Hall.

Brown, Lester (2008) *Plan B 3.0*. Washington, DC: Earth Policy Institute.

Daly, Herman (1990) "Towards Some Operational Principles of Sustainable Development", *Ecological Economics* 2, pp. 1–6.

Devall, Bill and George Sessions (1985) *Deep Ecology*. Layton, UT: Gibbs M. Smith.

Forestry Agency of Japan (2008) "Annual Report on Trends in Forest and Forestry Fiscal Year 2007 (Summary)", Forestry Agency of Japan, Tokyo.

——— (2009a) "Annual Report on Trends in Forest and Forestry Fiscal Year 2008 (Summary)"; available at www.rinya.maff.go.jp/j/kikaku/hakusyo/index.html.

——— (2009b) "The Current State of Forest and Forest Management in Japan"; available at www.rinya.maff.go.jp/j/kaigai/pdf/countryreport-japan-1.pdf (in Japanese).

Harbermas, Jürgen (1990) *Strukturwandel der Offentlichkeit*. Frankfurt: Fuhrrkamp Verlag.

Iijima, Nobuko (1996) "Experiences on Environmental Movements in Japan", *Contemporary Sociology* 25, pp. 143–160 (in Japanese).

Japan Forest Technology Association (1999) "Density Control Chart of Planted Forest", JAFTA, Tokyo (in Japanese).

Japan Low-Carbon Society Scenario Team (2008) "Japan Scenarios and Actions towards Low-Carbon Societies (LCSs)", National Institute for Environmental Studies; available at http://2050.nies.go.jp/index_j.html.

Ministry of Agriculture, Forestry and Fisheries (2009) "Annual Report on Food, Agriculture and Rural Areas in Japan, FY2008 Summary"; available at www.maff.go.jp/e/annual_report/2008/index.html.

Naess, Arne (1973) "The Shallow and the Deep Long-range Ecology Movement: A Summary", *Inquiry* 1(16), pp. 95–100.

Nash, Roderick (1982) *Wildness and the American Mind*. New Haven, CT: Yale University Press.

——— (1989) *The Rights of Nature*. Madison, WI: University of Wisconsin Press.

New Energy and Industrial Technology Development Organization (2008) *New Energy Guidebook 2008*; available at www.nedo.go.jp/kankobutsu/pamphlets/dounyuu/shinenegaido2008/ (in Japanese).

Numata, Makoto (1994) *The Idea of Nature Conservation.* Tokyo: Iwanami Shoten (in Japanese).

Stone, Christopher D. (1972) "Should Trees Have Standing? Toward Legal Rights for Natural Objects", *Southern California Law Review* 45, pp. 450–501.

Turner, Ralph H. (1981) "Collective Behavior and Resource Mobilization as Approaches to Social Movement Issues and Continuities", *Research in Social Movements, Conflict and Change* 4, pp. 1–24.

6-3

Urban stock management for sustainable urban renewal and development: A case study of Shanghai in China

Yugo Yamamoto and Tohru Morioka

6-3-1 Introduction

Large material stocks and flows have promoted rapid economic growth in Shanghai, China. In this chapter, using Shanghai as a case study, we evaluate the impact of energy and material metabolic activities induced by urban activities on resource depletion, land use and climate change. Moreover, we quantify the contribution of policy alternatives for urban renewal to urban sustainability from the viewpoint that, in addition to developing environmental technologies and equipment, changes to the core urban form itself are important when trying to bring about reductions in resource consumption and low carbonization in urban areas.

6-3-2 Environmental impacts of urban activities on natural resource consumption, land use and climate change

Urban metabolism driven by energy and materials consumption

In urban areas, which support large populations and much activity, material stock increases through the construction of infrastructure and housing using mineral resources extracted underground and biomass resources from the land surface. Stock waste passes from urban areas into the environment over time. This process of input, output and storage is the largest material metabolism in a region. Furthermore, the facilities and

Establishing a resource-circulating society in Asia: Challenges and opportunities, Morioka, Hanaki and Moriguchi (eds), United Nations University Press, 2011, ISBN 978-92-808-1182-7

products required to supply and utilize electricity, gas and water form the basis of urban life and economic activities. However, an increase in CO_2 emissions, resource consumption and waste generation is associated with this production, use and discarding of these resources. Thus urban metabolisms that are driven by energy and material consumption threaten global sustainability.

In recent years several megacities with populations of at least 10 million have evolved rapidly in the East Asian region, which includes China and India. Currently more than 200 cities in Asia have populations of 1 million or more. As reported previously (Shen et al., 2005), the expansion of urban activities due to increasing populations and the advancement of urbanization results in an increase in the energy and material metabolism of cities. Prediction, evaluation and management of urban metabolisms are thus essential points to consider when addressing improvements in urban sustainability. Particularly in China, which has 10 metropolitan areas represented by Shanghai and Beijing, the input of fossil fuels, metal, industrial and construction materials and biomass has increased year on year (Xu and Zhang, 2007). The transformation of urban structures and the achievement of sustainable urban development have been recognized as important policy concerns in China.

Urban metabolism is defined as the sum total of the technical and socio-economic processes that occur in cities, resulting in growth, production of energy and elimination of waste (Kennedy, Cuddihy and Engel-Yan, 2007). This concept was first developed by Wolman (1965). Since then, numerous efforts targeting various metropolises in the world have been made to quantify urban metabolism. In the field of civil engineering, Sueishi and Morioka (1976) developed a theory for regional planning for resource circulation based on the analysis of material flow and stock in an urban metabolism.

The key urban metabolism flows addressed in previous studies can broadly be divided into natural resources, energy, waste, nutrients and water (Decker et al., 2000). Because the order of the flows related to water and the atmosphere is significantly larger than other flows, comparisons of flows are not straightforward. Consequently, these types of flow are not always considered in general material flow analysis (MFA). However, urban metabolism flows cannot be ignored when evaluating urban sustainability.

Indicators of environmental sustainability

If we assume that urban activities are based on the levels of interaction and interdependence between industrial systems and ecosystems, the en-

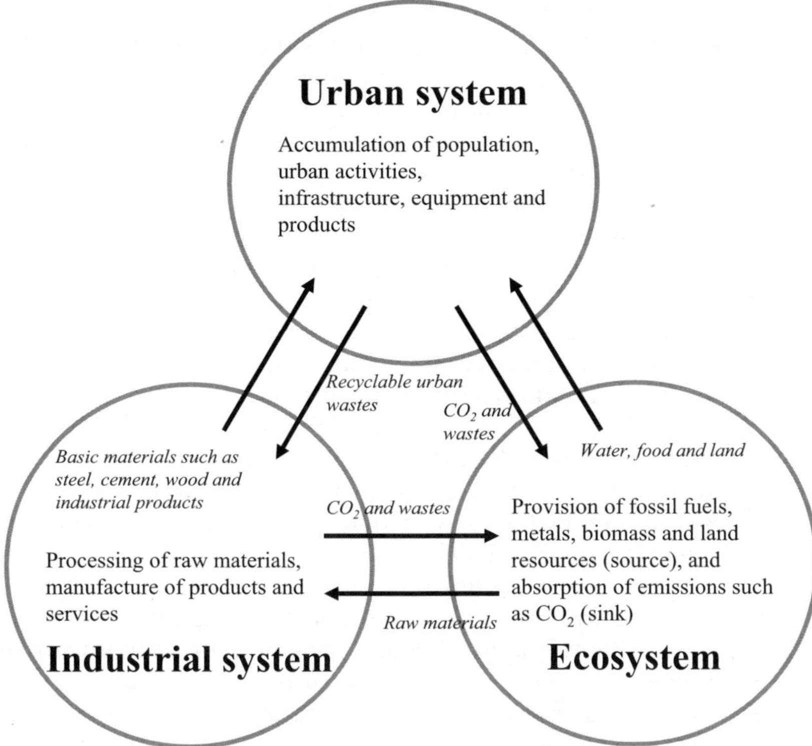

Figure 6.3.1 Conceptual scheme of industrial metabolism

ergy and material metabolism of a social system can be illustrated schematically as shown in Figure 6.3.1.

In urban systems, items necessary for activity and living, such as food and water, are taken from ecosystems and the CO_2 and waste resulting from socio-economic activities are then returned to the natural environment. Focusing on this relationship between urban environments and ecosystems, it can be seen that ecosystems are damaged by the direct land-use changes resulting from the physical expansion of urban areas, waste disposal sites and unplanned development of suburbs that are associated with increases in population and industrial growth. As a result, ecosystem services are disrupted in terms of mitigation of the urban heat-island effect, absorption of CO_2, food production and habitat provision for living creatures.

From the viewpoint of the anthropogenic impact on the ecosystem, increased attention is being focused on the analysis and evaluation of direct and indirect environmental burden using the ecological footprint (EF) indicator. The EF can be represented as the aggregate area of land and water in various ecological categories that is claimed by participants in that economy to produce all the resources they consume and absorb all the wastes they generate on a continuous basis, using prevailing technology (Wackernagel and Rees, 1997). The sustainability of human activities can then be estimated with reference to environmental carrying capacity. If the human race attempts to replace fossil resources with biological resources in efforts towards creating a low-carbon society, then the EF might exceed the biological capacity of the Earth.

The industrial system extracts raw materials such as fossil fuels, metals and wood from the natural environment and converts or processes these into usable forms and industrial products. The utilization of biomass resources therefore induces the consumption and degradation of terrestrial resources indirectly. Similarly, the so-called "hidden flow", which has been treated as a non-economic good in conventional MFA, is associated with the process of extracting underground resources such as fossil fuels and metal minerals. Taking mining as an example, "hidden flow" would refer to the soil and stone removed during the mining process, and the impurities removed when the ore is processed (Moriguchi and Hashimoto, 2006). Measuring this kind of indirect material flow and quantifying the total amount of resources required for urban and industrial activity have been referred to as the ecological rucksack or total material requirement (TMR) (Nakajima et al., 2006; Bringezu et al., 2004), and are useful in evaluations of urban sustainability.

For improving eco-efficiency and resource productivity in industrial systems, establishing an eco-industrial complex is an effective method, as reported in our previous research (Morioka, Yoshida and Yamamoto, 2003; Morioka et al., 2005).

6-3-3 Future trends in urban metabolism and environmental sustainability of Shanghai

The conservation and intensive utilization of land resources, energy, water and raw materials are one of the priority subjects in Shanghai's Eleventh Five-Year Plan and Three-Year Action Plan for Environmental Protection to promote the sustainable development of Shanghai's economy and society based on a circular-economy concept. In order to enhance urban sustainability, transforming social systems, including policies, human lifestyle and fundamental urban form, is as important as installing environmental technologies and equipment into urban systems.

In this section we introduce an urban metabolism case study targeting the city of Shanghai, focusing on our previous research that evaluated the effect of change in urban form (Imanishi et al., 2010).

Energy and material metabolism of Shanghai, 1995–2030

We previously developed a model to estimate the quantity of construction activity, electrical consumption, traffic/transportation and food and water consumption, based on future changes in an urban socio-economic structure. We then applied the model to the city of Shanghai, which is currently experiencing significant economic growth. Previous studies on urban metabolism tended to measure environmental burdens by modelling, individually and separately, activities such as construction and traffic/transportation. In contrast, the model we developed has a distinctive structural feature in that the urban metabolism and its sustainability are estimated together with socio-economic variables, such as population and GDP, as drivers. This made it possible to conduct future projections of urban metabolism and sustainability based on future scenarios for urban development and transition.

Figures 6.3.2 and 6.3.3 show the results of projected materials accumulation and quantities of demolition waste in Shanghai. Reflecting the construction bubble in the early 2000s, the material input in construction activities peaked in 2004. The quantities of natural resources stock in

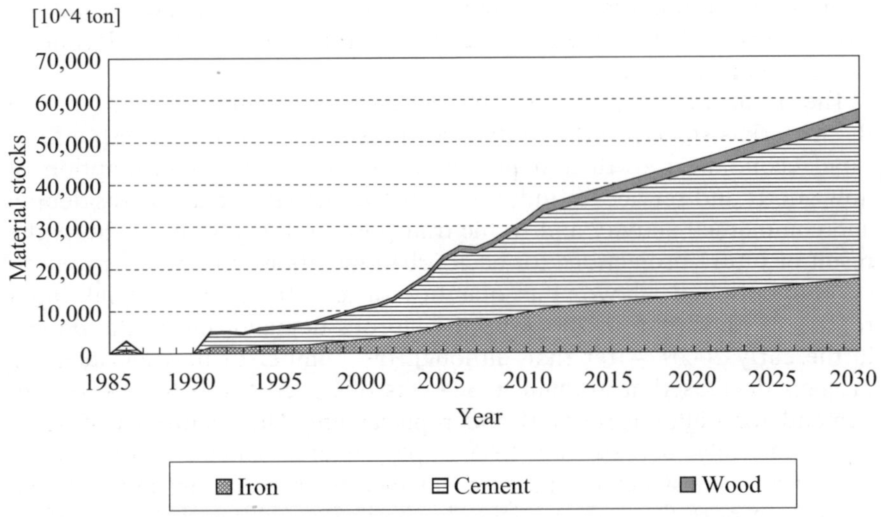

Figure 6.3.2 Material stocks in urban buildings of Shanghai

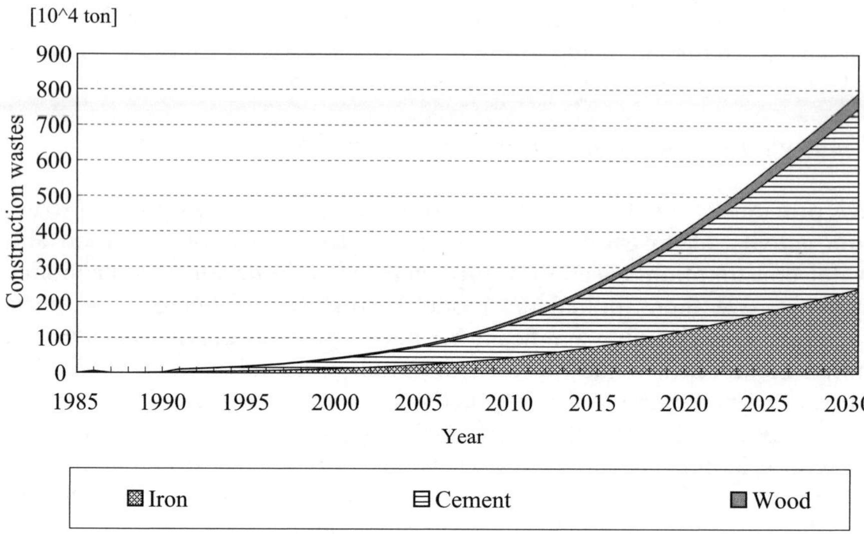

Figure 6.3.3 Construction wastes from urban buildings in Shanghai

constructed buildings and demolition waste in 2020 were estimated to increase by 2.5 and 5.6 times that of 2004. Consequently, enhancing the resource collection and circulating system within China is a necessary prerequisite for improving the utilization efficiency of stocked resources that have a "temporal lag" between their use and disposal. In the medium to long term, it is also necessary to design and select policy alternatives for urban development and renewal that can contribute to decreased resource consumption.

The urban metabolism has a characteristic structural feature wherein the materials stock in urban infrastructures is constructed in response to rapid economic growth and population increases. The consumption of flow goods and services is induced by urban activities such as residential and commercial activity and traffic/transportation. Figure 6.3.4 shows the result of future projections for each urban metabolism flow.

As mentioned above, the quantity of construction material input reached a maximum in 2004 due to vigorous demand during the bubble in the early 2000s. After that, although the number of new construction projects decreased, a gradual increase is observed towards 2030 due to demand for building renewal and replacement. The quantities of other flows generally increase due to a ripple effect in stock as urban infrastructure is constructed. Increases in electric power consumption and traffic/transportation are particularly significant, with increases of 104.3 and 126.3 per cent observed compared to 2004.

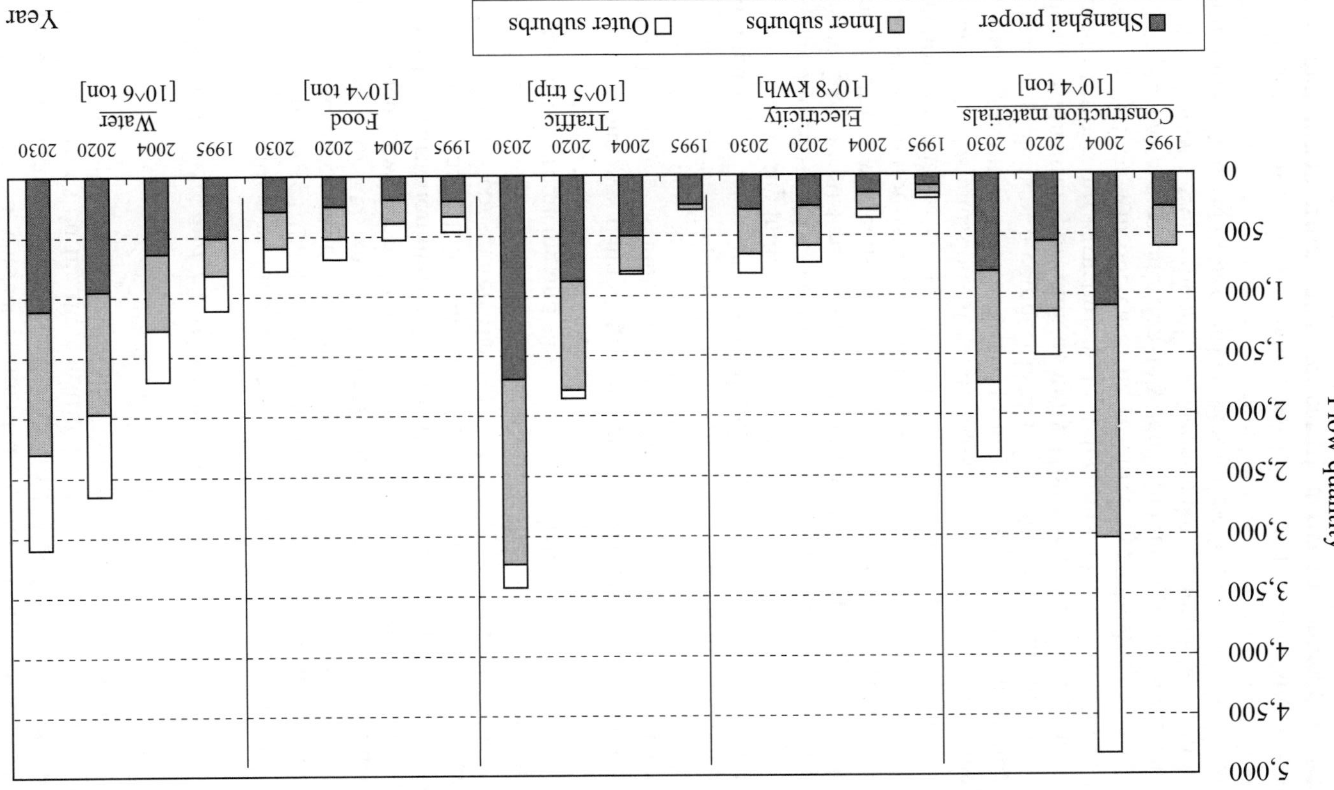

Figure 6.3.4 Flow quantities in urban metabolism in Shanghai and its environs

Examining the spatial characteristics of the different flows in Shanghai reveals that the accumulation of materials stock was dominant in the inner and outer suburbs during the construction bubble. However, at other times this urban activity is concentrated in central Shanghai proper and the inner suburbs.

CO_2 emissions, TMR and EF of Shanghai, 1995–2030

We evaluated the direct and indirect impact of the urban metabolism discussed above on the carrying capacity of the terrestrial environment and atmospheric resources using the three sustainability indicators of TMR, EF and quantity of CO_2 emissions. TMR was estimated using the quantity of "hidden flow" as an indirect burden underlying the direct consumption of construction materials (iron, cement and wood), oil and coal in power generation, fuels in transport activities and other related factors. To estimate EF we considered the land area occupied by urban infrastructure and buildings as a direct burden within the region, and the land area required for producing and supplying construction materials, energy resources, food and water as an indirect burden. To estimate the quantity of CO_2 emissions, we defined the emissions resulting from electrical power consumption in buildings and fuel consumption in transport activities as a direct burden, and the emissions derived from the production process of construction materials (e.g. iron and cement) as an indirect burden. Figure 6.3.5 shows the annual changes in the sustainability indicators, as well as in the indirect burdens.

Compared to 2004, TMR is expected to increase with economic growth, peaking in 2020 at 80.4 per cent. In addition, due to traffic/transportation and electric power consumption, the indirect burden associated with fossil-fuel consumption is dominant relative to the direct burden due to construction materials. Because these factors also lead to an increase in the quantity of CO_2 emissions, it is necessary to promote energy savings in the power generation and industrial production processes as a countermeasure, and implement a compact urban structure that contributes to a reduction in traffic/transportation quantity. However, accelerating the replacement of urban infrastructure and production technologies with high energy-saving effects will decrease the resource use efficiency of social stocks and generate disproportionately large amounts of resource consumption and waste. Consequently, decision-makers should be cautious regarding the implementation of urban renewal policies.

Regarding the EF, the vigorous demand for construction associated with the bubble resulted in the highest burden in 2004. Especially during periods of high urban growth, the indirect EF derived from construction materials becomes a significant part of the total EF. Thus the need to

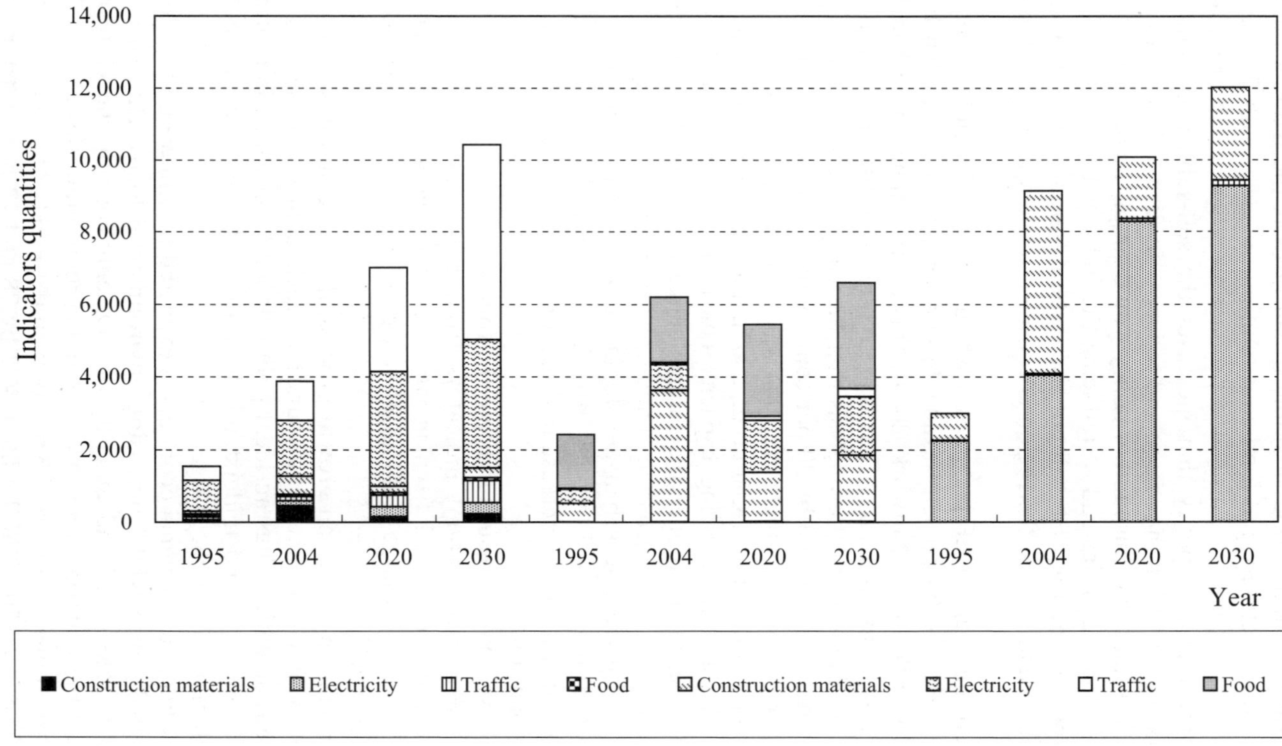

Figure 6.3.5 Environmental sustainability of Shanghai

limit overbuilding and/or excessive demolition is a significant policy challenge. However, in a period of stable urban growth, the indirect burden derived from electricity and food consumption increases with the expansion of urban activity. Because food production relies on land resources outside the region, a policy that increases the self-sufficiency ratio for food production within the region and reduces "food miles" is worth considering. It seems that this kind of policy would simply increase the direct EF within the region instead of reducing the indirect EF outside the region. However, the total EF will not rise if the difference in land productivity within and outside the region is considered when implementing the policy.

In 2006 the average EF per person worldwide was 2.6 global hectares while the average biocapacity available per person was 1.8 global hectares (Global Footprint Network, 2009). This means humanity is demanding 1.44 Earths. In China, 2.17 Earths are required to sustain the economy in 2006. We found from this analysis that the EF per person of Shanghai in 2030 would be reduced by 30 per cent compared with 2004. However, the EF per person of Shanghai in 2004 was 3.4 hm^2 while the biocapacity per person was 0.21 hm^2 (Kou et al., 2007), and Shanghai's economy has already overshot its carrying capacity considerably. Megacities should make more effort to reduce their dependence on the land resources of hinterlands outside the urban area and ecosystems outside the region and country for sustainable urban development. The quantity of CO_2 emissions in 2020 is expected to peak after increasing by 10.3 per cent compared to 2004 due to an increase in direct energy consumption caused by urban expansion.

The above analysis results indicate the following.

- In all of the sustainability indicators, from 2004 to 2030, the environmental burden derived from urban stock construction will decrease and, conversely, a large-scale negative ripple effect on urban stock will manifest itself.

- Depending on the urban growth process, the three sustainability indicators exhibit different behaviours and each indicator is sensitive to different activities. Thus an ideal policy depends on which indicator is used to measure and understand the effects of environmental policy and planning as a policy target.

Meanwhile, the Shanghai economy is expected to achieve mid- to long-term growth, even while increasing environmental loads. Therefore, we divided the TMR, EF and quantity of CO_2 emissions by the GDP and calculated the material, land resource and carbon intensities for use. The results are shown in Figure 6.3.6. Compared to 2004, the land resource and carbon intensities can be improved by 78 and 72 per cent for 2020,

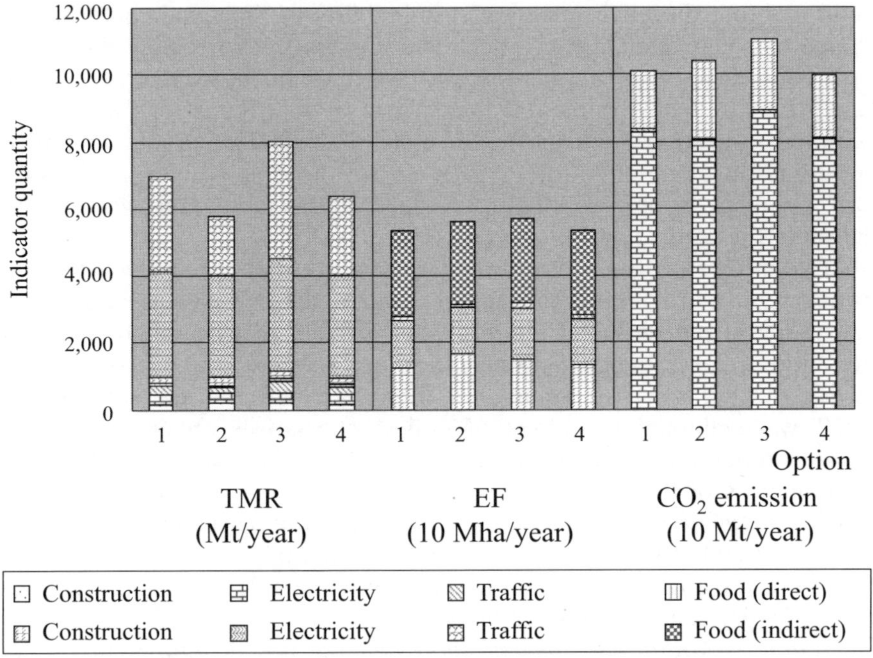

Figure 6.3.6 Environmental load intensity in Shanghai

respectively, and 84 and 80 per cent for 2030. The improvements in land resource intensity resulting from reductions in the environmental burden from construction (indirect), food consumption (indirect), carbon intensity (indirect) and energy consumption (direct) were particularly remarkable. Although the reduction rate of material intensity (including hidden flow) was low in comparison, the possibility exists of a 55 per cent improvement in 2020 and 60 per cent in 2030 when compared to 2004.

6-3-4 Effect of alternative urban renewal patterns on urban metabolism

Kennedy (2007) discussed "urban form" and "the evolution of transportation technology", which are among the main factors contributing to the change in urban metabolism, stating "urban form, including density and morphology, and the evolution of transportation technology can influence both energy and material flows. Sprawled, low-density cities have higher per capita transportation energy requirements than compact cities." This indicates that the environmental sustainability of Shanghai could be enhanced through a change in urban form that aims at correcting the excessive concentration of population and activities in the centre of the city and its related environmental loads, such as CO_2 emissions associated with transportation. Actually, the Shanghai municipal government planned an urban development strategy to construct three new towns in the suburbs (Lingang, Songjiang, Jiading) to decentralize the overcrowded population in the central part of the city (Haixiao, 2006).

To identify the effects of alternative urban renewal policies on the improvement of urban metabolism and sustainability, we developed four urban renewal patterns and set the value of permanent population ratios for three areas (Shanghai proper, the inner suburbs and the outer suburbs). Furthermore, assuming that these urban forms are achieved in 2020, we evaluated the effect of policy alternatives on environmental burden reduction using the three sustainability indicators of TMR, EF and quantity of CO_2 emissions.

- *Option 1: Current trend distribution pattern.* The permanent population ratio of 2006 for the three areas will be maintained until 2020: 36 per cent of the entire permanent population will reside in Shanghai proper and 38 per cent in the inner suburbs.
- *Option 2: Multipolar concentration pattern.* The development of the three new towns currently being planned by the Shanghai municipal government is promoted for 2020. The goal is to keep the Shanghai proper population at 8 million or less and guide immigrants who would cause a population increase into areas where the new towns are located (Lingang, Songjiang, Jiading). The permanent population ratio of Shanghai proper in 2020 would be held at 19 per cent of the entire city.
- *Option 3: Unipolar concentration pattern.* In this option, Shanghai proper experiences further overcrowding. The permanent population ratio of Shanghai proper will increase to 44 per cent by 2020.
- *Option 4: Pattern of diffusion into outer suburbs.* This is an option in which the permanent population ratio becomes uniform throughout Shanghai due to expansion of the city in all directions as land prices for the central area increase. This is a current fear of the Shanghai government.

We also set exogenously fixed values for household composition, which influences electricity consumption and floor area of buildings in the residential sector. Specifically, we set the average number of people per household to be high in areas where the permanent population is concentrated and low in areas with low permanent population density. Table 6.3.1 shows the values set for Shanghai proper as well as the inner and outer suburbs in each urban renewal option.

Table 6.3.1 Values set for urban renewal patterns in the target year of 2020

	Permanent population ratio			People per household		
	SP	IS	OS	SP	IS	OS
Option 1	0.36	0.38	0.26	2.27	2.20	2.22
Option 2	0.19	0.43	0.38	2.13	2.42	2.28
Option 3	0.44	0.30	0.26	2.38	2.17	2.09
Option 4	0.35	0.32	0.33	2.26	2.24	2.22

Note: SP = Shanghai proper, IS = inner suburbs, OS = outer suburbs.

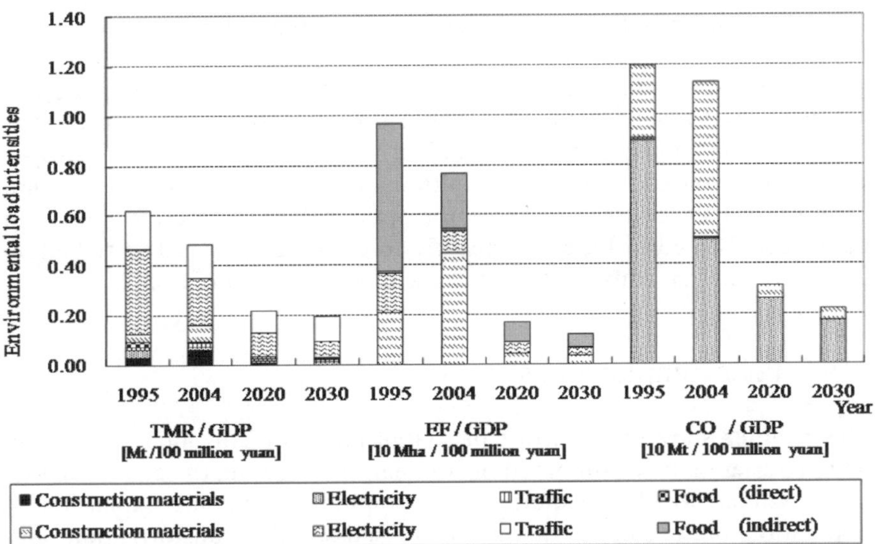

Figure 6.3.7 Effect of urban renewal patterns on environmental sustainability of Shanghai in 2020

Figure 6.3.7 shows results obtained for the three sustainability indicators. The effect of TMR reduction in option 2, which achieves a compact city with a multipolar concentration pattern, is notable. The TMR of option 2 in 2020 can be reduced by 18 per cent compared to option 1. In contrast, option 3, which achieves a compact city through a unipolar concentration of the population, has a TMR in 2020 that is 4.5 per cent higher than that of option 1. Consequently, it is believed that developing a compact urban form with a multipolar concentration pattern is an effective option for Shanghai when taking into consideration its sustained increase in population, urban activity expansion and the need to reduce direct and indirect resource consumption.

The EF originating from energy consumption decreases slightly in options 2 and 4. However, the total EF increases for each option due to the increase in the quantity of materials input during construction activities. The increase ratios for options 2, 3 and 4, in comparison to option 1, are 6.0, 7.3 and 0.1 per cent respectively.

Similarly, quantities of CO_2 emissions derived from electricity consumption and materials input during construction show different increasing/decreasing trends for each option. When compared to option 1, the total quantity of CO_2 emissions in option 4 decreases by 1.3 per cent, but CO_2 emissions in options 2 and 3 increase by 3.0 and 9.6 per cent respectively.

The analysis results clarified that the quantity of environmental loads will increase for all sustainability indicators in option 3, so future over-concentration of the population and urban activity in Shanghai proper should be avoided. Additionally, although a slight increase in EF and quantity of CO_2 emissions is seen for options 2 and 4, these options can be expected to contribute significantly to TMR reduction. The reduction effect of resource consumption is especially notable in option 2.

6-3-5 Policy implications

This chapter showed the effect of spatial management policy on energy and material metabolism based on an analysis targeting the city of Shanghai in China, which is experiencing a rapid and ongoing expansion of population and urban activity. We also discussed the transformation policies of urban structures towards the achievement of a sustainable urban metabolism.

During the process of urban growth, resource consumption increases exponentially and materials that have accumulated in urban areas eventually generate immense waste flows. Additionally, further energy-saving renovation for existing urban buildings is required to accelerate sustainable green building innovation, as we can see, for example, in the Empire State Building, Leadership in American Progress in Sustainability initiative that aims at reduction of energy use by up to 38 per cent. These decreasing social demands for energy and resource consumption will emerge not only in Shanghai but in metropolises around the world. Thus careful management and wise utilization of the stocked resources accumulating in our societies are common issues shared when working to establish resource-circulating and low-carbon societies across the world.

Furthermore, in order to reduce resource consumption and promote low carbonization in urban areas, where substantial amounts of material stock and flow are generated, changing the fundamental urban form itself is as essential as developing environmental technologies and equipment in the medium and long term.

The results of case studies on the city of Shanghai indicate that policy discussions with the following scopes are necessary for urban renewal alternatives.

- Instead of an urban policy that promotes excessive and rapid unipolar population concentration, a policy of controlling urban development patterns and their degree of concentration/dispersion could enhance urban sustainability. Conversely, deregulated expansion of low-density urban areas is not a desirable renewal alternative because it causes an increase in hidden material flows.

- Achieving a compact city with a multipolar concentration pattern is effective for reducing resource consumption. Additionally, this type of urban renewal has a greater possibility for contributing to reducing environmental burdens resulting from traffic than a unipolar concentration pattern. However, construction of new cities results in an increase in CO_2 emission quantities. Thus a policy that simultaneously improves the carbon balance in urban areas is necessary in new population hubs. This includes introducing energy-saving technology across the board at the housing and building level when constructing these new hubs, as well as developing environmental infrastructures to increase overall energy efficiency in the region.

- The three sustainability indicators (TMR, EF and CO_2) show different changes depending on the different factors for each urban growth process. Furthermore, trade-offs occur among these indicators. Thus the ideal solution is to choose a management indicator, monitor and measure it continuously, and review the obtained numerical targets based on environmental policy goals.

- Developing Asian countries, which are currently experiencing rapid economic growth and urbanization, will find it necessary to design, evaluate and select urban development and land-use plans that consider the particular state of urbanization in each country. For example, they will need to decide between "central city or suburbs" in areas earmarked for development, "concentrated or dispersed" when considering population and building density, and "unipolar or multipolar" for the number of hubs. These choices will, as a result, have a significant influence on their future urban metabolism and waste management methods.

REFERENCES

Bringezu, S., H. Schütz, S. Steger and J. Baudisch (2004) "International Comparison of Resource Use and Its Relation to Economic Growth: The Development of Total Material Requirement, Direct Material Inputs and Hidden Flows and the Structure of TMR", *Ecological Economics* 51(1/2), pp. 97–124.

Decker, H. Ethan, Scott Elliott, Felisa A. Smith, Donald R. Blake and F. Sherwood Rowland (2000) "Energy and Material Flow through the Urban Ecosystem", *Annual Review of Energy and the Environment* 25, pp. 685–740.

Global Footprint Network (2009) "Humanity Now Demanding 1.4 Earths"; available at www.footprintnetwork.org/en/index.php/GFN/blog/humanity_now_using_the_resources_of_1.4_planets/.

Haixiao, P. (2006) "Shanghai from Dense Mono-center to Organic Poly-center Urban Expansion", Institute for Global Environmental Strategies; available at http://enviroscope.iges.or.jp/modules/envirolib/view.php?docid=787.

Imanishi, M., Y. Yamamoto, A. Tokai, A. and T. Morioka (2010) "Future Estimation of Urban Metabolism and Environmental Sustainability Driven by Urban Activities in Shanghai, China", *Journal of Environmental Systems and Engineering, Ser. G* 66(2), pp. 65–74 (in Japanese).

Kennedy, Christopher (2007) "Urban Metabolism", Encyclopedia of Earth; available at www.eoearth.org/article/Urban_metabolism.

Kennedy, C., J. Cuddihy and J. Engel-Yan (2007) "The Changing Metabolism of Cities", *Journal of Industrial Ecology* 11(2), pp. 43–59.

Kou, X., G. Li, Q. Wang, L. Yang and H. Xue (2007) "Application Research of Ecological Footprint: Time Sequence and Comparative Analysis of Selected Chinese Cities", paper presented at International Ecological Footprint Conference; available at www.brass.cf.ac.uk/uploads/Xiaodong_M101.pdf.

Moriguchi, Y. and S. Hashimoto (2006) *Material Flow Data Book: World Resource Flows around Japan*, 3rd edn, National Institute for Environmental Studies; available at www-cger.nies.go.jp/cger-e/e_report/r_index-e.html#2006.

Morioka, T., N. Yoshida and Y. Yamamoto (2003) "Cycle-closing Product Chain Management with Appropriate Production Site Metabolism toward Zero Emission in an Industrial Machinery Corporation", *Clean Technologies and Environmental Policy* 6(1), pp. 7–17.

Morioka, T., K. Tsunemi, Y. Yamamoto, H. Yabar and N. Yoshida (2005) "Eco-efficiency of Advanced Loop-closing Systems for Vehicles and Household Appliances in Hyogo Eco-town", *Journal of Industrial Ecology* 9(4), pp. 205–221.

Nakajima, K., K. Halada, K. Ijima and T. Nagasaka (2006) "Estimation of Total Materials Requirement: Energy Resources and Industrial Materials", *Journal of Life Cycle Assessment, Japan* 2(1), pp. 152–158 (in Japanese).

Shen, L., S. Cheng, J. A. Gunson and H. Wan (2005) "Urbanization, Sustainability and the Utilization of Energy and Mineral Resources in China", *Cities* 22(4), pp. 287–302.

Sueishi, T. and T. Morioka (1976) "Regional Planning on Waste Recycling System for Urban Metabolism", in HESC Organizing Committee, Science Council of Japan (ed.) *Science for Better Environment: Proceedings of the International*

Congress on the Human Environment. Tokyo: Asahi Evening News, pp. 317–327.

Wackernagel, M. and W. E. Rees (1997) "Perceptual and Structural Barriers to Investing in Natural Capital: Economics from an Ecological Footprint Perspective", *Ecological Economics* 20(1), pp. 3–24.

Wolman, Abel (1965) "The Metabolism of Cities", *Scientific American* 213(3), pp. 179–190.

Xu, M. and T. Zhang (2007) "Material Flows and Economic Growth in Developing China", *Journal of Industrial Ecology* 11(1), pp. 121–140.

7

Conclusion: Challenges to a resource-circulating society in Asia

Tohru Morioka, Keisuke Hanaki and Yuichi Moriguchi

7-1 What are Asian roles in a future transition to a resource-circulating society?

It is virtually impossible to achieve an effective global resource-circulating system without promoting development of policy-making and practices of resource-efficient production and consumption in Asia. In this sense the policy directives towards the vision for a resource-circulating society are advancing in Asia, and this trend is perceived positively by the global community. However, there are still many difficult tasks ahead. For instance, unlike the IPCC task of tackling climate change, the resource-circulating society challenge is not yet integrated and unified in academia. This book intends to raise awareness of resource-circulating attempts in Asia and explore the challenges and opportunities for academia, governmental sectors and business firms.

The rapid economic growth in Asian emerging nations like China and India is having a great impact on the environment, including resource depletion, huge waste generation and environmental degradation. The scenario writing of a resource-circulating society is a very important first step to address this threat. As a conventional top-down approach, we discuss the benefit of the scenario approach for framework setting. We have examined mid-term socio-economic scenarios, developed a macro-level accounting system for natural resources and conducted an analytical evaluation based on selected indicators and assessment methods. Since there are different images of Asian-scale resource-circulating societies, we make

Establishing a resource-circulating society in Asia: Challenges and opportunities, Morioka, Hanaki and Moriguchi (eds), United Nations University Press, 2011, ISBN 978-92-808-1182-7

a few assumptions that reflect the characteristics of the region and then set a simulator system that can interpret both the knowledge information and the goal-achievement approach.

In Asia it would be relatively easy to apply the "grow first, clean up later" approach. Government regulations are necessary for sanitation practices and resource circulation with minimum environmental burden. In this sense, international official development assistance programmes are necessary to enable developing countries to establish their fundamental plan for resource circulation, ensure governmental regulation capability and construct waste treatment facilities to meet basic needs.

Since there are different levels of socio-economic development across Asian countries, we tried to introduce as many representative examples as possible, besides the practices in Japan. Our intention is not simply to apply the successful experience of developed countries in developing ones; instead, we first focus on the actual conditions in these countries on a bottom-up or case-by-case basis, and then evaluate the effectiveness of measures in terms of planning, regulation and construction.

The resource-efficiency concept in industrial society and modern corporations has been applied successfully in the research arena and could be an effective tool for Asia. The process of improving resource efficiency involves the monitoring, calculation and assessment of the flow of materials, energy and resources across countries. The results of country-based or worldwide pilot projects could be important references for Asia. From the characterization of the various cases we can get a sense of the different patterns of development countries are undertaking.

The "circulation" concept is not a simple scheme. It has a variety of implications or functions, including production efficiency improvement, promoting biomass utilization, transboundary trade of recyclable wastes and revitalization of nature-dependent regional communities. The concept also stresses the importance of coexistence between environmentally sound economic growth and diversity of eco-activities and attitudes in Asia. While the target is not as clear as carbon decoupling in climate change, the resource-circulating society goes beyond science alone and encompasses aspects such as traditions, values, culture and beliefs.

7-2 Characterized research perspectives in frameworks, exploration and policy implications

Scenario topology groups a wide variety of cases at different levels. The authors proposed a support tool for scenario designers. The focal point in scenario design starts from the various ideas of a resource-circulating society and considers not only macro factors such as industrial production and population but also market commercialization of resources in the Asian region.

The issue of an Asian resource-circulating society inherently contains a wide variety of topics and covers various regions that in most cases lack reliable fundamental data, especially in developing countries. The authors proposed that, in describing Asian resource-circulating society scenarios under these conditions, they take a bottom-up and flexible approach, which may be rephrased as scenario planning or option design for alternative future visions and their evaluation.

Interpreting knowledge linkages can be a powerful tool for characterization of a resource-circulating society. For instance, from the examination of development of environment-related technologies to some extent in Asian contexts, it becomes clear that the "reduce" strategy first prioritized in the 3Rs (reduce, reuse and recycle) seems to be isolated from voluntary pledge-reporting actions in industrial firms. While the authors highlight the improvement in resource efficiency and the 3R Initiative, the central focus is the design of a roadmap towards a resource-circulating society by 2020.

Chapters 2-3 and 2-4 demonstrated the importance of indicator systems as an instrument to support stakeholders' decision-making in the achievement of a resource-circulating society. Indicators could play an essential role in measuring or assessing the status of a society and eventually provide channels to the pathways towards sustainability. Since sustainability remains a big task ahead in Asia, despite economic development, socio-economic change has been monitored in terms of an appropriate set of indicators in research. In the case of China, for instance, while the quality of the environment could be improving in large metropolises, some surrounding areas are experiencing decline in the quality of their environment due to the huge pollution caused by the industrialization and urbanization of those metropolises.

Chapter 2-5 summarized international initiatives and networking associated with sustainable development and a resource-circulating society in Asia. The identified scope and activities of major research institutions in Asia suggest their preference for a more comprehensive domain of sustainability, multiple perspectives or multiple-benefit approaches.

7-3 Implications from Asian initiatives and projects for a resource-circulating society

As reviewed in Chapter 3, recent initiatives such as zero emissions, eco-towns and the 3Rs collaboratively undertaken by industry, local and national governments and academic experts have played key roles in spreading the concept and practices of a resource-circulating society to Japan, Asia and other parts of the world. For example, the Zero Emissions Forum (ZEF) has played a central role in disseminating the concept and best practices of zero emissions (ZE), which was originally proposed by the United Nations University, through partnerships among industries, governments, academics and civil societies, particularly in East and Southeast Asia. Such efforts by the ZEF and exemplar cases such as the implementation of environmental management based on ZE by a world-leading photocopier manufacturer give a lot of insights for a transition from industrialized society to a resource-circulating society.

Industrial symbiosis is another conceptual keyword to realize sustainable resource circulation through collaborative networks among industries and between industries and other sectors. The synergetic opportunity offered by geographic proximity has been proven by successful practices in eco-industrial parks and developments. Findings from qualitative characterization of Japanese eco-towns being developed through a national governmental programme and an in-depth quantitative analysis of the Kawasaki eco-town can be applied to urban industrial development in Asia.

In spite of opportunities of loop-closing resource-circulation systems based on the ZE concept at a local scale, as in the case of eco-towns, large amounts of recyclable end-of-life products such as waste PET bottles and so-called e-wastes are traded beyond national boundaries, driven by increasing demand from rapidly developing economies in Asia. However, the regulations governing the trade of recyclables have not been sufficiently established and enforced.

National and international policy for environmentally sound management of massive flows of materials should thus be well designed. The case of the Japanese sound material-cycle society is a unique example of putting the concept of a resource-circulating society into practice by national policies, and this experience is being disseminated through international activities such as the 3R Initiative. Mutual learning through exchange of data, knowledge and practical experiences in the field of resource and waste management is a fundamental step for realizing the concept of a resource-circulating society reflecting local and regional specificities.

7-4 Appreciated outcome of utilized resources in urban-rural partnership

There used to be symbiosis between nature and human society, like Satoyama and similar systems in the monsoon Asian region. However, such interactive relationships between urban and rural areas have been lost in many industrialized countries. Urban-rural partnership is indispensable for forming a resource-circulating society. There should be mutual flows of material, energy, information, money and people in such partnerships. Unlike industrial symbiosis, this symbiosis encompasses different sectors with various spatial scales. Proper symbiosis helps circulation of materials.

There are many possibilities for urban-rural symbiosis depending on local factors. Local customs or practices often derive from the historical wisdom of that area. However, such traditional customs often need to be changed because social circumstances in most of the world have changed dramatically during the last century. We are living in an industrial world with much higher material consumption and more information than in the time before the Industrial Revolution. Therefore a new style of urban-rural symbiosis should be developed as the fruit of modern wisdom.

Characterization of urban and rural areas through analysing flow and stock of materials with consideration of environmental, economic and social aspects is necessary. First we need to know the ecological impact in the actual world to understand the current situation. With such understanding we will be able to propose the enhancement of the human-environment symbiosis system. Analysis of feasibility and effects of such symbiosis needs to be done before full policy implementation to change society's production and consumption patterns.

Various cases of symbiosis are discussed in Chapter 4. The field surveys or models in Japan, China, Thailand and Myanmar are introduced here. Learning from successful cases provides knowledge and experiences which can be applied elsewhere. Learning from unsuccessful cases or obstacles is important as well. On the one hand, symbiosis should be based on local circumstances, but on the other hand successful and unsuccessful cases of symbiosis should be compiled and shared for better practice. Though the examples shown here are limited from the viewpoint of diversity around the world, this book provides typical cases. Such knowledge accumulation would help the reader propose and implement local initiatives as urban-rural symbiosis for a sustainable society.

7-5 Appraised biomass exploitation for carbon-neutral resources

Solar energy is converted to biomass such as trees, plants and crops either intentionally as agriculture and forestry or non-intentionally in nature. Organic solid waste derived from food and paper, sewage and sewage sludge are typical biomass in urban areas. These wide varieties of biomass are known as biotic resources. Their utilization as an energy source can reduce the use of fossil fuel and hence reduce carbon dioxide emission because these resources are so-called carbon neutral. In addition to being a source of energy, biotic resources could provide various materials. Their utilization is an essential part of a resource-circulating society with low carbon emission.

Biotic resources are nature's blessings in rural areas, especially in developing countries where other resources are scarce. In urban areas, use of solid waste and sewage, which would otherwise cause an environmental burden, as an energy source can contribute to the environment twofold, through avoidance of fossil-fuel consumption and prevention of pollution.

However, biotic resources should be used in a sustainable manner. It is claimed that biofuel production from crops competes with food supply and large-scale planting of energy-producing plants, such as oil palm, harms the ecosystem. Care should be taken to avoid such side-effects. Biotic resource management in urban areas needs improvements in both social and physical infrastructure. For instance, the use of sewage sludge requires urban sewerage systems, while food waste utilization requires a sorted waste collection system.

Evaluation of technology can be done in a comprehensive manner by using life-cycle assessment. In addition to technological relevancy, economic feasibility and social consequences of the technology are also important. However, this must be carried out paying special attention to the local society.

Four examples of biotic resource utilization are discussed in Chapter 5. Bioethanol production from rice chaff and stems can be applied to agricultural areas in monsoon Asia. The use of Eucommia for various production purposes is an example of biotic industrial development. One example is the comprehensive design and management of urban biomass utilization. Development of new technology for urban biomass conversion is also demonstrated. These are typical cases applied in Asian countries and the rest of the world depending on climate condition, agricultural background and enabling factors.

The development of technologies alone does not create a resource-circulating society. It should be noted that the applicability of technologies and institutional schemes differs from one country to another. Academia and practitioners need to play roles in this regard.

7-6 Acknowledged virtual, indirect and invisible effects due to urban activities

Asia has experienced and will continue with rapid urbanization. In order to achieve a sustainable Asia, we need to tackle three major threats faced by megacities: urban population explosion, per capita resource consumption increase and higher environmental impact per resource use. When urban developers or stakeholders include the indirect consumption related to goods and services such as extracted resources, the amount of water, minerals and energy used during production processes and the land use associated with those activities, they will understand that cities have a huge footprint on the environment. Cities and their surrounding areas or city-regions should consider the following guides when taking the lead in terms of resource-circulating initiatives.

Cities must minimize as much as possible their local environmental impacts associated with urban infrastructure, production systems, etc. For this purpose, while promoting zero-emission and recycling initiatives, cities should also pursue the transition to a low-carbon economy. Concrete aspects of low-carbon urban design are addressed in Chapter 6-1.

Cities must take responsibility for the indirect burden caused by their increasing demand for resources by minimizing their virtual burden such as ecological, water and carbon footprints, etc. They must also develop policies that encourage the industrial sector to provide energy-efficient products and services, and especially focus innovations on products with high energy consumption in the use phase.

When corporate firms or developers extract underground resources there is concern that they are exceeding the Earth's carrying capacity, even with the use of large-scale solar power generation, wind power or biomass, etc. in rural or neighbouring conservation area and relying on the eco-system services. The exploitation of woody zones without any consideration of rural communities and their culture also poses risk. When urban development sectors or consumers look for a symbiotic system with nature, they have to understand the cultural traditions and community-based customs, and incorporate this understanding in the concept of sustainable forest (Chapter 6-2).

In order to minimize the environmental impacts associated with urban growth, special focus should be put on resource use efficiency, especially in use of scarce land. Urban decision-makers need to find appropriate patterns between centralized and decentralized urban design that prioritize eco-efficient mobility and improve floor-space use efficiency in buildings. Attention must also be put on the indirect pressure on both inside and outside urban land. One effective way to minimize the indirect environmental burden is to promote the design of compact cities and avoid the construction of extra-large-scale infrastructure (Chapter 6-3).

When we set up the options for urban shape in 2020, we estimated the environmental impacts associated with the huge amount of materials consumed, land use (indirect) and CO_2 emissions from a life-cycle perspective. The moderately distributed type of cities tends to have less environmental impacts, as demonstrated by Shanghai. Growing cities in Asia should design a plan that takes into consideration both infrastructure maintenance and upgrading and environmental management. While this is important, it is also imperative to include the low-carbon and resource-circulation aspects in urban design. In this sense, the future outlook should consider the environmental implications of land, resources and energy saving simultaneously.

Index

ISBN 978-92-808-1180-3 • paper • 488pp • US$37.00

Sustainability Science
A Multidisciplinary Approach

Edited by Hiroshi Komiyama, Kazuhiko Takeuchi, Hideaki Shiroyama and Takashi Mino

Sustainability Science

Contents overview:

Sustainability science: Building a new academic discipline
Hiroshi Komiyama and Kazuhiko Takeuchi

The connections between existing sciences and sustainability science
Contributors include: Yuya Kajikawa, Hiroshi Komiyama, Riichiro Mizoguchi, Kouji Kozaki, Osamu Saito, Terukazu Kumazawa, Takanori Matsui, Takeru Hirota and Kazuhiko Takeuchi

Concepts of "sustainability" and "sustainability science"
Contributors include: Motoharu Onuki, Takashi Mino, Masaru Yarime, Kensuke Fukushi and Kazuhiko Takeuchi

Tools and methods for sustainability science
Contributors include: Hideaki Shiroyama, Hironori Kato, Mitsutsugu Hamamoto, Masahiro Matsuura, Nobuo Kurata, Hideyuki Hirakawa, Makiko Matsuo and Hirotaka Matsuda

The redefinition of existing sciences in light of sustainability science
Contributors include: Akimasa Sumi, Hiroyuki Yohikawa, Mitsuru Osaki, Gakushi Ishimura, Magan Bailey, Takamitsu Sawa, Jin Sato, Makio Takemura and Kazuhiko Takeuchi

Education
Contributors include: Mitsuhiro Nakagawa, Michinori Uwasu, Noriyuki Tanaka, Makoto Tamura, Takahide Uegaki, Hisashi Otsuji, Harumoto Gunji, Motoharu Onuki, Takashi Mino, Akihisa Mori, Michinori Kimura, Keishiro Hara, Helmut Yabar, Yoshiyuki Shimoda, Nobuyuki Tsuji and Yasuhiko Kudo

Building a global meta-network for sustainability science
Kazuhiko Takeuchi

Designing Our Future
Local Perspectives on Bioproction, Ecosystems and Humanity

Edited by Mitsuru Osaki, Ademola K. Braimoh and Ken'ichi Nakagami

Sustainability Science

ISBN 978-92-808-1183-4 • paper • 504pp • US$39.00

Contents overview:

Introduction: From global to regional sustainability
Contributors include: Mitsuru Osaki and Norihito Tambo

Sustainable land management
Contributors include: Masakazu Komatsuzaki, Hiroyuki Ohta, Ademola K. Braimoh, Anthony R. Chittenden, Yutaka Saito and Makoto Ogawa

How to make food, biological and water resources sustainable
Contributors include: Fumitaka Shiotsu, Taiichiro Hattori, Shigenori Morita, Takashi S. Kohyama, Akihiko Ito, Noriyuki Kobayashi, Masahide Kaeriyama, Michio J. Kishi, Sei-Ichi Saitoh and Yasunori Sakurai

Regional initiatives for self-sustaining models
Contributors include: Ken'ichi Nakagami, Kazuyuki Doi, Yoshito Yuyama, Hidetsugu Morimoto, Nobuyuki Tsuji, Toshiki Sato, Juzo Matsuda, Shiho Ishikawa, Marianne Karpenstein-Machan, Peter Schmuck, Ryoh Nakakubo, Søren Hermansen and B. Mohan Kumar

Self-sustaining local and regional societies
Contributors include: Yoshiki Yamagata, Florian Kraxner, Kentaro Aoki, Noriyuki Tanaka, Kazuhiko Takeuchi, Makoto Inoue and Hiroyuki Matsuda

Bridging between sustainability and governance
Contributors include: Nobuo Kurata, Yuka Motoda, Yasuhiko Kudo, Nobuyuki Tsuji, Hironori Kato, Hideaki Shiroyama and Seiichi Kagaya

How to sustain social, cultural and human well-being
Contributors include: Osamu Saito, Richard Bawden, Tatsuji Sawa, Koji Yamasaki, Kiyoto Kurokawa, Takumi Kondo, Hong Park, Yoshifumi Miyazaki, Bum-Jin Park, Juyoung Lee, Tatsuo Omura, Fumikazu Yoshida and Motoyoshi Ikeda

Achieving Global Sustainability

Policy Recommendations

Edited by Takamitsu Sawa, Susumu Iai and Seiji Ikkatai

Sustainability Science

Contents overview:

Introduction,
Takamitsu Sawa

Global sustainability
Contributors include: Michinori Uwasu,
Kazuhiro Ueta and Takamitsu Sawa

Paradigm shift of socio-economic development
Contributors include: Kazuhiro Ueta, Takashi Ohshima and Masayuki Sato

ISBN 978-92-808-1184-1 • paper •
375pp • US$37.00

Strategies for sustainable society
Contributors include: Seiji Ikkatai, Satoshi

Konishi, Shiro Saka, Akihisa Mori, Kosuke Mizuno, Haris Gunawan and Yukari Takamura

Adaptation for environmental change
Contributors include: Hans-Martin Füssel, Susumu Iai and Jiro Akahori

Policy recommendations towards global sustainability
Contributors include: Takamitsu Sawa, Kazuo Matsushita and Seiichiro Hasui

Climate Change and Global Sustainability
A Holistic Approach

Edited by Akimasa Sumi, Nobuo Mimura and Toshihiko Masui

Sustainability Science

Contents overview:

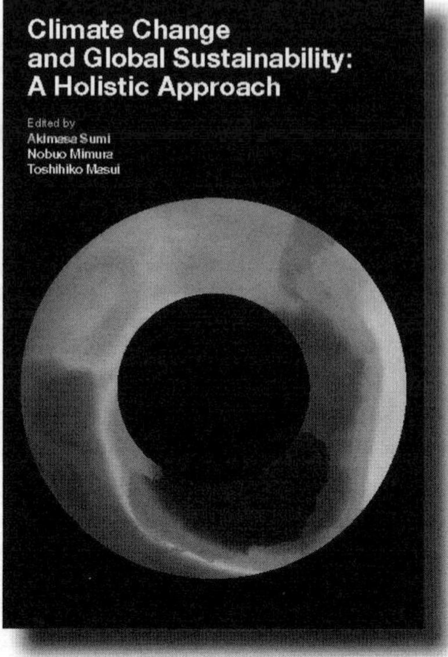

Introduction: From climate change to global sustainability
Akimasa Sumi and Nobuo Mimura

Structuring knowledge of climate change
Ai Hiramatsu

Communicating climate change risk
Seita Emori

Climate change impacts and adaptation
Contributors include: Nobuo Mimura, Yasuaki Hijioka, So Kazama, Hiroyuki Kawashima, Yasuhiro Yamanaka, Masahiko Fujii, Hisamichi Nobuoka, Satoshi Murakami and Makoto Tamura

ISBN 978-92-808-1181-0 • paper • 325pp • US$35.00

Designing climate policy
Contributors include: Hiroshi Hamasaki, Tatsuyoshi Saijo, Seiji Ikkatai, Shell International BV and Shunji Matsuoka

Transformation of social systems and lifestyles
Contributors include: Keisuke Hanaki, Tokuhisa Yoshida, Hideo Kawamoto

Integration of a low-carbon society with a resource-circulating and nature-harmonious society
Toshihiko Masui

Future vision towards a sustainable society
Akimasa Sumi

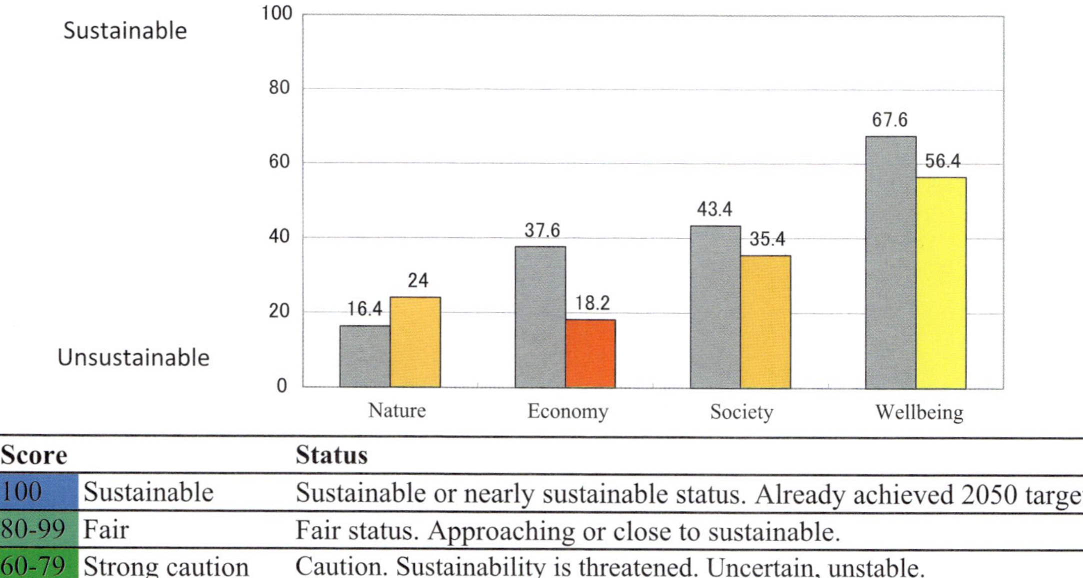

Score		Status
100	Sustainable	Sustainable or nearly sustainable status. Already achieved 2050 targets
80-99	Fair	Fair status. Approaching or close to sustainable.
60-79	Strong caution	Caution. Sustainability is threatened. Uncertain, unstable.
40-59	Dangerous	Danger. Phenomenon harmful to sustainability becoming manifest. Insufficient.
20-39	Very dangerous	Very dangerous. Moving further away from sustainability. Unsatisfactory.
<20	Disastrous	Disastrous. Unsustainable, markedly inferior to other countries. Difficult to justify.

Figure 2.4.2 Results of evaluation of Japan using JFS index
Note: Please see page 80 for this figure's placement in the text.

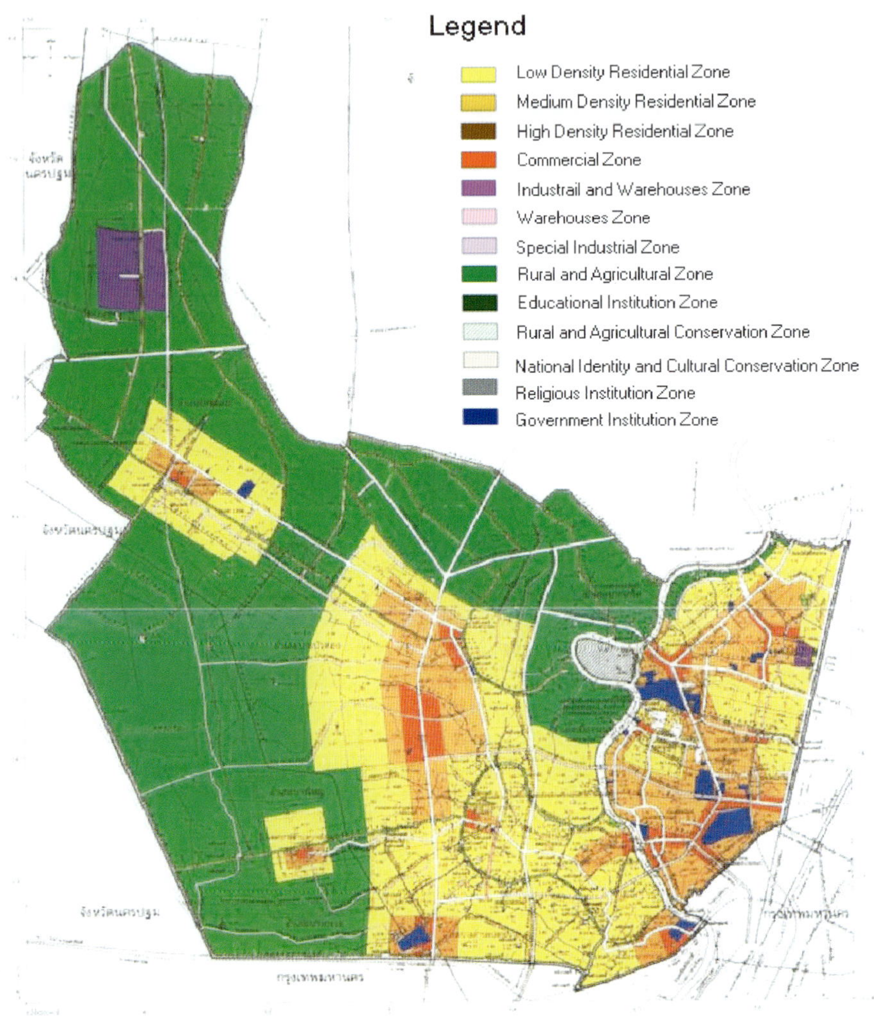

Figure 4.5.6 Current zoning map of Nonthaburi province showing land-use planning, which is based on the existing road network without any consideration of irrigation districts

Note: Please see page 258 for this figure's placement in the text.

428

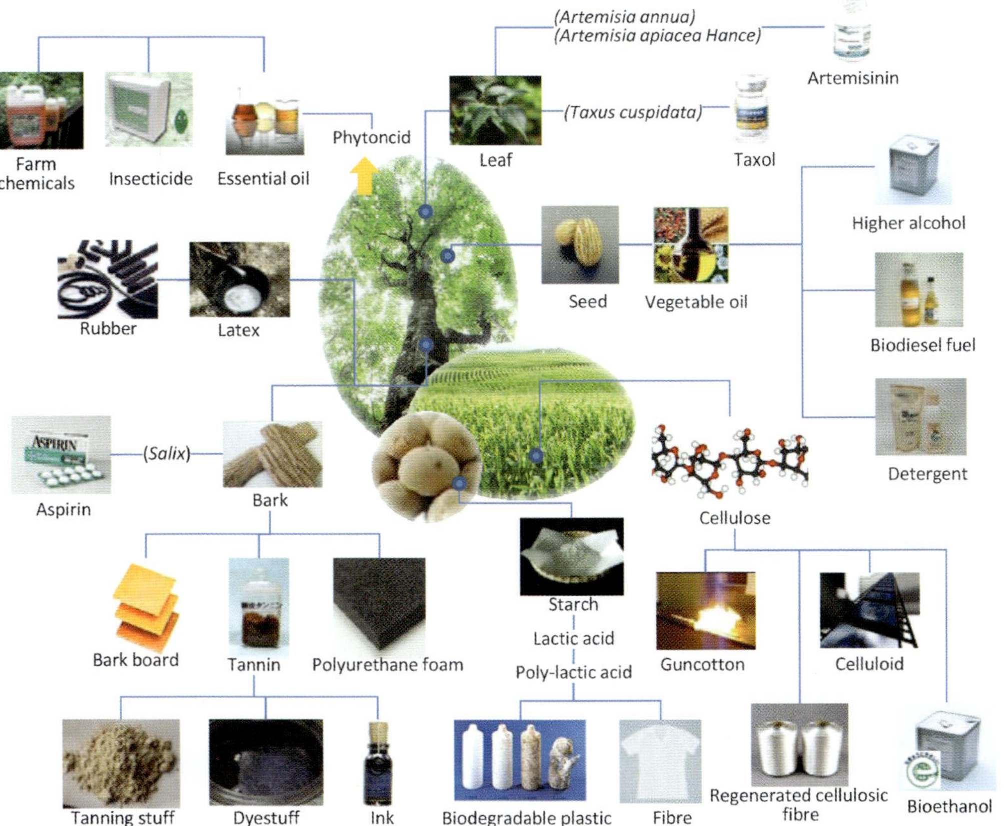

Figure 5.2.3 The mandala of high-order plant biomass utility
Notes: 1. Thousands of plant species including trees, crops, grasses, and seaweed provide us with a greater range of valuable and indispensable materials than mineral and fossil-based resources do.
2. Please see page 292 for this figure's placement in the text.

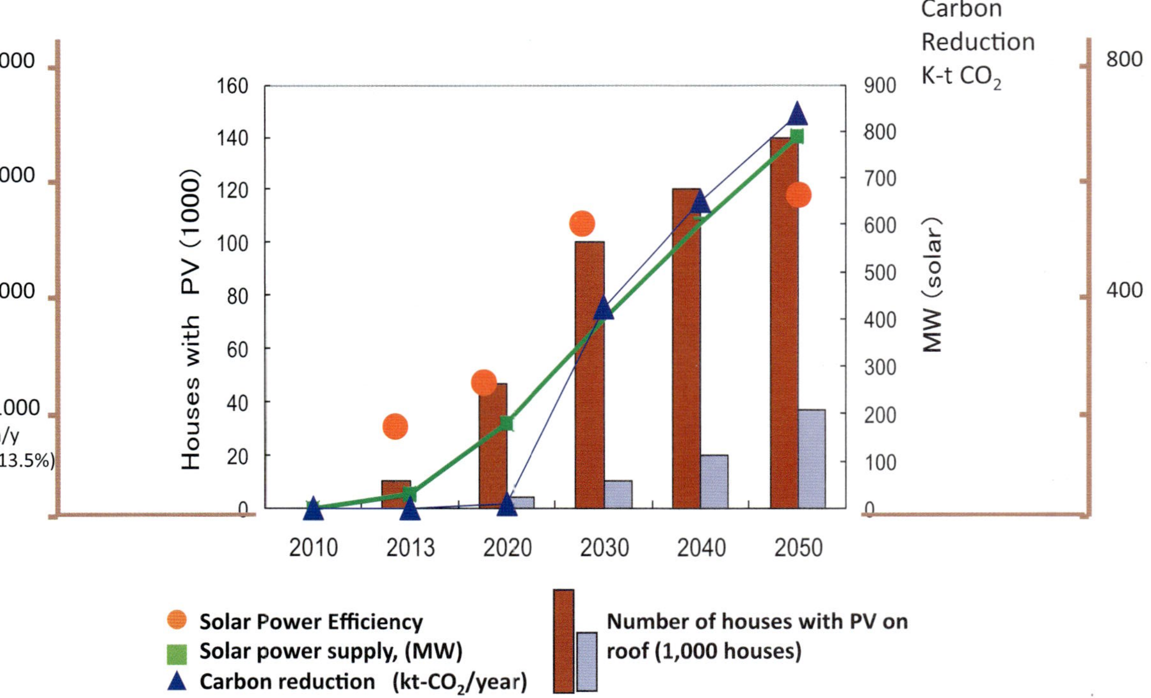

Figure 6.1.5 Performance of lifestyle innovation in terms of PV cells on buildings and changes to electricity use

Note: Please see page 339 for this figure's placement in the text.

Plate 3.3.1 Second-hand appliance market, Tianjin
Note: Please see page 164 for this plate's placement in the text.

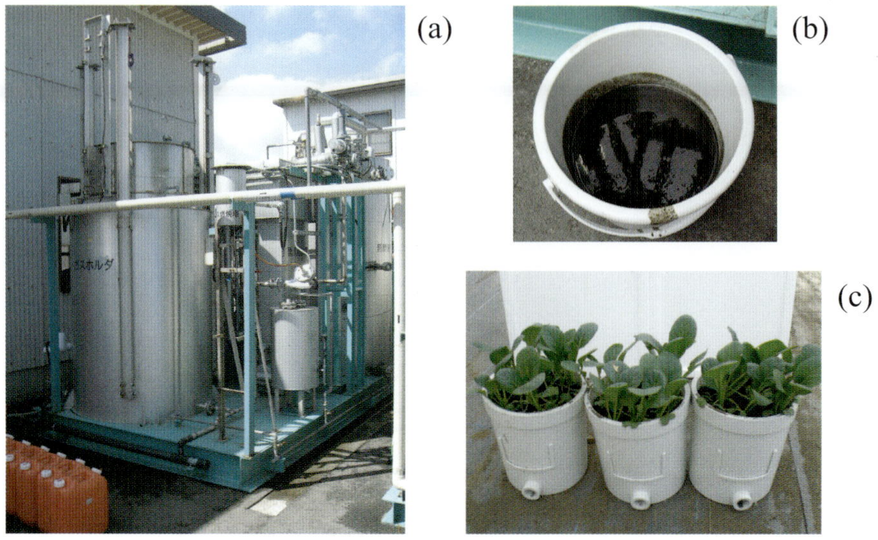

Plate 4.3.1 (a) Methane fermentation test plant, (b) bucketful of digested liquid, (c) pot test of Komatsuna (*Brassica rapa* var. *peruviridis*) with digested liquid
Note: Please see page 222 for this plate's placement in the text.

Plate 4.3.2 Sweet sorghum (var. FS902) cultivated at Ibaraki University, Japan (36°02′10″N, 140°12′43″E), in the suburbs of the Tokyo metropolitan area. The height of the bar is 4 m (October 2008)
Note: Please see page 226 for this plate's placement in the text.

Plate 5.2.1 Soil erosion observation plot installed at the Eucommia plantation
Note: Please see page 289 for this plate's placement in the text.

433

Plate 4.5.1 Typical features of the study area: (a) paddy field, (b) orchards and gardens, (c) canal transport, (d) garbage collection truck
Note: Please see page 250 for this plate's placement in the text.